Visitors From Time

The Secret of the UFOs

Revised Edition

MARC DAVENPORT

Greenleaf Publications
P.O. Box 8152
Murfreesboro, TN 37133

D1563331

COVER DESIGN: David K. Brunn
David Brunn began designing art on the Macintosh when the machine was first released in 1984, and he received his M.F.A. from the University of Oregon in 1986. Dave creates his covers by using Adobe Photoshop on a Macintosh to "stitch" together his own photographs.

Library of Congress Cataloging-in-Publication Data

Davenport, Marc 1952-
        Visitors from time: the secret of the UFOs/
        Marc Davenport.—Rev. ed.
                        p. cm.
        Includes bibliographical references (p. 241) and index.
        ISBN 1-883729-02-5: $16.95
        1. Unidentified flying objects—Sightings and encounters.
        I. Title.
        TL789.3.D37 1994
        001.9 ' 42—dc20   94-36813
                        CIP

Library of Congress Catalog Card Number 94-36813

Second edition, Fourth printing
Printed in the United States of America

Printed in the United States of America

Address all inquiries to

Greenleaf Publications
P.O. Box 8152
Murfreesboro, TN 37133
USA

AUTHOR

Marc Davenport has researhed UFOs and abductions intensively for twenty five years. He studied chemical engineering and worked as a manufacturing engineer for a number of years before becoming a full-time freelance writer in 1985. He is the author of *Dear Mr. President: 100 Earth-Saving Letters* (New York: Citadel Press 1992). He has also written articles that have appeared in *Analog Science Fiction/Science Fact, UFO Universe, UFO,* and *International UFO Library Magazine.* He edits works by other ufologists and has appeared on numerous radio and television programs. Marc is very active in the UFO field, lecturing to audiences around the world regarding his theory of UFOs and how they may be traveling to Earth.

to

my father

Table of Contents

Acknowledgments

Grateful acknowledgment is made for permission to reprint from the following works:

Healing Shattered Reality: Understanding Contactee Trauma by Alice Bryant and Linda Seebach M.S.W. (1991), published by Wild Flower Press, Newberg, Oregon.

The Watchers by Raymond E. Fowler and Betty Ann Luca (1990), published by Bantam Books, New York.

The Roswell Incident by Charles Berlitz and William L. Moore (1980), published by Grosset & Dunlap, New York.

Casebook of a UFO Investigator by Raymond E. Fowler (1981), published by Prentice-Hall, Inc., Englewood Cliffs, New Jersey.

Aliens From Space by Donald E. Keyhoe (1973), published by Doubleday & Company, Inc., Garden City, New York.

What We Really Know About Flying Saucers by Otto Binder (1967), published by Fawcett Publications, Inc., Greenwich, Connecticut. Reprinted by permission of Random House, New York.

UFOs: Operation Trojan Horse by John A. Keel (1970), published by G.P. Putnam's Sons, New York.

Our Haunted Planet by John A. Keel (1971), Published by Fawcett Publications, Inc., Greenwich, Connecticut.

The Mothman Prophesies by John A. Keel (1975), published by The Saturday Review Press/E.P. Dutton & Co., Inc., New York.

Disneyland of the Gods by John A. Keel (1988), published by Amok Press, New York.

Preface

I love a mystery. I guess most people do. When human beings first lashed logs together and set out to cross vast oceans,
the seductive lure of mystery must have inspired them. I think
it is that same lure that today drives our relentless searches for
the ultimate subatomic particle, the secret of the genetic code,
the most distant galaxy and the oldest civilization. Mysteries are
candy for the curious, fascination for the fearful and allure for
the adventurous. And no mystery I have ever encountered has
been as compelling, or as intriguing—or as disturbing—as the
mystery of UFOs.

I literally cut my teeth on UFOs. Not on real ones, but on
artists' renderings that appeared on the covers of *Fate* magazine in the 1950s. We called them flying saucers back then. My
father, an electronics expert and amateur astronomer who had
been a member of the U.S. Army's Eighth Air Force during
World War II, had become interested in them before the government began its campaign to deny their existence in 1947. He
often had a magazine or book about them on his nightstand or
by his chair.

So it was only natural that I, too, developed an interest in
the subject. But I was skeptical. Like a lot of other boys in the
1950s, I followed the space race religiously and dreamed of becoming an astronaut. Like a lot of other students in the 1960s,

I studied science and learned all I could about space. The more I learned, the less likely it seemed that UFOs were real.

Then a silver disc landed in a pasture in a remote rural area within driving distance of my home. I made the drive. I saw and touched the scorched circle on the ground and noticed how the cows wouldn't go near it. And I interviewed the witness, Mr. S., a solid, no-nonsense tee-totaler with a firm handshake and a level gaze, who obviously worked from dawn to dusk to scratch out a living in the poor soil of those Missouri hills. He said he supposed he could answer a few questions while he ate his lunch, but then he would have to get back to plowing and I would have to leave.

He had seen the landed disc at dawn, when he went to feed his hogs. He assumed it was a fallen aircraft fuel tank or a silver tarpaulin that had blown there. He finished his chores first, then took the tractor to drag it out of the pasture. Before he reached it, it rose 20 feet in the air, showing its saucer shape, then streaked away like lightning and merged with a large cylindrical object high in the sky.

There are times when you are absolutely sure a man is telling you the truth, and for me, this was one of them. Mr. S. believed lying was a sin. He had never heard of UFOs. He didn't know what this one had been and didn't care, but he didn't want them in his pasture. Nor did he want people in it bothering his stock and degrading his fence. He had only mentioned the incident to the sheriff because he thought it might be important.

After that I was hooked. Starting that day I studied UFOs at every opportunity. I spent 15 years reading, talking to people about their experiences, scratching my head and looking puzzled. Then one day I used a technique I had learned as a manufacturing engineer. I turned the problem upside-down and looked at it from a different perspective. And finally things began to make sense. So I took a few more years to make a careful, step-by-step examination of all the UFO encounter reports at my disposal. And things *still* made sense.

I don't claim to have found all the answers to the UFO mystery, but I do think I have made some progress. This book is to share with you how I arrived at a working hypothesis that explains some UFOs *and* fits the relevant data—something I believe no other book has done.

I hope it is as intriguing to read as it was to write.

1

The medical examinations that report-edly occur aboard alien vehicles are pain-ful and extreme: Biopsies (later appearing on the skin as long, straight cuts or simply as scoops) are performed on arms and legs. Transponder implants that enable aliens to track their subjects like caribou are inserted in the eyes, nose, ears, and even the brain. And most disturbing of all, painful surgical procedures remove human eggs and sperm. The result, many abduct-ees contend, is a race of human-alien hy-brids....

—*Pamela Weintraub*[1]

We Are Guinea Pigs

We are being victimized. Somebody is abducting us in the wee, dark hours of the morning, paralyzing us, examining us against our will, brainwashing us and apparently even raping us. Sometimes they stop our cars on lonely roads in the middle of nowhere. Sometimes they invade our bedrooms while we sleep to carry us off. More than five mil-lion Americans may have been abducted.[2] Those who have been re-turned are changed. Some families have suffered these horrifying intrusions for several generations. Nobody is exempt—not even in-fants. Nobody has been able to stop the abductions—not even our armed forces. The number of victims is growing at an alarming rate. You or your loved one might be a victim tonight.

But surely the people who report such abductions are crazy, aren't they? Or mistaken? Or publicity seekers? Surely unidentified flying ob-jects—UFOs—are just hoaxes or hallucinations or misperceptions of meteors, airplanes or swamp gas? Many high-level government officials would like you to believe that. Many UFO occupants would like you to believe that. Yet nothing could be further from the truth. Author and *Omni* editor Pamela Weintraub writes:

> *Hundreds of people worldwide, in countries from Canada to Bra-zil, now claim the abduction experience. What's more, the strange de-tails they conjure up—from the appearance of the visitors to the surgical procedures they perform to the symbols on the alien ship—are*

1. Pamela Weintraub, "Secret Sharers," *Omni*,
   Dec. 1987, p. 54.
2. Telephone interview with Budd Hopkins, 1 June 1992. Hopkins' information is based on data from three polls by the Roper organization. See Bigelow Holding Corporation, *Unusual Personal Experiences: An Analysis of the Data from Three National Surveys* (Las Vegas, Nevada: Bigelow Holding Corporation, 1992).

*often uncannily similar. And the half dozen respected psychiatrists and psychologists who have studied this odd group find no evidence of psychopathology....the question of whether abductees are **crazy** can be unequivocally answered with a no.*[3]

Dr. J. Allen Hynek was a highly respected astronomer. He was Chief of the Section of Upper Atmosphere and Satellite Tracking, Associate Director of the Smithsonian Astrophysical Observatory, and Chairman of the Department of Astronomy and Director of Dearborn Observatory at Northwestern University. For 21 years he was also a special consultant to the Air Force on the subject of UFOs. Dr. Hynek coined the terms "close encounters of the first, second, and third kinds," and until his recent death, he was widely regarded as the world's foremost authority on UFOs.

Hynek began the UFO-related part of his career as a sort of "debunker" of UFO reports. He believed they could all be explained as natural phenomena if only enough data were available, and when the U.S. Air Force asked him to do just that, he was happy to comply. After several years though, he began to change his mind about the phenomena. Just as many other skeptical investigators that followed were to do, he eventually became a believer.

One reason for Hynek's reversal was that the Air Force insisted on mundane explanations for UFO reports whether the data supported them or not. This was something Hynek's trained scientific mind simply could not tolerate. Another was that he could not help but be impressed by the quality of many of the witnesses who reported encounters.[4] In 1972, he noted that according to many psychiatrists, mental patients seem to have "little or no interest" in UFOs, and rarely if ever report UFO encounters. He cited a study done by Dr. Berthold Schwarz in which some 3,400 patients were examined and no UFO-related experiences were found.[5]

It has since been demonstrated that people who report UFO abductions do not exhibit psychopathology in particular. To illustrate: In 1981, Budd Hopkins, Ted Bloecher and Dr. Aphrodite Clamar hired a respected New York psychologist, Dr. Elizabeth Slater, for the blind psychological testing of nine UFO abduction victims. Dr. Slater administered tests including the Minnesota Multiphasic Personality Inventory, the Rorschach, the Wechsler Adult Intelligence Scale, the Thematic Apperception Test and a projective drawing test. She found no major mental disorders such as paranoia or schizophrenia, though all nine showed wariness and a lack of self-esteem that she might expect in someone who had undergone an experience as traumatic as a UFO abduction.[6]

3. Weintraub *op. cit*, p. 140.
4. Dennis Stacy, "Close Encounter with Dr. J. Allen Hynek," *MUFON UFO Journal*, Feb. 1985, pp. 3-6.
5. J. Allen Hynek, *The UFO Experience* (Chicago: Henry Regnery Co., 1972), p. 10.
6. Budd Hopkins, *Intruders: The Incredible Visitations at Copley Woods* (New York: Random House, Inc., 1987), p. 23.

When Dr. Slater was informed of the nature of the experience that the nine subjects shared, she was astonished. She wrote an addition to her report, stating firmly that the subjects' experiences were not caused by any mental disorder, that her tests showed none of them had any of the extreme disorders that could produce such fantasies or confabulations and that she could find no psychological explanation for their fantastic stories. She went on to affirm that the inner turmoil and distrust she found in all nine of the subjects should be expected of people undergoing an experience like abduction by flying saucer occupants.[7]

Early UFO investigators tended to discard all accounts that made even a passing reference to actual contact with "ufonauts." They considered them too fantastic to merit study—probably confabulations or hallucinations—and concentrated instead on explaining lights in the sky. Curiously, even after the theory that UFOs must be extraterrestrial spacecraft gained widespread acceptance, the idea that pilots of UFOs might be kidnapping people continued to be shunned, not only by scientists and the general public, but also by the very investigators who found themselves inundated by an ever-growing body of evidence in favor of such abductions.

The root of that paradox may have been more than just publicity seekers claiming everything from visits to tropical lunar forests to bowling tournaments on Jupiter while they fleeced their audiences. From the beginning, abductees with reputations for truthfulness and respectability described sexual encounters of one form or another. The thought of this was so loathsome and frightening that they were simply refused a fair hearing. They were branded as liars or perverts. Yet the fact remained that their friends and acquaintances swore that they were dependable, hardworking people not given to flights of fancy at all.

Often these individuals had nothing to gain and everything to lose by telling their stories. Still, many stuck by them even while they watched their jobs, reputations and marriages crumble before their eyes because others could not accept their allegations. Many abductees had never heard of UFOs or flying saucers, much less studied them in enough depth to know esoteric details that were not publicized. Nevertheless, percipients from all over the world described such details identically.

One of the first such stories investigators dared to publicize was that of a Brazilian farmer named Antonio Villas-Boas. Dr. Olavo Fontes, Professor of Medicine at the Brazilian National School of Medicine, documented the case exhaustively.

Antonio and his brother João had seen strange aerial lights on October 5 and 14, 1957. On October 15, while plowing a field early in the morning, Antonio watched a starlike UFO approach quickly, then hover. He could see that it was a bright red, egg-shaped object covered with small purple lights and with one huge red light. On its top something

---

7. *Ibid.*, pp. 23-25.

rotated, emitting a fluorescent red light that turned green as soon as the UFO slowed to land. His tractor's engine and lights failed, and he could not restart the machine.

The UFO landed a few feet away, resting on a tripod landing gear. The witness tried to run away, but he was caught by three small, helmeted beings who dragged him into the UFO, undressed him and sponged his body with a thick, clear liquid. Blood samples were taken, and he was put in a room that filled with a nauseating smoke that made him vomit.

A small, unusually beautiful, nude woman with thin, almost white hair, large, slanted, blue eyes, prominent cheekbones, slit-thin lips and a pointed chin entered the room. She seduced Antonio—twice—in an apparent attempt to become pregnant by him. After the copulation, she pointed to her belly and then to the sky.

The embarrassed witness' clothes were returned, and he was escorted out of the craft. The saucer-shaped object on top of the UFO spun faster and faster, the lights waxed brighter, and the craft rose, retracted its tripod and got brighter. The main light changed various colors, ending with bright red. The UFO buzzed, abruptly changed direction and flew off at the speed of a bullet.

Antonio suffered irritated eyes, nervousness, nausea, sleeplessness and many strange eruptions on his body following the encounter.[8]

Dr. Fontes, a respected man in his field, stated flatly that Antonio was obviously not suffering from a psychosis and seemed emotionally stable. In remarks similar to those of Dr. Slater, he reported to Aerial Phenomena Research Organization (APRO) founder Coral Lorenzen that it was normal for someone who had undergone such an unusual experience to show the uncertainty Antonio displayed.[9]

Mrs. Lorenzen noted:

> Preliminary examination by Dr. Fontes... seems to assure us that Villas-Boas is stable, not a liar, and certainly not knowledgeable about certain information which he would have to have in order to concoct such a **logical** tale.[10]

If Antonio Villas-Boas was not crazy or a liar, the only logical explanation seems to be that he may have impregnated a UFO occupant who apparently expected to bear a hybrid child. The idea would be absurd, were there not such a wealth of other stories to support it. For example, consider this statement by Brad Steiger and Joan Whritenour:

> The authors have on file the claim of a young California woman that she was raped by an occupant of a UFO. There is also a deposition by her doctor who testifies to having treated the young woman for

8. Coral E. Lorenzen, *The Great Flying Saucer Hoax: The UFO Facts and Their Interpretation* (New York: William Frederick Press, 1962); rpt. *Flying Saucers: The Startling Evidence of the Invasion From Outer Space* (New York: Signet-New American Library, Inc., 1966), pp. 64-74.
9. *Ibid.*, p. 72.
10. *Ibid.*, p. 73.

a premature delivery of a stillborn baby that seemed to have been the product of a highly dubious mixed breeding.

...the woman's highly distraught condition was responsible for her miscarriage...,

...it would be far more effective to operate a program of inter-breeding as the aliens did with Antonio Villas Boas. Bring a female, whose egg is ready to be fertilized, to the earthman... douse the man with a powerful aphrodisiac to help him overcome any innate shyness and fear... The alien woman waits out her gestation period in comfort, tended to by her own kind, and the earthman is left with either a memory lapse or a story that no one will believe. [11]

Early on an April morning in 1970, a Wisconsin attorney was driving alone on a rural highway when he heard static on his car radio and felt the car's interior grow hotter. He suddenly, unaccountably, turned onto a dead-end gravel road in an uninhabited area miles from his home. He had to skid to a stop to avoid hitting a "flying saucer," which then glowed blue-green. He tried to drive away, but the car's engine, lights and radio failed. He saw shadows moving around the car and lost consciousness.

He arrived home at dawn with a welt on his neck, suffering a loss of memory of the intervening time. He then became inexplicably obsessed with politics to the exclusion of his law practice, argued with his wife and law partner and suffered from anxiety and headaches.

Under hypnosis, details of his UFO encounter surfaced. He had been abducted from his car, tranquilized, and taken aboard a silver, saucer-shaped UFO on a tripod landing gear by a group of humanoids who had been gathering samples of sticks, rocks, etc. They had long, flat faces, light, thin eyebrows, heavy eyelids, thin lips and flat noses. They were muscular, with large chests, and they wore boots, gloves with a thumb and four fingers, coveralls and belts with a boxlike device attached.

The "captain" asked him what type of time we use. He said we should learn to use time correctly, that it doesn't exist and that his people could "distort time as we know it by speeding it up, slowing it down, or stopping it." He said they traveled faster than light and that we couldn't visit them (the way they visit us) because of our ideas about time.

They put a cone-shaped device on his head, and he felt as though his "brain were being scrambled." He later thought that they had programmed him to be interested in running for Congress. They told him that they had altered others to act as their agents, and that they used people and animals for *breeding experiments.* [12]

---

11. Brad Steiger and Joan Whritenour, *Flying Saucers Are Hostile* (New York: Universal Publishing and Distributing Corporation, 1967), pp. 66-67. See also Brad Steiger with Sherry Hansen Steiger, *UFO Abductors* (New York: Berkley Publishing Group, 1988).
12. Warren Smith, *UFO Trek* (New York: Zebra Books-Kensington Publishing Corp., 1976), pp. 114-132.

In 1966 John Fuller, in his bestselling book, *The Interrupted Journey*, introduced both the fact that abductees were being given some sort of powerful "posthypnotic suggestion" to prevent them from remembering their experiences and the use of the hypnosis method in retrieving their repressed memories. In this book Fuller carefully documented the experiences of Betty and Barney Hill.

While driving late at night in the mountains of New Hampshire, the Hills were frightened by a disc-shaped UFO the size of an airliner that emitted red, amber, green and blue light. Then it changed to a white glow. Barney likened its motion to that of a paddleball. It made 180-degree turns at great speed with no turning radius.

Barney, normally very cautious, left the car in the center of the highway with the door open and walked into a field toward the UFO to observe it. He could not hear Betty's screams for him to return to the car. He then saw several uniformed figures inside the UFO watching him, and became very frightened of being captured. He rushed to the car and drove on. The Hills heard a series of beeps at the back of the car, then lost consciousness.

Their next memory was of hearing more beeps many miles further along the road. They arrived home, confused and disturbed, hours later than expected. Barney felt a strange urge to inspect his groin and found unusual scuff marks on the tops of his shoes. Betty unaccountably packed away the clothes she had on and never wore them again. Both felt somehow unclean. Both of their wrist watches had stopped. They found numerous circular spots of high polish on their trunk lid, each of which caused a compass needle to spin.

A perfect circle of warts developed on Barney's groin. Suffering apprehension, anxiety, insomnia and nightmares about being abducted, the Hills began a series of therapy sessions with noted Boston psychiatrist Dr. Benjamin Simon, who hypnotized each of them and regressed them to the time of their encounter.

Under hypnosis, they recalled that they had made an inexplicable, sharp turn off the main highway. Their car's engine then failed, and they were approached by five-foot-tall, hairless humanoids with large slanted eyes, large heads, underdeveloped mouths, noses and chins, overdeveloped chests and pallid, bluish skin.

The humanoids somehow tranquilized the Hills. They were walked into separate, pie-shaped, hospital-like examining rooms inside the UFO, where they were placed, nude, on tables and examined.

Barney recalled that skin samples were taken and a cuplike device was placed on his groin. Betty recalled that samples of her skin, hair, fingernails and ear wax were taken, and her nervous system was tested with probes. A long needle attached to a tube was then inserted painfully into her navel. It was explained to her that this was a "pregnancy test." The humanoids seemed startled that Barney's teeth came out, but Betty's did not.

Speaking in English with an accent, the humanoids asked Betty many questions about time: "What is age? What is old age? What is a year?" They also wanted to know the length of the human life span. Betty was told, "Don't worry, if we decide to come back, we will be able to find you...We always find those we want to." The humanoids said they didn't have much time. They showed her a star map but laughed when she asked where their home was and would not tell her. They did not allow her to keep a memento so she could not prove that the incident had happened.

The Hills were escorted back to their car. Barney noticed a marked difference in the atmosphere between the interior and exterior of the UFO (though neither of the Hills mentioned an air lock). They were both given a strong posthypnotic suggestion that they would forget the entire abduction. They watched the UFO change from orange to brilliant silver and fly away.[13]

Dr. Simon pioneered the use of hypnotic regression in the investigation of a UFO encounter because the Hills showed evidence of amnesia about the incident. He expected to uncover some traumatic event that caused that amnesia. He no doubt hoped a specific pathology could be pinpointed and treated, and he was surprised to uncover such a consistent story when he regressed each of the Hills separately.

The Hills did not want publicity, but eventually their story leaked out. Because both they and Dr. Simon were of unquestionable integrity, the story became both an international sensation and the standard by which investigators measured subsequent stories of abductions. No firm explanation for their experience was ever found, although much of their anxiety was relieved when their repressed memories were revealed to them, and they were able to lead relatively normal lives.

Betty seems to have undergone laparoscopy as part of her examination in 1961, years before the procedure was invented. Her captors may have intended to gather ova. The cuplike device placed on Barney's groin may have been a sperm-collection device. At the time, these details seemed more enigmatic than significant, since the idea of breeding experiments had not yet been seriously considered.

The Hill case was extremely important, though. Since it was publicized, hundreds of other UFO kidnappings have been brought to light through the use of regressive hypnosis.

One important case is that of a Massachusetts woman named Betty Andreasson, who seems to have experienced contacts throughout her life. UFO investigator and author Raymond Fowler published the results of his exhaustive study of the case in *The Andreasson Affair*, *The Andreasson Affair, Phase Two*, and *The Watchers*.

Betty's first known encounter took place in 1944, when she was just seven years old. While playing alone in a hut in the back yard of her rural Massachusetts home, she was somehow anesthetized, and a chorus of voices told her that she was being prepared for a meeting with "The One." She was told that she had been watched, was

---

13. John G. Fuller, *The Interrupted Journey* (New York: Dial Press, 1966).

progressing and would not remember the encounter.[14]

In 1949, at age twelve, Betty was playing alone in the woods when she came upon an entity about three feet in height with gray skin, large eyes and a face shaped like a teardrop. She threw rocks at it. They seemed to silently strike an invisible barrier and fall to the ground an arm's length before reaching it. She was once again anesthetized. She was "checked," and told that part of her had not matured enough, and that it would be another year before she was ready.[15]

A year later, Betty saw a UFO that looked like "a big moon" approaching her. Then she found herself in a white room surrounded by small humanoids. She was told she would be taken "home," and then she experienced a bizarre series of events, during which she seemed to be transported in a UFO to a network of icy tunnels underneath an ocean. There she saw what she described as a "museum of time" with dioramas including human specimens from all time periods in apparent suspended animation, what was apparently an extremely sophisticated interactive holographic record of nature, and a "Great Door," behind which she experienced some kind of ecstasy. She was transported instantaneously in a pod-like, mirrored device and met tall, robed humans with white hair. Then she was transported back to a place containing many UFOs.

She then underwent a series of tests and surgical procedures. The apparent purpose of these was to implant tiny, bead-like and sliver-like devices into her body to monitor and control her actions and act as communicators. One of her eyes was removed, and at least one of the BB-sized objects was implanted behind it. She was then placed in a liquid-filled chamber and returned in a UFO to the woods near her home, where she was given a posthypnotic suggestion to forget the experiences.[16]

In 1961, Betty heard a strange sound and felt a compulsion to leave her sleeping young children alone in the house and walk into an isolated area. She was met by another of the large-headed humanoids, who told her telepathically that she was chosen to experience esoteric events and bring a message to others. Certain events would happen in the future. There were bad forces that wanted to destroy man. She interpreted the encounter in terms of her strong Christian beliefs. She was told she would not remember, and she was returned to her house.[17]

In 1967, Betty was at home with her seven children and her parents when the electrical power in the house failed. She saw a pink light outside the window that got brighter, changed to red-orange, and pulsated. All nine of the others became paralyzed "*as if time had stopped for them.*"

14. Raymond E. Fowler, *The Andreasson Affair, Phase Two* (Englewood Cliffs, New Jersey: Prentice-Hall, Inc., 1982), pp. 42-56.
15. *Ibid.*, pp. 80-91, 255.
16. *Ibid.*, pp. 94-185.
17. *Ibid.*, pp. 190-197.

Betty then watched four humanoids similar in appearance to those described by the Hills enter the house through the *closed* door. Her father and daughter Becky also saw them.

The leader told Betty his name was "Quazgaa." She handed him a bible, which he somehow duplicated instantly, and he gave her a book in return. Becky also saw the book. Quazgaa said that they had come to help the world, because it was trying to destroy itself. He told Betty to stand behind him and in front of the other three beings. All five then levitated through the closed door in single file, Betty always staying the same distance behind Quazgaa. This outlandish method of transportation was used several times throughout her encounter.

In her yard, an oval, domed UFO sat on struts. Quazgaa somehow made part of the hull transparent. Betty was floated inside. She felt weightless. She was told to stand under a "cleansing" light, then she was asked to change into a garment like a hospital gown.

She was floated onto and strapped to an examination table. A long needle was inserted painfully through her left nostril and into her head, breaking through tissue in the process. When the needle was removed, she could see a tiny ball with pointed projections on the end of the needle. Apparently, one of the devices that had been implanted earlier had been removed. A long needle was inserted into her navel. She was told this was a procreation test, and that some of her parts were missing (she had had a hysterectomy). Her abductors seemed surprised at this.

She was floated through a tunnel to a chamber where she was put in a form-fitting, liquid-filled, plastic chair, and then she experienced a dreamlike series of events. She seemed to be flown to another place, and floated through tunnels and caverns where she observed numerous things alien to her, including a swarm of monkey-like creatures. Then she was taken to witness the phoenix-like transformation of a huge bird-like creature. She attached religious significance to this experience.

She was then returned home by the same methods by which she was taken. Her family was again animated. Quazgaa left her with the messages that humanity is taking the wrong path, that they had come to help, that "All things have been planned." "The future and the past are the same as today to them," Betty told Fowler while under hypnosis. "Time to them is not like our time, but they know about our time...they can reverse time."[18]

The book Quazgaa gave her remained in her possession for ten days after the encounter. She was to study it, but not let anyone else see it. Its pages were luminous and contained symbols. After the promised ten-day period, it disappeared from the place she hid it.

Betty and her daughter suffered paranormal manifestations related to the incident—even after moving to another home. Eventually they

18. Fowler, *The Andreasson Affair* (Englewood Cliffs, New Jersey: Prentice-Hall, Inc., 1979), pp. 143-144.

moved to Florida, where Betty met (by a very strange coincidence) Bob Luca, whom she was later to marry. Luca had apparently been contacted as a five-year-old child in 1944. He had been abducted and examined in Connecticut in 1967 by beings similar to those described by Betty.[19, 20]

While Betty was conversing with Luca by telephone once (before she married him), the conversation was interrupted by an angry voice speaking in an unrecognizable language. She sensed it was a prophetic warning that the humanoids were going to arrange something, and she reported this to Fowler. The next day, two of her sons died in an auto accident. By another strange coincidence, Betty's first husband was hospitalized due to a very serious auto accident at the time of Betty's 1967 abduction.[21]

Betty and Bob have suffered more paranormal manifestations since their marriage, and Betty seems to have undergone another contact experience in 1975.[22] (Fowler has stayed with the investigation. His persistence has paid off with some astounding findings, which we will look at in Chapter 13.)

The fact that the ufonauts invaded Betty's house implies that she was very important to them. Instead of following their usual pattern of capturing victims on isolated roads late at night, they were bold enough to land in a populated area at an hour when many people were awake and then enter a house containing no fewer than ten witnesses. They were sloppy in their methods, as if they were in a hurry; Betty and others in her family remembered details they shouldn't have. Why did they deviate from the pattern investigators had become familiar with?

The fact that Betty had seven children implies that she was very fertile and therefore a good candidate for breeding experiments. Consider for a moment the following scenario: Betty is part of an experiment. The tiny sphere in her sinus is a monitoring device similar to the collars that biologists attach to endangered animals to watch their movements or record their pulse rates.[23] It might measure levels of hormones in her body and transmit a homing signal when ova were ripe for collection or fertilization.

Then Betty has a hysterectomy—which may or may not be related to her body's reaction to the experimentation. The time for egg collection comes and goes several times, but the transmitter does not alert the ufonauts. Something must be wrong.

A team is sent to take corrective action. The transmitter is retrieved. It is in perfect working order. The team concludes that it must be the subject who is malfunctioning. A needle is inserted into her navel for a "procreation test"—the same type of laparoscopic procedure that Betty Hill and scores of other abductees have reported and that

19. *Ibid.,* pp. 195-196.
20. Fowler, *Phase Two,* pp. 14-41, 57-78.
21. Fowler, *The Andreasson Affair,* pp. 196-197.
22. Fowler, *Phase Two,* pp. 198-199, 260.
23. Fowler, *The Andreasson Affair,* pp. 190-191.

UFO investigator and author John Keel has found in stories up to 500 years old.[24] The test reveals that some of the subject's parts are missing! She is no longer capable of procreation. Years of careful undercover work and scientific research must be scrapped! To cut their losses, the team decides to reprogram the subject for another type of experiment, the purpose of which is even more enigmatic to us.

Of course this is pure conjecture, but Betty Andreasson is not the only victim to have been used in this manner. There have been many others—far too many. Fowler refers to another case in which a tiny, buckshot-like thing was inserted into an abductee's side with a needle. She was told that it was for "better communications and power" and that it would be activated up to a month later, after it was determined that her body was not going to reject it. Her "doctor" said that he hoped her body would not reject the device—which is curious, since we think of hope as a distinctly human attribute.

Soon other incidents involving probes began to surface. In August of 1975, Sandra Larson was driving near Tower City, North Dakota, with her daughter, Jackie, and a friend at 4:00 in the morning. After a bright flash and thunderous explosion, they saw eight or ten brilliant, spherical, orange UFOs surrounded by smoke-like vapor descending about 150 feet from the car. Several of the UFOs stopped abruptly in midair above a grove of trees; the rest soared away at great speed. Mrs. Larson felt as though the car were barely moving, even though it was traveling about 50 m.p.h. It was as if she were "frozen for a second." Jackie, who had been sitting in the front seat, was now unaccountably sitting in the back seat. They continued to Tower City, where the friend reported the incident to the police and Sandra noticed that they were missing a full hour of time.

Under hypnosis, Sandra recalled that the car had stopped by itself and had been pulled up to a round, house-sized UFO that hovered close to the ground. She felt dizzy and numb. She was floated into the UFO by some outside force. Her clothes were removed, and she was examined by a being with unblinking eyes, whose face was wrapped in material. Her body was washed with an alcohol-like liquid. A scan of her abdomen was taken. A thin instrument was painfully inserted into her nose, and she experienced odd sensations, as if her brain were removed, examined and reconnected differently so she would have no control over what she said. She was told she would not remember, and then she was floated back to her car.

In February 1976, investigator Jerome Clark hypnotically regressed her. She remembered having once been abducted from her home by similar creatures, floated through the wall of her house to an identical UFO and placed in a transparent container molded to fit her body. She was then taken to a strange place surmised to be another planet. She had the impression that she was on display for others to see. She experienced the same dizziness and nausea as during her first

24. John A. Keel, *Disneyland of the Gods* (New York: Amok Press, 1988), pp. 103-104.

encounter. She was returned (once again through a wall), and again she was told not to remember.

Before the first encounter, Sandra had suffered from a severe, protracted sinus condition. Afterward she had no further problems. The obvious inference is that a foreign object was removed from her sinus during the encounter.[25]

Budd Hopkins has perhaps done more than anyone else to bring the shadowy mystery of UFO abduction into the light. Hopkins became interested in the UFO phenomenon after a personal experience in 1964. He has since worked intensively with hundreds of abductees.[26] He often uses hypnosis to uncover deeply repressed memories. In 1981, he published *Missing Time*, followed by *Intruders: The Incredible Visitations at Copley Woods* in 1987. Both books have been extremely important in the unraveling of the UFO mystery.

In *Missing Time*, Hopkins began to show definite patterns to the abduction phenomena:

A woman born in 1943 recalled abduction experiences in 1950 and 1960. She remembered being taken to a UFO, where entities examined her and probed inside her left nostril. Her blouse became bloodied as a result. The other members of her family were witnesses both to the fact that she had been inexplicably missing and to the blood on her blouse (this was coincidentally documented in home movies), for which they had no explanation. She was apparently given a posthypnotic suggestion not to remember the experience.[27]

A young man was driving late at night between Pikesville and Frederick, Maryland, when he saw two lights high in the sky. Although he was driving quite fast, his car suddenly jerked violently to the right side of the road and stopped without skidding—as if sucked sideways by a huge magnet. Several small, chalky-complected entities immobilized him with a clamp-like device and took him up a ramp to a saucer-shaped object. He was examined and a sperm sample was taken. He was apparently given a posthypnotic suggestion not to remember the incident.[28, 29]

After studying many such episodes, Hopkins logically suggested:

> *One inescapable inference to be drawn from this pattern is that a very long-term, in-depth study is being made of a relatively large sample of humans, and that this study may involve mechanical implants of some sort. Perhaps Virginia Horton, Betty Andreasson, and others as children had tiny monitoring devices installed high in their nasal cavities, much as terrestrial ecologists and zoologists install implants to monitor wildlife. A neurosurgeon informed me that certain brain op-*

25. Coral and Jim Lorenzen, *Abducted!* (New York: Berkley Medallion Books-Berkley Publishing Corporation, 1977), pp. 52-69.
26. *The Mike Murphy Show*, prod. Chris Stoner, KCMO Radio, Kansas City, Missouri, 14 May, 1992.
27. Budd Hopkins, *Missing Time* (New York: Richard Marek Publishers, Inc., 1981), p. 205.
28. *Ibid.*, pp.51-58.
29. Hopkins, *Intruders*, p. 22.

erations—tissue biopsies, for example—can be carried out by entering the brain from below, through this convenient channel. If such a long-term system is going on, it would help explain the decades of surreptitious UFO behavior and the absence of direct communication.[30]

By 1987, when *Intruders* was published, the disturbing patterns—much as we might wish to deny them—were all too clear. The book centers around the bizarre experiences of a young woman whom Hopkins referred to as "Kathie Davis." This name is a pseudonym designed to protect the woman's privacy. (Contrary to popular opinion, the vast majority of UFO witnesses are not publicity seekers in the least. In fact, most go to extreme lengths to assure that no one learns their identity. They are frequently confused by—and ashamed of—the unwanted experiences that have been thrust upon them.)

At 8:45 P.M. on June 30, 1983, Kathie saw an odd-colored light in the pump house near her family's swimming pool and noticed that the pump-house door was open. Her mother also saw the light. A few minutes later, the light had been extinguished and the door had been shut. Taking a rifle, Kathie investigated. She later returned—minus the rifle—and told her mother everything was all right.

She proceeded to a neighboring house to invite two girlfriends to come for a swim (and in so doing lost an hour of time between 8:00 and 9:00). The friends accepted. One of them experienced tingling and numbness in her bare foot when she stepped onto a portion of Kathie's yard, which she said felt hard, like concrete, and warm. All three women felt nausea and chills. Kathie suffered blurred vision and burning eyes (she was later told by her doctor that it was due to something similar to conjunctivitis). They noticed that it was very foggy.

On that same evening, at 8:45, Kathie's neighbor saw a flash in the direction of the Davis backyard and violent vibrations shook her house. Her television's picture turned completely red and the lights in her house dimmed and flickered. All the digital clocks in her house were flashing afterward and had to be reset. She was terrified by the incident.

Kathie's neighbor to the west was also terrified by a nearly identical occurrence (she could not be sure whether the date was June 30). She also experienced a power interruption in her home. Three digital clocks on the bedroom side of her house were affected and had to be reset, but three other digital clocks on the other side of her house were not affected. Her closest neighbors on the unaffected side did not notice any vibrations, nor was their power interrupted.

The grass in a circular area and a straight swath of Kathie's backyard (where her girlfriend had stepped) died. Nothing would grow there for years afterward, and nearby shrubbery withered. Soil from outside the affected area had the same crystalline structure and chemical composition as soil from inside it, but had to be heated to 800 degrees to attain the same color. The ground had apparently been subjected to ra-

---

30. Hopkins, *Missing Time*, p. 217.

diation that had heated and dried it, and it was still warm when Kathie's friend stepped on it.

Kathie suffered hair loss and did not feel well for several days after the encounter. She experienced pain in her right ear and hearing impairment for several days afterward.

By gleaning information from hypnosis sessions with Kathie, subsequent consciously recalled details provided by Kathie and interviews with Kathie's family, neighbors and friends, Hopkins pieced together an incredible series of encounters with UFO occupants spanning much of Kathie's life.

Kathie's mother appears to have been the victim of UFO abductions of her own, both as a child and as an adult. Kathie's first UFO experience may have occurred when she was two or three years old. She has recurrent dreams about her mother taking her into a closet to hide from some type of threat in the sky.

The next episode appears to have happened when Kathie was about seven, when she and her sister Laura were visiting friends. Kathie wandered away from the house and into the open door of a "house" occupied by strange people. A being she first thought of as a boy, but later saw as a small figure with gray skin and a large head, took her into a white, round room with no windows. It made an incision on her leg, which scarred. Kathie's mother, her closest friend and her next door neighbor now have scars on their legs nearly identical to Kathie's. All of them may have resulted from UFO abductions.

In July 1975, Kathie was visiting Rough Rider State Park, Kentucky, with friends. She observed four brilliant, pinwheel-like lights and experienced a power failure in the truck she was sitting in. She and her friends were then paid a strange, hours-long visit by three odd young men. They arrived in a vehicle with an odd configuration of headlights and no taillights. It glided smoothly over the pot-holed road.

One of the men bore a strong resemblance to Kathie. He did all the talking. He seemed somehow familiar to her, and she became infatuated with him. The other two visitors were tall, thin and dressed alike. They stood silently off to the side. Later, neither Kathie nor her friends could remember anything more about them, nor could they remember much of what had been said during those hours. Kathie did recall that at one point her friends seemed to be in a state of suspended animation. One of them later had at least one independent encounter when Kathie was not present.

In December 1977, when Kathie was 18, she and two girlfriends were driving in the country late at night. They saw a strange flashing light descending to the ground. The friend stopped the car and Kathie was abducted. She underwent a painful penetration of her uterus, which may have been an artificial insemination. This was at about the same time Kathie had begun dating the man that she eventually married.

Shortly after the experience in the car, Kathie found that she was pregnant. Her doctor confirmed this, both by urinalysis and blood test.

In March of 1978, Kathie was abducted from her sister Laura's house. She was apparently anesthetized and dilated, and her baby was removed.

Later, Kathie's doctor, who knew nothing of the UFO abductions, was mystified by the disappearance of her pregnancy. She did not suffer a miscarriage; she was simply no longer pregnant. This was subsequently confirmed by tests.

In the spring or summer of 1979, Kathie, then pregnant with her older son, was abducted from her apartment. She was floated into a UFO and onto a table, where she underwent yet another gynecological examination. Probes were forced into her nose, and apparently broke through into her sinuses, making it difficult for her to swallow and causing her to taste blood. She felt pressure in her neck and abdomen. She saw the small man with gray skin and large black eyes, whose appearance both frightened and reassured her. She awakened in her bed. Two beings stood nearby and moved in unison. They showed her a "shimmering box," then took it away, conveying to her telepathically that she would understand what it was for the next time she saw it.

In 1980, during her pregnancy with her younger son, Kathie was plagued by strange telephone calls every Wednesday afternoon. They involved indecipherable moaning sounds. Her mother and one of her friends also answered and heard the weird sounds. Kathie changed her number to an unlisted number, but immediately afterward she received another of the calls. She felt that the sounds seemed angry this time. The calls continued until her son was born, then they ended suddenly.

When her son was born, he did not talk until very late, but instead made moaning sounds similar to the calls Kathie had received. Speech therapy was required before he could make himself understood. The cause of his speech problem is unknown.

On June 30, 1983, the experience by the swimming pool occurred. When Hopkins hypnotized Kathie and regressed her to the time of the incident, he learned these details: Kathie had apparently been given a posthypnotic suggestion not to remember the experience. She felt that she might die if she tried to remember. She then recalled an egg-shaped UFO resting on four legs on the place where the scorched circle was later found in her yard. She also recalled being paralyzed and in pain while a blinding ball of light moved up and down her body, and she remembered that her arm had been held while something was poked into her ear.

On the night of October 3, 1983, Kathie had an urge to drive to a convenience store for a soft drink. Her car exhibited strange characteristics—as if the electrical system were delayed in responding. She saw a rotating UFO with multiple lights; there ensued a conversation with the gray-skinned being. She then experienced amnesia. Her next recollection was of returning home without the soft drink. She feared something was going to happen, felt cold and tingly and saw strange lights moving through the house.

Once again she fell into a trancelike state, and was taken from her bedroom. Once again she underwent a probing examination by the gray-skinned being, whom she felt she knew.

Six female entities presented a tiny, pale child with thin white hair, a large forehead, small low ears, and big blue eyes. Kathie instinctively knew that this was her daughter—a hybrid between herself and the gray-skinned being! She felt overwhelming emotion toward the child. She was told that the little girl was a part of her and was promised she would get to see her again.

She was then somehow transported out of the UFO, during which procedure the air pressure surrounding her apparently changed abruptly. She found herself lying in her yard in her pajamas. She saw the UFO leaving, then discovered she was locked out of the house. She called to her mother, who inexplicably let her in without saying a word about her bizarre predicament.

One night in November of 1983, Kathie awoke to the desperate screams of her terrified four-year-old son. He had been paralyzed while he watched a "man with a big head" with "lights around his head" materialize through his wall and communicate to him telepathically that he wanted the boy's three-year-old brother. Kathie saw a flash and a shadow disappearing from the room.

Kathie was apparently taken captive again that same evening. As she lay on a table with her nightgown pulled up, she felt bloated, as if her uterus and rectum were filled with air, and as if her insides were being moved around. She described sensations identical to those reported by women undergoing laparoscopic examinations. The same gray-skinned, large-eyed entity asked how she felt. She answered that she had cramps, whereupon he patted her belly pleasantly and said, "That's good." The following day she suffered from ovarian pain, cramps and unusual vaginal discharge. She discovered from her calendar that she expected to be ovulating. The obvious inference is that the ufonauts had either removed an ovum or artificially inseminated her.

One morning about a week later, she found her younger son and his room spattered with blood from a severe nosebleed. An emergency-room doctor found a puncture wound high in the boy's nasal cavity.

In February of 1986, Kathie was awakened by the older son, who was frightened by a strange light in his room. A few minutes later, she clearly saw one of the gray-skinned beings walk through the hall past her bedroom door from the direction of that room.

In April of 1986, Kathie was again abducted from her home. She was again shown her "daughter," along with a pitifully small, pale infant. The entities conveyed to her that these were the oldest and the youngest of her nine hybrid children. The purpose of the meeting was to have her hold and love the infant so that they could observe and learn how to do so themselves. They asked her to name all nine children. When she held the baby, she got the impression that it was very "wise." It seemed to gain strength from her touch.

In September of 1986, Kathie, while driving her sons to her apartment late at night, twice sighted large, luminous, oval UFOs hovering above the tree tops. She arrived at the apartment more than an hour late and was unable to account for the missing time. A few hours later her older son suffered a severe nosebleed. It is thought that Kathie and her son may have been abducted and that the son's nose implanted with a monitoring device.[31]

If Kathie Davis' unbelievable story could not be substantiated, one could dismiss it as imaginative fiction and rest easily at night. Unfortunately this is not the case. Kathie's accounts are borne out by her doctor, neighbors, sister, mother, sons, girlfriends, etc. Her body and her mother's bear identical scars of a type common among abductees. The scorched circle in her yard was studied by many others. The details of her adventures are not at all uncommon, and there is very little chance that she could have heard of and repeated certain details common to other cases, since those cases were not publicized.

Hopkins has found many corroborations for almost every detail of Kathie's story. Some of the information comes from disturbing "dreams" that the percipients remember, some comes from hypnosis sessions, some is from consciously remembered details and some is from the testimony of friends, neighbors and families of the witnesses (as was the case with Kathie). When it is all considered as a body, it exhibits astounding degrees of continuity and congruence.

The UFO sightings, the odd way of being rendered immobile and floated through the air into the UFO for examination, the identical scars, the pattern of multiple experiences, the implants, the penetrations of vaginas, navels, noses and ears, and the pregnancies that disappear are all described similarly—and sometimes even using exactly the same terms—by many witnesses who are totally unaware of one another.

One girl became pregnant at age 13. She had not had intercourse, but she remembered a "dream" of being paralyzed while a bald man with funny eyes inserted a sharp object into her vagina that caused a burning sensation and made her stomach feel like it would explode. One woman was able to make a drawing of a double-bladed instrument

---

31. Hopkins, *Intruders*. An odd event occurred when "Kathie" was in her teens. It is not known to have a connection to her UFO-related experiences, but Hopkins told me in an interview on June 1, 1992, that he believes it could be a clue that she was implanted with a monitoring device. Kathie noticed a little bump on the front of her shin that she couldn't explain. There was a round object under the skin that she could move around. Assuming it to be a cyst, her doctor tried to dissolve it by injection. The needle would not penetrate it and finally broke off. Later the doctor removed it surgically. When he first pressed the skin with a scalpel, a small, calcified object shot into the air like a missile, striking the lamp in the surgery and startling the doctor and nurses. The nonplused doctor caught it before it fell to the floor. Apparently it had been in Kathie's body long enough to form calcium deposits (one is reminded of pearls forming in oysters) and for a pad of fat to have formed beneath it to protect the bone. Unfortunately, the idea that abductees might be implanted had not yet surfaced. The doctor discarded the object. Now he does not wish to become involved in the controversy surrounding such experiences, so the matter must rest there.

that was used to snip something in her cervix. Such surgical procedures and instruments are described identically by many women.

Several men report having sperm samples extracted with a funnel-like vacuum device. One man had several such experiences as a young man. When he was older, he was again abducted, and underwent a "rape" similar to that described by Antonio Villas-Boas. Afterward, the entities collected his semen and became angry. Apparently they had discovered that he had had a vasectomy. Of course this would throw a wrench in their plans, just as Betty Andreasson's hysterectomy had!

Hopkins has discovered so many instances in which two or more generations of the same family have experienced these abductions (like Kathie, her mother, her sister and her sons) that he has concluded that the abductions may "represent a genetically focused study of particular bloodlines."[32] He remarks:

> In a Canadian case, a father was abducted as a young man and decades later his son experienced a series of such encounters. In an Erie, Pennsylvania, family, both mother and daughter have apparently undergone the same abduction experiences over the years, while in Connecticut, Vermont and Florida cases mothers and sons were separately picked up and "examined" by UFO occupants.... the human species itself is the subject of a breeding experiment.[33]

Most of the victims of these events seem to be taken first when they are about six or seven years old, then they undergo several other experiences until they are about forty. Many of the accounts parallel one another. People born in the same years seem to be abducted in the same years.[34]

UFO investigator and author John Keel even found that contactees may be likely to have identical birth dates. At one time he was corresponding with several people who claimed contact with UFO entities and who were all born on September 6.[35]

Abductees other than Kathie recount having their babies taken away and then shown to them later. They describe them as pitifully thin, pale and "wise." Pamela Weintraub writes:

> Other abductees recalled special incubation rooms, weird incubation vessels (Hopkins will not describe them for publication), and bizarre, high-tech nurseries in which tiny babies were raised. People consistently describe the unusual way the hybrid babies were dressed. Still other abductees, both men and women, claimed they were taken for the distinct purpose of touching these baby hybrids.[36]

The tiny, BB-like implants are described time and again. Hopkins notes:

---

32. *Ibid.*, p. 26.
33. *Ibid.*, p. 27.
34. Hopkins, *Intruders.*
35. John A. Keel, *The Mothman Prophesies* (New York: The Saturday Review Press/E.P. Dutton & Co., Inc., 1975), p. 197.
36. Weintraub *op. cit.*, pp. 137-138.

...apparent implants...have been recalled, both with and without the aid of hypnosis. ...The object most often described is a tiny ball, only two or three millimeters in diameter, that is put in place by means of a long needle.[37]

An analogy which immediately springs to mind is the human study of endangered animals, in which zoologists tranquilize and tag or implant transmitters in sample animals to trace their subsequent wanderings.[38]

Noted author Whitley Strieber has suffered from shadowy, frightening abduction experiences involving four different types of humanoid beings—and one entity in particular—throughout his life. He was unaware of them until the entities made the mistake of allowing him to see them when they stole into his bedroom one night in 1985 (without tripping his burglar alarm). In 1987 he risked a well-established reputation by publishing the true account of his experiences in *Communion: A True Story*. It became a #1 best seller that shocked many out of their blithe opinion that UFOs were funny lights in the sky and into awareness of the true nature of the UFO phenomenon.[39]

One night Strieber awoke to find himself paralyzed. He couldn't open his eyes. He felt something probing deeply in his left nostril. When he tried to move, he heard a sound "like an apple crunching between my eyes." He then lost consciousness, but the next morning experienced nasal bleeding. His nose was sore and had a "knot" in it. Coincidentally, both his wife and son had had identical symptoms a few days earlier. Strieber later recounted this about "intrusions":

...I met a woman who has had the visitor experience....the visitors inserted a probe into her nose, which made a sound "like an apple crunching," between her eyes. She had even drawn pictures of the probe and of the entity that had inserted it. The probe was a businesslike affair, a needle with a small, knifelike handle. The entity was familiar to me because I had seen such beings also.

I then asked Budd Hopkins for information, from his cases, of reports of intrusions into the head. Of his hundred cases, four including me reported intrusions in or behind the ear, three under the eye, and eleven, again including me, up the nose.[40]

Strieber's story involves three generations of his family, and details of it were corroborated by family, friends and neighbors. It includes many outlandish details, such as power failures, entities dressed in hilariously outmoded clothes, obsessive behavior, etc.[41] As we shall see, these are hallmarks of the contact experience.

---

37. Hopkins, *Intruders*, p. 26.
38. *Ibid.*, p. 7.
39. Whitley Strieber, *Communion: A True Story* (New York: Beech Tree Books-William Morrow and Company, Inc., 1987).
40. *Ibid.*, p. 129.
41. Strieber *op. cit.*

Hopkins stated in 1981 that he felt about 500 of the witnesses were probably abductees.[42] And since he found that some individuals remember nothing of their encounters until placed under hypnosis—not even that they saw a UFO—he thought there could be thousands of others. He wrote:

> *...how could one guess how many other abduction experiences lay buried and ticking within how many other unconscious minds? The prospect was staggering; if it happened once, it could happen ten thousand times and no one would necessarily know!*[43]

Based on an analysis of data from three 1991 national surveys conducted by the Roper organization, Hopkins has now come to the chilling conclusion that the 10,000 figure may be thousands of times too low. In all, a random, balanced sampling of 5,947 adult Americans was taken, and represents a population of 185,000,000. The surveys did not ask if respondents had been abducted by ufonauts, but did ask five key questions that Hopkins and others consider indicators of possible abductions. (In simplified terms: Have you awakened paralyzed with a sense of a strange presence in the room? Have you experienced missing time? A feeling of actually flying? Balls of light in the room? Do you have puzzling scars that neither you nor others can identify?) Two percent of the respondents (119) answered a definite yes to four or more of these questions. This indicates "there is a strong possibility that individual is a UFO abductee." Two percent of the total population represented would be 3,700,000.[44] And two percent of the earth's entire population (not accurately represented by the poll, but necessary to consider, since the UFO is a global phenomenon) *would be more than 100,000,000 people!*

We can no longer afford to hide our heads in the sand about this thing that is happening to us. The stories the abductees tell are unpalatable, unacceptable, unbelievable—but they are nevertheless unavoidable. Hundreds of people are not having identical hallucinations. And hallucinations do not cause power failures, scorched earth and holes in peoples' skulls.

The common complaint that the use of hypnosis to learn details invalidates the whole study has little validity itself. Sixteen of Hopkins' subjects recalled their entire stories without hypnosis; 23 others volunteered for hypnosis, thinking they had been abducted, and subsequently found out that they had not been abducted.[45] UFOs can no longer be called "odd lights in the sky." They are real, they are intrusive, and we need to face those facts and deal with them. We need to look for patterns that will help us determine what they are, what they want and how we should react. Although I have only reviewed a few of the best-documented cases here, several patterns that I believe may be

42. Hopkins, *Missing Time*, p. 23.
43. *Ibid.*, p. 73.
44. Bigelow Holding Corporation, *op. cit.*
45. Weintraub *op. cit.*, p. 140.

crucial to the solution of the UFO mystery are already beginning to emerge.

The occupants of the UFOs, though often described as short with large heads and eyes and small features, are usually humanoids very much like ourselves. As we shall see in later chapters, many of them are indistinguishable from humans. And, much as we might wish to deny it, they have apparently successfully interbred with us.

The most popular theory to account for UFOs proposes that they are extraterrestrial spacecraft piloted by beings from other planets. But, as every geneticist knows and everyone who remembers his high school biology lessons can guess, the idea that life forms closely resembling humans could have evolved independently on another planet is at best highly unlikely. And the idea that such life forms could mate and crossbreed with us is patently absurd. We have been creating hybrids for centuries now. We know that only species with relatively recent common ancestry—i.e. those whose DNA molecules are substantially identical—can be crossbred. Horses and donkeys can interbreed, for instance, to produce mules, but men and chimpanzees (whose genes are only 99% identical) cannot. The chance of a species with DNA nearly indistinguishable from ours evolving independently on another planet constitutes such an astronomical improbability that there is no scientific choice but to consider it impossible.

Since it has been well established that the witnesses are not lying, we are left with only a few explanations:

(a) We and those ufonauts who interbreed with us have a common ancestor (or were created with identical genes).

(b) They are human.

(c) For reasons we do not yet understand, evolution results in DNA structures almost identical to ours, even if it occurs independently on other planets.

At first glance, all three of these scenarios appear preposterous. But I will try to demonstrate that, once we learn more about the universe, one or more of them are actually not only possible, but probable.

Another pattern that is extremely important concerns the tiny objects that ufonauts have implanted in abduction victims. Many UFO investigators believe them to be miniature monitoring devices. Some suggest that they may be receivers that cause abductees to hallucinate. Hopkins says it's anybody's guess how many abductees have implants, because although some can be detected with X rays, CAT scans, or magnetic resonance imaging, most cannot. But he estimates that "the majority of abductees describe a process occurring during the abduction which would seem to be putting an implant in place."

If these devices are implanted in even a tenth as many victims as investigators suspect, scientists should be able to locate and isolate them and study them under laboratory microscopes. Pertinent data can be published. This procedure can be *repeated* and the results *compared*. The physical evidence can be analyzed, classified, catalogued, and placed in museums with dinosaur bones and meteorites. In June of 1992, Hopkins told me he knew of four of these devices "being studied right now by major people."[46]

For years, UFO investigators have been searching in vain for incontrovertible physical evidence to prove the existence of UFOs and reveal concrete facts about UFOs' origin and purpose. They know that until it is found, research grants and scientists willing to study the problem seriously will likely remain scarce. These little devices may well be the "smoking gun" they have been seeking.

And finally, a pattern emerges that may prove the most important of all: *Ufonauts seem to measure time differently than we do, and time seems to be somehow affected when they or their craft are present.*

The Wisconsin attorney said his kidnapper asked him what type of time we use and said we should learn to use time correctly, that it doesn't exist and that they could "distort time as we know it by speeding it up, slowing it down, or stopping it." He was told we cannot visit them as they visit us because of our ideas about time, and that they traveled faster than light.

Betty and Barney Hill's wrist watches stopped. Their abductors asked Betty, "What is age? What is old age? What is a year?" They wanted to know how long the human life span was and said they didn't have much time.

Betty Andreasson's family became paralyzed "as if time had stopped for them." Betty told Raymond Fowler, "The future and the past are the same as today to them. Time to them is not like our time, but they know about our time. They can reverse time."

Sandra Larson felt her car was barely moving, even though it was traveling at 50 m.p.h. She said it was as if she were "frozen for a second."

Kathie Davis said at one point her friends seemed to be in suspended animation. Later her car's electrical system acted as though it were delayed in responding.

Although the anomalous behavior of time in the vicinity of UFOs and the ufonauts' preoccupation with time have been dutifully reported by investigators for decades now, they have been largely ignored. But as we shall see, they are universal characteristics of UFO phenomena. I believe that makes them very important. In fact, I hope this book will demonstrate that they may well prove to be the long-sought-after keys that ultimately unlock what is perhaps the most intriguing mystery in history—the secret of the UFOs.

46. Telephone interview with Budd Hopkins, 1 June 1992.

The many rumors regarding the flying disc became a reality yesterday when the intelligence office of the 509th Bomb Group of the Eighth Air Force, Roswell Army Air Field, was fortunate enough to gain possession of a disc....

The flying object landed on a ranch near Roswell sometime last week....

Action was immediately taken and the disc was picked up at the rancher's home. It was inspected at the Roswell Army Air Field and subsequently loaned by Major Marcel to higher headquarters.

—Roswell Army Air Field press release, July 8, 1947[1]

We Are Being Lied To

From July to September of 1977, UFOs of all shapes and sizes, from starlike to twice the length of a 737, hovered and maneuvered over the island of Colares and the beach of Baia do Sol, island of Mosqueiro, Brazil, at the mouth of the Amazon River. Every night, they were seen by hundreds, perhaps thousands of witnesses. Some came from the sky, some rose out of the ocean. They were photographed by scientists, military teams, and journalists. The entire area was in a panic. Some 20 people were injured by beams of light from the objects. They were treated by Dr. Wellaide Cecim Carvalho de Oliveira, the director of a community health center on the island of Marajo.

A Brazilian military investigation was launched first. A team of soldiers took extensive measurements. They sent a comprehensive report up through military channels to the Brazilian capital, where it is off-limits to the public. Then reporters and camera crews arrived on the scene. They took some excellent photographs, many of which were subsequently published in Brazilian newspapers.

If you study the archives of Brazilian newspapers for the summer of 1977, you will find a lot of UFO photographs. But photographs printed on newsprint are of course of such poor quality as to be virtually useless for scientific study, or even as proof of anything. If you want proof, if you want something to study in a laboratory so as to ferret out clues as to what UFOs are, you need negatives. But the negatives are not available. Check with any of the newspaper publishers; you will find that their negatives were bought and taken out of Brazil by

---

1. Charles Berlitz and William L. Moore, *The Roswell Incident* (New York: Grosset & Dunlap, 1980), pp. 22-24.

someone from a nameless American company.[2]

Dr. Jacques Vallée, astrophysicist, computer expert, and longtime UFO investigator and author, investigated the Colares and Mosqueiro wave of encounters. According to Dr. Vallée:

> *Somebody in the United States owns a collection of records that contains proof of the reality of the phenomenon....*
>
> *The evidence that has now been obtained by the major powers is so valid and it has such devastating implications for future military systems that the decision has been made to keep it under lock and key....[3]*

Dr. Vallée's statement implies that the American firm that bought the pictures was a front for an agency of the U.S. government. If so, it would not be the first or last time a U.S. military/intelligence coterie has used taxpayers' dollars to cover up important evidence of UFO activities. This group has, in fact, consistently and deliberately misled us and lied to us about UFOs for more than 40 years.

World War II pilots encountered luminous globes, which they nicknamed "foo fighters." American pilots thought they must be some new German invention. Later, studies of German records showed that the Germans didn't know what they were either. They thought that perhaps they belonged to the Allies.

After the war, mysterious "ghost rockets" began appearing, mainly over Scandinavia. They outperformed existing aircraft, and, like the foo fighters, were never identified. Nerves were jittery. The ghost fliers appeared in corridors where they had no permission to fly. Were they secret weapons? Were Scandinavian countries about to be attacked by Russia or some other air power?

The Japanese attack on Pearl Harbor had made Americans suspicious of any foreign aerial contraption. Our fledgling radar sets had detected the Japanese planes as they approached Hawaii on that fateful day but were disregarded. Americans were determined never to err so again. When the war ended, the horror of Hiroshima and Nagasaki haunted us. We had to be ready for foreign attack from the air.

So in 1947, when unidentified flying objects began violating U.S. sovereign air space and ignoring challenges to identify themselves, military officials became alarmed. Orders were issued; paper chains were set up. Information was to be collected as quickly as possible. Fighter planes were scrambled to chase the intruders and blow them out of the sky. All military personnel were to report any UFO in detail. We wanted one of those discs captured. The generals were "by God going to get to the bottom of this flying saucer business!"

As data mounted, tension increased. The unknowns were easily outperforming every aircraft we had! They were flying at incredible speeds without burning up, and turning corners at speeds that would

---

2. Jacques Vallée, *Confrontations: A Scientist's Search for Alien Contact* (New York: Ballantine Books, 1990), pp. 220-226.
3. *Ibid.,* p. 225.

crush pilots and destroy aircraft. Nobody on Earth could have built them; they must be from another planet—maybe Mars!

A blanket of secrecy was thrown over the subject. Joint Army/ Navy Air Publication 146 warned servicemen not to leak information about UFOs to the public. The punishment was a $10,000 fine and up to ten years in prison. Air Force Regulation 200-2, paragraph 9, provided for defusing public interest in UFOs:[4]

> *In response to local inquiries, it is permissible to inform news media representatives on UFOBs when the object is positively identified as a familiar object.... For those objects which are not explainable, only the fact that ATIC will analyze the data is worthy of release....*[5]

The public was told that the answer had been found. There was nothing to the UFOs. As many as 90 percent of them were identified as hoaxes, hallucinations, misidentified balloons, airplanes, stars, meteors, etc., and if there had been enough information, the others could be also.

Witnesses were harassed, threatened and badgered. Physical evidence was confiscated. Those who reported close encounters were publicly ridiculed. Statements they made that could be questioned were stressed, while unquestionable ones were suppressed. "Flaps" or "waves" of reports were labeled hysteria.

At the same time, "fringe" groups consisting of obvious charlatans and fanatical followers of ludicrous claims (of rides to the jungles of the moon in Venusian space ships or mental contact with beautiful space women) were not interfered with. There is even some evidence that they were encouraged. George Adamski, the controversial contactee who claimed he had talked to and taken rides to other planets with "spacemen," and who produced photographs of their "spaceships," toured the world, lecturing, and calling himself "Professor" (even though his credentials consisted of having run a hamburger stand near the Mount Palomar astronomical observatory). In *Dimensions: A Casebook of Alien Contact*, Dr. Vallée makes these intriguing observations:

> *...Adamski has confessed that four U.S. government scientists were responsible for launching his career as an ambassador for the Space Brothers. These scientists were from the Point Loma Naval Electronics Laboratory near San Diego and from a "similar setup" in Pasadena. They asked him if he would "cooperate in the collective attempt to get photographs of the strange craft moving through space." Adamski's major supporter abroad was a former intelligence officer with the British Army, with whom I have personally met....A man who hosted Adamski during his tour of Australia told me that "Good old George" was traveling with a passport bearing special privileges.*[6]

4. Ralph and Judy Blum, *Beyond Earth: Man's Contact With UFOs* (New York: Bantam Books, Inc., 1974), pp. 101-102.
5. From AFR 200-2, para. 9, Aug. 1953. ATIC is Air Technical Intelligence Command. "UFOBs" (instead of "UFOs") was a U.S. Air Force designation for unidentified flying objects at the time the regulation was written.
6. Jacques Vallée, *Dimensions: A Casebook of Alien Contact* (Chicago: Contemporary Books, 1988), pp. 247-248.

While all this was going on behind the scenes, the Air Force set up projects to give the public the impression that it dutifully studied each sighting and found mundane explanations for almost all of them. Project Bluebook, which succeeded earlier projects, was the most widely publicized. In reality, reports were screened first. Those that seemed to have mundane explanations, either directly or by stretching the truth a little, were handled by the projects. The others—those that contained truly damning evidence—were sent into the intelligence underground under TOP SECRET classification.

Civilian UFO investigators were put under surveillance. The most outspoken group against government secrecy, National Investigations Committee on Aerial Phenomena (NICAP) was eventually infiltrated by intelligence agents and effectively neutralized. It became, for all practical purposes, an intelligence-community collection point for UFO reports and soon afterwards dissolved.[7]

For some reason, certain government officials wanted very badly to keep what they knew about UFOs hidden—so badly, in fact, that UFO-related documents were more highly classified than information about the hydrogen bomb.[8]

But, as is the case with any government project, mistakes were made. Press releases were issued and then withdrawn. Air Force officials gave preposterous explanations. People who reported seeing navigable machines at close range were said to have been fooled by "swamp gas" or stars that were not even visible from their hemisphere.

And mass sightings of UFOs continued all over the world, some involving hundreds or even thousands of witnesses. In July of 1952, 67 UFOs were either seen or tracked by radar in the Washington, D.C., area by an estimated 250,000 witnesses. Two years later, thousands of witnesses watched as a UFO hovered and maneuvered around the sky over Rome. In August of 1965, 100,000 people from North Dakota to Texas saw "a fleet" of the objects. During the following three months, they flew over Mt. Yokohama several times as U.S. Air Force pilots and Japanese citizens that altogether numbered in the hundreds of thousands looked on. Since then, as many as 300,000 people, including policemen and the mayor, have from time to time seen them over Wanaque, New Jersey. Color photographs were taken of a UFO that flew over Perth, Australia, in 1966, and was observed by as many as 10,000.[9]

Despite the incontrovertible evidence, the Air Force stuck to its claims. People who had seen the craft were understandably outraged. Cries of "cover-up!" grew louder. Anxious to escape the burden of public vehemence, the Air Force paid the University of Colorado half a mil-

7. Timothy Good, *Above Top Secret* (Sidgwick and Jackson Limited, 1987; rpt. New York: William Morrow and Company, Inc., 1988), pp. 346-352.
8. *Ibid.*, pp. 183, 520.
9. Otto O. Binder, "10,000,000 UFO Witnesses Can't Be Wrong!" *Mechanix Illustrated*, Jun. 1967, pp. 61-63, 144-145.

lion dollars to study UFOs "independently" and determine whether continued study was warranted.

Again mistakes were made. Dr. Edward Condon, who was to head the investigation, indicated a negative conclusion before the data had been studied. Project Coordinator Robert Low implied the project should be a whitewash. Condon publicly emphasized and ridiculed obviously spurious UFO reports, while ignoring puzzling "unknowns." A scandal erupted when Condon's negative attitude resulted in his firing of dissenting professors. Even though several unknowns were uncovered during the course of the investigation, the final published report said basically what the Air Force wanted it to say—that there was nothing to UFOs. Dr. David R. Saunders, Co-principal Investigator for the project, then published his own book, *UFOs? Yes! Where the Condon Committee Went Wrong*, in which he blasted the project's findings.[10] But Project Bluebook was officially closed down, and the Air Force claimed neither it nor any other government agency would be investigating UFOs henceforth.

Again civilian researchers weren't fooled. They pressed the issue for years, finally turning to the courts to get at the truth. Using channels spelled out in the Freedom of Information Act, they forced the release of documents. The Air Force resisted, but finally had to comply. The paper trail was followed, and led inevitably back to the CIA, the NSA (National Security Agency), the FBI, etc.

These agencies were targeted next for Freedom of Information requests. First they denied the documents existed, then they kicked and screamed "national security!" in much the same way they later protested during the trial of Lt. Col. Oliver North. But eventually some documents were forced out of them which prove that they were involved in the UFO situation from 1947 to the present. The end of Project Bluebook in 1969 was *not* the end of government involvement.

Clear Intent, by Lawrence Fawcett and Barry J. Greenwood, and *Above Top Secret,* by Timothy Good, document dozens of instances in which officials of the U.S. government and other governments were caught lying about their involvement with UFOs. Often the evidence is clearly visible in declassified documents obtained through Freedom of Information Act requests.[11, 12] But release of many of the requested documents is still being refused. As I prepare this book for publication, the DIA (Defense Intelligence Agency) still refuses to release six UFO-related documents. The CIA refuses to release 50 others. And, by its own admission, the NSA is still withholding more than 100 more.[13] These are undoubtedly not the only ones these agencies are withhold-

10. David R. Saunders and R. Roger Harkins, *UFOs? Yes! Where The Condon Committee Went Wrong* (New York: World Publishing Co. 1968; rpt. New York: Signet-New American Library, Inc., 1968).
11. Lawrence Fawcett and Barry J. Greenwood, *Clear Intent* (Englewood Cliffs, New Jersey: Prentice-Hall, Inc., 1984).
12. Good, *Above Top Secret*
13. Patrick Huyghe, "What the Government Isn't Saying about UFO's," *Omni*, Dec. 1990, p. 94.

ing; they are only the ones we know about. Furthermore, much of the information contained in documents that have been released was blacked out prior to release.

The intelligence agencies claim this secrecy is only to protect their methods of operation, but why should we believe that or anything else they tell us? Deception is their business—espionage, disinformation, psychological warfare, propaganda and brainwashing. They have gigantic budgets and are often not accountable to anyone. And because of the way they are compartmentalized on a need-to-know basis, some of their operations are so secret that even the President is not privy to them!

UFO investigators have long contended that the "protection of intelligence methods" story is just a cover to allow these agencies to keep certain information under wraps. They have usually entertained the ideas:

(a) UFOs are interplanetary spacecraft piloted by extraterrestrial beings possessing a superior technology

(b) The government knows this

(c) Officials don't want to tell us because they fear panic similar to the reaction to Orson Welles's famous *War of the Worlds* broadcast, or collapse of society's economic and religious structures, etc.

One of the chief reasons for this belief in a cover-up is that scores of witnesses claim the government has recovered crashed UFOs and their occupants on at least one and perhaps several occasions.

The "crashed saucer" story begins on July 2, 1947, when something exploded in the air and fell to the ground over Lincoln County, New Mexico. KSWS radio station reporter and part owner Johnny McBoyle went there. He called Lydia Sleppy, teletype operator at sister station KOAT in Albuquerque, to tell her it was a flying saucer, and he had seen it—it was "like a big crumpled dishpan." He said the Army had closed off the whole area, and told her to get the story out on the ABC wire right away. After only a few sentences, the teletype machine in Albuquerque stopped by itself and printed out a warning. It said in no uncertain terms to stop transmitting immediately. Lydia asked McBoyle what to do. McBoyle said she was not supposed to know about what had happened. He told her, in effect, to pretend the whole incident had never happened and not discuss it with anyone.[14]

On July 8, Roswell Army Air Field public information officer Lt. Walter Haut issued the press release quoted at the beginning of this chapter, saying that one of the flying discs had been recovered. It was picked up by both the Associated Press and the *New York Times* wire service. Papers across the U.S. and abroad printed it. The story also broke on New Mexico radio stations.[15]

14. Berlitz, *op. cit.*, pp. 14-15.
15. *Ibid.*, pp. 22-23, 45-46.

Then Brig. Gen. Roger M. Ramey took command of the situation, personally broadcasting the cover story that the "gadget" had only been the remains of a weather balloon. Meanwhile, he saw to it that what had really happened was buried as deeply as possible. Torn pieces of a weather balloon that had nothing to do with the incident were shown to newsmen and later to the public. They were told that the saucer story had just been a big misunderstanding by an excitable public information officer. Some witnesses who had actually seen the wreckage were told it was their patriotic duty to keep silent about it forever because national security was at stake. Others were threatened directly or it was implied to them that their families might be in danger if they ever talked about what they had seen. Meanwhile an intensive recovery and study effort was going on behind the scenes.

Ramey's efforts to keep the real story hidden from us very nearly worked. For years his cover story was widely believed. But the witnesses grew older, and eventually some of them lay on their deathbeds. They knew the long arm of Uncle Sam could no longer hurt them, and they yearned for deliverance from the awful burden of the secret that had weighed so heavily on them for so many years. Some of them talked.

Most of the stories were dismissed as delirium, but after a while they began to filter down to UFO investigators, some of whom still remembered the premature press release from Roswell. Knowing that the government, especially the military, often disseminated disinformation, they wondered if the stories might have some truth to them. They made a few inquiries, and soon they found themselves knee-deep in evidence that the crashed saucer story was true!

In 1980, authors Charles Berlitz and William L. Moore published *The Roswell Incident*, which presented the astounding results of detailed investigations they and physicist Stanton Friedman had made of the Roswell case. Their evidence had to be pieced together from various sources, many of which were secondhand, but it is remarkably cohesive, and debunkers have failed to discredit it.

Apparently what happened was that a UFO was struck by a lightning bolt or another UFO on that July night in 1947. An explosion resulted, which littered a remote area of William W. (Mac) Brazel's ranch with debris. The saucer-shaped craft was able to fly on for several miles before it crashed into another remote part of the New Mexican desert.

Brazel later came across the debris field. When he reported it to military authorities, he was held under armed guard for about a week, questioned and sworn to secrecy. He was told it was his patriotic duty not to tell anyone about the debris (some researchers believe he may also have received threats against himself or his family). He refused to talk about the subject to his death, 16 years later.

Meanwhile, intelligence officer Maj. Jesse Marcel was sent to collect every scrap of the debris from Brazel's ranch. It was flown by special plane to Wright Field for scientific examination under the direction of Lt. Gen. Hoyt Vandenburg, Deputy Chief of the Air Force, while Gen.

Ramey arranged for the torn pieces of weather balloon to be displayed at Roswell for newsmen to examine and photograph.[16]

Maj. Marcel told Friedman and Moore that the pieces of metal he collected were as thin as the foil in a pack of cigarettes and extremely light, but it could not be bent, cut or torn, even with a 16-pound sledgehammer. He affirmed that Gen. Ramey's weather balloon was a fake cover story, and that he, Marcel, was restricted from telling the press anything other than what he was told to say.[17]

The main body of the saucer and its dead small humanoid occupants were seen by many witnesses, notably one Grady Barnett, "a civil engineer working for the federal government in soil conservation." Military officials cordoned off the area, swore the witnesses to secrecy and sent them away. Teams of experts were brought in under strict security to study the disc and were also sworn to secrecy.

Both the wrecked craft and the "little men" were collected and sent to Air Force bases for study and storage, as witnessed by numerous military personnel along their routes and later at their destinations. The bodies were autopsied and found to be similar to humans, but hairless and small in stature, with large heads and underdeveloped limbs and features. They were then preserved in glass cases. The disc was studied and attempts were made to duplicate it.[18]

Everything was placed under such strict security that even years later, Sen. Barry Goldwater, a high-ranking reserve officer, was unable to find out anything about it. While visiting Gen. Curtis LeMay at Wright-Patterson AFB, he asked LeMay if he could see the "Blue Room" exhibits, where he had heard UFO artifacts were kept. LeMay told him, "Hell, no. I can't go, you can't go, and don't ever ask me again!"[19]

As of this writing, investigation of the Roswell case is still in full swing. Moore, Friedman, Capt. Kevin Randle, Don Schmitt and others have now interviewed scores of firsthand, secondhand, and thirdhand witnesses who swear they either saw, or talked to others who saw, the damaged saucer, the bodies of small "aliens" or both. A few witnesses have now come forward to claim that at least one of the occupants was still alive when it was taken away. Randle has even spoken with a former USAF sergeant who admits having followed orders handed down from the Pentagon to take weather balloons to several locations, including Roswell, to make people believe they had seen weather balloons instead of the UFOs they actually saw.[20]

The astonishing story these investigators have managed to piece together is as cohesive as cases prosecutors use to convict murderers. Statements made by one witness are often corroborated by others who had no prior knowledge of either those statements or of the original wit-

16. *Ibid.*, pp. 28-33.
17. *Ibid.*, pp. 66-68.
18. Berlitz, *op. cit.*
19. *Ibid.*, p. 124.
20. Kevin D. Randle, *The UFO Casebook* (New York: Warner Books, Inc., 1989), pp. 124-127. For more information, see Kevin D. Randle and Donald R. Schmitt, *UFO Crash at Roswell* (New York: Avon Books, 1991).

ness. And the common thread that holds them all together is the fact that *all* the witnesses (whether they were at the crash site, or were involved in transporting the debris, the saucer, or the bodies, or were present at the autopsies, or saw the bodies or the saucer in storage later) were told to keep quiet about what they had seen—forever. Some were told that national security was at stake, some were threatened and at least one man has complained of threats against his family.[21]

Perhaps the most damning evidence of all is the lack of evidence. The files of Project Sign, the Air Force project set up that year to explain away UFOs, contain no reference to the Roswell event.[22]

Many believe that the Roswell affair will eventually be the "Achilles' heel" that will expose the government cover-up of UFOs. More than perhaps any other incident, it has produced proof that the U.S. government knows far more about UFOs than it is telling. It is not, however, the only persistent story of crashed saucers and little men.

In 1950, syndicated columnist Frank Scully published *Behind the Flying Saucers*, which contained unsubstantiated secondhand and thirdhand accounts of crashed flying saucers and occupants being retrieved by American scientists.

An alleged informant, "Dr. Gee," implied one saucer had been built using feet and inches, and said its bottom part was encircled with a gear that engaged a gear on its cabin. This is surprisingly mundane machinery for a spacecraft, but could very well be found in a terrestrial aircraft of unusual design. His description of the occupants sounded as if they could have been human children, all with perfect teeth, dressed in clothing resembling the styles worn in 1890.[23] This sounds like disinformation. But was it?

Scully indicated that the saucers were dismantled and that they and their occupants were shipped to air bases to be studied and stored.

The story was widely scorned as a hoax. Many believed Scully had been duped and that the whole affair was an elaborate fiction.[24] But was it really? Or was Scully the victim of unfair criticism? Berlitz and Moore write in *The Roswell Incident*:

> *...Mrs. Frank Scully, widow of the writer, interviewed by Bill Moore at her home in June and December 1979, steadfastly maintained that the basic story behind her husband's book was correct and that he had been vilified because of it—particularly by J.P. Cahn, a "most unscrupulous journalist from San Francisco" who may have been paid off to do "the hatchet job" on Scully. It is true that Cahn's article on Scully and his book is full of exaggerations and inaccuracies.[25]*

21. Huyghe, "What the Government Isn't Saying," p. 93.
22. Randle, *Casebook*, p. 10.
23. Frank Scully, *Behind the Flying Saucers* (New York: Henry Holt and Company, 1950), pp. 24, 129-133.
24. Ronald Story, "Scully Hoax," in Ronald D. Story, ed., *The Encyclopedia of UFOs* (Garden City, New York: Dolphin Books-Doubleday & Company, Inc., 1980), p. 326.
25. Berlitz, *op. cit.*, p. 47.

They also learned that Scully's scientist informant had told Mrs. Scully details about the "alien bodies," and that former Project Bluebook head Capt. Edward Ruppelt had told her that *Behind the Flying Saucers* had caused the Air Force "headaches" because it had been fairly accurate. They speculated that the government may have used psychological warfare tactics. Scully could have been fed information that would later be used to discredit him, and thereby discredit the whole concept he was trying to expose.[26]

Even after Scully was discredited, rumors of crashed saucers continued to surface, but witnesses were afraid to give their names. Military historian Fletcher Pratt announced publicly in 1950 that he had received similar information about a crashed saucer and humanoid bodies, but even he protected his sources.[27] Most subsequent stories were also secondhand and thirdhand accounts, but contained remarkably similar details. Many of them could not be traced back to Scully. Often they were told by former military men, intelligence officers or civilian employees of Air Force bases. The tellers were always adamant that under no circumstances must their real identities be revealed. They said they had been sworn to secrecy and feared retribution if the government were to find out they had talked.

UFO investigator and author Leonard Stringfield detailed three deathbed confessions of crashed saucer/little men stories in *Situation Red, The UFO Siege*.

One of the cases involved a minister and his son. They had stumbled upon preserved small humanoid bodies in glass cases in what was guessed to be a Security Intelligence Corps office in Chicago's Museum of Science and Industry. The minister was immediately seized by several men, forced into another room and detained. He had to sign some papers before being allowed to leave.

Another case concerned a dying woman who had a top security clearance while working at Wright-Patterson Field. She had seen a damaged saucer and an intact one in a secret hangar and had processed paperwork for the autopsy report of two preserved "creatures" secreted in another building.

The third story involved a similar confession from a man who had worked with Project Bluebook.[28]

Stringfield continued to collect similar stories (and still collects them today). In 1980, he stated that he had reliable data from almost 50 sources that the military had retrieved crashed UFOs and/or bodies of occupants. Five of the sources were firsthand and had served in military capacities. Some of those had been in intelligence. One of his informants worked in a hospital where humanoids had been autopsied. The information was enough to convince Stringfield, a former skeptic,

---

26. *Ibid.*, pp. 48-50.
27. *Ibid.*, p. 50.
28. Leonard H. Stringfield, *Situation Red, The UFO Siege* (Garden City, New York: Doubleday & Company, Inc., 1977), pp. 177-178.

even though the military documentation is still classified "above TOP SECRET."[29]

Raymond Fowler presented more accounts of retrievals of crashed UFOs in *Casebook of a UFO Investigator.* One was almost identical to the New Mexico accounts but took place outside Mexico City. Another occurred very early on a Sunday morning in 1953 or 1954 at Mattydale, New York.

Fowler's strongest case involved an engineer of excellent reputation holding degrees in mathematics, physics and engineering. He had held management and engineering positions at Wright-Patterson AFB. During the incident, he was working within "the Air Material [sic] Command Installations Division, within the Office of Special Studies...." He was project engineer on an Air Force contract with the Atomic Energy Commission for "Operation Upshot-Knothole," measuring blast effects on structures. Although he would not allow publication of his real name, he gave Fowler a signed affidavit testifying to his story. Fowler refers to him by the pseudonym "Fritz Werner."

On May 21, 1953, Werner and 15 other specialists reported for special duty. They left their valuables with military police at Indian Springs Air Force Base, and they were then flown to Phoenix. They were not allowed to talk to one another. They then boarded a bus with blacked-out windows. They were driven to a destination in the desert, where a silver, saucer-shaped craft had crashed and stuck in the sand at an angle. It was night. Bright lights had been set up, and the site was surrounded by guards. Also guarded was a tent containing the dead body of a four-foot-tall humanoid in a silver suit. The specialists were escorted to the disk one at a time to gather data for reports (Werner's report was to be written in longhand and not reproduced, and was picked up later by special Air Force courier). They were subjected to recorded interviews, escorted back to the bus and sworn to secrecy by an Air Force Colonel. The Colonel told them the craft was "a supersecret Air Force Vehicle."[30]

In 1984, TV producer Jaime Shandera received a document supposedly prepared for President Eisenhower in 1952. It is classified "TOP SECRET/MAJIC/EYES ONLY" and describes a supersecret panel of generals, admirals, intelligence heads and highly distinguished scientists formed by President Truman in 1947 to investigate UFOs and report to him. The retrieval of crashed saucers and the bodies of small humanoids are stated as facts. The panel is referred to as "Majestic 12" (also "Majic-12" or "MJ-12"). The entire document is reproduced as an appendix in *Above Top Secret,* and in Howard Blum's *Out There.*[31, 32]

In 1989, Shandera claimed to have a dozen very high level "deepthroat" informants to corroborate the story. He was speaking of people

---

29. Story, *op. cit.,* p. 353.
30. Raymond E. Fowler, *Casebook of a UFO Investigator* (Englewood Cliffs, New Jersey: Prentice-Hall, Inc., 1981), pp. 196-203.
31. Good, *Above Top Secret,* pp. 544-551.
32. Howard Blum, *Out There* (New York: Simon & Schuster, 1990), appendix.

on the level of members of Congress.[33] Two witnesses to the MJ-12 affair were seen in silhouette with their voices disguised on the two-hour TV special *UFO Cover-Up... Live,* which aired October 14, 1988. They allowed themselves to be identified only by the code names "Falcon" and "Condor."[34]

Government officials deny any knowledge that the MJ-12 group ever existed, and debunkers are still searching for some inconsistency in the document that could prove it is a fake, but so far these efforts have failed. The document is written in the correct style, with appropriate date codes, etc. Every member of the panel listed in the document would have been logical choices to sit on just such a panel at the time the document was allegedly written. And as Pulitzer Prize nominee Blum showed us in *Out There,* a supersecret panel of military, intelligence and scientific experts could have been convened to deal with the UFO question then because *one exists now.*

Like the Roswell case, which was probably the reason the MJ-12 panel would have been convened in the first place, the MJ-12 story defies all attempts to squash it. It refuses to die. And it is only one of many flashing red arrows suggesting a government cover-up that makes Watergate look like child's play.

When he was 12 years old, an acquaintance of mine—I'll call him "Bob"—saw a fascinating example of the way the government cover-up works. The place was a farm in Michigan. The year was 1961. Bob had gone to a friend's house to spend the night. He had not been there long when a UFO "shaped like a fried egg" descended near the barn, not more than 50 feet away. It was bright, with lights on the bottom, lights and "portholes" on the top, and a rotating dome.

Bob and his friend's family watched in amazement as the object made a whirring sound, extended a tripod landing gear, and settled to earth. The friend's mother ran to the house and called the police. Before she could hang up the telephone, the craft had risen back into the sky and flown away.

Minutes later, a motorcade from the air base 14 miles away rushed into the farm's driveway and skidded to a stop. An Air Force colonel listened to the story and examined the burned circle the craft had left on the ground. He told everyone they were not to say a word about what they had seen. He then told the farmer he wanted him to plow the landing site under and hose it down—*and handed him five $100 bills.*

The colonel and several Air Force personnel stood by until the farmer destroyed all traces of the landing site, then drove back the way they had come. Bob, who had been closest to the object, had trouble with his eyes. He had never needed glasses before the incident, but afterward he had to be fitted with thick glasses, which he still wears.

Author and UFO investigator Warren Smith personally felt the pressure of government efforts to maintain secrecy on at least one oc-

33. *The Mike Murphy Show,* KCMO radio, Kansas City, Missouri, 6 Feb. 1989.
34. *UFO Cover-Up...Live,* produced by LBS Communications and Michael Seligman, hosted by Mike Farrell, 14 Oct. 1988.

casion. After having obtained a piece of metal from a farmer who said he found it on the ground under where a UFO had hovered, Smith suffered break-ins and searches of his hotel room, interference with his telephone messages and hotel records and finally a visit by two men who made veiled threats against his wife, children and publisher. When he asked to see identification, the men told him they had IDs from NORAD, the USAF, the FBI or any other agency Smith wanted to name. After forcing Smith to hand over his artifact, the two men left the southern Wisconsin town in a car bearing an Illinois license that Smith later determined had never been issued. He came to the conclusion that the men must have been CIA agents.[35]

UFO literature is replete with instances of officials pressuring people to keep silent about their encounters. Raymond Fowler writes:

> I have come across several cases where investigating Air Force officers specifically told police, airline pilots and government employees not to talk about their UFO sightings—and threatened investigators for releasing data to the public.[36]

In *Casebook of a UFO Investigator*, Fowler gives numerous examples of UFO witnesses and investigators being subjected to surveillance. Their cars are followed, their houses are watched, their telephones are tapped, etc.[37]

A common complaint of witnesses is that a few hours or days after UFO encounters, a man or men will come to their doors and demand that they keep quiet about what they have seen. The demands often involve vague threats that are not carried out.

Fowler gives a typical example in *The Andreasson Affair, Phase Two*. A person living in Oxford, Maine, experienced an apparent UFO abduction on October 27, 1975. Two days later, a stranger about 5'7" tall wearing sunglasses and dark blue clothes arrived at his front door and asked if he had "seen a flying saucer." When he answered affirmatively, the man told him that if he knew what was good for him, he had better keep his mouth shut.[38]

The mystery of these cases is that often the witness has not yet had a chance to tell anyone about his encounter. So how does the man who comes to threaten him know about it? There are numerous accounts of this intriguing paradox to be found in UFO literature. The obvious implication is that these government agents, or whoever they are, were either present at the time of the UFO encounter, or are in communication with the ufonauts. The subject will be probed in depth in Chapter 14.

Percipients of UFO encounters have also reported being followed by unmarked, flat-black helicopters. One hovered over Betty Andreasson while she worked in her garden in Ashburnham, Massachusetts, where her famous abduction took place. Later, she married Bob Luca,

---

35. Smith, *op. cit.*, pp. 210-219.
36. Fowler, *Casebook*, p. 165.
37. *Ibid.*, pp. 172-181.
38. Fowler, *Phase Two*, pp. 217-218.

who had a UFO experience of his own (see Chapter 1), and they moved to Connecticut. Right away they noticed black helicopters with no identification markings flying illegally low over their house. Neighbors said it was unusual.

Luca photographed the machines and complained to the authorities. One FAA official told Luca his description of the events brought to mind CIA activities. The Lucas continued to be plagued by the helicopters while driving, while vacationing, after moving to another house, etc. Bob continued to photograph them and complain to various authorities, but no explanation was ever given. He sent photos to Bell Helicopter, and was told that they looked like Huey UH-1Hs, and that the military may have modified them.[39]

"Stealth" helicopters have been reported for years in connection with UFOs, especially in cases involving livestock mutilations. One of the most astounding cases was related by Jenny Randles in *The UFO Conspiracy: The First Forty Years*.

On December 29, 1980, Betty Cash, Vickie Landrum and Colby (Landrum's young grandson) were driving through a pine forest at night near Huffman, Texas. They saw a silent, diamond-shaped UFO appear ahead of them. It was "pouring out flame and light." The car became very hot, and they exited it. Betty felt her wedding ring burning her finger. The Landrums got back in the car. A large number of Chinook helicopters arrived and ushered the hovering UFO away.

After the incident, the witnesses suffered vomiting, diarrhea, headaches, hair loss and burns as if their skin had been cooked. Betty Cash was in intensive care for an extended period, and was hospitalized on several occasions, altogether covering most of seven or more years following the encounter. Houston space shuttle engineer John Shuessler, NASA scientist Dr. Alan Holt and members of the Mutual UFO Network (MUFON) located corroborating witnesses. The U.S. government denied any knowledge of the affair—even of the presence of the helicopters. The witnesses sued for damages.[40]

It is of course absurd to suppose military authorities really had no knowledge of the affair. Large contingents of Chinook helicopters are not something one can charter at a local airport. What is most intriguing about this case is that the helicopters did not dive at the UFO or shoot it down—they simply escorted it away. It appears as if there was a degree of cooperation. Perhaps there was a greater degree than we think. One of the informants interviewed on the *UFO Cover-Up...Live* program claimed the "Cash-Landrum" UFO was being test-flown by military personnel who had trouble controlling it!

What do we really know from all this impossible muddle of rumor, innuendo, subterfuge, claims, testimony and downright solid evidence? Does it mean we know there are aliens coming to Earth in spaceships?

39. *Ibid.*, pp. 210-215.
40. Jenny Randles, *The UFO Conspiracy: The First Forty Years* (Poole, England: Blandford Press, 1987), pp. 147-149.

Not necessarily.

It means the government knows more about UFOs than it's telling. It means there is at least one important reason why government officials are resolute about keeping UFO evidence out of the glare of public scrutiny. It means we will probably see a protracted series of allegations, denials and political tooth-pulling equal to Watergate and Iran/Contra combined before the truth is admitted—if it is ever admitted. And even then, we will probably not learn the whole truth and will always have to doubt what we do learn.

Dr. Vallée says he thinks the cover-up is bound to fail despite the protective shell of ridiculous disinformation.[41] But I'm not so sure. These intelligence agents are professionals. Concealment and disinformation is their business. They know exactly how to confuse us. And until they decide that they are ready to level with us, if we do manage to pry any facts out of them, each one will have two red herrings attached. That golden fleece of *ultimate truth* that UFO investigators have been seeking so aggressively is buried under so much red tape, compartmentalization and cloak-and-dagger rigmarole that even its keepers probably don't know how to get at it anymore.

So how do we solve the mystery of the UFO? By examining the data we already have.

Take a moment to ask yourself, "Why all the secrecy?" Is it because the government wants to prevent panic? Not likely. Polls show that a large fraction of the population already believes in extraterrestrial life, and a large portion of that population believes we are being visited. There doesn't seem to be any panic. Of course, Orson Welles's broadcast of *War of the Worlds* did cause a stir 50 years ago, but we were much less informed and sophisticated then. Besides, the Martians in that bit of fiction were supposed to have been systematically demolishing whole cities with "death rays," while real UFO occupants seem much less belligerent.

Is it because they fear collapse of economic or religious structures? Maybe, but the hundreds of people who have been contacted—the Betty Andreassons and Kathie Davises—haven't quit working and attending church. And if collapse is so worrisome a probability, why does it appear that nothing is being done to prepare us for the day when it inevitably must come?

Is it because some country might copy the UFOs before the U.S. does, and then they will have even more of an advantage over Americans than Americans had over everyone else when the U.S. alone had atomic bombs? Perhaps, but if we haven't been able to copy them after all this time, how can someone else? And if we already have, why haven't we used our copies to rid the world of the horror of nuclear weapons? A vehicle that could hover, stop instantly and travel through the atmosphere in any direction at thousands of miles per hour (as UFOs do) would be an invincible weapons delivery system, overwhelm-

---

41. Vallée, *Confrontations*, p. 226.

ingly superior to anything now being used. Since humans have existed, they have fought, and the axiom has always been that he who possesses the superior weapon uses it, either directly or as a threat, and prevails. Are we to believe that rule has been discarded?

Are officials covering up because our military forces are embarrassed to admit that their airspace is being violated? It's possible, but everybody already knows all about it. So why be embarrassed? And the airspace of every other country in the world is being invaded, too. Why be embarrassed?

Let's suppose for a moment that not all genuine, piloted UFOs are from the same source. Let's assume there are "good guys" and "bad guys." The bad guys might be comparable to the Mafia, which operates in secrecy right under our noses all the time. We squirm a little when we think about it, but we all know it exists, even though it is concealed. The good guys might correspond to undercover policemen, whose job it is to infiltrate the Mafia. Their need for secrecy is also intense. An undercover cop must always live in fear of "having his cover blown." Could the U.S. government and the governments of other nations be supporting some type of cosmic police action? Is that why they are lying to us about UFOs?

Buried in the mountain of data investigators have painstakingly excavated are patterns. I pointed out a few of them at the end of Chapter 1. Now we have another one—the government cover-up—to add to the list. As we continue our study of UFO reports, we will add others. If we can refrain from jumping to wild conclusions about "Moon maidens" and "Martian monsters" long enough to study these patterns carefully, we will find clues. And once we have enough clues, we can weave them together into an hypothesis which at last explains some of the UFOs *and* fits the relevant data.

Knowledge progresses by the refutation as well as the confirmation of hypotheses, and the only essential is not to persist stubbornly in obsolete habits of mind.

—*Aimé Michel*[1]

A Fresh Approach

An attendance list at a UFO conference can sometimes read like a who's who of "weirdos" and "kooks."

Believing what one wants to believe seems to be a universal human trait. A growing number want to believe that since ufonauts possess technology superior to ours, they must have come from other planets to help us clean up the mess we have made of Earth—that they must be "ethereal beings from a higher plane come to guide our spirits toward a more harmonious path." UFOs have become a sort of new religion for the disturbed and disillusioned who find no solace in the old ones. Where wishful thinking ends is impossible to say, even for psychologists. After all, there is no way of proving that Ms. X is *not* in mental contact with a gorgeous Saturnian Councilman or with an Elvis look-alike from the center of the hollow Earth.

And of course anywhere the gullible and confused congregate, the unscrupulous are sure to prey upon them. A lot of money has been paid for "Magic Powers Saucer Amulets" and "Ultimate Secret of the Ethereans" pamphlets. "The world is about to come to an end," one is likely to hear, "but you can get one of the few remaining seats on an intergalactic alien ship and avoid the catastrophe. All you have to do is sign over your earthly possessions, which of course will be useless anyway!"

As the previous chapters demonstrate, truth is stranger than fiction in this field, as in any other. Those who have undergone genuine

1. Aimé Michel, *Mysterieux Objets celestes* (Paris: Arthaud, 1958), trans. Civilian Saucer Intelligence of New York, *Flying Saucers and the Straight Line Mystery* (New York: Criterion Books, 1958), p. 206.

contact experiences relate stories of high strangeness. Many of them even suffer from poltergeist activity following their encounters.

So it's not surprising that even when scientists who could make substantial progress toward solving the UFO mystery become interested, they seldom let themselves become involved. Most depend on research grants from prestigious organizations. Letting their names become associated with "crackpots" could be professional suicide. And many are simply too annoyed by the fringe elements to become interested.

The government has been very successful in keeping scientific research out of the public eye. Several scientists have admitted to doing secret research for the government, studying crashed UFOs and their occupants. Others—Dr. Donald Menzel, for example—are rumored to have been employed by the government to debunk UFO sightings (incidentally, the MJ-12 document lists Dr. Menzel as one of the original members of the secret MJ-12 group). Still others have swallowed whole the "UFOs don't exist" charade the Air Force has fed us for years, and refuse to even consider examining any of the data.

Scientists who have not been approached to work on the problem *for* the government find there is no money for open research *from* the government. A huge portion of all research funds comes from defense– and other government-sponsored programs. Scientists know the government's hard-line position that UFOs don't exist. So, since they depend on research funds for their livelihoods, they don't study UFOs.

It is private researchers who have done the job. With very few exceptions, ufologists are amateurs. They do their sleuthing in their spare time, after work and on weekends. Using their own resources for support and their curiosity for incentive, they have compiled and painstakingly documented an immense—and impressive—amount of valuable raw data over the last 40 years.

The evidence speaks for itself. After known hoaxes, hallucinations and misperceptions are filtered out, the theories that UFOs are atmospheric animals, psychological constructs, fairies, angels or demons do not seem to fit the data. The "hollow Earth" hypothesis appears to be nonsense.

As we saw in Chapter 2, the idea that UFOs are U.S. secret weapons makes little sense. Neither do they seem to be Russian secrets. If the Russians had such advanced weapons delivery systems, would they make their people wait in line for hours to buy a loaf of bread so they could build costly arsenals of outdated conventional weapons? Would they have let thousands of their soldiers die in Afghanistan? Would they have lost the fight in Afghanistan? Would they be so fearful of an American attack? Why would they risk flying their secret devices over American soil? Why would they be doing breeding experiments on us?

Before his death, the late Dr. Felix Zigel, hailed as the foremost authority on UFOs in what was then the Soviet Union, admitted being as puzzled as we are about them. He noted that UFOs of all shapes and sizes had been observed hovering, maneuvering, and streaking through the sky at 100,000 k.p.h. (without burning up), appearing and disappearing, and causing power outages and engine stoppages. As Jacques Vallée documents in his latest book, *UFO Chronicles of the Soviet Union: A Cosmic Samizdat,* scientists are studying numerous encounters of all types (including abductions) that have occurred in what is now the fledgling Commonwealth of Independent States.[2,3]

The popular idea that UFOs are extraterrestrial spacecraft piloted by super-intelligent beings from other solar systems ostensibly explains some UFO encounters nicely. But for many others, it is no better than the other theories mentioned because it simply *does not fit the data.*

One problem with the extraterrestrial hypothesis is that in the vast majority of cases the occupants of UFOs appear human or humanoid. As Dr. Vallée comments:

> Contactees tell us they have met the denizens of other planets. In some cases the beings turn out to be robots or dwarfs in diving suits, but in most incidents they were humanoid, and they could breathe our air. They walked normally on our planet. In a variety of sightings they were accompanied by human beings. Occasionally, the occupants were completely human and spoke human languages.
>
> However, visitors from outer space would not necessarily be human in shape. They would certainly not breathe our air (for fear of viruses). They might have serious problems with the earth's gravity.[4]

Vallée's point is well taken. If the occupants of UFOs evolved independently on distant planets, would they resemble us so closely? It seems highly unlikely. In fact, exobiologists have often suggested that independently evolved alien life forms are likely to be so different from us that we might be unable to recognize that they are intelligent or even alive at all. The probability of such a scenario is one of the chief arguments against "terraforming" other worlds.

On the other hand, if life on Earth did *not* evolve independently of life elsewhere, then the similarity of DNA is not an obstacle to the theory of extraterrestrial UFOs, but instead is significant evidence for the theory. Consider the relative youth of our solar system compared to the billions of presumably life-suitable and Earth-similar planets elsewhere in our galaxy. Humanoid life might have evolved elsewhere millions of years before Earth was ready. Such advanced civilizations might have long ago colonized other planets or even conducted genetic engineering experiments, combining their DNA with that of indigenous life forms on various planets. Such intentional seeding activities would create "punctuated evolution" such as the sudden rise of Cro-Magnon man and leave DNA compatibility and interbreeding between aliens

2. Gordon Creighton, "Dr. Zigel and the Development of Ufology in Russia: Part II," *Flying Saucer Review,* 27, No. 4 (1982), p. 18.
3. Jacques Vallée, in collaboration with Martine Castello, *UFO Chronicles of the Soviet Union: A Cosmic Samizdat* (New York: Ballantine Books, 1992).
4. Jacques Vallée, *Messengers of Deception* (New York: Bantam Books, Inc., 1980), pp. 30-31.

and earthlings merely a predictable and continuing consequence of our
true history.

Although disembodied brains, beer-can-shaped creatures, or "liz-
ard men" are reported on occasion, UFO occupants are almost always
humanoid. Do human beings and "ufonauts" have a common heritage?
What is our connection to them? How can we ever cut through all the
spurious information surrounding the UFO subject to get at the under-
lying facts and solve the puzzle?

Perhaps we have taken the wrong approach.

Maybe we have been asking the wrong questions. Why not forget
the big "Where did UFOs come from?" and "Why are they here?" questions for a while and see if some of the smaller ones can be answered
by analyzing that mountain of observational data we have collected?
Why not form hypotheses that can be tested experimentally? No competent scientist jumps immediately to final conclusions without first
forming a foundation of knowledge based on observations and then
building on that foundation; why should ufologists?

There are plenty of other questions to ask:

Q: Why do automobiles, televisions, even the electrical systems
   of entire cities sometimes—but not always—cease to function in the presence of UFOs?

Q: How can UFOs fly at such incredible speeds in our
   atmosphere—speeds that would incinerate conventional
   aircraft?

Q: How do they perform right-angled turns at these speeds?

Q: How do they hover soundlessly without moving the air?

Q: How can they appear, disappear, and change shape?

Q: Why are they sometimes not detected by radar?

Q: Why are they sometimes detected by radar but not seen?

Q: How can there be so many different types of craft and occupants?

Q: Why aren't there any good photographs?

Q: Why do some abductees suffer paranormal manifestations
   following encounters?

Q: What is the connection between the government and UFOs?

Maybe we should change our methods of examining data a little,
too. Several past studies failed to reach conclusions for several reasons, not the least of which was that researchers, determined to filter
out all irrelevant data, "threw the baby out with the bath water." The
following statement by Dr. Hynek is an excellent example:

> The "repeater" aspect of some UFO reporters is sufficient cause,
> in my opinion, to exclude their reports from further consideration, at
> least in the present study.[5]

---

5. Hynek, *Experience*, p. 30.

Thus, the Kathie Davis story is not admissible evidence. Betty Andreasson and Whitley Strieber must be excluded from consideration. In fact, *most* abduction stories can't be used, since most abductees report multiple encounters. Unfortunately, the fact that the same witnesses often see UFOs on more than one occasion may be one of the most important clues of all to the solution of the UFO mystery!

Dr. Hynek was not alone in his well intentioned attempt to "clean up" the data. It was years after accounts of contacts with "saucer people" began to reach the public before many investigators would accept even the slightest possibility that they might have validity. These accounts exhibited such a high degree of strangeness that they were completely disregarded. And so many charlatans tried to take advantage of public interest in the subject that researchers assumed any account that included occupants *must* be spurious.

In addition, only a tiny fraction of the percipients of UFO encounters dared to tell anyone of their experiences for fear of persecution. Those who did often remembered only parts of those experiences, and usually did not tell investigators vital details because they seemed too strange, embarrassing, or silly to possibly be true.

Most investigators had "pet" theories about what UFOs were, and many of them overlooked data that did not fit these theories. Some even twisted the truth to make sure the data would support their contentions.

Other researchers, frustrated by the anecdotal nature of the information, approached the problem the same way that a court of law would handle evidence in a criminal trial. Accounts of encounters with fewer than two unrelated witnesses were not considered substantial evidence. Testimony from criminals, drug users, children—anyone whose character was less than model—was stricken from the record. Any accounts of UFO encounters lacking exact place, date or time could not be used. If witnesses would not allow their names to be published, their stories were unacceptable. Such stringent screening criteria eliminated most of the pertinent data. Conclusions became impossible.

This study is different. I did not follow the commonly accepted rules of journalism that require two firsthand sources for each fact. The degree of strangeness of an account did not keep it out of these pages. Instead, what I used as a criterion for inclusion was repetition. For each of the cases considered here there are 10 or 100 or 1,000 others that contain similar—sometimes identical—details. Any of the accounts I have included might be a mistake or deception, but each similar account adds weight to the others. If there are enough accounts, that weight can become overwhelming, especially when witnesses have never heard of one another (or of UFOs), and when they want nothing to do with publicity.

The scientific method dictates that conclusions drawn from observational data be used to form a hypothesis, which must then be tested repeatedly through experimentation and found to be correct before it may be accepted as scientific fact. But UFO data are *anecdotal* rather than *empirical.* While UFOs may be in government hands, they are not available to us for laboratory study.

The accounts in this work are not the control and experimental data that will be used to arrive at scientific fact, but observational data that will enable us to form a working hypothesis. The difference could be analogous to the difference between a congressional investigation and a trial. We can read any information we want to into this record. At this stage, there is no distinction between admissible evidence and inadmissible evidence. We are trying to get to the bottom of this mystery. *All* the evidence is pertinent.

Much as we might wish to keep the data we like and discard the rest, let's *try* to keep an open mind. We should remember that there was a time in our history when a man who stated that the sun, not the earth, was the center of our solar system was in danger of being burned at the stake. The assertion that the earth was spherical was the merest nonsense to the scientists who "knew" it was flat. As late as the last century, there were no such things as meteors; everyone "knew" there were no stones *in* the sky, therefore no stones could possibly fall *from* the sky. Air travel, then supersonic flight, then space flight, then lunar landings were all preposterous notions to most people a few years before they happened...but not to people with open minds.

*The premise that UFOs, or at least **some** UFOs, are associated with strong magnetic fields is only tenuously supported at the present time.*
—Allan Hendry[1]

"Electromagnetic" Effects

There are hundreds of cases in UFO literature of automobiles being affected by the close approach of a UFO.

Sometimes the cars just slow down. A Mr. T. Untiedt experienced this on November 16, 1965, while driving near Cyrus, Minnesota. When his car came to within a quarter mile of a fluorescent red UFO enveloped in a white glow, it slowed down. The UFO then flew away.[2]

Levelland, Texas, Fire Marshal Ray Jones reported a similar effect in the wee hours of November 3, 1957. Driving north of the Oklahoma Flat near Levelland in an attempt to see UFOs that had been reported by numerous citizens that morning, he noticed his car's headlights dimmed and its engine sputtered just as he saw a "streak of light."[3]

At 7:45 on the morning of November 7, 1957, the engine of Mrs. Frank Lain's new car also sputtered—and then died. Looking above her, she spotted a silver, disc-shaped UFO hovering at an altitude of about 200 feet above her Lake Charles, Louisiana, location. After the saucer sped away, she had no trouble restarting the car.[4]

Most of the reports do involve engines failing completely. It was a rash of such reports around Levelland that had prompted Ray Jones to go hunting for UFOs in the case mentioned earlier. Jim Wheeler, a resident of Whitharral, was among the many witnesses who reported

1. Allan Hendry, *The UFO Handbook* (Garden City, New York: Doubleday & Company, Inc., 1979), p. 190.
2. From *Flying Saucer Review*, 66, No. 6, as reported in Jacques Vallée, *Passport to Magonia* (Chicago: Henry Regnery Co., 1969), pp. 320-321.
3. Hynek, *Experience*, p. 127.
4. From *Saucer News*, Feb.-Mar. 1958, as reported in Alexander D. Mebane, "The 1957 Saucer Wave in the United States," appendix in Michel, *Straight Line Mystery*, p. 263.

engines stalling when they approached UFOs during a two-hour period that night. At about midnight, Wheeler was driving a few miles east of Levelland. A brilliantly lit, egg-shaped UFO about 200 feet long rested in the road, casting a bright light over the area. Wheeler's car engine and headlights quit. When he got out of his car, the UFO ascended to about 200 feet and the light went out. He could then start his engine. A few minutes later, another Whitharral man, Joe Alvaraz, called authorities with an identical report.[5, 6]

At the same time, Texas Tech student Newell Wright was driving east of Levelland when his car's engine sputtered, its ammeter fluctuated, its headlights dimmed and failed, and its engine quit. He saw a glowing, oval, blue-green UFO about 100 feet long in the road ahead. He could not start his car until the "aluminum-like" object shot up vertically to disappear "in a split instant." Another nearly identical encounter was reported a few miles north. When the UFO shot up vertically to about 300 feet, extinguished its lights and disappeared, the car's headlights came back on and the engine could be restarted.[7, 8]

During a wave of French sightings in October, 1954, two mechanics were baffled by a similar occurrence at Cuisy, Seine-et-Marne, at about 9:20 at night. André Bartoli saw a yellow-orange cigar-shaped UFO; his car's engine and headlights failed and his car stopped suddenly. Jean Jacques Lalevée witnessed the incident. After the UFO left, Bartoli was able to restart the car and the headlights worked.[9]

The same thing happened to Julia Juste and two other women near Châteauneuf-sur-Charente in November. The glowing, globe-shaped UFOs stopped, moved back and forth and stopped again. One grew brilliant white with a red halo.[10]

During that same wave, Henri Gallois and Louis Vigneron felt paralyzed as if by an electric shock when their vehicle's engine and headlights failed near Sassier at 4:30 in the morning. They then noticed a round, landed UFO and three figures about 150 feet away. When the figures boarded the craft and left at high speed, the men could move, and the car worked.[11]

The paralysis is not at all uncommon. On March 9, 1967, at 1:00 in the morning, a couple driving near Leominster, Massachusetts, spotted a bright, oval, humming UFO, and stopped to look. When the driver exited the car and pointed at it, the car's lights, engine and radio all quit, his arm was thrown back against the car, and he was paralyzed. His wife, still inside the car, was not affected. After 40 seconds, the UFO flew away, and the car's lights and radio resumed functioning.[12]

5. Hynek, *Experience,* pp. 124-125.
6. Paris Flammonde, *UFO Exist!* (New York: G. P. Putnam's Sons, 1976), pp. 289-290.
7. Hynek, *Experience,* pp. 124-125.
8. Flammonde, *op. cit.,* p. 290.
9. Michel, *Straight Line Mystery,* pp. 150-151.
10. *Ibid.,* p. 160.
11. *Ibid.,* p. 158.

In June of 1964, the engine of another couple's car quit at Pajas Blancas, Córdoba, Argentina, and they saw a very large, bright UFO in the road. After the bright lights went out, and only a violet light remained, a man came to their car to tell them they should not fear and that the car would then work if they started it. It did, and the stranger and two others boarded the craft, which left.[13]

Some cases involve several vehicles and several witnesses. On November 6, 1957, at 5:40 A.M., the cars of Richard Kehoe, Ronald Burke and Joe Thomas were stopped on the Vista del Mar highway near Playa del Rey, California. All three drivers saw an egg-shaped UFO enveloped in a blue haze resting on a nearby beach. Two men with yellow-green complexions who wore black leather pants and light jerseys spoke to them in English that was hard to understand. They asked the drivers *what time it was*, who they were, etc. Of course when the UFO took off, all three cars could be started.[14] The sallow skin tone of the ufonauts could easily have been exaggerated by the very early morning light near the ocean. They appeared normal otherwise.[15]

An even more startling case occurred in September, 1956. Just before 8:00 A.M. a domed disk landed less than 50 yards from busy U.S. 70 highway near Holloman Air Force Base in New Mexico, stalling cars and creating a traffic jam for ten minutes. Among the many amazed witnesses were "two air force colonels, two sergeants, and dozens of base employees...." Air Force Intelligence and CIA operatives from Washington interrogated all base employees and swore them to secrecy.[16]

Cars are not the only vehicles affected. At dusk on November 8, 1954, André Chaillou's motorcycle succumbed to a blue, disc-shaped UFO at La Tessoualle, France. Chaillou himself was paralyzed.[17]

Ray Hawks's tractor similarly stalled in Left Hand Canyon, near Boulder, Colorado. The date was August 11, 1960. Hawks heard a muffled explosion and saw a gray disc descend vertically through a cloud. It wobbled "as a coin wobbles when thrown upon a table," and hovered at about a 200-foot altitude. A platelike structure was replaced as if a repair had been effected. The UFO made a humming sound that increased in pitch, then it appeared to be enveloped in a "shimmering field," as if it were very hot. The object sped away upward instantly. Hawks then felt as if he were "coming to his senses" and was able to restart the tractor, which worked normally from then on.[18]

Baptiste Jourdy's milk truck was temporarily put out of commission near Fronfrède, Loire, France, when a large, luminous, multicol-

12. Fowler, *The Andreasson Affair*, pp. 164-166.
13. Coral and Jim Lorenzen, *Flying Saucer Occupants* (New York: Signet-New American Library, Inc., 1967), p. 112.
14. John A. Keel, *UFOs: Operation Trojan Horse* (New York: G. P. Putnam's Sons, 1970), p. 211.
15. Lorenzen, *Occupants*, pp. 126-127.
16. Blum, *Beyond Earth*, p. 102.
17. Vallée, *Magonia*, p. 243.
18. Coral E. and Jim Lorenzen, *UFOs: The Whole Story* (New York: Signet-New American Library, Inc., 1969), pp. 223-225.

ored UFO passed over his route at high speed. When it was gone, the headlights came back on and he could restart the engine. Jourdy's encounter occurred on October 11, 1954, during a wave of French sightings.[19]

A brilliantly-lit, yellow and white "torpedo" 200 feet long streaked over Pedro Saucedo's truck and caused the headlights and motor to fail during the November 2-3 Levelland flap. Saucedo, who had been driving a few miles west of Levelland with Joe Salaz, felt heat from the UFO.[20] He could not stand the glare, which changed from blue-green to red.[21] Saucedo's sighting was at 11:00 P.M. At 12:45, another truck driver reported a similar incident just west of Levelland, and at 1:15, yet another trucker became a victim. All the trucks' engines and lights worked normally after the objects departed.[22]

On August 31, 1978, Giglio Martin and Nazareno de Cesare experienced an even more bizarre truck stoppage in the mountains of San Juan, Argentina. At 2:00 A.M., a fleet of UFOs dropped down and circled their truck, killing its engine. They watched them maneuver for four hours from a hiding spot in the bushes. After the encounter, when it became light, they found dead birds and goats, and raised circles of earth at the site.[23]

A bus was stopped near Hook, Hampshire, England, on October 26, 1967. W. Collett had been driving a load of titanium parts toward Reading at 4:30 in the morning. When the engine, lights and radio failed, he felt air pressure on his eardrums (which he equalized) and a feeling of "oppression" similar to the feeling one experiences before a storm. He noticed a smell reminiscent of film floodlights (ozone perhaps). He saw a dark, domed, disc-shaped UFO with a conical bottom hovering above the road. It was about 60 feet wide. When it left, he was able to restart the bus's engine.

Despite a 20-minute delay, Collett arrived 15 minutes early. He was confused about how he could have finished the unfamiliar trip without thinking about it. He had trouble operating the gearshift and accelerator. The return trip required three gallons more gas than the trip there.[24]

Aircraft are not exempt from the effect. Leonard Stringfield was a Fifth Air Force specialist on board a C-46 flying between Ie Shima and Iwo Jima on August 28, 1945. As he saw three brilliant teardrop-shaped UFOs approach the plane to fly on a parallel course, the left engine feathered, causing the plane to lose altitude. At the same time, "navigation-instrument needles went wild." The pilot told the crew to

19. Michel, *Straight Line Mystery*, pp. 157-158.
20. Hynek, *Experience*, pp. 123-124.
21. Frank Edwards, *Flying Saucers: Serious Business* (New York: Lyle Stuart, Inc., 1966; rpt. New York: Bantam Books, Inc.-Grosset & Dunlap, Inc., 1966), p. 13.
22. Hynek, *Experience*, pp. 125-126.
23. From *La Crónica* (Buenos Aires, Argentina), 29 Sept. 1978, as reported in Alex Evans, "Close Encounters in Argentina," *UFO Report*, Sept. 1979, pp. 20, 58.
24. R. H. B. Winder, "Vehicle Stoppage at Hook" in *Encounter Cases From Flying Saucer Review*, ed. Charles Bowen (New York: Signet-New American Library, Inc., 1977), pp. 11-17.

prepare to ditch. As soon as the formation of UFOs disappeared into a cloud bank, the engine revved up; the plane regained altitude, and continued to Iwo Jima.[25]

Commander Jorge Campos Araujo and a crew of four had an equally terrifying trouble at about 9:00 on an August evening in 1957. Five minutes past Joinville, Santa Catarina, Brazil, on their way to Rio de Janeiro, a luminous yellow saucer with a luminous green dome flew to the left of their Varig C-47 cargo plane, shot ahead at supersonic speed, crossed to the right, stopped and dived into clouds. While it was near the right side, the plane's engines coughed and sputtered, and the cabin lights dimmed considerably.[26] Radio reception also failed.[27]

A Russian aircraft flying over the Ukraine between Zaporoje and Volgograd dropped to an altitude of half a mile when a passing UFO caused its engines to fail. When the UFO disappeared, the engines started up again, and the plane finished its flight. The incident happened on September 29, 1967.[28]

Even ships sometimes lose power when UFOs are near. The Brazilian Navy's Hydrography and Navigation Division ship *Almirante Saldanha* lost electrical power while its captain and 100 others watched a UFO at midday on January 16, 1958. As the object undulated in bat-like flight, photographer Almiro Barauna snapped four pictures, which were later pronounced genuine by the Cruzeiro do Sul Aerophotogrammetric Service. The UFO was Saturn-shaped, silent, dark gray, and surrounded by a luminous green mist, mostly ahead of it. At times it glittered, and once it appeared to stop in midair. It was estimated to be about 24 feet tall and 120 feet in diameter. The Navy was very concerned, and there was even a congressional investigation.[29]

One of the most spectacular of the vehicle stoppages occurred at Nha Trang, Vietnam, on June 19, 1966. Sgt. Wayne Dalrymple and others were watching a movie outdoors at 9:45 at night. A round, brilliant UFO about 50 feet wide descended to an altitude of about 400 feet over the camp, stopped, illuminated the entire area brightly, and ascended so quickly that it was out of sight in three seconds or less. During the sighting, six 100-kilowatt diesel-powered generators, eight diesel bulldozers, two Skyraider aircraft, cars, trucks, and even an oil tanker anchored offshore experienced complete failure for four minutes. Dalrymple checked the generators and found no problem then or subsequently. He said the incident was reported on the radio in

25. Stringfield, *Situation Red* (Doubleday), pp. 9-10.
26. Lorenzen, *Startling Evidence*, pp. 153-155.
27. Edwards, *Serious Business*, p. 31.
28. From *Sovietskaia Latvia*, Dec. 1967 and *Veac Nou*, 28 Nov. 1968, as reported in Ion Hobana and Julien Weverbergh, *UFOs From Behind The Iron Curtain*, trans. A. D. Hills (London: Souvenir Press Ltd., 1974) rpt. New York: Bantam Books, Inc., 1975), p. 289.
29. Lorenzen, *Startling Evidence*, pp. 164-174.

Vietnam, and officials flew from Washington to investigate.[30, 31]

A few people have speculated that vehicle stoppages may be caused by strong electric fields that ufonauts use to prevent us from taking aggressive action against their craft. Most ET proponents assume they are side effects of some type of antigravity system that employs strong magnetic fields to traverse magnetic lines of force. They have been dubbed "electromagnetic effects," or "EM effects."

Unfortunately, the EM theory, like the ET theory, leaves important questions unanswered. As John Keel points out:

> The Ford Motor Company, working with a UFO investigating group at Colorado University, found that a magnetic field strong enough to stall an automobile engine would also bend the car itself.[32]

Dr. David R. Saunders writes of a case investigated by physical chemist Roy Craig in 1967. The witness saw a glowing UFO near the Riverside cutoff on the Los Angeles freeway at about 2:00 A.M. His car's engine and clock failed, and an audio tape became distorted. Craig tested the magnetic signatures of the witness' car and another car of similar make and model. He found "no appreciable difference."[33]

Bill Moyer, of Ford Motor Company, found that it took an intense magnetic field to stall an engine, and it was reasoned that such a field would alter the affected car's magnetic signature.[34]

Residual magnetism is not found in the vehicles affected. They are not bent. The extremely delicate components in car radios function normally again after the UFO leaves the area—which would seem unlikely, had they truly been exposed to an electromagnetic field of such magnitude. One would instead expect induced currents to destroy components like capacitors, transistors and integrated circuits. This is not the case.

Moreover, diesel engines would probably not be affected by strong magnetic fields. Once started, they rely on the heat of compression to ignite their fuel. After a diesel is running, its battery and all its wiring can be removed with little difference in its operation. Power is boosted by simply dumping more fuel into the cylinders. But diesel engines have failed in the presence of UFOs.

All these arguments pale in comparison with one other. Vehicles stalled in this way for a few seconds, minutes, or even hours would have no way to restart of their own accord, with no help from their drivers. But in some cases, that is exactly what happens.

A Frenchman from Montceau-les-Mines had to push his motorcycle when it stalled on the road between St.-Romainsous-Gourdon and Brosses-Thillot, Saône-et-loire. Then "a bright light burst out about 50 yards in front of him," and he saw a UFO shaped like an upside-down

30. Nigel Blundell and Roger Boar, *The World's Greatest UFO Mysteries* (London: Octopus Books Limited, 1983; rpt. New York: Berkley Books, 1990), pp. 14-16.
31. Raymond E. Fowler, *UFOs: Interplanetary Visitors* (Jericho, New York: Exposition Press, 1974), pp. 101-103.
32. Keel, *Trojan Horse*, p. 63.
33. Saunders, *op. cit.*, p. 177.
34. *Ibid.*, pp. 229-230.

plate. Retreating from the frightening apparition in fear, he came to the place where his motor had stopped. It started again! The incident took place on October 14, 1954.[35]

Not long after sunset on December 8, 1957, an aircraft company employee and two passengers were driving in a wooded area between Woodward and Seiling, Oklahoma. When they approached a hill, they saw a bright light ahead. The car slowed to a stop of its own accord, and the electrical system, including heater, wipers and radio, quit working. A 50-foot, Saturn-shaped UFO flew over with a high-pitched noise, giving off a stream of hot air. "Portholes" were visible. As the disc ascended, "the car started by itself." Later, while talking to officers from Kirtland AFB for four hours, the driver was told about other encounters like his. However, Project Bluebook never learned of the incident.[36]

Robert Collins had a similar experience in his pickup truck just before sunrise on January 13, 1959. He was driving over Pymatuning Lake in Pennsylvania when lights as bright as arc lights flew toward him from the east and hovered about 2,000 feet above his truck, illuminating an area of a hundred yards. The truck stalled, and the radio and electrical system failed. After a few minutes, the UFO left at high speed, and the pickup's "engine, lights, and radio came to life."[37]

Minnesota played host to at least two such events in the 1960s. At approximately 7:15 P.M. on October 23, 1965, James Townsend had to skid to a stop when he came around a curve at a good clip near Long Prairie, and confronted a cylindrical UFO something like a squat rocket sitting in the road on fins. The car's engine, lights and radio failed, and he was unable to restart it. Three robot-like "creatures" retreated into the UFO, which ascended atop a brilliant light beam as it made a loud hum. Townsend's car then *began running by itself.*[38]

Villard, Minnesota, resident Robert Blaine and five passengers were driving two miles east of Farwell at about 7:30 one winter evening in 1967, when their car's engine and headlights failed. An orange and red flash of light passed by the windshield. After the car coasted awhile, "the engine and lights came on again without warning or aid." The car was checked and found to be in working order, and it had no subsequent trouble.[39]

Another of the enigmatic sightings occurred in Bucharest, Rumania, at 1:30 in the morning on December 14, 1970. Author Julien Weverbergh and his wife were awakened when a light lit the sky red. Weverbergh heard a "pulsating sound." The red light changed to white. Weverbergh's wife and mother observed a pulsating, white-blue, spherical UFO hovering over a car. The sphere suddenly disappeared just be-

35. Michel, *Straight Line Mystery*, p. 175.
36. Vallée, *Magonia*, pp. 267-268.
37. Lorenzen, *The Whole Story*, pp. 95-96.
38. Brad Steiger, *Strangers from the Skies* (London: Universal-Tandem Publishing Co. Ltd., 1966; rpt. London: Tandem Publishing Ltd, 1975), pp. 126-128.
39. Coral and Jim Lorenzen, *UFOs Over The Americas* (New York: Signet-New American Library, Inc., 1968), pp. 25-27.

fore the author arrived at the window, then all three saw the car start
by itself.[40]

On October 8, 1973, Forrest County, Mississippi, constable Char-
lie Delk answered Petal residents' complaints about a bright aerial
light. He followed it to the Jones County line and toward Tallahalla
Swamp. When he got close to it, his car's engine and police radio failed
for fifteen minutes, then "started up like nothing was wrong."[41]

The Belgian UFO investigation group Sociéte Belge d'Étude des
Phénomènes Spatiaux (SOBEPS) investigated a self-starting car case
that took place southeast of Bruxelles, Belgium, in 1974. At 4:00 P.M.
on January 24, a clear day, Mme. N.D. was driving her Volkswagen at
highway speed when she saw a red UFO resting on the ground to the
left of the road nearly 500 feet ahead. The car's engine slowed to a stop
and its engine and radio failed (although the radio's light stayed on).
By then, the witness was only about 33 feet away from the object. It
looked tiny—only about 40 inches in diameter and 20 inches tall. It
had a double row of "spots" around its circumference, and a flattened
dome on top, and appeared to be made of dull metal.

Twice it rose about 20 inches off the ground, then it ascended to
10 or 12 feet and hovered over the Volkswagen for a few seconds. The
witness noticed the bottom of it was gray and flat. Then it flew away
silently and disappeared in the east-northeast, at which time the car's
engine started running by itself without any help from Mme. N.D. Since
the transmission was still engaged in fourth gear, the car moved forward. [42]

A number of UFOs were seen in Belgium that year. One spring
evening an encounter similar to Mme. N.D.'s took place on a plateau
near Koningslo. A resident of Vilvorde, Flanders, was driving with his
wife and cousin. They spotted a luminous UFO that looked a bit like a
"second moon." Their car's engine sputtered and died and the lights
failed. The engine could not be restarted. About a minute later, the
UFO flew away, and "the engine started up again by itself without any
action by the driver." Since the car was still in third gear, it continued
on. The witness had reported several other sightings.[43]

Yet another of the fantastic encounters is an Italian case that was
part of an intense wave of sightings during 1978. At 8:15 P.M. on September 17, Signora Ultimina Boscagli and her son were in the street in
front of their house in Torrita Di Siena when they heard a sound like
an artillery round. They saw a bright, round "fireball" with a reddish
bottom, a very bright white top, yellow-orange contours, and a reddish
trail. It vanished in a blinding flash. Signora Santina Faralli, who was

40. Hobana, *op. cit.*, p. 271.
41. Associated Press, "Forrest Constable Chases UFO Through Two Counties," *Mobile*
    (Alabama) *Register*, 9 Oct. 1973; rpt. in Blum, *Beyond Earth*, pp. 27-28.
42. Richard Hall, "Woman Says UFO Restarted Her Auto," *Skylook*, Feb. 1976, p. 10. It
    should be mentioned that later, in the spring, the car developed engine problems
    and its distributor had to be replaced.
43. Jean-Luc Vertongen, "The Vilvorde Humanoid," *Inforespace*, No. 18 (Brussels, 1974);
    rpt. *Flying Saucer Review*, 20, No. 6 (1974), pp. 13-17, 22., trans. Gordon
    Creighton.

watching television in her house nearby, also saw the flash. Her electric light suddenly went off and then came back on.

At about 9:00, her son, Rivo, left in his Fiat. The electrical system failed, stalling the car, and an orange, domed disk about ten feet wide followed a red light beam and landed in the street in front of him, lighting the whole area. It seemed to be supported a few feet off the ground by three light beams that changed color from yellow, to green, to red, to blue.

A door opened. Two helmeted humanoids about three and a half feet tall wearing green coveralls exited, circled the car and returned. The UFO rose straight up for about 30 feet, then streaked away, leaving a trail of light. The Fiat's headlights came back on by themselves, and "since the gears were still engaged *the car started to move forward* without any action by Rivo Faralli."

Several televisions on the next street were reported to have gone off and returned to normal. Physical traces were found at the site, and Rivo suffered burning eyes for three days.[44]

The evidence is clear. Magnetic fields do not satisfactorily explain vehicle stoppages. But what else could be causing them? What special condition exists in the vicinity of UFOs that sometimes causes cars to stop running one minute and start the next?

It may be what science fiction writers call a "time warp."

Contrary to popular belief, nobody knows what time really is. Some highly qualified physicists who study time contend that it is not linear, like a river, as most of us imagine. They say the flow of time exists only in our imaginations. According to Dr. Paul Davies, Professor of Theoretical Physics at the University of Newcastle-upon-Tyne, England, lecturer in applied mathematics at Kings College, University of London, and visiting fellow at the Institute of Astronomy, Cambridge, England:

> There seems to be no strong reason for supposing that the flow of time is any more than an illusion produced by brain processes similar to the perception of rotation during dizziness.[45]

Also contrary to popular opinion, *physicists have proven that time travel is a reality.* Again to quote Dr. Davies:

> The concept of elastic time was quite a shock when Einstein introduced it in 1905, but since then many experiments have confirmed its reality....
>
> A good check on the effect was made at CERN in Geneva in early 1977.... It confirmed the amount of time dilation predicted by the theory of relativity, to an accuracy of 0.2 per cent.
>
> One intriguing possibility opened up by the time dilation effect is time travel. By approaching closer and closer to the speed of light, an astronaut can dislocate his time scale more and more violently relative to the rest of the universe. For example, rocketing to within one hun-

44. Roberto Pinotti, "Landing E. M. Effects and Entities at Torrita di Siena," trans. Maurizio Verga, *Flying Saucer Review*, 25, No. 4 (1979), pp. 3-6.
45. Paul Davies, *Other Worlds* (New York: Simon & Schuster, 1980), p. 190.

*dred m.p.h. of the speed of light, he could accomplish a journey to the
nearest star (more than four light years away) in less than one day
though the same journey measured from Earth takes over four years.
His clock rate is thus about 1800 times slower when observed from
Earth than when observed from the rocket....*

...time dilation is definitely science fact.[46]

By observing light from distant galaxies and measuring the
amount of Doppler effect, astronomers have determined that some of
them are rushing away from us at such extreme speeds that time is indeed actually passing more slowly for them than for us. And since that
light has taken millions of years to reach the earth, what they see when
they look through their telescopes is not what those galaxies are like
now, but what they were like millions of years ago. They are looking
back into time.

And then there are tachyons—atomic particles whose *minimum*
speed limit is the speed of light. They can never quite go as *slowly* as
light. Their entire existence is spent traveling backward in time. Of
course tachyons are theoretical. No one has ever seen one. But the theory has been around long enough to have been tested many times, and
there is evidence to support it.

Einstein's theory of relativity states that time is relative, that time
and space are interdependent, forming a four-dimensional continuum,
and that the presence of matter warps the space-time continuum.
What if we were to discover a way to warp the space-time continuum
even more by creating some sort of field around ourselves? Would we
have found a short cut to time dilation? Could we perhaps change our
rate of travel into the future, like the hypothetical astronaut Dr. Davies
suggested, but into the past as well, as tachyons do? Could we avoid
the necessity of expending the almost limitless amounts of energy that
rockets would require to approach the speed of light (and therefore
make use of time dilation)?

Suppose for a moment that we were somehow able to use this
knowledge to learn how to manipulate space-time (and therefore time)
in a manner similar to the way we manipulate electromagnetic energy.
What if we could build a machine—like a generator—that could form a
field around itself, and inside that field time would not flow at the same
rate as outside it? Yes, it sounds like fanciful science fiction; science
fiction writers have been writing such scenarios for a long while. H. G.
Wells wrote about time travel in 1895.[47] But science fiction frequently
becomes science fact—as when Neil Armstrong stepped onto the moon.

If we set the controls of our hypothetical "time-warping" generator
to "stop" time inside the field, and if we place the generator close
enough to a running automobile, won't the automobile's engine appear
to stop? Won't the electrical energy in the wires be frozen on its way to
the spark plugs, unable to get to them? Won't the interval required for

46. *Ibid.*, pp. 41-42.
47. H.G. Wells, *The Time Machine: An Invention* (Holt, 1895).

the crankshaft to rotate become longer? If we then suddenly turn the generator off or remove the field from the area of the car in just the right way, won't the engine, its rate of revolution then returned to normal, continue to operate normally, provided the ignition key is left in the "on" position?

Of course, such a hypothetical time-warping field would not preclude electromagnetic effects. Matter, energy, space and time are inextricably interlocked. Any field capable of warping time might produce electromagnetic by-products and many other unusual effects, perhaps even distortions of gravity strong enough to allow levitation.

Could it be that ufonauts have learned to understand black holes and tachyons? Have they discovered how to generate fields that warp time?

If the recent, controversial claims of a young physicist named Robert Lazar are true, it would appear that they may have done just that. Lazar swears that between December 1988 and March 1989, he worked for the U.S. Department of Naval Intelligence north of Las Vegas, Nevada, at "S-4," a supersecret area next to Papoose (Dry) Lake in Emigrant Valley. His job—classified 37 levels above Top Secret—was to determine how to duplicate the propulsion system of one of nine captured alien flying saucers stored in a camouflaged underground hangar under tight security.

Lazar claims that the propulsion system consisted of a basketball-sized, hemispherical chamber in which a super-heavy element (115) was bombarded with protons to produce antimatter, and above it, a central column that acted as a wave guide to propagate a "gravity field." This field, he says, is used to "fold" time and space to enable the craft to travel vast distances virtually instantaneously. It selectively warps space in the direction it is pointed. With distant space close at hand, the craft moves into that space. Turning off the generator then allows space to spring back to its original form, taking the craft far away immediately, with no need to laboriously traverse the intervening reaches of space. Lazar has been accused of being a crank and/or a disinformation agent, but neither of these charges has been proven.[48]

Are time- or space-warping fields what power UFOs? Are they the cause of vehicle stoppages? Could they be the culprits that cause houses, towns, even whole states to experience power failures sometimes during UFO sightings?

On November 14, 1957, there was a ten-minute electrical power failure in "a four-mile area" of Tamaroa, Illinois, just after a UFO emitted a bright flash.[49, 50]

Mogi Mirim, Brazil, was the scene of a UFO-related outage just eleven days later. Three glowing, disc-shaped UFOs flew over the city

48. Timothy Good, *Alien Liaison* (London: Century, 1991; rpt. London: Arrow Books Limited, 1992), pp. 147-186.
49. Binder, *What We Really Know*, p. 76.
50. Donald E. Keyhoe, *Aliens From Space* (Garden City, New York: Doubleday & Co., Inc., 1973, p. 207.

and all city lights failed. An important pattern was noted in this case: The failure was inversely proportional to the distance from the UFOs. Lights farther away from them only dimmed.[51]

Another important case is also Brazilian. As a bright, round, silent UFO followed power lines and passed overhead, illuminating the area with its glow, automatic keys at the Uberlandia power station and another power station nearby disconnected power to all trunks. After it disappeared over the horizon, the keys turned on automatically, returning the stations to normal operation. That incident occurred on August 17, 1959.[52]

On April 18, 1962, electrical power failed at a substation in Eureka, Utah, during the 42 minutes that a UFO sat on the ground near it. The UFO then flew away and was subsequently chased by armed jet interceptors until it exploded over the Mesquite Range 70 miles south of Reno, Nevada. Light from the explosion lit Reno streets and was seen over a five-state area. It was being tracked on radar at the time—it had been tracked from New York.[53]

Manuel Arias and his wife saw a brilliant, cylindrical UFO hovering near a power line during a power blackout in Nicanor Olivera, Buenos Aires, Argentina, at 9:50 P.M. on August 31, 1978. Other witnesses reported like sightings during the same outage.[54]

Argentina has had far more than its share of UFO-related power failures. UFOs were seen when Salta was blacked out on July 22, 1958, January 22, 1959, and June 22, 1959.[55,56,57] Córdoba had the same problem on September 6, 1978, and Roberto Francisco Torres reported seeing a domed, oval UFO with lighted "windows" just as a blackout hit Venado Tuerto, Santa Fe.[58]

At midnight on September 2, 1965, Sgt. Robert Mark and two airmen were at the main gate at Pease Air Force Base near Portsmouth, New Hampshire. They saw a silent UFO that resembled car headlights approaching the guard shack at high speed about 350 feet up. As it passed over various lights, the lights failed then returned when it left.[59]

The St. Paul Pioneer Press and other papers carried the account of a similar occurrence witnessed by Nick de Vara and Mark Wilcox in St. Paul, Minnesota, on November 26, 1965. They saw a brightly-lit service station black out as a UFO passed overhead, then return to normal as it flew away. The UFO had blue, blinking lights and emitted blue flashes as brilliant as a welder's flame. Police officers and others reported to Northern States Power Company that they had experienced a power failure while two UFOs flew over and emitted blue and orange flashes.

51. Edwards, Serious Business, p. 144.
52. Lorenzen, Startling Evidence, pp. 179-180.
53. Edwards, Serious Business, pp. 151-152.
54. Evans, op. cit., p. 58.
55. Edwards, Serious Business, p. 144.
56. Keyhoe, op. cit., p. 207.
57. Lorenzen, Startling Evidence, p. 178.
58. Evans, op. cit.
59. Fawcett, Clear Intent, pp. 58-59.

The company found no reason for the outage.[60]

Gov. Emilie Riva Palacie, Mayor Valentin L. Gonzales, Gen. Rafael Enrique Vega and most of the local residents saw a glowing, disc-shaped UFO flying over Cuernavaca, Mexico, "at low altitude" then stopping to hover. The city's electrical power failed for the few minutes that the UFO hovered overhead, then returned when it "climbed swiftly out of sight." The date was September 23, 1965.[61, 62]

Robert Moses, Robert McCambly and many others watched a domed, oval UFO with lights around the bottom that changed from red, to white, to green during an April 12, 1966, power failure in Dorchester, Massachusetts. It executed maneuvers, then landed on the Oliver Wendell Holmes grade school.[63] Just before midnight on January 18, 1967, a luminous, domed UFO was seen hovering near Williamstown during a blackout there.[64]

Sometimes there are huge numbers of witnesses to these UFO-related outages. At 9:00 P.M. on January 5, 1969, hundreds of people in small towns around Jacksonville, Florida, watched lights of different colors in the sky. By 9:30, a series of power failures had occurred.[65]

Hundreds in Florida, Uruguay, watched a globe-shaped UFO with colored lights meandering overhead during an eighteen-minute power failure in 1981.[66]

On August 3, 1958, power failed in a large part of Rome, Italy, until a large, glowing UFO flew away.[67, 68]

Officials of the Bogotá Power Company found no cause for a power outage that left two million people in the dark just after UFOs were seen over Bogotá, Columbia, on September 7, 1966.[69]

The most publicized power failure in history happened during a UFO flap, and it has been linked to UFOs. On November 9, 1965, parts of Canada and the entire northeast corner of the United States, including New York City, were without power all night. For the first time in memory, the great city was dark. Hundreds were trapped in subways and elevators. In all, 30 million people were without power. UFOs were seen before, during and after the blackout. Flight instructor Weldon Ross and student James Brooking reported seeing a red, glowing, spherical UFO over power lines from the Niagara Falls generating plant.[70] At dawn, the famous actor Stuart Whitman heard a whistling noise outside his twelfth-story New York City window. He saw one orange and one blue UFO and heard an announcement—in English—

60. Edwards, *Serious Business*, p. 149.
61. Keyhoe, *op. cit.*, p. 207.
62. Edwards, *Serious Business*, p. 145.
63. From *Flying Saucer Review*, 66, No. 4, as reported in Vallée, *Magonia*, pp. 328-329.
64. Fowler, *The Andreasson Affair*, p. 163.
65. Keel, *Trojan Horse*, p. 162.
66. "UFO Update: Turn Off the Lights," *UFO Annual Report*, 10, No. 1 (1981), p. 10.
67. Edwards, *Serious Business*, p. 144.
68. Keyhoe, *op. cit.*, p. 207.
69. Steiger, *Flying Saucers Are Hostile*, p. 69.
70. Edwards, *Serious Business*, pp. 145-148.

that "the blackout was a 'demonstration.'"[71]

UFO literature contains hundreds of accounts similar to the ones I have listed. Witnesses from all over the world who have never heard of one another and who have never heard of UFOs have reported identical events. Skeptics who complain that one report contains no date, another is from a secondary source, or another cannot be confirmed because the witness is now deceased are completely missing the point—which is that the collective weight of the evidence is too much to ignore, regardless of how many witnesses can be discredited, regardless of how much data one chooses to throw out.

I believe our failure to solve the UFO riddle after nearly half a century of study stems not from a paucity of data, but from a refusal to accept the data we have.

These power failures are good examples. A lot of researchers insist that they must be by-products of some form of electromagnetic (EM) propulsion. But we know that magnetic fields strong enough to produce the results observed at the speeds reported would destroy sensitive electronic components with induced currents and would probably cause irreparable damage to electrical distribution systems as well. Transformers would explode, wires would melt, light filaments would vaporize. Magnetic signatures would be imprinted everywhere. Tripped circuit breakers would remain off until reset by power company employees instead of turning themselves back on.

But none of these events is being reported. In other words, the data and the EM hypothesis do not match.

The existence of time-warping fields surrounding some UFOs, however, could easily explain such outages. If a trunk line were affected, then as soon as the field were removed, current would once again be allowed to flow and power would be restored. This has happened in many UFO-related outages—to the bafflement of power-company officials, who are sometimes unable to find anything wrong with any of the affected equipment.[72]

Could it be that the things ufonauts tell abductees have a basis in fact? Can they really "distort time as we know it by speeding it up, slowing it down, or stopping it?" Perhaps we should have listened to Betty Andreasson's words when she said, "The future and the past are the same as today to them. Time to them is not like our time, but they know about our time. They can reverse time."

The hypothesis that UFOs can generate fields capable of warping time does not clash with the data we have looked at so far. It suggests a reason for ufonauts' preoccupation with time and a mechanism for their "powerfailing" of vehicles and cities that is more plausible than other, more popular theories. Does it tell us why the bizarre "breeding

---

71. From *Flying Saucer Review*, 66, No. 6, as reported in Vallée, *Magonia*, p. 320.
72. Fuller, *Incident at Exeter*, p. 204.

experiments?" And what of the thousands of reports that contain accounts of other enigmatic phenomena—photographic anomalies, "impossible" maneuvers, disappearances, shape changes? Can time-warping fields explain them too?

Where Are the Photographs?

Since World War II, a vast number of UFOs have been sighted by people with easy access to cameras. But clear, close-up photographs of UFOs are rare. When known and suspected hoaxes and forgeries are eliminated, the remaining collection of photographs available for study consists largely of distant shots and improperly exposed, vague blobs.

Many who prefer to deny the reality of UFOs use this fact to support arguments against their existence. "UFOs must not exist," they say, "because if they did we would have clear photographs of them." This is a premature conclusion for several reasons.

To begin with, many of the UFO occupants' actions, such as choosing out-of-the-way landing spots in the middle of the night and fleeing when they are seen, indicate that they wish to keep a very low profile. And they have consistently demonstrated the ability to paralyze machinery and the minds and bodies of percipients. It is quite possible that they are using a superior technology to systematically prevent witnesses from obtaining close-up photographs, simply because they do not want us to have proof of their existence. Several reasons for this will become evident later in this book.

Secondly, we *do* have clear photographs of UFOs. Some, like the now-famous ones taken by contactees Eduard (Billy) Meier and Ed Walters, are widely suspected of being faked, but this has never been proven. In fact, quite the opposite seems to be the case. Photography analysts Jim Dilettoso and Gem Cox, at the March 1992 National New Age and Truth about UFOs conference in San Diego, declared publicly that, after having subjected Meier's photos to the latest computer analyses for authenticity, "It is no longer a matter of *believing* that these

---

1. Hynek, *Experience*, p. 58.

photos are genuine. We *know* they are genuine." Many other photos of UFOs have been examined by teams of experts—along with the photographers who took them—and pronounced genuine. I have seen some of them myself, and I can tell you that those who declare they do not exist are mistaken.

That we have any UFO photographs at all is remarkable when one stops to consider how few photographs exist of events like automobile collisions. Such collisions occur hundreds of times daily, yet there are almost no photographs of them happening. Like UFO encounters, they are always surprises. Nobody plans them. Nobody knows when they are going to happen. Nobody wants them to happen. The duration is extremely short—seconds or less. The personal experiences of the victims are often shocking, traumatic and terrifying. The last thing most people think about when an accident is in progress is photographing it.

UFO encounters are similarly often over in seconds and are similarly shocking to percipients. It is not surprising that few of the witnesses who have cameras have the presence of mind to use them.

On April 3, 1967, John Keel, an experienced journalist and seasoned UFO researcher, parked on a lonely hilltop near Gallipolis Ferry, Ohio, where many UFOs had been seen. It was 1:35 A.M. A brilliant, colorful, circular object with a green upper surface topped by a red light and with red "portholes" flew "within a few hundred feet" of Keel on Five Mile Creek Road. Although he had been watching and waiting for just such an event and had a camera lying right beside him, he was taken by surprise. He didn't think of using the camera until it was too late. A few seconds later, the UFO was gone, and Keel probably considered kicking himself. His only record of the event was a mild case of klieg conjunctivitis (an eye irritation) that lasted several days.[2]

On July 16, 1975, Betty Bodian observed an odd, white, glowing sphere over Provincetown harbor (Cape Cod). Three miles away, Dan and Jan Boynton (who owned, edited, and wrote and photographed for the *Provincetown Advocate*) watched an object of similar description in the same location at the same time for about two minutes without thinking to photograph it—even though all their camera gear was in the back seat of the car they were in.[3]

Cascade County, Montana, Sheriff's Department Captain Keith Wolverton didn't have time to photograph the UFO he sighted on the evening of November 11, 1975. He and a deputy were driving from Missoula, Montana, to Great Falls at 50 m.p.h. when "a very large orange light descended, lighting up both sides of the road." It sailed directly overhead at an altitude of 200 feet, traveling "from horizon to horizon in four seconds." The cruiser was carrying thousands of dollars' worth of photographic equipment, but the incident was over too quickly for anyone to use it.[4]

2. Keel, *Mothman Prophesies*, p. 123.
3. Hopkins, *Missing Time*, p. 29.
4. Fawcett, *op. cit.*, pp. 34-35.

The following year an Idaho state trooper, Dennis Abrams, skidded his car off the road an hour after midnight to watch a pale green, seemingly self-luminous oval object rise from trees and hover without a sound about 60 feet away. He was four or five miles northeast of downtown Soda Springs. He radioed to an officer west of town, who saw an orange-pink light to the north. Both officers had loaded cameras, but neither thought of using his.[5] (Corporal E. H. Christensen saw the UFO ten seconds after it had left Abrams' position. His own position was about 20 miles away.[6] This translates to a velocity of about 7,200 m.p.h.)

Recently another seasoned UFO investigator and author was caught "with his pants down." Bob Oechsler is a former NASA Mission Specialist. As a State Section Director for MUFON, he was doubtless aware that Keel and the others had missed chances to photograph UFOs. In December of 1988, he was riding across the Three Mile Bridge toward Pensacola, Florida, with contactee Ed Walters in Walters's truck. They spotted an unidentified object only 200 feet to their left at an altitude of only 50 feet. It was so close they could see the reflection of its glowing, orange bottom ring in the bay. They watched until it moved out of sight near a Pensacola pier two or three minutes later. An automatic camera lay in Oechsler's lap the whole time; neither he nor Walters thought of using it until after the object was gone.[7]

Others have taken photographs, only to have them confiscated. Marine Corps photographer Ralph Mayher shot 40 feet of 16-millimeter movie film of a bright UFO that passed over Miami, Florida, on July 29, 1952. He called the Marine Air Station, and an officer was sent, who took the film with him. Copies were sent to the Air Force, which later denied it had ever received them. Mayher contacted the Marine Air Station. The commanding officer wired back that his "saucer film" had been given to the Air Force two days after he shot it.[8] In 1975 William Spaulding, of Ground Saucer Watch, sent a series of queries to the CIA and found that some data concerning the film were classified information.[9]

Witnesses are often accosted by a man or men wanting both prints and negatives a few hours or days after photographing UFOs. They often say they are from the Air Force, NORAD or some other government agency, which agency invariably denies their existence. If the witness refuses to turn his photos over, he is often threatened. Sometimes he later finds them missing from their hiding places.

UFO photos are frequently "lost" in the mail, "misplaced" after being sent to government agencies, etc. Investigators sometimes receive mailed packages from contactees, and find that they were opened in

5. Hendry, op. cit., pp. 116-117.
6. Tim Anderson, "Smokey and the UFO," UFO Report, Sept. 1979, pp. 14-17.
7. Bob Oechsler, "Investigation: The Gulf Breeze Sightings," International UFO Library Magazine, 1, No. 3 (1992), pp. 7-8.
8. Leonard Stringfield, Inside Saucer Post...3-0 Blue (Cincinnati, Ohio: Civilian Research, Interplanetary Flying Objects, 1957), pp. 70-71.
9. Stringfield, Situation Red (Doubleday), p. 154.

transit and important photographs removed. Witnesses who send originals to the Air Force complain of getting only crude copies back. Researchers even cite stories that film developers have, as Leonard Stringfield puts it, "played a *sub rosa* intermediary role in monitoring UFO film."[10]

Much of this suspicious activity is doubtless attributable to the work of agents of Air Force Intelligence, the CIA and other government agencies. But there is another aspect to the problem. In many cases, would-be collectors of photographs and other evidence show up asking about an encounter that took place in the middle of nowhere in the middle of the night, *before* the witness has told a soul about his experience. These mysterious visitors, dubbed "men in black," will be discussed in more detail in Chapter 14.

Be all this as it may, one still finds that distant photos of UFOs far outnumber close-ups, not just because more are taken, but because *the closer one's camera is to a UFO, the less likely it is to function properly.* Keel mentions several instances of malfunctioning cameras. In one case, a cameraman for a television station in New York state photographed a UFO, but the developed film showed nothing. In another, professional photographer Daniel Drasin, who was trying to film a UFO documentary in the Point Pleasant, West Virginia, area, could not get his battery-powered photographic equipment to work when he saw lights in the sky. Later, he believed he had captured some images, but the film was "accidentally ruined" when he sent it to be processed in New York.[11, 12]

Atlanta *Constitution* reporter Tom Winfield went to a Gainsville, Georgia, motel at 11:00 P.M. on July 14, 1964, where a motel employee pointed out a bowl-shaped, orange UFO that seemed to be glowing. It moved, stopped to hover, moved back, then shot upward out of sight. Winfield tried to capture whatever it was on film, but when the film was developed, nothing showed up on it.[13]

Two police officers' attempts to photograph UFOs were foiled at 2:00 A.M. on August 12, 1972, at Gem, Kansas. John Calkins was awakened by barking dogs. He saw a brilliant, domed, saucer-shaped UFO about 30 feet in diameter landing on a Quonset building 150 feet from his mobile home. It made a high-pitched noise that apparently disturbed his dog, and it illuminated the area. He also saw two other illuminated UFOs. He called the police.

Colby police officers Paul Carter and Dennis Brown responded, following the lights to Calkins' home. Both officers saw the UFOs at close range. Carter used all the film in his Polaroid camera and Brown used all the film in his Instamatic, but neither ended up with any photographs of the UFOs. Carter watched one UFO hover over a field, pro-

10. *Ibid.*, p. 155.
11. Glenn McWane and David Graham, *The New UFO Sightings* (New York: Warner Paperback Library-Warner Books, Inc., 1974), p. 31.
12. Keel, *Mothman Prophesies*, pp. 43, 130-131, 179.
13. Jeffery Liss, "UFOs That Look Like Tops," *Fate*, Nov. 1964, p. 71.

duce a brilliant light, then shoot up so quickly that it was out of sight within three seconds, extinguishing the light and making a "whooshing" sound as it did so.[14]

Is it possible that the same invisible force that stops automobiles could cause camera malfunctions? Perhaps. During a Point Pleasant, West Virginia, sighting on April 5, 1967, a newsman's camera failed to operate, just as a glowing UFO passed overhead at an altitude between 100 and 200 feet. Cars also failed to start at the same time.[15] Maybe the cars are clues. Maybe time-warping fields were responsible.

The fact that we have not yet discovered how to manipulate time by producing a time-warping field does not mean that when such a field is discovered it will defy the laws of physics. We have no reason to doubt that it would conform to the same inverse square law governing other fields—the one that says the strength of a field is inversely proportional to the square of the distance from its source.

If that is true, then the shutter of any camera close to the UFO (and therefore within the influence of its field) might be operating at a different speed than that of a distant camera. If time within the field were passing very slowly, the shutter would open very slowly. The film could be overexposed. If time were passing very quickly, the film might not be exposed at all. The reaction time of the emulsion itself would of course be affected as well, as would the rate at which the photographer's hands shake the camera. Depending on the strength of the field and the closeness of the camera, the lens, shutter and film might actually be in three different time zones. Anyone familiar with photography can see that a clear photograph under such circumstances could only be obtained by a coincidence of accidents.

Conversely, the camera placed at a distance sufficient to be effectively outside of the time-warping field's sphere of influence would not be affected. This would make distant photos easier to obtain.

Camera problems have been occurring at least since September 14, 1908. On that night, in Worcestershire, England, David Packer photographed what appeared to him to be a diffuse, cloud-like auroral display. When the film was developed, "a large disc or sphere" was evident. It was not a film flaw or the result of a light leak in Packer's camera.[16]

Packer's invisible UFO may have been emitting ultraviolet light, or infrared rays, or some other type of invisible radiation that he could not see, but that affected the emulsion of his film.

Two similar cases were reported from Colorado. When Robert Rinker, a professional meteorologist, was photographing winter landscapes at his home near Climax, he accidentally obtained a photograph of a large, luminous, disc-shaped UFO with a definite rim. He had not seen the UFO at all, but learned of it only after the film was

14. McWane, *op. cit.,* pp. 52-53.
15. Keel, *Mothman Prophesies,* pp. 130-131.
16. M. K. Jessup, *The Case for the UFO* (New York: The Citadel Press, 1955), p. 173.

developed.[17]

Another Colorado photo came from Commerce City, an industrial part of metropolitan Denver. On October 26, 1967, 12-year-old Dan Kiscaden saw a red, spherical UFO. He ran to get his mother's camera, took two daylight photographs, then ran home, frightened. The images on the film appeared disc-shaped—not round like Dan's eyes had seen them.[18]

Another broad-daylight photo opportunity went awry in 1952 at Tucson, Arizona. Two metallic-appearing, disc-shaped UFOs were watched by many witnesses for a considerable length of time as they maneuvered over Davis-Monthan Air Force Base. An intelligence officer and a sergeant each took about 40 photographs using fine-grained 4x5 film. The developed images appeared as "black ovoid blobs" instead of the metallic discs the witnesses had seen.[19]

Chief of Police Gerald Buchert, of Mantua Village, Ohio, tried unsuccessfully to get a clear picture at dawn on April 17, 1966. Portage County Deputy Dale Spaur, East Palestine Deputy Wayne Huston and others chased a bright, cone-shaped UFO at speeds of up to 90 m.p.h. toward Pittsburgh, Pennsylvania (after it was seen by hundreds in or near Ravenna). About 40 feet in diameter, the UFO "appeared round until it was some distance away, then it appeared like two saucers, lip-to-lip." It appeared to have an antenna-like protuberance. At times it ascended very rapidly or hovered. Buchert took a photograph, but it just showed a blob.[20]

A doctor of aeronautical engineering in Bahía Blanca, Argentina, met with similar difficulties in 1950. The witness was driving along an isolated highway. He came upon a landed disk that appeared metallic, but felt resilient like rubber. Entering an open hatch, he smelled ozone and garlic and found the bodies of three small humanoids with brown skin, wearing tight, brown coveralls. He became frightened and rushed back to his hotel to tell friends about the encounter.

The next morning they accompanied him to the site. Only a warm pile of ashes remained where the disc had been. Their hands turned green when they touched them. They saw a cigar-shaped object and two discs in the sky. The engineer took five photographs of the closest disc, but only two showed it "with any degree of clarity." The discs merged with the cigar, which turned blood-red, ascended quickly and left. The witness suffered for weeks from fever and from skin irritation and blisters on only the portions of his body that were exposed.[21]

In some cases, film is fogged by UFOs. One witness to this was trying to photograph eagles one October morning in 1978 near Jaraba, Zaragoza, Spain. He used a Canon camera with a 200 millimeter objective and Kodachrome film. He noticed silence, reflections in his view

17. Hans Holzer, The Ufonauts: New Facts on Extraterrestrial Landings (Greenwich, Connecticut: Fawcett Gold Medal-Fawcett Publications, Inc., 1976), p. 35.
18. Lorenzen, UFOs Over the Americas, p. 177.
19. Lorenzen, Occupants, pp. 151-152.
20. Lorenzen, Startling Evidence, pp. 250-251.
21. Ibid., pp. 58-60.

finder, a weak buzzing sound and "metallic teeth." The hair on his neck stood on end, and his camera and watch felt warm.

Turning, he saw an ovoid object about 16 feet in diameter, surrounded at the middle by antenna-like protuberances. It was only about 65 feet away. He also saw two blond entities more than six feet tall. One carried a box above which a sphere hovered. The other bent over a metal tube in the ground. Speaking to them, he heard his voice distorted. He felt the sensation of heat. The entities returned to the object. The buzzing increased, and the UFO rose to hover six feet off the ground. The witness snapped some pictures, while once again feeling the hair rise on the nape of his neck. The UFO rose again and disappeared, but the metallic taste remained for about two days. The developed film was completely fogged.[22]

Another case of fogged film occurred at dawn on a September, 1950, flight over Korea. The witness was a radar gunner on one of three U.S. aircraft-carrier fighter-bombers on a strafing mission. He saw two huge, round shadows on the ground, then saw two mirrored UFOs more than 600 feet in diameter. They were shaped like coolie hats and surrounded by red glows. They moved at over 1,000 m.p.h., then stopped and fibrillated (this odd motion was not shared by a circular, inky-black area on the bottom of each of the UFOs). Each object had "ports," from which shone green light that changed color. All the gun camera film on all three planes was fogged or exposed, *even though the cameras had not been used.*[23]

The bombers seem to have been exposed to some type of radiation capable of penetrating the camera bodies and ruining the film inside. Perhaps the UFO was emitting X rays similar to those that ruin our high-speed film at airport security booths if we forget to ask for a hand check. The various physical effects described in the Jaraba case, on the other hand, indicate something more along the lines of microwaves.

Those images that are invisible to the naked eye but nevertheless appear on the developed film, and those that appear differently on the film than to the eye might be caused by emissions of ultraviolet or infrared frequencies, both of which are invisible but can affect photographic emulsion.

Other cases offer a wealth of evidence indicating that UFOs can emit electromagnetic radiation across the entire spectrum of frequencies—from radio waves to hard X rays.

One such case ended in tragedy for residents of Walesville, New York. It happened at midday on July 2, 1954. Griffiss AFB radar operators detected a UFO 75 miles northeast of Rome, New York. An F94-C Starfire of the 27th Fighter Interceptor Squadron piloted by Lieutenant William E. Atkins was scrambled from a training mission to intercept, along with another jet. Atkins' radar observer was Lieutenant Henry F. Coudon. Atkins and Coudon spotted the UFO but had to bail

22. F. Louange and J. L. Casero, "Unusual Encounter in Jaraba, Spain," *Flying Saucer Review*, 26, No. 2 (1980), pp. 4-5.
23. Lorenzen, *Startling Evidence*, pp. 30-32.

out when the cockpit suddenly became intolerably hot. The F-94C crashed into the middle of Walesville, killing four people.[24]

Other pilots have experienced these heating effects. On May 5, 1958, a pilot had to take off some of his clothes when he encountered a brilliant UFO near San Carlos, Uruguay.[25]

Some ufologists have concluded that the planes in these accounts were attacked by a "heat ray weapon" beamed into their cockpits. While it appears that the UFOs were emitting some type of heating radiation, perhaps in the microwave range, a more logical conclusion might be that the pilots had fallen victim to a by-product of the UFOs' propulsion mechanisms. They were, after all, chasing the UFOs, which were obliged to put on bursts of speed to elude them.

Heating effects are common features of UFO close encounters. A Frenchman named Roger Réveillé encountered heat near Troyes, l'Aube, France, during the great October, 1954, wave of sightings there. While walking along a road in the Lusigny forest, Réveillé saw an elliptical UFO about 20 feet long at treetop level above him. It produced a rustling like a flock of pigeons. Réveillé experienced intense heat. It was raining, and the heat produced dense fog. It grew so hot that he had to back away. Fifteen minutes later, the site was completely dry, although it was still raining.[26]

Both heat and a power failure figure in a bizarre and frightening account of a Brazilian close encounter that took place on November 4, 1957, at 2:03 A.M. Two sentries atop the Itaipu fort watched a brilliant, star-like light descend silently at tremendous speed, slow, then stop and hover 120 to 180 feet above the highest turret. It was a disc 100 feet or more in diameter, surrounded by an orange glow. It began making a humming sound. The sentries were badly burned by a sudden heat wave, and they screamed, waking the garrison. Abruptly, all electrical power failed; later it returned when the UFO shot straight up and flew away very fast.[27, 28]

On that very same day, at 1:10 P.M., another "hot" UFO was reported from Orogrande, New Mexico. James Stokes, a Holloman AFB high-altitude missile engineer and Navy veteran, was driving south from Alamogordo to El Paso, Texas, when his car radio faded, then failed and his car's engine stopped. Several other cars were also stopped, and the drivers were pointing northeast. An egg-shaped, pearlescent UFO twice passed overhead, performing shallow dives and sharp turns at 2000 m.p.h. Stokes felt a heat wave as the UFO flew over, and suffered a sunburned face.[29]

24. "Abandoned Jet Kills 3 in Car, 1 in House," *New York Times*, Late City Ed., 3 July 1954, Sec. A, pp. 1, 6.
25. Binder, *What We Really Know*, p. 82.
26. Michel, *Straight Line Mystery*, p. 204.
27. Lorenzen, *Startling Evidence*, pp. 155-157.
28. Keyhoe, *op. cit.*, pp. 23-26.
29. From the *Alamagordo* (New Mexico) *Daily News*, 5 Nov. 1957, *APRO Bulletin*, Nov. 1957, and *Writer's Digest*, Dec. 1957, as reported in Mebane, p. 240.

The presence of heat and the sunburn imply that the UFO was emitting radiation in both the ultraviolet range and the infrared or microwave range. The case is reminiscent of the Cash-Landrum case (Chapter 2), in which the witnesses felt heat and later developed symptoms of radiation sickness.

Just two days after Stokes' New Mexico encounter and the Itaipu incident, at 9:00 P.M., Jacques Jacobsen and three of his friends saw a UFO from their hunting lodge at Lake Baskatong, Quebec, Canada. It was brilliant, yellow-white and spherical. It hovered over a hill at a distance of about two or three miles. It projected cone-shaped light beams from its top and bottom, lighting up trees under it and clouds above it. The group's shortwave radio could not receive anything but a strange, strong, modulated noise on one particular frequency while the UFO was present. When the UFO moved southward into the clouds about 15 minutes later, the same radio functioned normally.[30]

Another encounter resulting in both sunburn and radiation burns took place that same night on a farm near Merom, Indiana. René Gilham went outdoors to investigate a strange light. He observed a bright, glowing UFO about 40 feet in diameter hovering at an altitude of about 1000 feet and illuminating his farm. He watched for about ten minutes, during which time the UFO was joined by a smaller one. They ascended vertically and flew away westward, the light increasing in brightness. Gilham heard a "whirring noise like a high-speed electric motor gaining revolutions."

The witness suffered such severe sunburn on his face that he consulted a doctor. Two days later, he had to be hospitalized. No visitors were allowed, and the hospital staff would not talk to reporters. The Terre Haute, Indiana *Tribune* reported that military authorities had been informed about the case.[31] Gilham was hospitalized for 11 days.[32]

Just four days later, yet another case involving possible radiation burns was added to the list for that frightening week. This one occurred in Madison, Ohio, at 1:25 A.M. Mrs. Leita Kuhn suffered partial vision loss and a body rash after watching a bright, acorn-shaped UFO 35 to 40 feet wide that hovered behind her garage at an altitude of about 100 feet about 100 feet away. During the 30 minutes she watched it, she detected no noise or odor and felt neither cold nor hot. Her doctor said her eyes looked as if she had been burned by radiation.[33]

A night case involving sunburn, swollen eyes and television interference was reported from Tallulah Falls, Georgia, on July 7, 1964. Jimmy Ivester and eight others saw a silent, bright red, bowl-shaped UFO flying at treetop height 300 feet away after TV interference became so severe that the television set was turned off. The UFO hovered low

30. From *APRO Bulletin*, Jan. 1958, as reported in Mebane, pp. 248-249.
31. From the Sullivan, Indiana, *Times*, 11 Nov. 1957, and the Terre Haute, Indiana, *Tribune*, 12 Nov. 1957, as reported in Mebane, pp. 249-250.
32. Binder, *What We Really Know*, p. 82.
33. From the Painesville, Ohio, *Telegraph*, 27 Nov. 1957, as reported in Mebane, pp. 266-267.

over Mrs. Russell Hickman's garden, across the highway. The UFO extinguished its red and "clear" lights and ascended, shining a brilliant, green light from the bottom and lighting up the countryside. The witnesses (and Habersham County Sheriff A. J. Chapman, who arrived a few minutes later) smelled an odor similar to embalming fluid. Mrs. Hickman suffered burning arms and face afterward, and her daughter, Diane, suffered a red, drawn face and swollen eyelids the next day.[34]

A Baden, Pennsylvania, man suffered sunburn over his whole body and lost vision in both eyes for several days following a close encounter on August 13, 1965. The UFO was disc-shaped and more than 300 feet in diameter. It had orange lights all around it, which dimmed when a bright blue light shone for three seconds. Tree leaves were disturbed by a "shock wave."[35]

Early on August 20, 1966, Otto Becker and two relatives awoke to a bright light in the house. They saw a "six-story" UFO 200 feet from their position at treetop height. It emitted "rainbow colors which appeared to pour off its edges 'like water.'" Domestic animals were upset. The witnesses heard what sounded to them like the sound of an engine when the UFO ascended vertically. They suffered inflamed eyes for several days.[36]

The transmitters that we use to produce microwaves are very different from those that produce radio signals, television signals, ultraviolet light, visible light or X rays. An X-ray machine could no more produce light than a light bulb could broadcast radio programs. Yet UFOs seem to be able to give off any or all forms of radiation in all directions at any time. How is this possible? Do they lug around a dozen different types of transmitters and beam various signals at different wavelengths, using their hulls as antennae? For what purpose?

The answer to the riddle may come from studying the tiny portion of the electromagnetic spectrum that we can see—visible light. Witnesses who see UFOs at night almost invariably say they are self-luminous. They glow. Daytime witnesses sometimes notice the glow too. The degree of luminosity varies from very dim to brighter than the sun. (Dr. Vallée analyzed a typical sighting and calculated that the light energy emitted by the object was on the order of 2.3 million watts—about the same as 23,000 100-watt light bulbs would give off.)[37] Dark UFOs sometimes begin glowing dimly and increase in brilliance until they are as bright as an arc welder, or vice versa. The change can be gradual or sudden.

They are also apt to glow with light of any and all possible colors, including colors witnesses say they have never seen before and find impossible to describe. Often these glows enshroud the UFO like a mist, and can change through the full color spectrum, either gradually or

34. From the Atlanta, Georgia, *Constitution*, as reported in Liss, pp. 70-71.
35. From Air Technical Intelligence Center files, as reported in Vallée, *Magonia*, pp. 313.
36. From *The NICAP Reporter* (Robert Gribble, 5108 South Findlay St., Seattle, 18, Washington), Jan. 1967, as reported in Vallée, *Magonia*, pp. 334-335.
37. Vallée, *Confrontations*, p. 30.

suddenly, while witnesses watch. The glow is separate from the lights, and often there are no lights involved at all.

If we were to try to duplicate this effect, we would find it impossible. Lasers can produce monochromatic light of a particular color, but we would have to have a different laser for each color, and they would have to be trained on the UFO from a distance and somehow diffused evenly around it. The only other way we have of producing light of specific colors is to pass white light through filters of different colors, like the lenses of stop lights, or like color slides or movie film. There is no way to make a blue light bulb shine with a red light. Of course, there are no projectors pointed at UFOs. They are just giving off a glow, either from the entire surface of their hulls, or from something surrounding them. They are simply doing things we cannot duplicate.

If we accept the possibility that UFOs are sometimes surrounded by time-warping fields, though, at least one explanation naturally follows. It has to do with something called the "Doppler effect."

Named after the 19th-century Austrian physicist, Christian Doppler, the Doppler effect is the apparent change of frequency of waves, such as sound waves or light waves, varying with the relative velocities of the source and the observer. Astronomers can tell how fast stars are moving away from the earth by measuring how far their light is shifted toward the red end of the light spectrum. The distance a star has traveled between one sine wave and the next gets added to the wave itself, making it appear to stretch, as observed from the earth. The faster a star recedes from the earth, the more "red shift" its light is subject to. If it were able to move away fast enough, its light would never reach us.

If stars were hurtling toward us rather than away from us, their light would appear to be shifted toward the violet end of the spectrum instead. The sine waves would apparently be compressed. The motion of the star between one sine wave and the next would make it seem to an observer on the earth that waves were emitted at a higher frequency than they actually were.

Perhaps a better example to explain the Doppler effect is the sound a moving automobile horn, siren or train whistle makes. An observer at a railroad station hears the whistle of an approaching train. Because the train is moving toward the station, the whistle sounds to him to be higher in pitch than it really is. The faster the train approaches, the higher the pitch. If the train could go fast enough, the pitch of the whistle would increase into the ultrasonic range and become inaudible to the observer.

As the train rushes past the station without slowing, the sound suddenly shifts to a lower pitch. The engineer hasn't done anything to the whistle; it still sounds the same to him. But because the train is now moving away from the observer, that observer hears the whistle at a lower pitch. The faster the train accelerates away from him, the lower the pitch will sound. That's the Doppler effect.

The electromagnetic spectrum includes energy waves of all wavelengths. If the wavelength is shorter than a billionth of a centimeter, we call them gamma rays. If it is between one billionth and one millionth of a centimeter, they are X rays. If it is between one millionth and four hundred-thousandths of a centimeter, the waves are ultraviolet rays. Visible light covers wavelengths from four hundred-thousandths of a centimeter on the violet end of the spectrum to eight hundred-thousandths on the red end. If the wavelength is between eight hundred-thousandths and a tenth of a centimeter, the waves are called infrared, or heat waves. Radio waves can have wavelengths from a tenth of a centimeter to several miles.[38]

Keeping that in mind, let's take another look at the hypothetical time-warping field I suggested earlier. Let's say we have built a capsule around our generator, and we have our generator turned on in such a way that time inside the field (and thus inside our capsule) is almost "stopped" in relation to time outside it. We're sitting inside our capsule on a highway. A car approaches. As it nears us, it is affected by the field. Time passes more and more slowly for it. The headlights are in the front, so they enter the field first. They begin to dim. Next comes the engine. It sputters and coughs. The car slows. By now the entire electrical system has been slowed to such a degree that, for all practical purposes, it has ceased to function altogether. The car stops. The driver feels the effects, but since his mind and body are affected equally, the effects are less dramatic for him. He gets out of the car and approaches us, slowing with each step. At some point, he can no longer move, and feels paralyzed.

Another witness watches from some distance away. He decides to throw a stone at us. Before it reaches us, it slows to a halt and falls harmlessly to the ground. He yells at us, but as the sound of his voice enters the field, it is slowed, or "Dopplered." The first witness hears the yell as a slow, low-frequency tone, like a fog horn. The frequency is so low by the time the sound reaches us that it is below the range of our hearing. We hear nothing at all.

A third witness, also standing at a distance, shines a flashlight at us. As the light enters the field, it is Dopplered, so that its wavelength is lengthened. The first witness sees it as a deep red, and by the time it reaches us, the wavelength is lengthened beyond the visible spectrum. We feel only a little heat.

Inside our field, crickets and frogs are singing, but the witnesses can't hear them, because their sound is Dopplered by the field. Its frequency is so high by the time it reaches their ears that it is beyond the range of their hearing. The ultrasonic vibrations do make them feel inexplicably frightened, though.

Now we decide to turn our radio transmitter on. The outer hull of our ship acts as our antenna. Since the time-warping field is still turned on, the radio waves are Dopplered as they pass through it. By the time they reach witness number one, they have been compressed enough so that he feels heat. To the second witness, it appears that our

---

38. Fred Hoyle, *Frontiers of Astronomy* (New York: Harper & Row, 1955), p. 41.

ship has suddenly begun to glow red, because the radio waves have been Dopplered so much by the time they reach him that the wavelengths are short enough to be barely visible to his eyes.

He decides to approach us and photograph us. Since it is night, he sets his camera shutter at a speed of one eighth of a second. As he gets closer, the glow fades, but he can now feel heat. He raises his camera and trips the shutter. But he is now far enough within the influence of our field that his film and shutter are in different time zones. For all practical purposes, his shutter stays open only about a tenth as long as needed to take a good photograph. The exposed film will show only a blob.

Now we decide to crank our radio transmitter up to full power and transmit on a much higher frequency. The witnesses are suddenly blinded by an orange light that appears to be bathing our ship. We switch to a higher frequency; the light appears to them to have turned some color between green and blue. Then we shine a spotlight at them. Like everything else, the light is affected by the field. Its wavelength is shortened to such an extent that by the time it reaches the witnesses, it has been Dopplered into the same wavelength as ultraviolet. Although they don't see the light at all, their eyes are damaged by the radiation, and they will suffer from sunburn. Had the light been in the ultraviolet range to begin with, it would have been Dopplered into the wavelength of either X rays or gamma rays. The witnesses might have been seriously injured or killed.

The person with the camera is taking another photograph. Since his film is sensitive to ultraviolet light, this one will show a bright image of our spot light, but our ship will still not produce an image. He will not understand why the image he saw is different from the image on the developed photograph.

Now all this is highly speculative. Since no one has yet determined how to construct a time machine (so far as we know), we can't be sure if ultraviolet light can be changed into something analogous to visible light, if visible light can be changed into something like infrared, and so on. If it is happening somewhere in the universe, we don't currently have a way of measuring it. But astronomers studying black holes, quasars and pulsars may someday make a breakthrough discovery. They already tell us that when we look at certain stars, we see light that left them millions of years ago. Perhaps even they don't understand time as well as they think.

In the meantime, the Doppler idea does seem supportable, provided there is an exchange of energy. In order to shorten the wavelength of a radiation, energy must be added; when it is lengthened, energy is released. Thus, we can deduce that a time-warping field might both produce and absorb energy.

To explain the peculiar characteristics of UFOs, we must take only one small step—that of supposing they might be surrounded by time-warping fields. As we will see, that step allows for explanations of a number of other situations that have historically made UFOs seem supernatural. For example, it could explain how one witness could see a UFO while another witness not far away does not, or why ambient insect and animal sounds often give way to absolute silence near a UFO. It allows for at least one additional reason for the lack of close-up photos of UFOs, since a time-warping field may sometimes have such profound psychological and physiological effects on percipients that they cannot operate cameras.

The apparently clear, close-up and purportedly genuine photographs that Eduard Meier has taken of many UFOs may at first seem to fly in the face of this hypothesis. On further reflection, however, it must be remembered that Meier has reported that the photography sessions were *invited* by the Pleiadeans. If this were true, then it is conceivable that the time-warp effects that would normally disrupt photography were intentionally controlled so that Meier's film would develop normally.

At any rate, the time-warp hypothesis is much more palatable than the "magnetic star drive" idea that has historically dominated UFO literature. That idea presupposes that the various frequencies of radiation are either consciously projected by ufonauts from some sort of hypothetical "ray guns," or are by-products of a potent magnetic field used to propel the craft. Unfortunately, the effects are noted not only when UFOs are in flight, but also when they are at rest on the ground (i.e. propulsion is not engaged), and even when they are unoccupied. Nor do witnesses (like the pilots who had to abandon their plane over Walesville) report seeing any type of weapon or nozzle that might project rays toward them. Instead, the effects are widespread, and seem to emanate from the craft in all directions—like a field.

...the most uniform features of their behavior in flight are: (1) oblique position of the object during acceleration and deceleration; (2) ability to stop completely at any altitude with no appreciable noise; (3) change of color as a function of acceleration; (4) ability to travel extremely fast over short distances; (5) in discontinuous flight, frequent periods of "dead leaf" maneuvers bringing the object to a lower altitude....

—Dr. Jacques Vallée [1]

"Faster than a Speeding Bullet..."

New Mexico, where the White Sands missile range is located, and where observers often watch the skies with special instruments to track missiles and weather balloons, has been the site of several UFO sightings indicating astounding speeds.

On April 6, 1948, a scientist and Navy missile trackers tracked an oval UFO through a theodolite and computed its speed to be 18,000 m.p.h.—30 times the speed of today's jetliners. It then climbed steeply 25 miles, gaining altitude at the rate of 9,000 m.p.h.[2]

A year later, on the 24th of the month at 10:30 A.M., members of Cmdr. R. B. McLauglin's crew spotted a silver or white elliptical UFO while observing a weather balloon through a theodolite at White Sands. They tracked it for about 60 seconds. Judging by the mountainous background, they were able to estimate that it was about 40 x 100 feet and flying about 25,000 m.p.h.[3]

A similar incident occurred at 11:00 A.M. on January 16, 1951. The manager of the Artesia Municipal Airport, an aeronautical engineer who tracked research balloons and four other men saw two gray, disc-shaped UFOs maneuvering in the vicinity of the Skyhook balloon they were tracking. They thought the UFOs were at about the same altitude as the balloon (100,000 feet), and twice its size or more. The objects made at least one abrupt 90-degree turn and moved through an arc of

1. Jacques Vallée and Janine Vallée, *Challenge to Science*, (Chicago: Henry Regnery Co., 1966), p. 186.
2. Keyhoe, *op. cit.*, pp. 46-47.
3. Edward J. Ruppelt, *The Report on Unidentified Flying Objects* (Garden City, New York: Doubleday and Company, Inc., 1956; rpt. New York: Ace Books, Inc., n.d.), pp. 97-98.

45 degrees in two to three seconds, which computes to a velocity of more than 18,000 m.p.h.[4]

Near Albuquerque, Julian Sandoval saw a UFO about 300 feet long on June 23, 1966. It left at "incredible speed, swiftly reaching six Machs" (more than 4,000 m.p.h.).[5] Sandoval, an Apollo Space Project engineer, was a pilot and former Air Force navigator with 7,000 hours of flying time. He watched the UFO fly around for 51 minutes. It was tetrahedral, luminous "like a light bulb," and had four blue-green lights at the rear. Its glow got brighter whenever it had moved to a new position.[6]

At least two very speedy UFOs were reported from Indiana in the summer of 1952. Three Civil Aeronautics Agency control-tower operators calculated the speed of a "saucer" that passed over the Terre Haute airport at 42,000 m.p.h.[7] The friction at the 3,000-foot altitude they estimated would vaporize any known aircraft.

From about 1:00 A.M. to about 5:00 A.M. on July 28, 1952, Patrolmen Jack Moore and Kenneth Rund and Capt. Lee Sloan of the Franklin Police Department watched three luminous, disc-shaped UFOs. One was larger and yellow; the others were orange and red respectively. They appeared to be flying at between 1,500 and 10,000 m.p.h. at 14,000 feet. The smaller ones performed various dramatic aerobatics at these speeds, including right-angled turns and yo-yo up-and-down motions. They flew southward until they disappeared into the distance, then returned almost instantly. Their outlines were indistinct, even when binoculars were employed to watch them. The smaller UFOs seemed to merge with the larger one, which flew away westward. The sighting was corroborated by the Edinburg, Columbus, Seynour, Greensburg, North Vernon and Connorsville police departments, and by Camp Atterbury.[8]

That same year, on December 6 at 5:24 A.M., Capt. John Harter, radar operator Lt. Sidney Coleman, navigator Lt. Cassidy, flight engineer Bailey, and S. Sgt. Ferris were making a routine practice run in a B-29 bomber over the Gulf of Mexico south of Louisiana. They watched a group of four UFOs on radar as they made three passes at the aircraft at more than 5,000 m.p.h. They approached, then veered off. Both Coleman and Ferris were able to catch glimpses of the UFOs as they shot past, but the relative speed was so great that they could only discern blue-white streaks of light. On the last pass, the UFOs cut across the B-29's path (behind it), turned to follow, stopped suddenly then began following the aircraft. Then a huge blip flared on the radar screen. The smaller ones merged with it; it flared even more brilliantly; and it

4. Vallée, *Challenge to Science*, pp. 1-3.
5. Keyhoe, *op. cit.*, p. 122.
6. Dale White, *Is Something Up There?* (New York: Doubleday and Company, Inc., 1968; rpt. New York: Scholastic Book Services—Scholastic Magazines, Inc., 1969), p. 136.
7. Binder, *What We Really Know*, p. 33.
8. Albert K. Bender, *Flying Saucers and the Three Men* (New York: Paperback Library, Inc., 1968), pp. 34-35.

streaked off the radar screen at 9,000 m.p.h. Intelligence officers questioned the men when they landed.[9, 10]

On June 23, 1955, the crew of a Mohawk Airlines DC-3 saw a light gray, near-round object with windows, which emitted bright light that changed from green, to blue, to green. The object was reported seen by Albany, New York and Boston, Massachusetts control-tower personnel on the Victor Two airway. Speed was computed at 4,500 m.p.h. or more. Altitude was estimated at 3,500 feet. Even though the UFO passed only 500 feet over the plane, *no sonic boom was heard.* The UFO was also reported by the crews of a Colonial Airlines flight and another commercial flight. It was estimated to be 150 feet long.[11,12]

Waldo J. Harris reported another broad-daylight sighting on October 2, 1961. Shortly after leaving the Salt Lake City, Utah, airport in his private plane, Harris saw a disc-shaped, aluminum-colored UFO about 52 feet in diameter hovering with a rocking motion. He approached it, and it ascended 1,000 feet in altitude abruptly. He again approached it, and it shot away, disappearing into the distance in two or three seconds (which computes to more than 5,000 m.p.h.). At least eight people on the ground at the airport also witnessed the incident.[13]

On the afternoon of January 5, 1965, satellite tracking chief Dempsey Bruton tracked a "huge" disc-shaped UFO that flew over the Wallops Island, Virginia, NASA station. He computed its speed at more than 6,000 m.p.h. Radar tracked a UFO making "a sharp turn at 4,800 miles an hour" at Maryland's Naval Air Test Center the same day.[14]

Seven months later, seven to ten UFOs were tracked on radar by personnel at the U.S. Air Force Radar Base in the Keweenaw Peninsula. They flew in a "V" formation at altitudes of between 5,200 and 17,000 feet over Lake Superior.[15] Even at 9,600 m.p.h. there was no sonic boom.[16]

The year 1967 produced several amazing reports from astronomers at the Soviet astronomical station at Kazan and the astrophysical station at Kislovodsk of orange, glowing, crescent-shaped UFOs well over a quarter of a mile wide flying at unimaginable speeds overhead. The speed of one that passed over the Kazan station just after twilight on July 18 was calculated at 11,160 m.p.h.[17]

The power in Bill Pecha's Colusa, California, house failed after midnight on September 10, 1976. He stepped outside, felt his hair prickle, and saw a UFO with a white underside, rotating rim and pro-

9. White, *op. cit.,* pp. 102-109.
10. Aimé Michel, *Lueurs sur les Socoupes Volantes* (Paris: Mame, 1954), trans. Paul Selver, *The Truth About Flying Saucers* (New York: Criterion Books, 1956; rpt. New York: Pyramid Books-Pyramid Communications, Inc., 1974), pp. 95-97.
11. John G. Fuller, ed., *Aliens in the Skies* (New York: G. P. Putnam's Sons, 1969), pp. 35-36.
12. Keyhoe, *op. cit.,* pp. 262-263.
13. Binder, *What We Really Know,* pp. 7-8.
14. Keyhoe, *op. cit.,* p. 106.
15. Edwards, *Serious Business,* pp. 167-169.
16. Frank Edwards, *Flying Saucers—Here and Now!* (New York: Lyle Stuart, 1967), p. 181.
17. Keyhoe, *op. cit.,* pp. 154-155.

jections hanging down. It hovered about 55 feet up and was about 150 feet in diameter. A large white light beam that projected downward extended only *halfway* to the ground. The UFO shot away westward between two other distant UFOs and into foothills, then it returned, covering 18 to 20 miles in two or three seconds. Its speed would have to have been at least 21,600 m.p.h. There were other witnesses—Gayle Arant described the object as a domed disc.[18]

On September 20, 1976, a UFO easily outraced an Iranian Air Force jet over Teheran, and at one time put on a burst of speed so intense that the movement was visible on the radarscope from a distance of 28 miles. At around 11:00 P.M. on the 19th, Teheran residents called Houssain Perouzi (chief air traffic controller at Mehrabad Airport) to report a hovering, multicolored UFO. Perouzi spotted it with binoculars and notified Gen. Youssefi, who also saw it. Youssefi scrambled a jet, which left at 1:30 A.M. He instructed the pilot to get close enough to identify the object.

The pilot chased the UFO at Mach II toward Afghanistan, turned back and found that *the object had beaten him back to Teheran.* Each time he got within 20 miles of the UFO, his instrumentation failed.

A second jet—an F-4—was scrambled. It chased the UFO at 1,500 m.p.h. but could not catch it. The UFO moved away at a speed that could be seen on the radar screen, then it maintained a distance of 28 miles. It produced a radar return similar to that of a 707 tanker and flashed bright red, green, orange and blue lights in quick succession. At one point, a smaller UFO broke off from the original and sped quickly toward the F-4. The pilot tried to fire an AIM-9 missile, but his weapons control panel and communications suddenly ceased to function. He took evasive action; the bright light pursued him, and ground observers reported a dark rectangular object on top of his plane. The light returned to (and merged with) the original UFO. Another UFO descended from it at great speed, landed and lit an area more than a mile in diameter.

The crew of a civil airliner and the F-4 pilot both reported communications failures when near the object. Citizens in a nearby house reported a loud noise and lightning-like light. Gen. Abdullah Azerbarzin confirmed the incident, saying one of the pilots had passed under the UFO and described it as a domed disc with a yellow-lit "cockpit."[19]

New Zealand was the scene of an incident in the early morning hours of December 21, 1978, during a "down under" wave of sightings. Capt. John Randle, piloting an Argosy, reported unidentified bright lights over the ocean off Kaikoura on two different flights, at 1:20 A.M. and 4:06 A.M. Wellington radar tracked coinciding UFOs. At 3:28 A.M., Capt. Vernon Powell was piloting an Argosy bound for Christchurch. A UFO approached his plane at 10,000 m.p.h., "leaving a trail on the radar screen," then veered off and vanished from the screen. Then a

18. Hendry, *op. cit.*, pp. 117-118.
19. Bruce Maccabee, UFOs—Still Unexplained," *Fate*, Mar. 1984, pp. 72-75.

flashing white light appeared 23 miles away, paced the aircraft for 12 miles and changed color. Wellington radar tracked it. Numerous other UFOs were seen in the area in December and January.[20]

Observers frequently describe UFOs as "moving so fast their lights appear to leave a trail" or "streaking away as fast as a meteor" or "shrinking away into the distance in the blink of an eye." The fact that UFOs are capable of such outlandish speeds has added fuel to the ET argument. Supporters of the ET hypothesis say, "Other planets are billions of miles away; therefore, if their inhabitants visit Earth, they must be able to travel at extremely fast speeds. UFOs travel at extremely fast speeds; therefore they must be spaceships from other planets."

This reasoning works as long as the "spaceships" stay in space, where there is almost no friction. But how do they travel at thousands of miles per hour through the earth's heavy atmosphere without burning up? Is their technology so advanced that they have found a way to avoid friction?

The Concorde supersonic transport, although very streamlined, heats up to hundreds of degrees when traveling at its top speed of about 1,800 m.p.h. Its skin has been engineered to withstand temperatures that would severely damage ordinary aircraft. Were it to reach a speed of 4,000 m.p.h., friction would probably rip it to pieces and incinerate it.

Our early space capsules depended on heat shields to protect them from the searing heat of friction upon re-entry into the atmosphere. Every inch of their re-entry trajectories was painstakingly planned. The slightest error, the tiniest bit too much angle, could cause them to burn up before they reached the ground. They scrubbed off speed by skipping gingerly on the thin, uppermost layer of the atmosphere just enough to keep their heat shields from vaporizing. The capsules bucked and quivered, and particles of the burning heat shields enveloped and trailed them like incandescent comets. The ionized particles made communication impossible during re-entry. By the time the capsules finally sizzled to their splashdowns in the ocean, their heat shields were nearly destroyed and the astronauts inside were sweating from the extreme cabin temperature.

Today our efforts are more sophisticated. The world's most advanced materials engineering knowledge has gone into making special heat-dissipating silicon tiles that are glued onto the space shuttle's skin. Even so, the reentry must be performed at precisely the right angle to scrub off momentum gradually. If the shuttle tried to fly straight up, straight down or at low altitudes at even a fraction of the speeds UFOs do, those tiles would burn up. As it is, tiles frequently need replacement between missions.

It is conceivable that the builders of UFOs have developed a technology so far in advance of our own that they can build aircraft out of

---

20. Kevin R. Berry, "The Kaikoura Controversy," *Flying Saucer Review*, 26, No. 2 (1980), pp. 13-15.

materials we have not yet discovered—materials that can withstand incredibly high temperatures. The fact remains, though (at least as far as
we know), that any material object traveling at thousands of miles per
hour through air makes a terrific racket. The Concorde and most other
supersonic flights have been outlawed in all but a few areas of the U.S.
because of the noise they make. We know of no aircraft shape—including the commonly reported UFO configurations of spheres, cigars, and
discs—that will not create a sonic boom when passing through air at
more than the speed of sound (about 750 m.p.h.). Yet UFOs often produce no sound at all, let alone sonic booms. And they are often reported to zip around at thousands of miles per hour while tilted at steep
angles, which would seem to defy everything we know about aerodynamics.

The problem has prompted some frustrated investigators to pro-
pose that UFOs are not material objects at all, but projections—like the
images in a "3-D" movie. But of course that hypothesis doesn't match
the data either. UFOs press dents into the ground, break tree limbs,
set grass and pavement ablaze and splash into oceans. They drag cars
sideways, disturb animals and reflect radar signals. People have
walked around inside them and rapped their knuckles on their floors,
walls and examining tables. These are without question physical objects!

So how is it possible that they can fly silently through the atmosphere at such tremendous speeds? Does their technology allow them
to circumvent the sound barrier as well as friction? Are they able to fool
all the laws of thermodynamics? Perhaps. But there may be a simpler
answer. They may not be subject to the same physical barriers our aircraft meet because they may be moving through *time* rather than simply through space.

Although few of us have ever thought much about it, we are all
constantly hurtling through the universe at incredible speeds in several different directions. Each day, our planet makes one revolution. That
means that, at the equator, the earth's surface—the ground people are
walking on right now—is spinning at more than 1,000 m.p.h. all the
time around an axis that runs through the north and south poles.
Once each year, Earth orbits the sun, which is 93 million miles away.
That means we are moving in that larger circle (which is tilted at a 23-
degree angle to the earth's axis) at more than 33,000 m.p.h. Our entire
solar system is orbiting the center of our galaxy in an even larger circle
at 500,000 m.p.h. (tilted at yet another angle). Our galaxy and other,
distant galaxies are moving away from each other at more than
136,000,000 m.p.h.![21]

Speed is measured in units of length divided by units of time—
miles per hour, feet per second, etc. If we could somehow change our
rate of passage through time, our apparent velocity relative to a stationary observer might change automatically.

---

21. Hoyle, *op. cit.*, pp. 226, 309.

For instance, let's say we are flying at 100 miles per hour. To an observer on the ground, we will appear to have traveled 100 miles in a space of one hour. If we then change our rate of passage through time relative to that observer so that one hour passes twice as quickly for us, it will appear to the observer that after one hour (his time), we will have traveled *200* miles. If instead we change our rate of passage through time so that an hour passes twice as *slowly* for us, it will appear to the observer that we have only traveled *50* miles in one hour.

This means that, were we to build a time machine surrounded by a field that warped time, we could *appear* to travel through space at very high speeds by simply changing the length of a second inside our time-warping field in relation to a second outside it.

If, for instance, we were suddenly to "stop" time inside the field by throwing a switch, our time machine would no longer be zipping along at the normal earthly velocity of 500,000 m.p.h. It would be stopped. But everything else *would* still be going 500,000 m.p.h. If we were lucky, we would have been on the "back" side of the earth when we threw our switch. An observer standing outside our field would seem to disappear instantly. And to him, we would seem to disappear instantly. Half an hour later (by the observer's time) we would be as far away from the earth as the moon is! If we weren't so lucky—if we had started out at some point in the earth's path as it followed its orbit—we might be slammed into the ground (or, more precisely, the ground might slam into us) at a relative velocity of 500,000 m.p.h. We don't know the physics of time travel yet, so we can't be sure of the outcome of that collision, but it seems reasonable to assume that a great deal of energy would be expended. We and our time machine might be vaporized.

But using this type of design, we could vary the apparent speed of a powered craft in relation to a fixed point by a tremendous amount. And even a capsule with no propulsion of its own could be made to move in various directions (which would depend on the attitude of that particular point on the earth as the earth followed its spin, solar orbit and so on at that particular moment).

Again, we don't know anything about the physics involved, but we can guess that our field, like all other fields we know about, would probably conform to the inverse square law. If so, air molecules that were in our path as we passed through the air would probably be affected by it more and more as they passed deeper into its sphere of influence, slowing to a stop within the field like bullets fired into sand, rather than striking it and bouncing away. And the kinetic energy they lost in the process would probably be released as heat and/or other forms of radiation. Depending on the degree of slowing, enough heat might even be generated to ionize the air in and around our field. It might begin to glow like the aurora borealis, especially directly in front of us, where the effect would be greatest. Our field would probably be shaped like other fields—spherical, egg-shaped, oblate or toroidal—so an observer would see a glow of one of these shapes enveloping us. Because the effect would not be sharply outlined, it would probably look hazy, like a mist.

The skin of our craft would probably experience some heating, but only a fraction of that experienced by conventional aircraft, because the molecules of air would be slowed to such an extent by our field that they would never actually strike it (indeed our field might also warp space itself in such a way that it would be impossible for them to strike it). There would be virtually no friction to contend with. Nor would our passage be likely to produce the types of sonic shock waves that cause the sonic booms associated with conventional aircraft, even when we moved at many times the speed of sound (relative to a stationary observer).

In other words, once one accepts that UFOs may indeed employ time-warping fields, witnesses' claims that they see UFOs enveloped in a "glowing haze" streaking through the air at thousands of miles per hour without burning up or causing sonic booms become evidence *in favor* of bona fide sightings, rather than *against* them.

7

...the Navy disclosed that two UFOs had been tracked by radar at the Naval Air Test Center in Maryland. One had made a sharp turn at 4,800 miles an hour.

—Maj. Donald Keyhoe
(USMC, Ret.)[1]

"Impossible" Aerobatics

One of the most famous UFO sightings of all time happened over the Mount Rainier Plateau in Washington State on the afternoon of June 24, 1947. Although UFOs have been reported throughout history, the Kenneth Arnold sighting is commonly regarded as the beginning of the "flying saucer era."

Arnold was an experienced mountain pilot, a member of Idaho Search and Rescue Mercy Flyers, and a deputy U.S. Marshal. While searching for a missing C-46 marine transport plane in his own light plane, he spotted a formation of nine shiny, crescent-shaped UFOs that emitted blue-white flashes from their wing tips and flew in an erratic pattern, "like a saucer would if you skipped it across the water," or like "speed boats on rough water."

Using mountains as landmarks, Arnold calculated their average velocity conservatively at 1,350 m.p.h. (months before the 750-m.p.h. sound barrier was broken). Arnold was quoted as saying, "this velocity, the human body simply could not stand, particularly considering the flipping, erratic movements of these strange craft."[2] Scores of witnesses watched blue and purple lights maneuvering in the sky above Seattle, Washington, until 11:00 that night.[3]

Aerobatics beyond the capabilities of conventional aircraft are hallmarks of the UFO phenomenon. In many cases it is this incredible maneuverability as much as their appearance that prompts witnesses to report sightings. This was the case on August 1, 1948, when the passengers and crew members of a Hong Kong-to-Saigon flight, including

---

1. Keyhoe, *op. cit.,* p. 106.
2. Flammonde, *op. cit.,* pp. 147-150.
3. Keel, *Trojan Horse,* p. 61.

French radio-television correspondent Samy Simon, saw a long, fish-shaped UFO that reflected sunlight as if it were metallic. Estimated to be twice the size of a large bomber, it executed a 90-degree turn without reducing its speed, and "vanished in the clouds."[4]

At 11:00 P.M. on October 15 of that same year, First Lt. Oliver Hemphill and his radar operator, Second Lt. Barton Halter, tried six times to close on a wingless, tailless UFO the size of a fighter plane near Fukuoka, Japan. The UFO repeatedly showed up on their radar. Each time, the UFO accelerated and easily outdistanced them. At one point, when they got to within 12,000 feet, the UFO made a 180-degree turn and dived under them. It ascended and descended almost vertically out of radar elevation limits.[5]

On July 2, 1952, warrant officer D. C. Newhouse and his wife were driving through Utah when they saw a group of UFOs in the sky. Newhouse got a movie camera out of his suitcase and photographed them. The photos were studied by the Photo Reconnaissance Laboratory, Wright Field Development Center, and by the U.S. Navy Photo Interpretation Center. They concluded that the UFOs were not birds, aircraft or balloons, and that they "would stop almost instantly and turn and change direction as no airplane could at that speed." The Air Force said it did not know what they were.[6]

Fifteen days later, at night, Capt. Paul L. Carpenter was flying an American Airlines DC-6 at 25,000 feet when he saw four bright UFOs zoom past at "fantastic speed." He had been alerted by the Denver, Colorado, airfield, where the objects had been tracked on radar at almost 3,000 m.p.h.[7] Three of the objects performed a 180-degree turn instantly.[8]

Not long after that, in August, a UFO was seen at Horn Island Pass, Mississippi. Oliver Bryant was operating a party–boat service based in Bayou La Battre. He and ten or twelve fishermen saw a domed, humming UFO almost 50 feet long with "lights all around." They watched it hover, ascend vertically and make instantaneous direction changes for 44 minutes, then they gave a signed report to the FBI in Mobile, Alabama.[9]

French customs agent Gabriel Gachignard encountered a UFO exhibiting instant acceleration at the Marignane Airport at 2:03 A.M. on October 27, 1952. Gachignard was eating a meal outdoors and saw a dim light approaching the airport on a low glide path at about 150

4. Jacques Vallée, *Anatomy of a Phenomenon: Unidentified Objects in Space—A Scientific Appraisal* (Chicago: Henry Regnery Co., 1965); rpt. *UFOs in Space: Anatomy of a Phenomenon* (New York: Ballantine Books-Random House, Inc., 1974), p. 59.
5. Blum, *Beyond Earth*, p. 188. Some information originally from James E. McDonald, *Symposium on Unidentified Flying Objects* (House Committee on Science and Astronautics, 29 Jul. 1968), pp. 69-70.
6. Frank E. Stranges, *Flying Saucerama* (New York: Vantage Press, Inc., 1959), pp. 28-29.
7. Renato Vesco, *Intercettateli Senza Sparare* (Milan, Italy: U. Mursia & C., 1968), trans. Grove Press, Inc., *Intercept—But Don't Shoot: The True Story of Flying Saucers* (New York: Grove Press, Inc., 1971), p. 58.
8. Flammonde, *op. cit.*, p. 263.
9. Blum, *Beyond Earth*, pp. 19-20.

m.p.h. When it touched the runway, it made a "dull" noise and stopped abruptly without slowing down. Walking toward it, he saw it was a dark, football-shaped object 15 feet long with four square "windows" that changed color from green, to blue, to red. After sitting at rest for a minute while the witness approached it, the UFO emitted a shower of sparks, and without acceleration, "changed instantly to a frightening speed, impossible to estimate," flew away back along the same low path and disappeared over a pond across the road from the airport.[10]

It is interesting to note at this point that UFOs are often reported to approach from a particular direction and leave along exactly the same route, as in this Marignane case, sometimes even disappearing for a time in between coming and going. This is exactly what one would expect if UFOs were traveling back and forth in time.

Aimé Michel presented an excellent case for the tendency of sightings to be arranged along straight paths in *Flying Saucers and the Straight Line Mystery*. Michel found that sightings did not necessarily occur in sequence; i.e., the two earliest sightings may be at the two extreme ends of a line hundreds of miles long, while later sightings may be at various points along the same line.[11] This apparent backtracking seems to make little sense if UFOs are extraterrestrial spacecraft performing a reconnaissance of Earth, but it is eminently logical if they are time machines trying to pinpoint an exact date and place, perhaps to search for something their pilots know happened in their past.

The shower of sparks produced when the Marignane object streaked away puts one in mind of the "rooster tail" of sparks made by a loose bumper dragged along behind a speeding car. Perhaps its pilots should have been more careful to ascend a few feet into the air before leaving at such breathtaking speed. They may have ground part of their machine off on the runway!

Air Force pilots thought they had caught a UFO over California's Sequoia-Kings National Park on August 1, 1953. They were circling above the park to investigate UFO sightings by Park Superintendent E. T. Scoyen and staff members during the previous three nights. Just before midnight, they saw a "disc slanting down at reduced speed" and followed, flying above it and matching its speed to force it to land. The UFO stopped instantly in midair without deceleration, then ascended steeply, eluding the jets.[12]

Nine UFOs were seen from Albuquerque, New Mexico, a "UFO hot spot," on July 3, 1954. They glowed with a green light and were described as "round." They hovered, and then made a 340-degree turn at an estimated 2,600 miles per hour.[13]

High-ranking Italian Army officers and military pilots were among thousands who watched a UFO perform breathtaking maneuvers over Rome at 6:28 P.M. on September 17 of that same year. For over an

10. Michel, *The Truth About Flying Saucers*, pp. 159-169.
11. Michel, *Straight Line Mystery*, p. 77.
12. Keyhoe, *op. cit.*, p. 49.
13. Binder, *What We Really Know*, p. 34.

hour, airport personnel tracked it on radar. They watched it accelerate from a dead stop to about 170 m.p.h. "almost instantaneously, only to stop suddenly again, drop down, then turn, rise, and so on." When the UFO moved, an antenna-like protuberance in its center appeared to be making a "short luminous trail."[14]

Dr. J. I. Bennet and his wife saw two silent, spinning, "powder blue" UFOs zipping around the sky "like fish in a tank." They abruptly paired and hovered, then shot away in different directions at very high speed. In the meantime, Bennet had taken photographs. The incident occurred at the Kilburn Estate in Singapore at 8:20 on the evening of July 26, 1956.[15]

Bright lights woke Mrs. Mary Starr in her Old Saybrook, Connecticut, cottage at about 2:30 A.M. on December 16, 1957. She saw a gray or black UFO about 20 feet long fly to a hovering position ten feet from her house and five feet off the ground. She observed figures moving inside through "portholes." The UFO turned luminous, and a glittering, antenna-like protuberance rose. The UFO hovered for five minutes, then moved sideways, executed an abrupt 90-degree turn, changed color to gray-blue (with circular lights where the portholes had been), tilted and shot away silently as fast as a jet.[16]

Another early morning encounter took place over the Pacific Ocean on July 12, 1959. While piloting a Pan Am flight to Hawaii, Capt. C. A. Wilson (a 19-year veteran), copilot Richard Lorenzon and their flight engineer saw a UFO in the form of a cluster of lights. It approached from ahead and to the left of the aircraft at tremendous speed, then turned sharply to the right "at a speed inconceivable for any vehicle we know of, and the light suddenly disappeared." Wilson reported that the UFO had approached at 180 degrees from his flight path, and made a 90-degree turn.

Other reports followed from at least eight other commercial flights. The Chief Air Traffic Control Officer at Honolulu called the Western Sea Frontier headquarters and the Pacific Air Force. Pilots were questioned by military intelligence officers, then by the press. The incident was reported in numerous newspapers. Project Bluebook personnel concluded that the UFO had been a meteor—even though it had made a right-angled turn and had left no trail![17]

A Trenton, New Jersey, man saw an orange, cigar-shaped UFO surrounded by a blue-green "area" just above the horizon at 7:45 P.M. on August 19, 1959. It made as many as ten right-angled turns in 25 minutes, and was accompanied by five shining companion UFOs.[18]

At 3:35 A.M. on March 23 the following year, a couple saw a UFO execute 180-degree and 90-degree turns over Indianapolis, Indiana. It was shaped like a kite, and seemed to be made of glowing beads. It re-

14. Vallée, *Challenge to Science*, p. 131.
15. Lorenzen, *The Whole Story*, p. 73.
16. Coral Lorenzen, "UFO Occupants in the United States," in *The Humanoids*, ed. Charles Bowen (Chicago: Henry Regnery Company, 1969), pp. 157-159.
17. White, *op. cit.*, pp. 59-64.
18. Vallée, *Challenge to Science*, pp. 178-179.

versed its course and flew away at a speed estimated to be about 18,000 m.p.h.[19]

A few minutes before midnight on August 13, 1960, another UFO reversed its course. This one was seen east of Corning, California, by Highway Patrolmen Stanley Scott and Charles Carson, who leaped from their patrol car to watch the elliptical object surrounded by a white glow and sporting red and white lights. They noticed "absolute silence." The UFO descended at a 45-degree angle to an altitude of 100 to 200 feet, not more than a mile away, then suddenly reversed course at high speed and rose 500 feet. It was 150 feet long and 40 feet tall, and made no sound.

Other officers were alerted, and several of them also spotted the object. Its presence was confirmed by the local radar base. For two hours, it was observed and chased while it performed unbelievable maneuvers, often hovering or reversing direction while moving at extremely high speed, and often sweeping the area with a red beam. The next day, Scott and Carson were not allowed to talk to the radar operator who had been on duty during the sighting.[20, 21]

At 7:18 P.M. on September 14, 1961, a white, circular UFO moved at irregular speed and direction over Korea's Osan Air Force Base. It traveled faster than an airplane, stopped, hovered, grew very bright, then ascended vertically as it changed color to red. When a jet approached the area, it executed 90-degree turns.[22]

While leading a squadron of Javelin delta-wing fighters over Egypt on the afternoon of September 11, 1962, an RAF pilot suffered a partial power loss. He descended 8,000 feet below the other planes. When he looked up at them, he caught sight of a bright white light, sharply defined against the vapor trails, which followed them at a speed of at least 1,500 m.p.h., passed them, and then stopped instantaneously. It executed an instantaneous turn of 150 degrees and sped away. Three other members of the squadron also saw the object; all deposed statements to RAF intelligence.[23]

Manuel Fernandez and his wife watched a large, red, domed disc take off as if shot from a gun at about 4:33 on the morning of July 12, 1965. It had approached quickly from the northeast, stopped abruptly and was hovering and rocking slowly over trees. Fernandez said it had a bright orange top and a dark rim with a "flickering" red light. It abruptly took off northward at high speed without any acceleration time. During the three minutes the UFO was near, Fernandez' radio changed from playing music to loud static then returned to music when it left.[24]

19. Binder, *What We Really Know*, p. 27
20. Testimony of Dr. James A. Harder before the House Committee on Science and Astronautics (29 Jul. 1968), as quoted in Fuller, *Aliens in the Skies*, pp. 134-136.
21. From a report given to the California State Highway Patrol area commander, as quoted in Lorenzen, *The Whole Story*, pp. 153-156.
22. Vallée, *UFOs in Space*, p. 174
23. David Apps, "Fighter Pilot's Sighting Over Egypt," *Flying Saucer Review*, 26, No. 1 (1980), pp. 32, iii.
24. Steiger, *Strangers from the Skies*, pp. 103-104.

Two months later, on the 9th, hundreds of residents of Cuzco, Peru, watched four metallic blue saucers hover, turn at right angles and otherwise fly in ways airplanes cannot for two hours. They also departed at "incredible" velocity.[25]

Another 4:30 A.M. sighting happened at Charleston, West Virginia, on May 4, 1966. An air-traffic-control-center operator watched an unidentified blip describe a 180-degree turn at 1,000 m.p.h. in a space of only five miles. At the same time, a Braniff pilot was watching a very bright light change colors in the same location.[26]

On September 20, 1966, veteran pilot James O'Connor was flying near Sebring, Florida, at mid-morning when a gigantic UFO (about the size of a football field) approached him quickly and hovered close above his plane. Terrified, O'Connor dove and took evasive action but could not shake his pursuer, which stayed in the same relative position. Eventually it flew away by performing an impossible maneuver, "a reverse peel in a 360-degree turn," as if it were "falling up."[27]

Next are two Rumanian cases. Engineering professor Bota Octavian witnessed the first incident at 10:30 P.M. on August 4, 1967 at Sîngeorz-Bai. A luminous, blue-yellow UFO approached in the same manner as a meteor. It slowed, changed direction, climbed steeply and changed color from bluish to white-yellow. It then executed a 90-degree turn without reducing speed, crossed half of the professor's field of vision and performed another right-angled turn, changing from yellow-white, to yellow, to rose-yellow.[28]

Another engineer witnessed a similar occurrence at Ploieçti the following year. Nicolae Rădulescu saw a glowing, red, disc-shaped UFO with a surrounding haze suddenly appear south of his flat. It moved north jerkily, returned south, suddenly executed a 90-degree turn and then vanished toward Strejnic Airport. It moved faster than a jet, yet it was silent.[29]

In 1976, at about 2:00 A.M., Idaho State Patrol Cpl. E. H. Christensen and a deputy sheriff saw a UFO perform unbelievable aerobatics. They watched through binoculars as an object with revolving blue, green and white lights moved erratically for more than five minutes, making 90-degree turns "at fantastic speeds," suddenly reversing direction and following a zigzag course. Christensen said the object had a rounded top and flat bottom. He also reported several other sightings in the Soda Springs area in 1976.[30]

Commandante Francisco de Tejada Lerdo had no choice but to shake up his 109 passengers when a stunt-flying UFO buzzed his Supercaravelle near Valencia, Spain, on November 11, 1979. The Commandante and his copilot spotted two bright red lights coming toward the aircraft at amazing speed. Lerdo reported, "I have never seen any-

25. Keel, *Trojan Horse*, p. 253.
26. Hynek, *Experience*, pp. 73-74.
27. Edwards, *Here and Now!*, pp. 109-111.
28. Hobana, *op. cit.*, pp. 156-157.
29. *Ibid.*, pp. 246-247.
30. Anderson, *op. cit.*, pp. 15-16.

thing like that speed." The lights appeared to be attached to an object. They approached to less than a half mile away, where they seemed to "play" with the liner, performing turns and maneuvers no aircraft would have been able to execute. The pilot had to turn the plane violently in a "break" maneuver and was followed by the UFO for about 30 miles. He landed at Valencia Airport, where the director, traffic controller and several ground personnel said they saw a UFO with several red lights hovering over buildings at the airport. The UFO was seen on Barcelona, Valencia and Air Defense Command Headquarters radars. Two F-1 fighters were scrambled to intercept.[31]

Many of the reports of these seemingly impossible feats of flying come from respectable and highly trained witnesses—missile trackers, air-traffic controllers, pilots, astronomers, meteorologists, policemen and CAA observers—people whose reports would ordinarily be considered beyond question. Commandante Tejada, for instance, had spent 8,000 hours flying; needless to say, he was familiar with aircraft. Yet the stories imply UFOs ignore the principles of thermodynamics and aerodynamics. Studies of depressions left in the ground by UFO landing gears imply they weigh tons, yet they hover with no noise and no movement of air—in stark contrast to helicopters or VTOL jets like the Harrier, which produce tremendous amounts of noise and wind when hovering. It has been estimated that some of the accelerations and hairpin turns observed (both visually and on radar) would produce inertial forces of 1,000 earth gravities—enough to crush any human pilot to a pulp, not to mention disintegrating any conventional aircraft.

How can this be possible? Once again the time-travel hypothesis may offer an answer.

Again, we can use our hypothetical time machine to illustrate. Let's assume once again that we have turned on our time-warping field in such a way that our seconds are lengthened, and the earth, which continues to follow its complex orbit through the universe, races away from us at some speed less than 500,000 m.p.h.—let's say 5,000 m.p.h. Since we are completely enclosed in our field, we do not notice the change in motion any more than a fly that is flying around inside a car notices that the car is traveling at 100 m.p.h. If we then shorten our seconds, that relative speed will reduce. If we shorten them enough, we will begin to gain on the earth, until eventually we are racing toward it rather than away from it. If we continue on, we will crash into it. If, before we reach the ground, we make the length of our seconds the same as Earth seconds, we will remain in the same position. We will in effect be in a suspended upward motion—we will be hovering.

So our machine can hover. But we are completely at the mercy of the earth's movements. We are still actually moving at exactly the same angular velocity as the surface of the earth, but the fact that we are

31. Juan José Benítez, "Jetliner 'Intercepted' by UFO near Valencia," trans. Gordon Creighton, *Flying Saucer Review*, 25, No. 5 (1980), pp. 13-15.

now above that surface (i.e. farther away from the center of the planet, and therefore farther from the axis around which it is spinning) makes us tend to drift and slowly be left behind. The higher we try to hover, the quicker we drift. And we have only three choices: moving away from the earth, moving toward the earth, and drifting as we try to hover. Our time machine is of little practical use, because every time we try to travel "back in time" (relative to an observer on the earth's surface), we fly off into space. And every time we try to visit the future, we get shoved into the ground in the opposite direction.

To travel backward and forward in time while staying in the same position relative to the earth, we need some type of propulsion—some way to compensate for our "absolute" motion. We could outfit our time machine with propellers or jets, but these would only work in the lower atmosphere (if they worked at all inside the sphere of influence of our time-warping field). They would be useless in space. Rockets would work in space, but even rockets would be pitifully inadequate to compensate for the immense speeds our time machine is capable of (remember, by stopping time, we can theoretically go 500,000 m.p.h. relative to the earth).

What we really need is to be able to distort the time-warping field itself, so that it extends farther in one particular area than anywhere else. Thus we could choose (to an extent) which one of the virtually infinite number of component vectors of the earth's complex angular motion we want to use in much the same way a sailboat can tack at various angles against the wind or let itself be blown by the wind at other angles.

Of course, doing this might be a very tricky proposition. Our motion would still be determined by the various vectors of our intrinsic angular velocity derived from all the different orbits and intergalactic movements. So, depending on what time of day it was and what time of year it was, we may actually have to extend a section of field pointing in one direction to move in an entirely different direction. Our equipment would have to include a computer capable of calculating all the relevant orbital mechanics at any given instant in time we might wish to visit. We would have to ensure that our field never became distorted in such a way that some piece of our time machine was outside of its influence, lest that part of the machine be left on the earth as the rest flies off into space. And we might be constrained within severe speed limits in certain directions (just as our sailboat counterpart is), so that we would find it necessary to follow a series of zigzags (tack) to move in some directions.

Perhaps a better analogy might be to liken our manipulation of our field to the subtle shifts of balance a surfer uses to vary his speed and direction (within limits) as he "harnesses" the immense power of the wave beneath his surfboard. We would be harnessing the power of planetary motion. Just as the surfer must be careful not to let a wave slam him into a pier or rock, we must be careful not to select the wrong direction in which to extend our time-warping field, lest we be hurled into the earth. As I said before, we have no way to know what the outcome of such a collision would be, but it is reasonable to assume that a tremendous amount of energy might be released, particularly if our time machine started out in the distant future, distant past or on some planet other than the earth, so that the relative intrinsic velocities were highly disparate to begin with. In this case, a collision causing the collapse of the field might be even more catastrophic.

Interestingly enough, there is some evidence to hint that just such a collision may have occurred during this century. On the morning of June 30, 1908, an unidentified something plunged to earth in the Tunguska area of Siberia. The flame of the explosion was seen for hundreds of miles. Black clouds billowed up to 60,000 feet, causing "black rain." Luminous, radioactive clouds crossed Europe and Asia. Hundreds of square miles of forest were destroyed, but no place was found where any meteor fragments had hit the earth. What *was* found appeared to be pieces of metal. Investigations revealed witnesses who claimed the object had been cylindrical, and had followed a zigzag flight path before exploding. The irregular shape of the blast pattern suggested that the explosion had been partially contained inside an artificial construction. Traces of radiation were found, and people in the area suffered from radiation sickness.[32]

Several books and many articles have been devoted to the mystery of the Tunguska event. Some suggest it was the end of an extraterrestrial spacecraft. Others say a comet collided with the earth. Whatever it was, it graphically illustrates what could happen if a (nuclear-powered) time machine were to malfunction or fall into incompetent hands. And it might help to explain the Roswell case and other reports of crashed saucers.

If ufonauts really do employ time-warping fields to perform their magic maneuvers, this danger of "zigging" when one should be "zagging" would pose a serious danger and might force certain characteristic behavior. For instance, we might expect that, even though UFOs race around at incredible speeds, they would land very carefully, so as not to effect a "hard" landing. They might sometimes hover a few feet off the ground rather than landing, so that fluctuations in their field could be compensated for before their landing gear was strained and damaged against the ground. Rockets or other types of propulsion might be needed. Computer-controlled automatic systems might constantly make minute adjustments in the shape (or strength) of fields to prevent the craft from drifting away or colliding with an object. The systems would have to counteract wind, fluctuations in the field or in time itself, the eccentricities of various orbits, etc.

Ufonauts using such a system might not wish to stay any longer than absolutely necessary to complete their missions, since their craft would be vulnerable to damage when on or near the ground. Any failure of power or control could trigger a catastrophic collision or cause

---

32. James E. Oberg, "Tunguska (Russia) event," in Story, *Encyclopedia*, pp. 371-372.

their craft to lift off and fly away without them. And we might also expect UFOs to land occasionally simply to "scrub off" differences in angular velocity to make their proximity to the ground safer and easier to maintain. This might be accomplished by landing briefly and very carefully altering the field so that unwanted kinetic energy is transferred through the landing gear to the ground.

This process could account for two very puzzling mysteries that crop up frequently in UFO reports. First, it might explain why UFOs often land for seconds, then take off again without even opening a door. Second, it might explain why UFO landing-gear "pods" leave depressions in the ground that indicate they are extremely heavy (it may be not only the weight of the craft, but also the downward vector of their own intrinsic motion that pushes them into the soil).

UFOs perform other unusual aerial maneuvers besides instantaneous hairpin turns. One of the most common and most baffling of them is what has been termed the "dead-leaf maneuver" or "falling-leaf descent," in which they follow a series of arcs similar to the path taken by an autumn leaf fluttering to the ground on a calm day. Some have likened the motion to that of a plate dropping to the bottom of a pond. Sometimes when they hover, this motion assumes a course like the swinging of a pendulum or the oscillation of a child's top about to fall. When they rise, it sometimes makes them appear to be climbing stairs. In flight, they sometimes appear to skip or bounce in wavelike undulations (remember Kenneth Arnold's analogies of skipping saucers or motorboats on rough water when he described the UFOs he saw speeding near the peaks of the Cascade Mountains).

One of the first to report a wobbling motion was Dr. Clyde Tombaugh, the famous astronomer who discovered the planet Pluto in 1930. On the afternoon of July 10, 1947, Professor Tombaugh, his wife and daughters were driving in New Mexico when he saw an almost immobile, shiny, elliptical object with a well-defined outline. It seemed to have a wobbling motion. It rose into clouds, reemerged and accelerated upward, reaching an estimated speed between 600 and 900 m.p.h. Dr. Tombaugh told the Air Force that the suddenness of its ascent convinced him it was something unprecedented.[33]

Another afternoon sighting occurred on June 12, 1952 in Paris. M. and Mme. Jean-Paul Nahon and two others saw a silver, elliptical UFO surrounded by a red glow through binoculars from Nahon's living room window. It first hovered at a 30- to 40-degree elevation, then it came closer while performing violent up, down and sideways maneuvers characterized by instantaneous accelerations and stops. It made ascents too fast to follow with the binoculars, followed by a slow, "fluttering-dead-leaf" descent, momentarily swung like a pendulum, then shot away at an angle.[34]

---

33. Flammonde, *op. cit.*, p. 153-154.
34. Michel, *The Truth About Flying Saucers*, pp. 173-174.

Many dead-leaf maneuvers were reported in France in 1954. Bernard Miserey watched one just before 1:00 on the morning of August 23, 1954, from outside his garage at Vernon, Eure. His attention drawn by a pale light illuminating the area, Miserey saw a huge, luminous UFO shaped like a cigar hovering vertically and noiselessly over the river 900 feet away. Four luminous discs—red in the center, fading out at the edges, and surrounded by halos that glowed brightly when they moved—dropped from the cigar and shot over the witness' head and away to the southwest at "prodigious speed." A fifth dropped from the cigar to a low altitude, swayed and wobbled as it hovered, then shot away to the north "like a flash," as the cigar faded into the dark. Two policemen and an army engineer also saw the phenomenon from separate viewpoints. The incident was reported in the August 25 edition of the Paris newspaper *Libération*.[35]

The following month, on the 19th, at 4:30 in the afternoon, Mlle. Delaire, Marie Christine, and Madeline Gauthier were picnicking at Beal pass on the Puy-de-Dôme/Loire border, when they saw a gray, metallic-appearing, disc-shaped UFO "appear suddenly in the north." It slowed to a halt, hovered with a swaying motion for about 30 seconds then flew away northwestward with quick acceleration.[36]

Then on the 26th, Dr. Martinet, his wife and 13 others near Col du Chat, Savoie, saw a gray, disc-shaped UFO that looked like aluminum at an altitude of about 1,500 feet over the 5,000-foot Croix du Nivolet mountain. It descended in a falling-leaf motion, hovered over a radio-station tower at Mont Revard, and "abruptly accelerated and disappeared in a flash." Martinet said the UFO had a lighter spot in the middle and dark spots all around it and that it changed color from gray to light gray. He had at one time been an artillery observer.[37]

At nightfall on October 16, near Baillolet, (Seine-Inférieure), Dr. Henri Robert saw four circular UFOs moving in a vertical formation at a moderate speed about 1,000 feet up. One of them dropped in a falling-leaf motion. As his car approached the UFOs, its engine and headlights failed, and he felt a sensation like an electric shock, which paralyzed him. The car stopped just as the UFO landed. Robert then saw a "creature" more than three feet tall, after which the light was extinguished, leaving Robert in total darkness and silence. The car's headlights then came on suddenly, and Robert saw the UFO flying away to the north.[38]

Mrs. Ivonne Torres de Mendonca, her driver, a servant and her children were driving from her farm to Ponta Poran, Brazil, when two silent, luminous, spinning, Saturn-shaped UFOs that wobbled as they flew dived at, circled, and followed their jeep for a considerable time, sometimes shining a light on it. The center, spherical part of the UFOs appeared to be metallic and about 15 feet in diameter. The rings and

35. Michel, *Straight Line Mystery*, pp. 19-23.
36. *Ibid.*, p. 62.
37. *Ibid.*, p. 81.
38. *Ibid.*, p. 184-185.

upper parts were red, and the bottom was enveloped in a silver or white glow. At one point, it dimmed when it hovered. The incident took place on December 21, 1957, at about 6:30 in the evening.[39]

Another Brazilian encounter happened at a few minutes after 3:00 A.M. on February 24 the following year near Conceição Almeida, Bahia. Dr. Carlos José da Costa Perieira, Manoel Mendes, and Antonio de Araujo were driving between Santo Antonio de Jesus and Conceição Almeida when their car's engine coughed and died. A silver-blue light approached. They could see it was a silent, Saturn-shaped UFO, about 65 to 70 feet in diameter and surrounded by a brilliant glow from its spinning ring. It descended like a falling leaf and stabilized about ten feet off the ground. When two witnesses approached it, it shot upward and flew about the sky performing maneuvers impossible for conventional aircraft. These included fast, vertical ascents, tight circles, straight flights made "more rapidly than lightning," falling-leaf descents and hovering. It was last seen at 6:30 as a silvery disc. As soon as it left, the witnesses were able to start their car normally.[40]

A sighting that later received extensive publicity occurred at 2:00 on the morning of September 3, 1965, near Kensington, New Hampshire. Norman Muscarello was hitchhiking along Route 150 when he saw a silent UFO about 85 feet in diameter with "brilliant, pulsating red lights around an apparent rim" moving slowly through the air toward him with a wobbling, yawing motion. It came so close that he dove to the road shoulder to avoid being hit. It hovered over a nearby house then moved farther away.

Patrolman Eugene Bertrand later accompanied Norman back to the site (Bertrand had heard a similar report from a woman on Route 101, who said the UFO had left at exceedingly high speed). They arrived at about 3:00 A.M. They shortly spotted a UFO as it hovered like a fluttering leaf 300 feet away and 100 feet up. Horses and dogs were disturbed. Houses were lit red from the UFO. It moved silently toward Hampton, performing erratic aerobatics. Bertrand said it "darted" and "could turn on a dime." Patrolman David Hunt then arrived, and also saw the UFO as it moved away. Large numbers of subsequent UFO reports came from the area, prompting John Fuller's famous book, *Incident at Exeter.* [41]

At 8:20 P.M on October 2, 1966, a Cincinnati, Ohio, woman suffered nausea and dizziness from an inexplicable foul odor in her house and felt as if someone were watching her. She then saw an oval, brightly-colored UFO hovering close to the ground in a wood. She alerted her husband and other relatives. They, along with a neighbor, Naval Reserve officer David Stites, watched the show. Stites used binoculars. The UFO was apparently about 75 feet in diameter and had red, green and white lights rotating quickly around its rim and yellow-lit, square "windows." It moved away, returned, ascended to an altitude of about

39. Lorenzen, *The Whole Story*, pp. 148-149.
40. Lorenzen, *Startling Evidence*, pp. 151-153.
41. Fuller, *Incident at Exeter*, pp. 9-15.

100 feet, hovered and wobbled. It moved slowly horizontally, returned, emitted a smaller, red, oval ball, which also wobbled and which moved erratically, then shot away southward.[42]

Bob Luca, who would later meet and marry abductee Betty Andreasson (see Chapter 1), underwent a frightening abduction experience of his own in June of 1967. While driving from Hammonasset Beach, Connecticut, Bob saw two large, bright, cigar-shaped UFOs. One of them dropped two smaller, oval, dull, metallic-looking UFOs. One of these flew away quickly, while the other descended with a falling-leaf motion about a quarter of a mile distant. Luca remembered fearing that "they" were "coming after" him. He could remember nothing else. Under hypnosis he recalled having been taken aboard a UFO, forced to take off his clothes, and examined on a table by humanoids.[43, 44]

For decades, investigators have been unable to account for the dead-leaf effect. Could it have something to do with orbital mechanics? Could UFOs simply be swaying in the breeze after avoiding the pull of gravity with time-warping fields? Are their positions in space being constantly adjusted to match their positions in time, thus to avoid obstacles? Must they generate fields continuously to visit our time frame? Is this why they sometimes hover instead of landing? Because it is difficult to match relative motions exactly? Could it become impossible for them to return home once they made the adjustments necessary to land and turn off their fields? If they have come here from Earth's future (or past), or from some other planet by manipulating fields that warp time, could it be that the farther away from us their time frame is located, the more compensation is required to hold a stable position near us? Could time contain eddy currents, and must constant adjustments be made to compensate for them? Would visitors from thousands of years in the future require more adjustments to stay stable in our time frame, and would their craft therefore wobble more than those of visitors from the not-too-distant future?

42. Stringfield, *Situation Red* (Doubleday), pp. 33-36.
43. Fowler, *The Andreasson Affair*, pp. 195-196.
44. Fowler, *Phase Two*, pp. 15, 57-58.

...a remarkable pattern emerges in which the color changes are almost certainly related to the UFO's movements—hovering, speeding up, slowing down, descending, ascending, and high-speed acceleration.
—Otto Binder[1]

A Rainbow of Colors, a Pot of Clues

Very early in the UFO guessing game, researchers noted that the incredible flight capabilities of UFOs appeared to be somehow linked to spectacular lighting displays. UFOs seen at night almost universally emitted bright light. The light frequently changed in brilliance, sometimes growing "brighter than the sun," and changed color—all seemingly in conjunction with changes in speed or direction. To quote science writer Otto Binder:

> *...all anomalous specimens aside, perhaps 80% of all the UFO's seen at night are "normally" lighted and display that strange pattern of color changes related to motion....*
>
> *Many investigators believe that the rainbow display of colors bears a direct relationship to the UFO's **propulsion** system and, in fact, is a clue to what amazing kind of engine and force drives them at such blistering speeds and in such dizzying maneuvers.*[2]

Aimé Michel was one of many other UFO investigators who also noted a relationship between changes of speed and changes of color on several occasions. *In Flying Saucers and the Straight Line Mystery*, he wrote this about a group of sightings made during the French wave of 1954:

> *(1) The object at rest is reddish, not very luminous, and maintains a vertical position.*
>
> *(2) On starting to move, it is seen to slant, and the color changes to white, then to blue. The white color corresponds to a slight angle of inclination and a slow start, the blue to a horizontal position and high speeds.*

---

1. Binder, *What We Really Know*, p. 48.
2. *Ibid.*, p. 58.

(3) On stopping, this sequence is reversed.[3]

In *The Truth About Flying Saucers*, he made these interesting observations:

> *The colors...seem associated in some way with the speed, or more probably with the rate of acceleration.*
>
> *...there is some relationship between the acceleration and the intensity of light. The silvery gray edged with red is really a barely luminous red, almost infrared...*
>
> *Certain movements at high but constant speed produce none of the strong colors, which seems to confirm the hypothesis that there is some relation between the color given off by the object and the power developed at each instant by the motor.*
>
> *...would it not account for certain sightings in February, 1954, when the witnesses felt a burning sensation in their eyes when they were watching a particularly violent maneuver? That sensation is perfectly familiar to the Alpine climber, who associates it with the ultraviolet of high altitudes and the well-known snow-blindness.*[4]

Here Michel seems to have made a very important connection between violent maneuvers and the emission of electromagnetic radiation in the ultraviolet range.

Veteran Pan Am pilots W. B. Nash and W. H. Fortenberry observed color changes while flying a DC-4 near Norfolk, Virginia, on the 14th of July, 1952. At 9:12 P.M. they saw six glowing, silver, disc-shaped UFOs about 75 feet in diameter flying toward them at 1,000 m.p.h. They were surrounded by red halos that occasionally changed to orange. When they slowed, their glows dimmed, and when their speed increased, they brightened. They made abrupt turns, one of which was more than 150 degrees, while flying in echelon formation. They were joined by two more objects that had been hovering at a lower altitude. They all abruptly turned dark, and when they once again brightened, they had formed a line. They climbed away at high speed, emitting brilliant, regular flashes.[5]

Two months later, on September 22, night-shift workers at the Mouguerre chemical factory near Bayonne, France, saw a UFO, the luminosity of which changed with its movement, and the color of which changed from red to blue. The object also oscillated.[6]

Exactly two months after that, a color-changing UFO was seen near Bocaranga, French Equatorial Africa at 10:00 P.M. Father Carlos Maria de Beata Assumptione and seven others were stopped on the road between villages when they saw four silver discs that alternately hovered, turned red, moved at the speed of a jet, climbed vertically, turned back to silver and hovered. They became brilliantly luminous just before they moved each time, and turned back to the original color

3. Michel, *Straight Line Mystery*, p. 29.
4. Michel, *The Truth About Flying Saucers*, p. 143.
5. Vesco, *op. cit.*, pp. 56-57.
6. Michel, *The Truth About Flying Saucers*, p. 140.

each time they stopped moving. Some appeared to be spinning. The sighting lasted 20 minutes.[7]

John Stewart reported an incident from Cincinnati, Ohio. He was driving when he saw a dark, elliptical UFO with a halo. It gave off light in pulses. After hovering seven or eight minutes, it flew away at great speed, changing color from blue-white, to yellow, to red as it did so. The date was March 9, 1954.[8]

On August 7, 1954, a first lieutenant in the Swiss Air Force was watching planes and a child's balloon with field-glasses from his Zurich apartment. He spotted a dark disc less than 50 feet wide. It had a large "crown," which constantly changed from silver, to red, to blue. The UFO's contours became indistinct *only* when the color was red. It wobbled like a child's top, and emitted brown smoke at intervals. There were several other witnesses.[9]

The Swiss sighting was followed by a rash of French night sightings. On September 30, at 10:00, Celeste Simonutti and two others saw a spherical, luminous UFO 40 feet in diameter hovering about three feet up near La Flotte-en-Re (on the Isle of Re). It turned red, then blue, then left the area.[10]

Two nights after that (November 2), the Croix d'Epine area was the scene of an encounter. Ernest Delattre was riding his motor scooter when he saw a brilliant, egg-shaped UFO the size of a bus land on the side of the road, 50 feet from his position. Dark shapes moved about the UFO. Delattre then sped up, and the UFO changed from orange, to blue, to gray-blue as it flew away.[11]

Then on the 10th, three people from Bordeaux came upon a UFO while driving at Tapignac, Charente-Maritime. It was disc-shaped, with an orange-red dome. It hovered at an altitude of about 30 feet, illuminating the landscape. Two of the three followed on foot when it moved behind woods, and saw four "little men" working outside it. When the witnesses were within 50 feet, the entities entered the UFO, which turned blue, orange and red, dazzled the witnesses and "left the ground at 'terrifying' speed."

At dawn that morning, a craft had been seen in a Heimersdorf (Haut-Rhin) pasture by Anny and Roselyne Pracht. It was luminous, disc-shaped and about six feet tall. When they approached, it took on a fiery red color and flew away very fast without sound. Two other Heimersdorf residents saw it shoot up and streak away.[12]

Near nightfall on the 14th, a farmer at Méral, Mayenne, saw an orange, dome-shaped, flat-bottomed UFO land near him. It gave off a brilliant light that lit up the surrounding landscape for 600 feet. It looked translucent, and he could see a silhouette inside it. After ten

7. *Ibid.*, pp. 120-128.
8. Binder, *What We Really Know*, p. 21.
9. Aimé Michel, "Flying Saucers in Europe: The Crisis of Autumn in 1954," *Fate*, Aug. 1957, pp. 28-35.
10. From *Sud Quest*, 2 Oct. 1954, as reported in Vallée, *Magonia*, p. 213.
11. Vallée, *Magonia*, p. 215.
12. Michel, *Straight Line Mystery*, pp. 159-160.

minutes the UFO abruptly changed from white to red and flew away very fast. A paraffin-like substance hung in the air like steam. It coated the witness' clothes then evaporated.[13]

A Cherbonnieres man was driving his three-year-old son toward Pouzou a week later when he felt prickling all over his body, and his son started to cry. The car's engine and headlights failed, and he saw a red glow changing to orange, which became brilliant as he saw an object hover briefly, then disappear. He was then able to restart his engine.[14]

While flying a National Airways DC-3 from Wellington, New Zealand, to Auckland on the last day of October, 1955, Capt. W. T. Rainbow and copilot S. G. Trounce were followed and overtaken by a UFO that fluctuated in brightness and changed from red, to yellow, to orange. Passenger A. R. Tuckett, an air-traffic-control officer and seasoned pilot, said it appeared "orange red at first, then it turned steel blue." The UFO flew away in a hurry.[15]

Just three days later, Roland Martin was one of many percipients of close encounters near Levelland, Texas, in the wee hours of November 3. Martin was driving when he saw a large red-orange UFO that resembled a ball of fire. It approached, landed in the road ahead of him and turned blue-green. His truck's engine and headlights failed. The glow from the object illuminated the cab of his truck. After about a minute, the object changed back to red-orange and rose vertically. When it was gone, his truck functioned normally.[16, 17]

A Painesville, Ohio, plasterer encountered another UFO just three nights later, at 11:30. Olden Moore was driving when he saw a bright UFO split apart. One part ascended vertically; the other grew in size, changing from bright white, to green, to blue-green, and landed 500 feet away with a "whirring" noise. Moore watched it for 15 minutes. It was circular ("shaped like a covered dish"), and 50 feet in diameter. It was surrounded by a blue-green fog and it pulsated. It appeared to have a mirrored surface. Footprints without beginning or end, strange holes and radioactivity were found at the site.[18]

At 3:20 A.M. on October 3, 1958, Cecil Bridge was fireman on a southbound Monon railroad train near Wasco, Indiana. He and four other crew members saw four silent, luminous white UFOs flying in a "V" formation across the tracks ahead at about 45 m.p.h. The objects suddenly stopped, reversed course and sped away eastward. They then returned, approaching from the south, and the crewmen could see that they were disc-shaped, about 40 feet in diameter. They glowed and

13. *Ibid.*, pp. 176-177.
14. Vallée, *UFOs in Space*, p. 140.
15. From the *New Zealand Herald*, 31 Oct. 1955 and 7 Nov. 1955, as quoted in Stranges, *op. cit.*, pp. 102-103.
16. Hynek, *Experience*, p. 125.
17. Flammonde, *op. cit.*, p. 291.
18. From an interview of the witness with Paul Colebrook of the Willoughby, Ohio, *Lake County Republican Herald*, 12 Nov. 1957, the Cleveland, Ohio, *Plain Dealer*, 8 Nov. 1957, The Cleveland *Press*, 8 Nov. 1957, and *APRO Bulletin*, Jan. 1958, as reported in Michel, *Straight Line Mystery*, pp. 252-253.

dimmed sequentially, and became brighter and whiter when moving faster, and dimmer and more yellow-orange when moving more slowly.[19]

Boianai, Papua, New Guinea, was the scene of multiple sightings in June of 1959. On the evening of the 26th, Rev. Father William Booth Gill and 37 others watched several UFOs during a period of several hours. One large one had what appeared to be a superstructure, and the witnesses saw beings aboard it. Others were smaller and disc-shaped. They were yellow or orange, and were very bright when in motion. When they left (at about 9:30), their color changed from white, to red, to blue-green. The next night another object appeared, and Gill and others waved to beings aboard it, who waved back. When they flashed flashlights at it, it wavered back and forth.[20]

One of the most bizarre of all accounts is from Argentina. Just before dawn on October 12, 1963, Eugenio Douglas was driving a truck-load of coal through the rain between Monte Maiz and Isla Verde, and he saw a blinding light ahead. He stopped, stepped from his truck and saw a circular, metallic-appearing UFO about 35 feet tall. Three 12-foot-tall men wearing antennae headgear exited the object through a lighted opening. A red light ray struck Douglas. He fled to Monte Maiz, the ray following. The street lights were turned "violet and green." He also smelled a pungent gas.

Douglas ran to a nearby house for help; the Ribas family who lived there said their candle flames and electric lights turned green. They also smelled the odor.

Douglas suffered burns on his face and hands, which a doctor said were caused by radiation similar to ultraviolet. Police received many reports of lights changing color. Villagers found 20-inch footprints at the site.[21]

Policemen and others watched several umbrella-shaped UFOs darting about the sky over Madras, Oregon, for hours on July 20, 1964. They sometimes hovered and sometimes shot away at "incredible speeds," changing color as they accelerated. As has been reported in many other cases, they were red when at rest.[22]

Even Antarctica, where the air is clear and aircraft are rare, has its share of UFO stories. On the evening of July 3, 1965, a very large, silent, solid-appearing, lens-shaped UFO flew over the Argentine base in a zigzag course. It sometimes moved at very high speed and sometimes hovered, and was reported to be mostly red and green, but at times changed to yellow, blue, white and orange. A meteorologist, three Chilean subofficers and 13 others were witnesses. Photographs were taken.

19. Edwards, *Serious Business*, pp. 62-66.
20. Lorenzen, *Startling Evidence*, p. 175-177.
21. From "Giants in Argentina," *U.F.O.I.C* (227 Bay Street, Brighton-le-Sards, Sydney, N.S.W., Australia), Jun. 1965, as reported in Vallée, *Magonia*, pp. 111-112.
22. Vallée, *Challenge to Science*, p. 40.

A similar UFO was seen that same afternoon at the South Orkney Islands Argentine base. The information was issued on July 6 in a report by the Argentine Navy Secretary. The Chilean and English bases on Deception Island also reported UFOs. Cmdr. Barrera of Chile's Pedro Aguirre Cerda base stated to the press that the UFO seen there was solid, moved at "incredible speeds," hovered for about 20 minutes, maneuvered, gave off a green light and affected instruments at the Argentine base.[23]

If Dr. Antonin Kulka's estimate of the date and time of his sighting is correct, it was exactly one month later that another colorful unknown was seen in the southern hemisphere. This time Carnarvon, Australia, was the setting. Kulka and Mrs. Audrey Lawrence saw an oval, orange UFO diving toward their car. They stepped from their car to watch. The UFO hovered near the ground, changed color to "fluorescent green" and left at high speed.[24]

From outside his rural Ann Arbor, Michigan, home, Frank Mannors saw a UFO at 8:00 on the evening of March 20, 1966. It resembled a meteor, but stopped abruptly just above treetop level. Mannors, his wife, his two grown children and his son-in-law watched as it landed and returned to treetop height, touching the trees. This was repeated several times. The color changed from red and blue in the trees to white on the ground each time.

Mannors and his son approached to within 1,500 feet. The UFO appeared to be a yellow-gray and shaped like a football with a pitted surface like coral. It had a pulsating white light on one end and a pulsating green light on the other. It hovered at an altitude of about eight feet, over a cloud of vapor. Both the lights had halos around them. It then turned hot-iron red, extinguished its lights and flew away at high speed, making a high-pitched whine. It and other UFOs were seen by numerous others, including several policemen.[25]

That same year, on June 11, a fisherman in Westport, Connecticut, saw a domed, plate-shaped UFO dive toward his car and hover at treetop height. It inclined to 45 degrees, ascended, executed a 90-degree turn and changed color from white, to yellow, to blue, to green as it accelerated. The incident occurred at 3:45 in the morning.[26]

The following month, another early morning report came from North Carolina. At 2:00 on the 25th, a man was followed by a pulsating, glowing UFO that flew within 328 feet not 50 feet up as he drove between Greenville and Vancehars. It changed color from orange, to red, to blue, to green, "wobbled on its axis," approached to within 100 feet and abruptly shot up vertically.[27]

On September 30, David Leer and another Anderson, Indiana, policeman saw a luminous white UFO the size of a jetliner fuselage flying

23. Lorenzen, The Whole Story, p. 245-248.
24. From NICAP, as reported in Vallée, Magonia, pp. 311-312.
25. Edwards, Here and Now!, pp. 21-27.
26. From NICAP, as reported in Vallée, Magonia, p. 331.
27. From Air Technical Intelligence Center files, as reported in Vallée, Magonia, p. 333.

below cloud cover. As it slowed, it changed from white, to pink, to red and then gave off a pulsating, blue-white light below it.[28]

The year 1967 gave us one of the most enigmatic close encounter cases of all. It happened at midday on the 20th of May in Manitoba, Canada. When he was prospecting north of Falcon Lake, Steven Michalak was silently approached by two UFOs, which appeared first to be cigar-shaped with bumps, then more oval, then domed discs. One of the objects stopped, hovered, then rose and departed quickly, changing color from red, to orange, to gray, to orange. The other landed on a large flat rock 160 feet away and changed color from red, to gray surrounded by a golden glow. It sat for 30 minutes and "radiated heat in rainbowlike colors." Brilliant purple light that produced red afterimages shone from openings in the UFO—*from inside it*—and lit its surroundings. Heat and a smell like sulfur seemed to come from the object, and it made whirring and hissing sounds.

Approaching, Michalak thought he heard voices. He called out in five languages but got no response. He walked directly to the UFO, flipped down welding goggles because of the extreme brightness (an amateur prospector, Michalak used a welding helmet as improvised eye protection against rock chips) and stuck his head inside, where he saw light beams and flashing lights. The wall seemed to be about 18 inches thick. The witness' hat and glove were melted and burned from contact with it.

The UFO spun and flew away, blasting Michalak with hot gas from a grid-like exhaust port, setting his clothes ablaze and leaving a smell like burning electrical circuits. The landing site appeared swept clean, except for a circular pile of pine needles, leaves, and dirt. Michalak's compass behaved erratically for a short time after the UFO left. He suffered headache, nausea, vomiting, weakness and severe burns in a pattern like the exhaust grill.[29, 30]

Pastor Estanislao Lugo Conteras watched a huge UFO change colors as it burst out of the ocean off the coast of Salina, Venezuela. It was just after dark on August 8, 1967. The pastor saw a large area of ocean about 1,650 feet offshore "wrinkle up," turn lighter blue, then white, then yellow, then orange. A huge disc rose up out of the water with a loud buzz, hovered, then flew away and was gone in seconds. The pastor felt tingling in his feet.[31]

A 73-year-old night watchman who encountered a colorful UFO in Argentina felt tingling in his legs—and has subsequently grown a new set of teeth! Ventura Maceiras was sitting outside his Tres Arroyos shack listening to a transistor radio at about 10:20 on the night of December 30, 1972. The radio quit working, and he heard a buzzing or humming sound. He then saw a brilliantly-lit UFO with a round cabin

28. Edwards, *Here and Now!*, p. 115.
29. Chris Rutkowski, "The Falcon Lake Incident—Part 1," *Flying Saucer Review*, 27, No. 1 (1981), pp. 14-16.
30. Lorenzen, *UFOs Over the Americas*, p. 39.
31. *Ibid.*, pp. 54-55.

with windows. Its color changed from orange to purple as he watched. He could see instruments, dials and two humanoids in gray, segmented suits inside it. It hovered over a nearby grove of eucalyptus trees, tilted, shot a blinding flash of light at him, then flew away, the hum rising in pitch.

Besides tingling legs, Maceiras suffered from headaches, nausea, diarrhea, hair loss, watery eyes, speaking difficulty and red pustules on the back of his neck for weeks afterward. Burned tree tops and dead fish in a stream were found at the site.[32]

Ventura Maceiras seems to be one of the many unwilling recipients of UFO radiation generated in sufficient quantity to induce illness. One is reminded of the Cash-Landrum affair, in which one of the witnesses had to be hospitalized for months following her encounter (see Chapter 2). Such illnesses have been reported many times, and occasionally a story involving a death has even been related to investigators.

The most intriguing aspect of the Maceiras case is the new set of teeth. Incredibly, rejuvenation and healing of wounds and diseases have been reported before in other cases. In one case, a witness had been bitten by a pet, and the bite had become infected, causing him pain. When the bite was irradiated during a subsequent UFO encounter, it miraculously healed. Abductees have been exposed to a light on examining tables aboard UFOs and told they were being cured of diseases. It seems that among the dozens of different wavelengths of radiation UFOs emit, some are harmful, some are not, and at least one stimulates cell growth.

As is the case with thousands of other anecdotes in UFO literature, the aged night watchman's story cannot be dismissed lightly. To do so, we must assume that an old man who is unable to read and who lives in the "boondocks" of Argentina somehow managed to expose himself to dangerous radiation, then concocted a story that meshes perfectly with obscure American reports never published in his language. Furthermore, we must suppose he climbed the eucalyptus trees armed with something to scorch their tops, killed a number of catfish in the stream below and successfully lied about his new set of teeth. We are confronted with the same enigma that haunts so many other cases. Even if the old man were nimble, clever and crazy enough to pull off such a splendid hoax, what possible motive could he have?

Even if we assume that the Maceiras case and 90 percent of all the other cases are spurious—and to do so would constitute total disregard for the painstaking documentation of these cases by investigators—we are still forced to conclude that UFOs do exist and do emit wavelengths of radiation spanning the entire known electromagnetic scale, from radio waves, to heat, light of all possible colors, X rays and gamma rays.

By observing the tiny portion of the spectrum we are able to see, we find clues to the mechanism of their emissions. UFOs often glow— that is to say light radiates outward from all their surfaces. The light

32. Blum, *Beyond Earth*, pp. 143-145.

can change gradually through a rainbow of different colors, can change quickly from one color to another, or can be a combination of different colors at once ("bluish-orange," "reddish-gray," etc.). The intensity of the light can change gradually from a dull glow to intense brilliance. The color and/or brightness often change just *before* the UFO shoots away at high speed.

The dull glow is usually red and is often associated with heat. The heat might be produced by the interaction of air molecules with a time-warping field, as outlined earlier, or by a number of other factors. At any rate, the hulls of the craft are known to be hot at times. They scorch vegetation and clothing, set lawns ablaze, bake moisture out of the soil, etc. From this we can deduce that at times the temperature of a UFO's hull might be 300 degrees or more. In other words, the entire surface of a UFO is as hot as the element on an electric range set at a moderate heat. A saucer 25 feet in diameter would have a surface area of about 1,000 square feet, which means that it might easily be giving off heat (infrared) energy on the order of hundreds of thousands of watts.

Infrared radiation has a wavelength just slightly longer than that of visible red light (its frequency is slightly lower than visible red light). If the wavelength of that infrared radiation could be compressed by as little as two or three hundred-thousandths of an inch, it would be the same as the wavelength of visible light, and would stimulate the retinas of a witness' eyes. In other words, were the heat from a hot flying saucer hull subjected to a Doppler effect by passing through a field that changes the nature of time, that hull could look like it was covered with thousands of 100-watt light bulbs. If the temperature were to rise as high as 1,000 degrees—which can happen with our own spacecraft—it could look like its entire surface was covered with high-intensity search lights. These conditions would be consistent with the calculated 2.3 million watts of light energy radiated by Dr. Vallée's example (see Chapter 5).

As our hypothetical model demonstrated in Chapter 5, an observer who approaches an object surrounded by a time-warping field might see a color change if he were to approach or retreat from the object (or vice versa), or if the field were expanded or contracted or its shape distorted. This is because the amount of Doppler effect between the object and the observer's eyes would have changed. The effect could be compared to the magnification or reduction of an image when it is viewed through convex or concave lenses of varying curvature, or to the change of color of an image viewed through filters of various colors. The intensity of the light could vary with the amount of heat being emitted and the portion of that heat that became visible due to the Doppler effect (heat radiates in a range of frequencies, just as light does).

A study of actual sightings shows that, time after time, UFOs have been observed to change color in three specific instances: (a) when they change speed or direction, (b) as they pass a witness, and (c) as they rise just prior to takeoff or descend just prior to landing. If UFOs really do move from one place to another by changing the shape of time-warping fields, these are precisely the effects we should expect to see.

Our hypothetical time machine can help us to explain why. Once again, let's suppose we have built a time machine. Inside is a generator, which radiates a time-warping field that completely surrounds the entire contraption. This particular generator happens to make a perfectly spherical field, so we have built a spherical hull around our time machine and placed the generator at its center.

It is midnight. We check our watches with a friend to make sure he has the same time. Then, while he stands ten feet away to observe, we enter our time machine and turn on the generator. Immediately, a field surrounds us, reaching out to about 20 feet beyond the hull in all directions. It's like an invisible bubble, and our "ship" is in its center.

It's a warm night, so the hull of our ship, like nearly everything else, is radiating some heat. Of course this is normally invisible, so our friend was unable to see it—until we turned on our generator. But now, the heat is being Dopplered as it passes through the field before it reaches his eyes. At this point, the field is still weak, and our friend is only looking through half of it, so the Doppler effect is slight. The infrared frequency is changed just enough to be seen dimly as red light. When we turned on our generator, it looked to our friend as if our hull suddenly began to glow a dull red (he may also have experienced some strange physiological effects).

We're ready to make a test flight now. We don't want to be crushed into the ground, so we are careful not to manipulate the field in such a way that movement will be applied in a downward vector in relation to the earth. We are in a forest clearing, so we must also take care not to move toward any particular side, lest we crash into the surrounding trees. What is called for is a vertical ascent.

We tell our computer we want to rise straight up. It calculates the complex orbital vectors that are in effect at that particular instant. If no vectors exist at that moment that we can use to ascend vertically, rockets or other auxiliary mechanisms may have to be employed until we have at least cleared the treetops and have more room to maneuver. (We may also choose auxiliary lift mechanisms to avoid affecting our friend, who may be so close to our machine that he would tend to be lifted along with us). Otherwise, the computer will manipulate the shape of our field so that our ship "sails" upward.

This change in shape of our field will not cause stress on our ship because the ship is completely enveloped by the field. Just as a fly can buzz around comfortably in a car traveling 70 m.p.h. without being affected by the air rushing by outside, our ship will not be distorted by the warping of the fabric of time and space that is occurring outside it.

Now we have cleared the treetops. The computer returns the field to its original shape, so that we are now hovering about 100 feet above the ground. As we rose, our observer friend was looking through more and more of our field, so the heat from our hull (and from our rockets, if we used any) was Dopplered more and more. To him, the red-glowing hull seemed to change to red-orange and then orange.

It is windy up here. The wind pushes against our field, which may or may not cause our ship to sway a little, depending on the strength and shape of the field at the time. Also, since we are a tiny bit further from the earth's axis up here while our angular velocity remains the same, our time machine slowly drifts away from the clearing. Our computer makes constant adjustments to the controls of our generator (and/or the auxiliary mechanisms) to compensate and hold our position.

Now that we are clear of the trees, we can really test the mettle of our time machine. We choose a direction and the computer manipulates the shape of our field in such a way that we move in that direction. When it does so, the thickness of field (and therefore the amount of Doppler effect) between us and our observer increases. To him, it now appears that our time machine has once again changed color—this time from orange to yellow—as we begin to move.

Our generator is working much harder now and is producing heat. To prevent our cockpit from becoming too hot, the heat is shunted to our hull. To our observer, it appears that the yellow glow brightens.

We want to go faster. We touch the appropriate controls, and our computer strengthens and/or distorts our field further to warp time even more severely around us. To the observer, it appears that our time machine suddenly shoots away eastward faster than a jet, turns blue-green and becomes so brilliant that he must turn his eyes away. Being completely inside the field, we feel no acceleration. But everything outside looks strange—all the lights are strangely different. In front of us—to the east—they are not visible at all. Everywhere else, the colors are all wrong. Stop lights and neon signs we expect to be green are red. Lights that we expect to be violet are yellow. Red and orange lights don't show up at all. Even the stars look red! We make a mental note that we will need a special computer program to adjust the pictures coming from video cameras pointed outside our time machine according to how much of a time warp we are producing, so that the Doppler effect will be undone and we will be able to observe things as they really are.

Once again we increase the strength of the time warp, and this time our observer, who has been watching us race away like a blue-green streak, sees us flash violet and wink out like magic. When we lessen the warp, we once again materialize in front of his eyes.

We are getting some distance away now, so we reverse the shape of our field. To the observer, it appears that we have made a sudden, 180-degree turn at high speed and are now racing back toward him. And once again we appear to him to have changed colors. Now he also notices a red haze surrounding our time machine at some distance. This is because air is being ionized as it enters our field and releases energy.

As we return, we decide to experiment. We give our computer new instructions, and it changes the angle of the strong part of our field slightly. Our observer sees our ship jump up higher in the sky, and since his angle of view through our field has changed, our violet color fades to indigo. As we race past over his head, he notices that the glow changes quickly from blue, to blue-green, to green, to green-yellow, and back to yellow.

Our time machine seems to work, so we decide to return to our clearing to land. We have overshot it, so we must reverse our course again. Again our friend sees the color changes. Eventually, we hover over the clearing by changing our time-warping field back to its original shape. Landing will be the most dangerous part of our flight. We need to go down, but using downward vectors could be a mistake. If the computer miscalculates one iota, we could crash into the ground before we have a chance to stop. Perhaps we should weaken the entire field until we are just barely supported and let gravity do the work.

We power down our generator, and our friend watches our yellow glow dim and change back through yellow-orange to orange. As the strength of our field lessens, we begin to float downward. Our weight is almost completely nullified, so the breeze sways us as we descend, and our computer adjusts our field to compensate, swaying us back the other way. We rock like a falling leaf. We are within 20 feet of our friend now. He sees the glow fade to red-orange. Now we are at ten feet. To his eyes, the glow has faded to red.

Finally, we land. Unfortunately, the pendulum motion of our descent has left us in an awkward position—the ship has landed on its side! Before we try another flight, we should fit our ship with a gyroscope to stabilize it. Maybe we could add a disc-shaped rim in the middle, and use gears to keep it spinning all the time. We could fix it to run off the excess heat from our field generator.

Now that we are on the ground, we very gradually lessen the strength of our field. Our friend sees our glow disappear, and now he can feel the warmth from our heated hull. Just as we suspected, our motion at rest no longer matches the motion of our landing site exactly. The hull of our ship strains against the ground, crushing the grass and pushing a concave impression of the side of our time machine into the soft soil. It's obvious that good stout landing gear is another improvement we need.

After our adventure, we compare notes with the friend who has been observing us. His watch reads 12:20. But ours reads 12:05. Since our test began, we have only aged 5 minutes, but our observer has aged 20 minutes!

Of course the time machine has not yet been invented (as far as we know), so the scenario I have just laid out may be completely wrong. It may not have any relation to what is happening with UFOs. On the other hand, it might be exactly right. It proposes not only a logical explanation for the perplexing luminosity and changes in color and brightness observed in hundreds of close encounter cases, but also may help to solve the riddle of how and why UFOs seem to emit other frequencies of radiation spanning the entire electromagnetic spectrum.

Visible light, we should remember, comprises only a small fraction of the total spectrum. All the other frequencies, from radio waves, to ultraviolet light, to X rays and gamma rays are invisible, but they are real nevertheless. And large amounts of them can be harmful or fatal.

That portion of the color changes due to changes in field strength while a UFO is in flight and performing violent maneuvers might be significant under certain circumstances. Such maneuvers might require drastic swings in field strength in both the original direction of travel and the new direction of travel. As Michel observed, strong ultraviolet light may be radiated at these times.

The huge UFOs encountered by the fighter bombers over Korea in September, 1950 (see Chapter 5) stopped abruptly while traveling toward the planes at a speed of 1,000 to 1,200 m.p.h. If they were operating the way we have surmised, the field surrounding them—which must have been of tremendous strength to begin with, since the objects were over 600 feet in diameter—must have been drastically changed for them to suddenly stop in midair. All the gun-camera film on the bombers was found to be fogged, even though the cameras had not been turned on. The implication is that the UFOs had emitted X rays or gamma rays as a result of the drastic change.

We know that they were emitting radiations on a variety of frequencies. They produced both radar and radio frequencies of such magnitude as to jam the planes' detection and communication equipment. They were surrounded by red glows. Green light that changed to pastel colors and back to green poured from their ports. Also, the middle of their undersides was coal black, and that black, circular area held steady, while the rest of the craft appeared to fibrillate. The indication here is that the strength or shape of the field underneath the craft was substantially different from the rest of the field. It might be analogous to the pole of a disc-shaped magnet. This same type of black area has been reported in many other cases, most notably the Maury Island case (which will be covered in Chapter 14).

The energy transmitted by many of our television stations amounts to a million watts or more. If a similar transmitter aboard a UFO were to be turned on and the craft's hull used as transmitting antenna—perhaps for radar signals—the results could be disastrous for nearby observers. Dopplered into heat, a million watts could be very uncomfortable. The Brazilian sentries who were scorched as power failed in their fort (see Chapter 5) may have suffered from just such an occurrence. Dopplered into the microwave range, a million-watt signal could easily produce the heating effects that made it necessary for the pilot of the pursuit plane over Walesville, New York, to bail out (see Chapter 5). Dopplered into visible light, a million watts would look as bright as a welder's arc, and UFOs are often observed to emit such brilliant light from all their surfaces.

Ultraviolet light is what causes welder's burn and sunburn. Large exposures cause skin cancer. Ultraviolet light has a wavelength just slightly shorter than visible violet light, which means that any infrared wavelength shortened just a bit more than was necessary to fall into the visible range would have a wavelength in the ultraviolet range. As Chapter 5 illustrates, burns from ultraviolet are common among UFO witnesses.

Of even higher frequency (and therefore of higher energy) are X rays and gamma rays. These are extremely dangerous. Seconds of exposure can be fatal. Instances of the apparent exposure of witnesses to these radiations are reported from time to time (the Cash-Landrum and Maceiras cases and the fogged gun camera film over Korea are examples), but are not nearly as common as reports of ultraviolet exposure. Several reasons for this can be deduced. One could be that ordinarily the time-warping fields that UFOs employ are simply not strong enough to raise the frequency of ordinary radiations to the level of these "hard" emissions, and only do so on rare occasions. Another could be that the ufonauts themselves are aware of the danger to us and avoid exposing us whenever possible. As we will see in Chapter 11, statistical studies indicate they stay as far away from populous areas as possible most of the time, and this may be one of the reasons for their reclusiveness.

If a UFO were to visit us from the past (rather than from the future), its time-warping field might have exactly the opposite Doppler effect. The wavelength of heat from its hull might be lengthened rather than shortened, so that it was the same as radio waves. It might produce "white noise" on one or several radio frequencies. Instead of being Dopplered into ultraviolet, light from this type of craft might be Dopplered into infrared or radio frequencies, so that the UFO might be invisible to an observer even in daylight, but he might be able to feel its heat.

Most people will conclude that the maneuvers UFOs perform require a great deal of energy from some type of power plant; however this may not be the case. Remember, they may actually be altering time rather than literally passing through space. Under the right circumstances, energy may be *produced* instead of used by the process, and their occupants may find themselves in possession of great surpluses of unwanted energy, which must then be "bled off," or "dumped." The dumping process might consist of landing and gradually reducing field strength so that kinetic energy is released by pushing against the ground, or it might be accomplished by heating the craft's hull (which would help account for some of the radiated heat discussed in this chapter) or by radiating radio waves.

Interestingly, time-warping fields do not necessarily clash with currently-accepted laws of physics. In order to accept them as possible, we need not insist that conventional equations are *wrong*, only that they are *incomplete*. That is, any mathematical expression that involves time might need an additional factor added—we might call it "@"—to represent the variability of time. For instance, the velocity of light is a universal constant in orthodox physics. It is the "c" in Einstein's famous equation $E = mc^2$, in which "E" represents energy and "m" represents mass. The velocity of light is generally expressed as 3×10^8 m/sec (300,000,000 meters per second). This might have to be changed to 3×10^8 m/@sec. Force is usually expressed in newtons, which are equal to 1 kg m/sec^2 (one kilogram-meter per second squared). This may need to be changed to 1 kg m/@sec^2. And so on.

The @ factor would simply have a value of 1 under most circumstances, so it would have no net effect on mathematical calculations. (Indeed, it has probably not been proven because it would have a value of 1 in virtually all experiments tried to date). But proof that its value could vary from 1 would have enormous implications. It would change physicists' entire picture of the universe. It could help explain the heretofore impenetrable enigmas of phenomena like black holes. It could result in the development of virtually unlimited power sources. And it could make travel to the future, to the past and to other planets possible. It could even make travel to other galaxies possible, because it would allow us to overcome Einstein's velocity-of-light speed limit. It may have already made all these things possible for countless intelligent races from countless planets.

But we are getting ahead of ourselves. These things will be determined by mathematicians and physicists, and only after the time-travel hypothesis is accepted as a possibility by the scientific community. And as yet, not enough evidence has been presented to convince most scientists that UFOs may indeed be generating fields capable of warping space-time.

Perhaps we should look at some of the other riddles the UFOs have served up to us; maybe they will lead to the same conclusion—that time is not as inflexible as most of us have always thought.

Another uncanny set of phenomena displayed by many UFO's, according to eyewitnesses, is the peculiar ways saucers will appear or disappear....
—Saucers that just fade from sight without growing smaller or receding in the distance.
—Bright saucers seen at night that suddenly "blink out."
—Saucers that have "fuzzy" outlines.
—Saucers that appear in a misty "cloud" of their own and usually "dissolve" into a cloud again.
—Saucers that seem to dive straight to the ground, leaving no wreckage....
—Otto Binder[1]

Now You See It; Now You Don't

The startling ability of UFOs to disappear before witnesses' very eyes has been a hotly contested issue, not only between dyed-in-the-wool skeptics and true UFO believers, but also between one group of researchers and another. That such reports are valid at first seems profoundly unlikely to one who undertakes to study the phenomenon. But there are hundreds of reports of such encounters—from credible witnesses, from all over the world and spanning many years.

A November 2, 1951, encounter serves as a good example. On that date, an hour before midnight, two California forest observers near Mojave saw a 30-foot, blue-green, disc-shaped UFO surrounded by a blue-green glow. They "signalled to the object," which approached and retreated as if playing. It then "vanished like a magician's trick."[2]

Santa Maria, Rio Grande do Sul, Brazil, was the scene of a vanishing act late one March afternoon in 1954. Rubem Hellwig saw a Volkswagen-sized, melon-shaped UFO landed near where he was driving. When he stopped to investigate, he encountered two normal-sized, blond, dark-complected men, one of whom was collecting grass samples. Although they used an unknown language, Hellwig thought he understood that they wanted ammonia. He told them to go to a nearby town. When the object left, it glowed, emitted blue and yellow flames and "vanished silently and instantly."[3]

At 3:12 in the morning on November 4, 1957 (just a few hours after the Brazilian sentries were burned by the glowing orange UFO atop their fort at Itaipu, and only about 24 hours after the rash of automo-

1. Binder, *What We Really Know*, p. 95.
2. From Air Technical Intelligence Center Files, as reported in Vallée, *Magonia*, pp. 196-197.
3. Lorenzen, *Occupants*, p. 109.

bile stoppages caused by glowing UFOs near Levelland, Texas), Patrolmen Joseph Lukasek and Clifford Schau and Fireman Robert Volt saw
a bright, red-orange, egg-shaped UFO hovering about 250 feet over an
Elmwood Park, Illinois, cemetery. It seemed to be "folding into itself."
When caught in the spotlight's beam, it appeared to swell, ascended
very quickly, and moved away. Ten minutes later, it disappeared after
seeming to "fold inward from the bottom." Officer Daniel de Giovanni
also saw it. The spotlight and headlights of the patrol car flickered during the encounter.[4]

On January 23, 1958, another glowing UFO vanished in the predawn sky of Sroarzedz, Poland. George Barroinski saw a green, phos-
phorescent cloud with a brilliant center. It turned deep red, then he
saw an oval object in its center, then a spark, then the whole thing vanished.[5]

On October 26 of that same year, while driving near Baltimore,
Maryland, Phillip Small and Alvin Cohen encountered a large, white,
egg-shaped UFO 100 feet in length hovering over a bridge. When the
car got to within 75 feet of the bridge, its engine and lights failed. They
watched for about a minute from outside the car. The UFO started
glowing and emitting heat. With a thunderclap, it shot up vertically and
disappeared. Both men suffered sunburned faces; Small's sunburn
was only on one side of his face. The incident occurred at 11:30 P.M.[6]

At 9:15 P.M. on May 3, 1975, Alois Olenick was driving his pickup
truck west on Mogford Road south of San Antonio, Texas. He saw an
amber UFO ascend quickly from among a grove of trees in a pasture
half a mile away. It dove at his vehicle at extreme speed, its light changing from amber to bright red in the process. The truck's engine and
lights died. The Saturn-shaped craft hovered above it for 10 to 20 seconds, during which Olenick saw two five-foot-tall, bald humanoids
with big ears and long noses through the UFO's transparent bubble
canopy. It then whooshed away, rocking the truck with air currents
and disappeared instantaneously, as if a switch had been flicked.[7]

It might be argued that any of the UFOs in these accounts disappear by simply flying away faster than the eye can follow. And that argument might be reasonable, especially in light of the extreme speed
allowed by the time-travel hypothesis. But not all disappearances are
so abrupt. A UFO with many "cells or 'windows'" *dematerialized* while
an Ardmore, Oklahoma, witness watched. It happened after 8:00 on
the evening of April 9, 1964.[8]

A terrifying incident including a similar disappearance happened
at about the same time of evening in Bealsville, Ohio, four years later,
on March 3. Mrs. James E. Wells's son Gregory was burned by a beam
of light from an oval UFO. He was knocked to the ground and his jacket

4. Lorenzen, *The Whole Story*, pp. 159.
5. Hobana, *op. cit.*, p. 211.
6. Lorenzen, *The Whole Story*, pp. 91-93.
7. Gary Graber, "Two Occupants in Craft," *Skylook*, Feb. 1976, pp. 3-4.
8. Vallée, *Challenge to Science*, p. 34.

ignited. Mrs. Wells and the boy's grandmother responded to his screams. Mrs. Wells said the UFO was red with red lights flashing around its middle and was bright enough to light the road. It did not leave the area, but "just faded away." Physical effects included the failure of a light on a nearby pole, television interference and the uncontrollable barking of the grandmother's dog. Gregory was treated for second-degree burns at Bealsville Hospital. He suffered scars. Numerous other witnesses saw UFOs in the area that night.[9]

At 9:00 the previous evening, Isopescu Vianora and "numerous witnesses" observed a large, orange, glowing, spherical UFO at Cimpulung, Rumania. It stood still, moved horizontally, then moved vertically. It then disappeared suddenly, but the halo surrounding it faded away slowly.[10]

At 4:45 A.M. on August 3, 1966, Donald Peck and William Rutledge of the Erie, Pennsylvania, police, watched a bright UFO move eastward, stop, turn red and disappear. It then *reappeared* as a blue-white light. At sunrise, the officers could tell it was a silver, metallic-type object before it flew away.[11]

Vivienne Roberts encountered a similar phenomenon in front of her Llanerchymedd home on Anglesey Island, North Wales, at about 9:55 P.M. on September 1, 1978. Miss Roberts caught sight of a star-sized, yellow light that disappeared instantly, then reappeared almost instantly in a slightly different location. It remained visible for about two seconds then disappeared again. Then a solid-looking, triangular, Prussian-blue object with two yellow lights and surrounded by a lighter, purple section, "burst into view." She got out of the car and watched the object as it glided slowly southward, lighting up the churchyard with a purple glow. Nearby horses were disturbed, and Miss Roberts later heard strange "voices" in her yard.[12]

A highway near Ririe, Idaho, was the scene of another incident in which a UFO appeared as if by magic. Two young native Americans were driving southward along Highway 26 at 9:30 on the night of November 2, 1967. Suddenly, they saw a brilliant flash that dimmed, and they could see an oval UFO, complete with two staring humanoids inside its transparent dome.[13]

Night watchman John Justice was leaving his Springfield, Ohio, job at 3:00 A.M. on the morning of January 8, 1974, when his car's headlights suddenly dimmed, and its engine failed. A rainbow-like light descended nearby in front of him, then "blinked out," leaving a brightly glowing, oval, gold, transparent UFO visible where it had been. Justice saw five identical, long-haired occupants in it. At 3:15, the UFO shot away at high speed at an angle to the ground and Justice's car "started instantly."[14]

9. Stringfield, *Situation Red* (Doubleday) pp. 197-198.
10. Hobana, *op. cit.*, p. 237.
11. Keel, *Trojan Horse*, p. 28.
12. Martin Keatman, "The Llanerchymedd UFO," *Flying Saucer Review*, 25, No. 5. (1979), pp. 20-21.
13. Fowler, *The Andreasson Affair*, p. 167.

Almost exactly two years later, a similar appearance was made by a UFO near Stanford, Kentucky. The case involved three very credible witnesses, who were the apparent victims of an abduction. It was exhaustively investigated, and details widely published.

It happened at 11:30 on the night of January 6, 1976. Mona Stafford, Louise Smith and Elaine Thomas were driving from Lancaster, Kentucky, to Liberty. A red glow descended to treetop height beside their car, stopped, hovered and formed into a sharply-defined, silent, disc-shaped UFO 100 feet wide with "windows," red and yellow flashing lights and a brilliant, blue-white dome. It maneuvered around the car, emitting light beams. Mrs. Smith stopped the car and stepped out, but seemed to be paralyzed. Mrs. Stafford pulled her back inside. Then they all experienced a strange total silence and darkness. Their skins tingled, they felt hot, and they suffered headaches, flowing tears, and painful eyes.

When Mrs. Smith drove on, the speedometer indicated 85 m.p.h. (much too fast for the road they were on) and she had no control over the car. The scenery became strange; they saw a straight road devoid of lights and houses, when they should have seen a winding road with lights and houses. Then the scenery became familiar once again, and they continued home at a normal speed, noting normal sounds and movements.

They arrived about 90 minutes later than they should have. Two of them had wrist watches; one had stopped; the other was 4 1/2 hours fast and the second hand and minute hand were revolving at the same speed. The witnesses suffered extreme thirst, burning red skin, burning swollen eyes, loss of appetite, weight loss, exhaustion and apathy following the incident. Mrs. Stafford's skin was blistered, even under her rings. Mrs. Smith's pet parakeet acted oddly, as if it did not know her and was terrified of her.

Police Detective James Young later performed a polygraph examination of the witnesses. He pronounced that all three were telling the truth about their encounter. Under hypnosis, the witnesses revealed that they had been taken aboard the UFO and examined by humanoids during their period of missing time. Mrs. Thomas described a "bullet-shaped" instrument that was placed on her left chest (she suffered pain and reddened skin there), and a choke-collar device that was used to control her. Mrs. Smith and Mrs. Stafford had inexplicable red marks on their necks.[15]

Although some have concluded the strange scene the women perceived while their car was under outside control was some sort of drug-induced or hypnosis-induced screen memory, it is intriguing to wonder if they were actually transported within the UFO's surrounding field to

14. Stringfield, *Situation Red*, (Doubleday), pp. 95-96.
15. Leonard H. Stringfield, *Situation Red: The UFO Siege* (Garden City, New York: Doubleday and Company, Inc., 1977; rpt. Fawcett Crest Books, 1977), pp. 228-242.

another dimension—*a different time frame, perhaps*—and then returned to their own.

A few months later, three witnesses whose credibility was even more unshakable reported seeing UFOs materialize out of thin air. At 9:00 P.M. on July 30, 1976, Capt. D. W. (a British Airways pilot for 20 years with 10,000 hours of flying), first officer C. T. (who had also been flying for 20 years), and second officer S. S. (a veteran of 5 years), were piloting a British Airways Trident 2 commercial flight 40 miles south of Lisbon, Portugal. After hearing a Lisbon air-traffic controller ask a nearby Tristar for confirmation of a UFO sighting, they saw a dazzling white light. As they watched, two brown, sausage-shaped UFOs enveloped in rectangular areas of mist materialized and hovered below the stationary light. Capt. C. T. announced the sighting to his passengers, who also watched. The pilot of a T. A. P. 727 also saw the phenomenon.[16]

Other pilots have reported "appearances." On the afternoon of July 4, 1981, Capt. P. S. was piloting a Lockheed L1011 on a coast-to-coast commercial flight. Over Lake Michigan, he saw a disc-shaped, metallic-looking UFO that appeared instantly, "...like the atmosphere opened up." He could discern six round, black markings, which he took to be portholes. He and his first officer saw a bright flash, which P. S. thought was reflected sunlight. P. S. also reported that an area of sky behind the object seemed darker than the rest of the sky, as if he could see "way out into space." The object approached the plane at an angle, then, as it got near, it turned and sped off the way it had come. P. S. described a halo that somewhat resembled cobwebs, and a round, black spot in the center of the underside of the object.[17]

Occasionally, the UFOs don't entirely appear or disappear, but parts of them seem to fade away—to become transparent. Young Christophe Fernandez was the percipient of such a trick at 6:00 P.M. on November 19, 1974. Through the windows of his house at Uzès, Gard, France, Christophe saw a bright, luminous, opalescent sphere with bubble-like circular patches of darker coloring in motion on its surface. While it hovered near or rested upon the ground, he took five photographs. One of them "was no good." Although the object was bright, it did not seem to illuminate the area around it. After a few minutes, the object rose to about 15 feet off the ground, lowered a blindingly bright three-foot-long cylinder and ascended vertically "with the speed of lightning. It was out of sight in a tiny fraction of a second." Fernandez said the object appeared at times to be transparent—he thought he could see through it to a stone wall behind it. It made a sound like a bottle being emptied.[18]

---

16. Omar Fowler, "UFO Seen from a Trident near Lisbon," *Flying Saucer Review*, 22., No. 4 (Nov. 1976), pp. 2-4, 19.

17. Richard F. Haines, "Commercial Jet Crew Sights Unidentified Flying Object," (Parts 1 and 2) *Flying Saucer Review*, 27, No. 4 (1982), pp. 3-6, and 27, No. 5 (1982), pp. 2-8.

18. Charles Gouiran, et al., "Report on a Landing at Uzès," *Flying Saucer Review*, 24, No. 4 (1979), pp. 3-7.

The failure of the light from the Uzès object to illuminate its surroundings may be significant, especially in view of the report of another transparent UFO seen in England four years later. At about 6:30 on the evening of January 26, Howard Honeywood and about 13 children watched as many as eight irregularly-flashing orange and white aerial lights silently performing "unbelievable aerobatics" near Paverham. They gave chase in Honeywood's van, passing through Paverham, West End and Carlton and were able to observe the UFOs at close range on several occasions in a span of about 40 minutes. Honeywood described the objects as transparent and dome-shaped, sporting orange and white lights. One such object, seen from about 150 feet away, could not be illuminated by the witness' headlights because it was surrounded by a kind of mist—this despite the fact that another car's headlights could be seen through it.[19]

The following year, in nearby Scotland, Bob Taylor was witness to a UFO that faded to transparency—and was apparently assaulted into the bargain! At mid-morning on November 9, 1979, Taylor had parked his car and was walking with his dog in the Livingston Development Corporation fir-tree plantation. He stumbled onto something he probably wasn't supposed to see—a dark gray, Saturn-shaped object about 23 feet in diameter resting in a clearing only 27 feet away. It had several propeller-like protuberances and "portholes." Although it appeared solid, parts of the dome faded away, becoming transparent, then reappeared in a pattern from left, to right, to center. Two smaller spheres with spikes suddenly hurtled toward him. He remembered a bad smell and taste before losing consciousness.

Taylor awoke with his face in the mud, feeling weak and sick, with a painful head and chin, and an itchy thigh. He heard a "whooshing" sound and the furious barks of his dog. The object was gone. He half crawled, half stumbled home (he was unable to drive), and arrived with torn clothes and marks on his chin and hip. Physical traces were found at the site.[20]

Skeptics are always outraged by Taylor's case and others like it. "Preposterous!" they declare. "Everybody knows a solid object cannot simply become transparent. And it certainly can't appear and disappear. The witnesses are either half blind or half crazy, or they are liars or fools or drunks. It's all hogwash!"

"It does seem impossible, doesn't it?" one UFO researcher admits. "Maybe they aren't physical at all. Maybe they are psychological constructs of some kind—produced by the collective unconscious of all the people wishing so hard for benevolent space brothers to bail us out of our troubles with the environment and impending nuclear war...."

---

19. Ken Phillips, "Bedfordshire Cross-Country Chase," *Flying Saucer Review*, 25, No. 3 (1979), pp. 28-31.
20. Martin Keatman and Andrew Collins, "Physical Assault by Unidentified Objects at Livingston—Part 1," *Flying Saucer Review*, 25, No. 6 (1979), pp. 2-7.

"They are probably just holographic images projected here from a distant planet by superintelligent beings to warn us and try to get us to stop killing each other," another offers.

"Nonsense! They are God's messengers and Satan's demons engaged in the holiest of struggles!"

"Swamp gas!"

"Corona discharge!"

"Temperature inversions!"

"Spirits from the other side!"

"No, no, it's Martians, and they are affecting our minds so we'll see things that aren't really there!"

Gentlemen, ladies, please! All of these things make for absorbing speculation, but none fit the data. We have a mountain of testimony by credible witnesses that say UFOs *do* appear, disappear, and become transparent. The fact that our own individual belief systems do not allow for this does not mean it is not happening—it merely means our belief systems are incomplete. We have done studies, and found that most witnesses are *not* crazy or liars or drunks, etc. Images do *not* make holes in the ground, take control of cars and people, break trees, etc., nor do temperature inversions, swamp gas, and corona discharges. Angels and demons may exist, but they aren't likely to collect grass and twig samples, as ufonauts are seen to do.

Not all researchers have offered such unlikely hypotheses. A few have seriously studied *all* the data, and have made some very astute observations. According to Raymond Fowler, one of the most meticulously honest of all the researchers:

> The paraphysical abilities of the aliens are mind-boggling. Their capability to materialize and dematerialize at will is most intriguing. This process of emerging into our space/time frame has been described as a conversion of energy and a change of vibration rate.[21]

Dr. Vallée, who is one of the world's foremost authorities on UFOs, writes:

> Both the UFOs and their operators are able to materialize and dematerialize on the spot and to penetrate physical obstacles.[22]

In 1974, Charles Bowen, editor of *Flying Saucer Review*, wrote that the materialization and dematerialization exhibited by UFOs seemed to support the idea that they might originate in a "time-space continuum" different from our own.[23] *Flying Saucer Review* is known for its dedication to honest appraisal of the UFO problem, and Bowen had firsthand knowledge of hundreds, perhaps thousands of cases.

John Keel has been a tireless seeker of the truth about UFOs for decades, refusing to discard data when they did not agree with precon-

21. Raymond E. Fowler and Betty Ann Luca, *The Watchers* (New York: Bantam Books, 1990), p. 183.
22. Vallée, *Confrontations*, p. 144.
23. Charles Bowen, "More Beliefs," *Flying Saucer Review*, 20, No. 6 (April 1975), p. 1.

ceived notions, regardless of how ridiculous those data seemed. Keel's approach led him to some very insightful conclusions:

> The phenomenon is mostly invisible to us.... It makes itself visible to us from time to time by manipulating patterns of frequency.[24]

> ...witnesses have clearly seen the objects in the process of materialization or dematerialization. A glow is observed first, usually a reddish glow marking the emergence of the object from the invisible band of the spectrum into infrared and then into the narrow band of visible light. Or, if the object is passing through the visible band to the higher frequencies it is cyan...before it fades into blue...and then enters the ultraviolet range....[25]

> UFOs often appear first as a purplish blob and then descend the visible scale until they turn red, at which point they sometimes solidify into seemingly material objects.[26]

Just as changes of light frequency (color) may explain the mechanism by which UFOs travel so fast, hover, etc., they may be significant clues to their method of appearing and disappearing.

Using the same type of hypothetical model as before, let us assume that the occupants of a time machine in our future set the controls of their time-warping field so that they are "moving backward through time." Their objective is to view some important event in history—the birth of Christ, for instance. Now they are already in Bethlehem, so they instruct their computer to automatically distort their time-warping field and/or employ auxiliary rockets or other means to make sure that their motion matches that of the earth as they regress. That way they can watch Bethlehem continuously.

Now if we were in Bethlehem in 1994, and were watching the same spot, our path might cross with that of the time machine. We might see a sort of cloud-like haze, out of which the time machine might form as a solid object. As the time machine continued on into the past while we remained in the present, it might again appear to dissolve into a hazy form and once again disappear.

If this passage were to happen while we were in daylight, we probably would notice little or no color effects, but such effects would almost certainly be visible at night. The fact that the object is moving *toward* us through time would probably cause any electromagnetic radiation radiating from it to undergo an apparent increase in frequency—a Doppler effect. Heat would be raised to the frequency of red light, or orange, or yellow, etc., depending on the extent of Doppler effect. If the time machine's rate of passage were extremely fast, it might even be raised to a higher energy frequency equal to that of ultraviolet light, X rays, etc. We might guess that the amount of Doppler effect would be directly proportional to the rate of passage, plus the additional amount

---

24. Keel, *Trojan Horse*, p. 51.
25. Keel, *Mothman Prophesies*, p. 42.
26. John A. Keel, *Our Haunted Planet* (Greenwich, Connecticut: Fawcett Gold Medal—Fawcett Publications, Inc., 1971), p. 169.

of Doppler effect created by the passage of the radiation through the field itself, as outlined in previous chapters.

As the time machine passed through our time and faded into the oblivion of the past, the color shift would probably reverse. Heat would tend to be Dopplered into radio waves, light into heat, etc. And of course the strength of the field itself, the degree to which it warped time would still be a major factor. If we stand on the same spot, we may be able to see a similar phenomenon as the time machine, its mission completed, returns to the future via the same route (provided, of course, that it is again compensating for the earth's motion somehow). Similar, but not identical. Since we and the time travelers from the future are now traveling through time in the same direction (albeit at different rates), the difference in our rates of travel would be less. The passage would probably appear to take longer, and the shifting of frequencies would be less profound.

If the pilots of the time machine see us watching them, they may decide to change the shape of their field a bit to match time with us. They might even decide to kidnap us and examine us, or offer us a ride in their vessel. During this period, they and their time machine would be as solid and real to us as a ton of bricks. But such an undertaking could be dangerous, especially in an area like Bethlehem. They might have to make a quick escape from Israeli war planes determined to blow them—or any other foreign aircraft that does not identify itself—out of the sky! If they were attacked, their field would allow them to outrun any airplane. It would also allow for a quick escape into the future or past. By strengthening and/or distorting their field dramatically and abruptly, they might be able to disappear on the spot, as if someone had snapped off a light switch.

Another uncanny "super power" that UFOs exhibit—their apparent ability to change shape—may be closely related to their appearances and disappearances.

At 9:05 P.M. on June 29, 1954, Capt. James Howard was piloting a British Overseas Airways Corporation airliner from New York to London. Southwest of Goose Bay, Labrador, he and his first officer sighted several dark UFOs pacing their plane at about the same altitude. The whole crew and some of the passengers watched. There was one large object that changed from a jellyfish shape, to that of a dart, to that of a dumbbell. Several smaller UFOs swarmed around it "like a group of fighters acting as a bomber escort." Goose Bay said there were no other aircraft in the area and sent a fighter plane to investigate. When the fighter approached, the UFOs faded into invisibility—except for one, which grew smaller and vanished. Capt. Howard had, by the way, flown 7,500 hours.[27]

Two months later, on the 19th, M. Pardon, of La Carondelet, Dôle, France, was awakened by a bright light outside the open window of his

27. Gray Barker, *They Knew Too Much About Flying Saucers* (New York: University Books, Inc., 1956), pp. 141-142.

apartment. He saw a huge, luminous blue, disc-shaped UFO. He woke his wife, and they watched it turn to white with a red halo and become exceedingly brilliant. It seemed to be spinning, and changed shape from circular to cigar-shaped, assumed a vertical angle, and made a buzzing noise.[28]

A rash of French sightings followed. M. Perrut saw one at Marcoing at 8:00 P.M. on October 3, 1954. It was circular, and had a luminous orange-red color. It hovered over the Gouillet woods. Below it a spot of light moved with a "see-saw movement." Perrut notified policemen and stopped passing bicyclists. All watched the UFO change shape to a cigar shape and the spot of light disappeared. Then the object moved away, changing again into a crescent shape. It returned to its original position, then shot away very fast toward Villiers-Plouich, emitting an intense light beam as it did so. In all, there were about 100 witnesses in 3 villages.[29]

An hour later a UFO changed shape at Milly-le-Fôret. M. Mourouzeau and three of his employees saw a red, half-moon-shaped UFO hovering almost motionless from outside his restaurant. It then became more sharply defined, changing in shape to a red cigar surmounting a smaller, shiny ring. It moved closer, lost altitude and finally disappeared over the horizon.[30]

Thirty minutes after that incident, Champigny-sur-Marne was visited. Claude Rigault, his sister and their parents watched an orange, cigar-shaped UFO in the direction of Orly Airport. It changed shape slowly, growing smaller and dimmer and dividing into two point sources of light. The lights then reunited, becoming clearer, changed into a saucer shape canted at an angle and grew larger. It then became smaller again, split into two parts, grew brighter, then left, fading away over the horizon.[31]

Offut AFB, Omaha, Nebraska, was the scene of an encounter on September 8, 1958. Maj. Paul Duich (USAF, Ret.) and 10 to 20 other officers watched a glowing UFO dim and change color to orange while changing from a "fuzzy," indistinct shape to a solid cigar shape. It then tilted from horizontal to nearly vertical, and a group of much smaller UFOs appeared at its lower end, darting around "like a swarm of gnats...."[32]

An engineer named J. Beck spotted a motionless UFO at midday in a cloudless sky on March 25, 1959. It was dumbbell-shaped, made up of a larger and a smaller sphere connected by a cylinder. It appeared to be constructed of aluminum. It turned, changing shape into a disc, moved toward Mlocin (Poland). Then it returned to its first position 1,300 feet above Warsaw's Palace of Culture and Sciences, whereupon it changed back to its original shape.[33]

28. Michel, *Straight Line Mystery*, pp. 27-28.
29. *Ibid.*, pp. 114-115.
30. *Ibid.*, p. 122.
31. *Ibid.*, p. 121.
32. Binder, *What We Really Know*, pp. 127-128.
33. Hobana, *op. cit.*, p. 212.

It was 10:15 at night when Elmore, Ohio, Chief of Police Richard Crawford spotted his UFO. The date was June 12, 1964. On patrol, Crawford saw a stationary, silent, blinking globe. It was 70 to 90 feet in diameter. It approached to within 500 feet. It was surrounded by an "aura," and seemed to respond to his spotlight by moving, blinking, ceasing to blink, and turning off its light.

At 11:30 he spotted it again. He radioed Deputy Carl Soenichsoen, who also saw it. The UFO sped up, changed from a globe shape to a wedge shape, abruptly changed course and passed within about 500 feet of the witnesses at very extreme speed—faster than anything Crawford had ever seen. Calls to the Toledo Express Airport elicited a negative radar report.[34]

At 4:36 A.M. on the morning of October 20, 1967, Georgia Bureau of Investigation officer Mixon and police lieutenant Niblett saw and followed a UFO while on patrol a few miles east of Midgeville on Georgia 22. The UFO turned red and left, but later returned to follow them. Before dawn Patrolman J. M. Poole and officer Alan Council joined them. All four men saw the brilliant object change from red-orange to blue, and from football shape to four-leaf-clover shape, then leave the area.[35]

The logbook of the Rumanian ship *Moldoveanu* states that the entire crew watched a radiant UFO between 3:00 and 4:00 A.M. on Christmas eve, 1972. It approached the ship at high speed, slowed overhead, and repeatedly changed shape from circular to elliptical as it changed color from red, to yellow, to blue-white. Then it ascended vertically, its image growing smaller until it disappeared.[36]

A Mrs. Cromwell spotted a UFO from her home in the Angeles Crest Mountains in Tujunga, California, on the evening of September 3, 1975. Mrs. Cromwell saw and heard a helicopter circling at a height of about 2,500 feet, then she sighted the UFO hovering above it at a height of about 3,700 feet. Through binoculars, she could see that it had a blue-green top, white middle, and red, glowing bottom, and it was disc-shaped. Its shape changed "from round to diamond, to chevron, and into a classic saucer." It flew in a zigzag pattern. The helicopter flew away quickly. Later two helicopters returned and continued the chase (if that is what it was). At about 11:00, the UFO flew away, with the helicopter following. Mr. Cromwell had also witnessed the incident, as had Mrs. Cromwell's sister, Mrs. Brandt. They all suffered painful, red eyes afterward, and Mrs. Cromwell's vision blurred.[37]

One of the strangest shapes was reported by Len Franklin, of Wantage, Oxfordshire, England. Franklin was walking a baby sitter home at about midnight one winter night in 1976 when he noticed a bright white, "nut-shaped" object in the sky, surrounded by a planar, amoe-

34. Richard D. Osborn, "UFOs Over Toledo," *Fate*, Nov. 1964, pp. 31-37.
35. Lorenzen, *UFOs Over the Americas*, pp. 170-171.
36. Hobana, *op. cit.*, p. 279.
37. Ann Druffel, "California Report: The Mystery Helicopters," *Skylook*, Feb. 1976, pp. 8-9.

ba-like cloud of small white bits with a white outline that constantly changed shape. Stars were visible through the flat "cloud." After five seconds or so, the central object glowed bright orange, dimmed, glowed again (while the surrounding cloud instantly took on a triangular shape), and the whole affair left at extreme velocity, covering the approximately seven miles to a landmark in about two seconds (this translates to over 12,000 m.p.h.). The baby sitter also saw the object, but was afraid to continue watching it.[38]

Another intriguing English encounter was reported by Mrs. Matilda Antell, of Bristol Way, Hollington. At 9:00 P.M. on October 4, 1981, Mrs. Antell and her daughter-in-law, Janette Antell, watched a golden-colored UFO that resembled a pair of plates for almost an hour as it changed shape into a ball, a cross and a cigar. It seemed to appear from a cloud, which it also seemed to hide behind whenever six fast planes and a helicopter got near it. Colin Carey, of Gladstone Terrace, Hastings, reported a yellow light with a white center from Plynlimmon Road at the same time.[39]

Some shape changes can doubtless be attributed to changes in altitude. A disc, sphere, cone, egg, football and cigar, for instance, will all look round to an observer who views them from exactly the right angle. Upon rotating, though, only the sphere will retain its apparent shape. The disc will take on an elliptical or cigar-shaped appearance, the cone will look triangular, etc. But not all of these changes can be explained away as optical illusions. Crosses, four-leaf clovers, chevrons, crescents and irregular "fried egg" shapes that change into triangles are somewhat more complicated to explain.

It is quite possible that the skeptics have jumped the gun by declaring that all such reports are "spurious because they are impossible." And researchers may not need to involve themselves in such convoluted theories as psychic manifestations and plastic life forms to account for these changes of form. The *actual* shape of the UFOs in question may not change shape any more than your body does when you look at its reflection in the distorted surface of a carnival mirror. Your body isn't really smaller than your head—the light you are seeing is just being twisted before it reaches your eyes.

Light passing through an area of space that subjects it to a Doppler effect may be changed in such a way that an observer beyond that area sees an image that bears little resemblance to the original. Some of it may be Dopplered to frequencies beyond those of visible light, and so would not be visible. If an observer were looking at a spherical object surrounded by a spherical field, light from the edges of the sphere would be passing through more of the field before reaching his eyes than would light from the center—just as light from the sun passes

---

38. Bob Webb, "Amoeba-like UFO Over Oxfordshire," *Flying Saucer Review*, 24, No. 4 (1979), pp. 26-27.
39. Johnathan Mendenhall, "Hastings UFO: 'Moonlight' Says Observatory," *The News* (Hastings, East Sussex, England), 8 Oct. 1981; rpt. in "World Round-up," *Flying Saucer Review*, 27, No. 4 (1982), p. 25.

through more of our atmosphere when near the horizon than when at the zenith, and therefore appears dimmer and redder when rising and setting. Light from the edges of the sphere would be subject to more of a Doppler effect than light from its center, perhaps even being shifted beyond the visible range. Or it might be simply shifted in color to a frequency more or less visible (yellow light, for instance, is more visible than violet). If the object or the field were some shape other than spherical, the effect would increase in some areas and decrease in others, creating even more of an illusion of shape change. A wobbling, rotating, domed disc covered with flashing lights of different colors—one of the most commonly reported types of UFOs—might under certain circumstances appear to be changing shape in quite spectacular fashion right in front of witnesses' eyes.

Infrared and other frequencies would be similarly affected. An object may be emitting heat or radio waves in all sorts of different patterns, perhaps because of uneven heating of the hull or because of the shape of broadcasting antennae. As these frequencies become visible due to Dopplering and as the object shifts attitude, speed, etc., these patterns would appear to shift as well. Any exhaust released would further enhance the appearance of change.

The transparent or hazy appearance of a time machine as it passed into our time frame from a foreign one, or vice versa, would no doubt exacerbate the effect. The part of the object closest to the observer might appear to wax visible first, then fade from sight before parts farther away became visible.

Warm air masses around the object might be visible one minute and invisible the next, or they might change shape due to their natural movement. Sometimes witnesses may be seeing the field around the UFO, not the UFO itself. An observer who sees a glowing, elliptical UFO might actually be looking at an egg-shaped field and might be astonished when the field is turned off and he finds himself looking at a craft shaped like a cross or a fan blade. And we can only guess at what other types of kaleidoscopic images might be produced by time-warping fields. They may, for instance, actually stimulate or deaden our optic nerves directly.

The end result of the interaction of all these different sources of flux could be incredibly confusing to an observer, especially if he is taken by surprise—as UFO witnesses invariably are—and is totally unaware of what it is he is actually seeing. When we see a stage magician change a motorcycle into a tiger, we know we have witnessed an illusion, but when we see a UFO that appears to change shape from a sphere to a disc to a sailboat, we can only report to others what our eyes reported to us.

In this regard, a radar set is no different. It operates by bouncing radio waves off an object and displaying the echoes on a screen. Radio waves are subject to the Doppler effect, just as light is. The wavelength of a radar beacon that passes through a time-warping field might be lengthened (or shortened) before striking the object inside it. After rebounding, it might be shortened (or lengthened), but the amount of foreshortening (or lengthening) may not necessarily correspond exactly to the original change—indeed it probably would not if the object and its field were moving through time. Naturally a radar receiver is tuned to the frequency of its corresponding transmitter, for maximum sensitivity and to avoid confusion with other transmitters. The result is that it will not interpret any signal of a different frequency as an echo.

In addition, a radar signal bounced off an object that is actually in a different time frame may actually arrive back at its source hours later instead of a split second after it was transmitted. Or it may actually arrive before it was sent! And a time-warping field might Doppler other frequencies into radar frequencies so that an extremely bright echo may appear inexplicably. A UFO that seems to be changing color or shape to an observer may be fading to invisibility on a radar screen. Or an observer might see a perfectly visible UFO blink out at the same instant an echo suddenly appears out of nowhere on a radar screen. In other words, the criterion that many have used as a prerequisite for acceptance of a report for study—that the UFO in question must have been seen visually and on radar simultaneously—may be possible only on rare occasions.

One of the earliest accounts of this type was reported over Speyer, Germany, on November 27, 1944. Pilots Walter Cleary and Henry Giblin both saw a huge, orange UFO in the form of a light 1,500 feet above their fighter plane. It was not detected by ground radar, but their own radar suddenly failed, and they had to return to their base.[40]

A red glow was seen at Goose Bay, Labrador, a few minutes after midnight on June 19, 1952, and was confirmed on radar. It abruptly "changed to a dazzling white and took off at tremendous speed." At precisely the same time, the radar blip became very vivid. One second later it had gone.[41]

When UFOs stormed our nation's capital late on the night of July 19, 1952, nervous radar operators could only shake their heads in disbelief. Harry Barnes and seven other air-traffic controllers under his supervision picked up seven UFOs. The other Washington control tower and the Air Force radar center at Andrews Air Force Base both confirmed the bogeys. They flew at speeds of from 100 to 7,000 m.p.h. all over the Washington area, including the restricted air corridors over the White House and the Capitol. They maneuvered until dawn, sometimes—but not always—corresponding to visual observations by commercial pilots.

The tower operator at Bowling Air Force Base sighted a UFO. Following directions from the radar tower, Capt. Casey Pierman and others aboard flight T807 saw six shining, circular lights that abruptly accelerated and disappeared. One UFO followed flight SP610 to within a few miles of its landing.

40. Vesco, *op. cit.*, p. 81.
41. Michel, *The Truth About Flying Saucers*, p. 92.

One of the UFOs made a 90-degree turn without decelerating. Another executed a 180-degree turn. At one point a very large orange sphere corresponding to a radar return was reported directly over Andrews radio range station. At times the UFOs vanished instantly from three separate radar screens. Radar sets were tested and found to be functioning normally. The UFOs disappeared each time jets were sent into the area to intercept them. Al Chop, the Pentagon's UFO spokesman, was alerted and was on the scene.[42, 43, 44]

The excitement continued exactly one week later, on the night of the 26th. At 10:30, Washington radar again picked up UFOs. They left, but were seen on Langley Air Force Base radar near Newport News, Virginia. Lt. William Paterson, piloting an Air Force F-94 interceptor scrambled from Langley, spotted one. As he gave chase, the luminous object suddenly winked out like a light being switched off; immediately, his radar locked on to the object.[45]

Responding to a midnight phone call by an FAA spokesman, Al Chop drove to Washington National Airport, where he and air-traffic controllers watched six to twelve UFOs on radar. They appeared on, and disappeared from, the screen in ways planes could not and moved too fast to be planes.

Chop requested an intercept and told the press they could witness it on the screen. He then received orders to remove the newsmen from the room. Two F-94s responded to the intercept request at 2:40 A.M., but as they appeared on the radar scope, the UFOs disappeared. The F-94 pilots flew around the area for a short time, then returned to base, at which time the UFOs returned to the scope.

Another intercept was ordered. One of the pilots saw the UFOs surrounding and closing in on his plane. He described them as "tremendous blue-white lights." They flew away after 20 seconds.[46]

Bentwaters A.F.B. and Lakenheath, England were similarly besieged by UFOs during a period of several hours on the night of August 13 and 14, 1956. Some exhibited speeds of 4,000 m.p.h., and perhaps as high as 18,000 m.p.h. Both visual and radar observations were made of hovering and abrupt stops and direction changes—without acceleration or deceleration time—at 600 m.p.h. One echo was tracked heading directly toward Bentwaters at 2,000 to 4,000 m.p.h. It disappeared from the radar screen when it was two miles east of Bentwaters, then immediately reappeared on the same course, three miles west of the station.

An RAF fighter pilot who was scrambled to investigate established visual and radar contact, but lost both inexplicably. Vectored to another target, he located it on his radar, reported that it was the clearest

42. Ruppelt, pp. 210-219.
43. Robert Emenegger, *UFOs, Past, Present and Future* (New York: Ballantine Books-Random House, Inc., 1974), pp. 42-43.
44. Michel, *The Truth About Flying Saucers*, pp. 86-88.
45. Geza Korcsmaros, Jr., "Radar—Clue to UFO Propulsion?" *Fate*, Aug. 1957, pp. 64-69.
46. Emenegger, *op. cit.*, pp. 43-45.

radar target he had ever seen and locked his guns on it. The target quickly circled behind him and followed him. He was unable to shake it with evasive maneuvers. It then stopped to hover once again. Another fighter was sent to investigate. Its engine malfunctioned and its pilot was forced to return to base.[47]

A year later, the perplexing phenomenon again appeared to an American military pilot, this time over Louisiana, near Winnsboro. Maj. Lewis Chase, USAF, was piloting an RB-47H aircraft on July 17. His crew included James McCoid (copilot), Thomas Hanley (navigator), and John Provenzano, Frank McClure and Walter Tuchsherer (electronic countermeasures monitors). At 4:10 A.M., Chase saw an intense, blue-white lighted UFO closing rapidly. It changed course instantaneously and flashed across his flight path at a speed greater than he had seen in 20 years of flying, then "blinked out." It was picked up on ECM where it had disappeared. It paced the aircraft through Louisiana and into Texas. The pilot and copilot then saw a huge, red, lighted UFO, which was tracked on ECM (electronic countermeasures monitors). They were told to pursue. Ground radar in Duncanville, Texas, confirmed the UFO.

At 4:50, the object stopped; the plane overshot it. It then disappeared from sight and from the ECM and ground radar screens. The RB-47 was turned around. The UFO was respotted and also again picked up on both ECM and ground radar, but the plane was low on fuel and had to return to base. The UFO had followed the plane for more than 700 miles, during which time it appeared and disappeared simultaneously to visual sight, ECM and ground-based radar several times. It also exhibited incredible speed and maneuverability.[48]

At 8:00 P.M. on April 7, 1959, control-tower observers at Canada's St. Hubert air defense establishment saw a red light hovering between 3,000 and 7,000 feet, then leaving at supersonic velocity. It did not register on radar, but was pronounced "unidentified" and "a genuine UFO" by Air Force spokesmen.[49]

On July 18, 1966, *Gemini X* astronauts Mike Collins and John Young saw a big, cylindrical object and two smaller, bright objects from their orbiting capsule. Although Young photographed the objects, NASA did not detect them on radar.[50]

At 10:00 P.M. on January 13 the following year, a National Airlines pilot and the pilot of a Lear jet near Winslow, Arizona, watched a red, flashing UFO that "quadrupled itself in a vertical position" as the controller in the Albuquerque control tower watched it on radar and communicated with both planes. The UFO showed up on the radar screen,

47. G. D. Thayer, "UFO Encounter II (Sample Case Selected by the UFO Subcommittee of the AIAA)," *Astronautics and Aeronautics*, Sept. 1971, pp. 60-64.
48. James E. McDonald, "UFO Encounter I," *Astronautics and Aeronautics*, Jul. 1971, pp. 66-70.
49. Lorenzen, *The Whole Story*, p. 100.
50. J. Allen Hynek and Jacques Vallée, *The Edge of Reality* (Chicago: Henry Regnery Company, 1975), p. 64.

but *only* when its light was on.[51]

A UFO that gave a strong radar return and exhibited the flight characteristics of an F-104 jet flew over the Colorado Springs, Colorado, airport on the night of May 13, 1967. It passed within 200 feet over the airport at high speed, but could not be seen by tower operators visually, even when they used binoculars. The radar operators were experts and were sure it was a solid object. When a Braniff airliner landed, the invisible UFO moved instantly to the side.[52]

When the time-travel hypothesis is taken into consideration, the inconsistency in radar data that has for so long confused and frustrated anyone trying to guess the true nature of UFOs suddenly becomes a help rather than a hindrance. Once one accepts that UFOs may be enveloped in fields that warp space-time, the inconsistencies become very consistent indeed—consistent with what witnesses report visually and consistent with the effects we can deduce should be taking place. If the time- travel hypothesis is correct, UFOs *shouldn't* show up on radar screens with any more consistency than they should show up on photographs or to the eyes of witnesses. The changes in echoes "painted" on the glowing green scopes in control towers everywhere correspond with the changes in color and shape reported by eyewitnesses on back roads and in fields and secluded forest clearings across our globe.

51. Hynek, *Experience*, p. 72.
52. Keyhoe, *op. cit.*, pp. 259-260.

10

The physical effects reportedly include...temporary paralysis, numbness, a feeling of heat, and other discomfort. "Interference" with the local gravitational field sometimes is also reported, as evidenced by the reports of some observers of temporary feelings of weightlessness or other inertial effects, as though the well-known laws of inertia had been temporarily abrogated.

—Dr. J. Allen Hynek[1]

Field Trips

In 1963, the state of Paraná, in the southern part of Brazil, was the site of an incredible UFO encounter. As a crowd of spectators watched one of the many destructive fires that raged through the Paraná forests that year, a shiny, basin-shaped saucer over 100 feet in diameter dropped down from the sky to hover silently 165 feet away *in the fire.* For 15 minutes it stayed about 13 feet above the ground. It had no visible support, but appeared to be enveloped in a protective field of repulsion. In front of the amazed onlookers' eyes, "two or three tall, good-looking 'people'" emerged from the object and strolled about inside the protected area to collect rocks and burned vegetation, unhampered by the flames and smoke raging outside it![2]

It appears that some force was surrounding the Brazilian UFO and formed a barrier through which the flames could not pass. Both popular UFO publications and scientific data bases are filled with accounts of witnesses encountering invisible barriers surrounding UFOs. An Englishman encountered one at Winkleigh Airfield in North Devon in May of 1957. While having a cup of coffee about 30 minutes before dawn, Mr. J. Payne saw a large, luminous, fluorescent blue, submarine-shaped UFO. He tried to walk toward it, but met with a barrier like a cushion of air that was so strong he could lean against it. It "seemed to completely surround the object." The UFO rose vertically and silently. It left a "faint black circle about 50 feet in diameter." The witness then

1. Hynek, *Experience*, p. 110.
2. From *Exchange Bulletin*, No. 4 (Oct. 1963-Feb. 1964) of Circulo da Amizade Sideral, Curitiba, Paraná, Brazil, as reported in Charles Bowen, "A South American Trio," *Flying Saucer Review*, 11, No. 1 (Jan.-Feb. 1965), p. 21.

discovered his watch was 20 minutes slow.[3]

Had time been passing more slowly for him when he was in contact with the cushion of air?

In the summer of 1961, two salvos of Russian ground-to-air missiles were fired at a group of disc-shaped UFOs that hovered 12 miles above a Rybinsk missile installation 93 miles north of Moscow. All of the missiles exploded harmlessly more than a mile away from the targets. The discs responded by powerfailing the whole missile base.[4] An identical incident was reported to have happened at a NATO missile installation on a Mediterranean island in 1975, but that occurrence cannot be substantiated.[5]

A Missouri farmer tried to throw stones at a gray-green, bowl-shaped UFO. It was 12 to 15 feet in diameter and six feet thick with flashing lights that continually changed color. The witness was only 30 feet from it, but his stone struck an invisible barrier 15 feet before it reached the craft and fell to the ground. He tried throwing another, higher up. It skipped silently off the barrier. When he tried to approach closer to the object, he was prevented by a "pressure" at the place the first stone had stopped. The UFO flew away without making a sound. The incident occurred at 7:00 A.M. on February 14, 1967.[6]

Sr. Nélson Vieira Leite and his nephew, Manoel Carlos Leite, encountered UFOs surrounded by barriers on two separate occasions at Itaperuna, Rio de Janeiro, Brazil. The first time was at 8:00 P.M. on February 7, 1969, when they were unable to approach closer than a block away from a luminous UFO that hovered about ten feet off the ground because of a barrier they could not see. Then in May of 1971, Nélson saw a brilliant, green UFO shaped like an upside-down plate descend nearby. He tried to approach it, but was 32 feet away when he discovered "that he was no longer walking" and had not been for several minutes. He "had by now somehow or other lost all sense of time" and felt "half-numbed." Manoel Carlos ran toward him, smacked into the unseen wall and was knocked unconscious for several hours. Both objects scorched the ground over which they had hovered.[7, 8]

Another Brazilian encounter comes from Itajuba, Minas Gerais. It was May, 1969. Sr. Clixto Borges de Mouros' car ran into an invisible barrier on the road between Pouso Alegre and Maria da Fé. Its wheels

3. From Richard Farrow, "Landing on Winkleigh Airfield" (Reader's Reports), *Flying Saucer Review Case Histories*, Supplement 8 (Dec. 1971), p. 16, and from Ron Toft, "The Alleged Landing at Winkleigh" (Reader's Reports), *Flying Saucer Review Case Histories*, Supplement 13 (Feb. 1973), p. 16.
4. From *Oltre Il Cielo: Missili & Razzi*, No. 105 (Jun. 1-15 1962, Rome), as reported in Gordon Creighton, "Amazing News From Russia," *Flying Saucer Review*, 8, No. 6 (Nov.-Dec. 1962), p. 28.
5. Vladimir Grigorievich Azhazha, "Life in the Cosmos" (lecture), trans. Gordon Creighton, *Flying Saucer Review*, 25, No. 1 (1979), p. 26.
6. From Ted Phillips, "UFO Events in Missouri 1957-1971," *Flying Saucer Review Case Histories*, Supplement 8 (Dec. 1971), pp. 10-11.
7. Walter Buhler, "Brazilian Cases in 1968 and 1969—4," *Flying Saucer Review Case Histories*, Supplement 5 (Jun. 1971), p. 10.
8. Gordon Creighton, "Itaperuna Again," *Flying Saucer Review*, 18, No. 2 (Mar.-Apr. 1972), p. 13. See also Carlos Chagas in the 17 October 1971 issue of *Domingo Ilustrado* (Rio de Janeiro).

spun, but it would not continue forward. A brilliantly-lit UFO could be seen overhead. The UFO also caused the car's headlights and the power in a nearby town to fail.[9]

Still another report is from Serra do Mouro, Santa Catarina. João Romeu Klein was returning home after visiting a friend at 7:00 P.M. on September 3, 1976. He saw a grayish disc about ten feet across with a rotating bottom part. A light on top varied from red, to orange, to yellow, to green, according to the speed of the object. When the UFO had come to a virtual standstill, the light dimmed and turned white. Three helmeted humanoids slowly descended to the road in a red beam of light and blocked Klein's path. He threw a knife at them, but it was deflected as if it had struck an unseen object. A humanoid shot his leg with a beam of blue light and he lost consciousness. The muscles in his leg remained rigid enough to impair his use of it for several days.[10]

It was at 11:15 on the night of October 7, 1973, that a Duluth, Minnesota, woman heard footsteps on her porch, then saw a faint silver cloud hovering over a tree in her backyard and shining a light beam into a neighbor's window. A street light blinked on and off, and nearby dogs were disturbed. About 15 minutes later, the cloud dispersed, and she was able to see a disc-shaped, domed UFO with projections hanging from its rim and an antenna-like protuberance on top. The bottom of it was red and luminous. She tried to get closer, but repeatedly encountered a barrier which stopped her and blocked her vision with silver light. At 12:15, the UFO left straight up, making a hole in overcast cloud in the process. The witness inexplicably forgot about the encounter the following day until one of the other three witness reminded her of it.[11]

The silver light that she encountered is intriguing. She said that each time she walked into the barrier, she couldn't see anything but the silver; each time she backed away, she could no longer see it, and her vision returned to normal. Could it be that the light was being Dopplered into a different frequency by a field with a well-defined perimeter? One is reminded of other accounts in which light beams appeared to shine only to a certain point and then stop, as if they had struck something. One witness said a light beam reached only *halfway* to the ground.

Edwin Pratt and Joyce Bowles saw an orange glow in the sky while driving on the Winchester Bypass at Hampshire, England. It was on the night of November 14, 1976, at 9:00 P.M. Their car shuddered violently, veered off the highway and stopped. The witnesses saw a cigar-shaped, orange UFO 15 feet in length hovering very close to the ground. "Jets" of "vapour" seemed to be issuing from its underside. A blond,

9. From *O Dia* (Rio de Janeiro), 30 May 1969, as reported in Walter Buhler, "Brazilian Cases in 1968 and 1969—Pt. 6," *Flying Saucer Review Case Histories*, Supplement 7 (Oct. 1971), p. 15, trans. Gordon Creighton.
10. Walter Buhler, "Extraterrestrial Dwarves Attack Farm Worker," *SBEDV Bulletin* (Rio de Janeiro), No. 136/145 (Sept. 1981-Apr. 1982), trans. Gordon Creighton, *Flying Saucer Review*, 28, No. 1 (1982), pp. 5-8.
11. "Cloud Hides UFO," *The A.P.R.O. Bulletin*, 22, No. 3 (1973), pp. 1, 4.

bearded, pink-eyed occupant six feet tall who wore a silver suit appeared to walk *through* the side of the UFO and to the rear of the car. The witnesses turned back toward the UFO, but could not see it. When they tried to drive forward, the car's wheels spun and its engine failed, as if an invisible object were stopping their progress.[12]

On the night of June 14, 1980, a Russian officer, Lt. Col. Oleg Karyakin, reported seeing a flying saucer hovering 100 feet from his house and exuding a glowing pink gas and a faint humming sound. When he tried to go closer, he came up against a barrier and was completely unable to advance. The saucer gave off blue-green flashes and flew off. Another witness said he had seen a human figure behind the craft's transparent dome.[13]

On May 22, 1973, at 3:00 in the morning, a Brazilian man experienced the opposite effect. Onilson Papero was driving south through rain north of Catanduva, São Paulo. His car's radio faded, and its engine sputtered and missed. He saw a bright blue light approach, then hover at an altitude of 33 feet, 50 feet away. He felt hot and starved for oxygen—even when he got out of his car. He then saw a gray, plate-shaped UFO 33 feet in diameter hovering with a buzzing noise where the light had been. A "transparent curtain" slowly encircled the UFO, then the feeling of suffocation ceased. Papero ran away, but felt as if he were being prevented by a "rubber lasso" after running only 100 feet. The UFO emitted a tubular light beam at Papero's car, which then became transparent, enabling him to see the engine and seats inside it.

Papero lost consciousness and was later found face down in the rain by passing motorists Valdomiro Barosco and Celso Aparecido Piu. His car's door was open, and the car's headlights were on. His suitcase had been ransacked, but nothing was missing. His car functioned normally. Papero struggled when police awakened him. He was taken to the Padre Albino Hospital in Cantaduva and released. He later developed bruise-like spots on his stomach, back, buttocks and hips, which Dr. Max Berezovski could not explain, despite extensive tests (all of which, including an electroencephalogram, indicated normal results).[14]

Papero's report that his car became invisible is fascinating. Could it have been fading into another time frame? Or could Papero himself have been doing so? Could he have been inside a field's influence? Is that why he had trouble breathing? And was he prevented from fleeing by a field, just as others may have been prevented from running toward UFOs by fields? The "transparent curtain" he reported seeing must have reflected, refracted or obscured some light (as a clear plastic shower curtain does). Otherwise, he would not have seen it at all. Could he have seen the effect of a field in much the same way he would

---

12. Leslie Harris, "UFO & Silver-Suited Entity Seen Near Winchester," *Flying Saucer Review*, 22, No. 5 (Feb. 1977), pp. 3-6.
13. Gordon Creighton, "Dr. Felix Zigel and the Development of Ufology in Russia: Part II," *Flying Saucer Review*, 27, No. 4, pp. 15-16.
14. "Follow Up," *The A.P.R.O. Bulletin*, Jul.-Aug. 1973, pp. 6-7.

see the interface between air and water when looking into a still, clear lake?

Wells Allen Webb may have seen the effects of a field surrounding a UFO in broad daylight. At 10:00 A.M. on May 5, 1953, Webb was seven miles east of Yuma, Arizona. He saw a white or silver, cloud-like, oblong UFO that changed shape to a circular configuration. When he looked at it through his Polaroid sunglasses, it seemed to be surrounded by a series of concentric, dark rings, but each time he took off the sunglasses, he could no longer see the rings.[15]

Webb's experience may be unique (it is, however, reminiscent of other cases in which percipients have reported that the UFOs they saw looked different to them when viewed through binoculars than when observed directly). Polaroid sunglasses polarize the light in a particular direction before it reaches the wearer's eyes. In simplified terms, they allow light with an up-and-down wave form to pass, while blocking out light with a side-to-side wave form. If light has already been polarized up-and-down before reaching the sunglasses, no light will pass through them. This is why two polarized lenses block out all light when one is rotated 90 degrees clockwise or counterclockwise.

The fact that Webb observed dark rings surrounding the UFO only when he was wearing polarizing lenses implies that an invisible something was causing at least partial polarization of light at intervals around the craft. The sunglasses apparently allowed him to "see" normally invisible "lines of force" in the same way fine iron filings sprinkled on a sheet of paper allow one to "see" magnetic lines of force from a magnet held beneath the paper. It is a pity that Webb did not take the glasses off and rotate them 90 degrees while looking through them at the UFO. Had he done so, he might have been able to supply even more valuable clues about the area immediately surrounding UFOs. At any rate, the circles he reported imply that some sort of field capable of polarizing light enveloped the UFO at the time of his encounter.

Another striking daylight sighting that also may have involved polarization occurred at 10:30 one August morning in 1952 at Catalina Island, California. About 300 Boy Scouts and 50 adults at Camp Fox saw a bright, metallic-appearing, lens-shaped UFO with "windows." One witness, Clyde Vrooman, of La Cresenta, California, estimated it to be 150 feet across at an altitude of 500 to 800 feet. It was first oriented vertically, but turned to a horizontal position. It left at incredible speed. The sky immediately surrounding the object was much darker blue or purple than the rest of the sky, and this area moved as the object moved. The camp director and all the Scouts wrote personal accounts of what they had seen and sent them to the Air Force. Vrooman received an acknowledgment from Col. Charles W. Bicking,

---

15. Testimony of Dr. James A. Harder before the House Committee on Science and Astronautics, 29 July, 1968, as recorded in Fuller, *Aliens in the Skies*, pp. 137-138.

Commander of March Air Force Base in California.[16] The description of the area is similar to that given by the captain of a Lockheed jetliner over Lake Michigan on July 4, 1981 (see Chapter 9). Capt. P.S. said that a fan-shaped area behind the UFO he saw was of a darker blue hue than the rest of the sky, as if he could see into outer space.

The sky itself is polarized in a plane passing through the sun. The maximum polarization occurs 90 degrees from the sun's position, and causes that area of (clear) sky to appear to be a darker hue of blue than the rest of the sky. Given that fact, we might extrapolate the hypothesis that the darker hues of blue surrounding the UFOs that the witnesses reported seeing resulted from a polarization effect created by an invisible something enveloping their craft. And we might assume that, in each case, that invisible something must have been a field of some sort.

The "envelopes" or "environments" that apparently surround UFOs much of the time are often detectable because of other physical effects. For instance, witnesses frequently describe the objects as being encased in a mist, haze or glow.

Georges Fortin and hundreds of others watched a gigantic cigar-shaped UFO that appeared to be a machine surrounded by a "luminous blue-violet mist" on September 14, 1954, in broad daylight. Fortin was watching from La Gabelière, Dept. of Vendée, France. The UFO descended, hovered and changed to a vertical angle. Then a smaller, metallic-appearing disc traced a helical smoke trail around the cigar, darted about the area at high speed, now and then stopped to hover and finally disappeared into the cylinder, which tilted and flew away into the clouds.[17]

Fortin's sighting took place during a wave of similar encounters. It was at 11:10 P.M. exactly two weeks later that railroad engineer Gérard and fireman Paroux saw a luminous, dark red, disc-shaped UFO surrounded by a violet glow at Butte du Rouge, Redon-St-Nicolas. It followed a few yards above their locomotive for ten seconds before leaving westward "at terrific speed." Paroux "suffered from nervous shock and fever" for days afterward.[18]

At 7:35 on the evening of October 13, Messrs. Perano and Oliver and another man encountered a red, disc-shaped UFO surrounded by a "misty glow." A humanoid in a shiny "diving suit" stood nearby. When one of the witnesses tried to approach to within 65 feet, he "found himself paralyzed." The UFO ascended quickly, and the witness was thrown down on the ground.[19]

Ufonauts may have some sort of "ray-gun" devices that can paralyze muscles by using beams to conduct electrical current. Many accounts exist in which percipients were stunned when a light beam

16. Dave Kenney, "1952 Catalina Sighting," The A.P.R.O. Bulletin, 27, No. 10 (Apr. 1979), pp. 4-5.
17. Michel, Straight Line Mystery, pp. 23-25.
18. From Parisien Libéré, 30 Sept. 1954, as reported in Michel, Straight Line Mystery, p. 95.
19. From Paris Presse, 15 Oct. 1954, from Libération, 15 Oct. 1954, and from La Croix, 16 Oct. 1954, as reported in Vallée, Magonia, p. 227.

struck them. But the paralysis experienced by Perano and Oliver and many others, whether they describe it as being caught in "rubber lassos," or stopped in their tracks by a "pressure" or "invisible wall," seems to result from their becoming "entangled" in some sort of invisible field.

Paralysis is common in close encounters and is often associated with other effects. In another French incident on September 17, 1954, as Yves David was riding his bicycle near Le Pontereau, Dept. of Vienne, he began to feel an itching or prickling reminiscent of an electric shock, then felt paralyzed. He saw a dark UFO nine feet long. A small "creature" approached him, touched his shoulder, said something in an unknown language, and returned to the UFO, which flew away at "amazing speed," emitting green light. David then found himself able to move. The encounter occurred at 10:30 at night.[20]

Then, on the evening of October 20, Jean Schoubrenner was driving through France's Turquenstein forest between Schirmeck and St-Quirin-en-Moselle, when he saw a luminous UFO on the road ahead. As he approached to within 60 feet, he felt paralyzed and his car's engine failed. The car rolled further, and Schoubrenner felt an increasing sensation of heat throughout his body. After seconds, the UFO flew away and the symptoms abated.[21]

A similar situation was reported from Williston, Florida, on November 2, 1955. C. F. Bell, Deputy-sheriff A. H. Perkins and twelve others watched six UFOs shaped like bells "moving by successive leaps." When one of the objects approached near their patrol car, the car's occupants' limbs "went dead," and their clothes felt very hot.[22]

Witnesses often faint when they come too close to UFOs. Lutz Holtmann was one. Holtmann lost consciousness when approaching a bright, round UFO with "a tripod landing gear and two rows of bright openings" in a forest at Werdehl-Eveking, Germany. He awoke to see it ascending straight up without a sound. The incident happened at 11:00 A.M. on August 25, 1959.[23]

Another apparent effect on people who come into contact with the field is weightlessness. One witness interviewed by Dr. Hynek knew what weightlessness felt like—she was a former Air Force stewardess. While driving near Cockrane, Wisconsin, on the evening of April 3, 1968, she saw another car's lights fail and pulled her own car to the side of the road as its lights began to dim. She then noticed a red-orange, crescent-shaped or triangle-shaped UFO approaching and hovering above the cars. Her engine, radio and lights failed, and she was unable to start her car—although she did say the starter groaned briefly. While the UFO was present, she felt weightless and experienced ab-

20. Michel, *Straight Line Mystery*, pp. 58-59.
21. *Ibid.*, pp. 203-204.
22. From Richard Hall, *UFO Evidence* (Washington: National Investigations Committee on Aerial Phenomena, 1964), as reported in Vallée, *Magonia*, p. 252.
23. From *UFO Nachrichten* (62 Wiesbaden, Schierstein, Milanstrasse 5, Germany) Oct. 1959, as reported in Vallée, *Magonia*, p. 277.

solute silence, hearing none of the usual background sounds. She also reported that her feet burned after the experience.[24]

The eerie silence—the total absence of the usual ambient sounds—is quite common. On the evening of November 4, 1975, six motorists observed a cylindrical UFO 75 feet in diameter with blue and green rotating lights and square windows hovering at treetop height over woods in Ross, Ohio. It began spinning, and a red sphere of light dropped from it. The witnesses' car's engine and lights failed, and insect sounds ceased. The sphere disappeared, and what appeared to be blue, glowing "landing gear" emerged from the craft. It appeared to land, then flew away, whereupon the car started and the insect sounds resumed.[25]

Nutria hunter Robert Melerine was paddling up the Dike Canal in St. Bernard Parish, Louisiana, at 8:45 on the night of January 21, 1977, when he was suddenly approached from the northwest by a glowing UFO. As it hovered overhead, lighting the area, Melerine felt warmth and was struck by the complete absence of the usual ambient sounds such as frogs croaking, duck calls and wind.

Melerine returned to camp and picked up his hunting partner, Irwin Menesses (a captain at the St. Bernard Fire Department). The two men motored slowly southeastward down the canal. The UFO returned and hovered about 65 or 70 feet over their boat. Again there was a complete absence of sound. They thought their outboard motor was still running, but it did not propel the boat, which remained dead in the water. Melerine's hair stood on end as the hunters watched the 15-to-25-foot round craft. It had a crosshatched appearance. When it flew away, the boat suddenly lurched forward, and both witnesses were thrown down into it.[26]

At about the same time of night on October 9 of that same year, Pinkerton security guard Holly Prunchak was the percipient of a similar occurrence at a Walcott, Iowa, French-Hecht plant. She reported that all noise from cattle and crickets ceased while a lighted, oval UFO descended across the road from the plant.[27] An AC-powered FM radio, battery-powered walkie-talkie, street light and nearby TV also quit temporarily during the encounter.[28]

The strange silence has long perplexed and frustrated researchers looking for answers. While physical effects like muscle paralysis, interference with automobile starters and perhaps even polarization of light might be explainable in terms of some unknown type of electric and/or magnetic field, electric and magnetic explanations seem to fall short of solving the "complete absence of sound" riddle.

If we accept that UFOs are at times encased in time-warping fields, however, such an effect would seem to follow quite naturally. Any kind

24. Hynek, *Experience*, pp. 116-118.
25. Stringfield, *Situation Red* (Doubleday), p. 20.
26. Ted Peters, "Warm Light Stops Everything!" *MUFON UFO Journal*, Feb. 1977, pp. 3-6.
27. "CE II in Iowa," *International UFO Reporter*, 2, No. 12 (Dec. 1977), pp. 4, 8.
28. Hendry, *op. cit.*, pp. 119-120.

of sound would of course be subject to the Doppler effect. Since the range of human hearing is very limited, only a slight Doppler effect could lower the frequencies of all audible sounds into the subsonic range or increase their frequencies into the ultrasonic range.

Witnesses who report that the "aliens" voices sound "high and singsongy" may be hearing evidence of this effect. To quote John Keel:

> ...I have pointed out the entities' obsession with time. Their be-
> havior...suggests their problems in adjusting to our time frame. For ex-
> ample, their rapid-fire unintelligible "language"...like "a speeded up
> phonograph record" could be caused by their failure to adjust to our
> time cycle when they enter our space-time continuum. They are talking
> at a faster rate because their time is different from ours.[29]

Some witnesses report that even their own voices change during close encounters. The harrowing January 20, 1988, experience of the Knowles family serves as a good case in point. At about 5:30 A.M., Faye Knowles, her grown sons, Wayne, Sean, and Patrick and the family dogs were driving eastward along the Eyre Highway in the middle of the barren Nullarbor Plain in remote Western Australia. They were somewhere between the Madura roadhouse and Mundrabilla when they spotted a group of lights in the predawn darkness. They began to hear static and noise on their car's radio, then saw a brilliant UFO, white with a yellow center, like an egg cup with an egg in it.

Sean made two U-turns to look, then the UFO sped up, landed atop the car and, while going 120 m.p.h., lifted it into the air! Faye reached up out of her window to touch the object. It felt hot and spongy. While the car was airborne, *their voices sounded deep and sluggish, like their speech was in slow motion.* A fine, black, ash-like dust covered the car inside and out. The dogs "went crazy." The Knowleses felt disoriented and thought they would die.

The UFO then lowered the car back down to the road (or dropped it), blowing out a rear tire in the process. The terrified family stopped the car and hid behind bushes until the object flew away, then changed their tire and fled.

The Knowleses felt ill. The hand and arm that Faye stuck out the window to touch the UFO swelled. Their dog's hair fell out in patches. The car's top had dents in each of its four corners. The tire was blown around the rim.

A truck driver and the crews of the tuna fishing boats *Monika* and *Empress Lady* independently reported sightings in the same area that morning (confirmed by police), and there were other reports before and after the incident. It was reported that *Monika's* crew also experienced the slow-motion speech, but this was later denied by her owner.[30, 31]

Jacques Vallée reported two cases of distorted sound in *UFO Chronicles of the Soviet Union: A Cosmic Samizdat.* The first occurred

---

29. Keel, *Mothman Prophesies*, p. 173.
30. Randle, *The UFO Casebook*, p. 205.
31. Paul Norman, "UFO Encounters Along the Nullarbor Plain," in *The UFO Report*, ed. Timothy Good (London: Sidgwick and Jackson, 1989; rpt. New York: Avon Books, 1991), pp. 146-163.

on July 18, 1967, at 2:47 in the afternoon at a place called Am-
vrosieyevka. Y. Divak, a student, was fishing with a friend when a UFO
with a dull finish passed overhead. The water reflected its image. During the incident, railroad sounds and noise from town sounded different or disappeared.[32]

The second encounter was more dramatic and is reminiscent of
the Knowles ordeal. At about 6:00 on the evening of October 11, 1989,
16-year-old Natasha Barinova was in her front yard in the village of
Maelski (in the Caucusus near Nalchik) when she felt as if something
lifted her up. A net with a bright white something in its middle fell out
of the sky toward her. When she reached out to shove it away, it
shocked her, burning her hands severely. She screamed and her voice
sounded strangely distorted—"sharp and shrill." Members of her family
hurried outside and saw her—in the air—less than 50 feet from a hovering flying saucer. The object disappeared. The witness was temporarily paralyzed. She was treated for stress at a hospital. The ends of
her fingers were enlarged, as if something had pulled at the skin.[33]

Another witness heard his own voice distorted when he attempted
to speak with the occupants of a UFO that he encountered near Jaraba, Zaragoza, Spain, on an October morning in 1978 (see Chapter 5).
He also experienced several effects that would seem to be electrical—
"metallic teeth," a buzzing sound and heating. Also the film he had
been using to photograph eagles was completely fogged.

Could it be that *both* electric/magnetic *and* temporal effects are
created by the fields surrounding UFOs? Could time-warping fields
have electromagnetic side effects? Or are time warps themselves
achieved via some type of electromagnetic forces?

Cameras, automobiles, radios and people are not the only things
to malfunction in the vicinity of UFOs. Other things that should not be
affected by electromagnetic fields are also affected. Italian farmer
Amerigo Lorenzini was unable to get his rifle to fire at "three dwarfs
dressed in metallic diving suits" who emerged from a bright UFO
shaped like a cigar. The little men talked to each other in a language
Lorenzini did not recognize and stole some of his rabbits. Not only did
his gun refuse to fire, but he grew so weak he could not hold on to it,
and it fell to the ground. The UFO flew away, "leaving a bright trail."
The incident occurred on the afternoon of November 14, 1954, at Iso-
la.[34]

Joe Martinez and Albert Gallegos were driving on the east side of
Santa Fe, New Mexico, when they saw a huge, bright, egg-shaped,
slow-moving, humming UFO pass over their car. The car's engine and
clock failed, and Martinez' wrist watch ceased to function.[35]

That incident came exactly three days after the midnight siege of
auto stoppages centered around nearby Levelland, Texas (see Chapter

32. Vallée, *Chronicles*, p. 191.
33. *Ibid.*, pp. 36-37.
34. From *Settimana Incom*, 17 Jun. 1962, as reported in Vallée, *Magonia*, p. 244.
35. From the Santa Fe *New Mexican*, 6 Nov. 1957, as reported in Mebane, p. 246.

4), during which another interesting case was reported that indicates the presence of a field. Frank Williams was driving near Whitharral (not far from Levelland) when he encountered a huge UFO that was pulsating with bright, then dim luminosity. His engine failed, and his headlights began pulsating bright and dim *opposite* the UFO's pulsations. The UFO finally ascended, producing a loud roar, and Williams was able to restart his car.[36]

Mr. R. Sullivan's headlight beams were subject to an even more bizarre field effect. While he was driving from Wycheproof, Australia, to his home in Maryborough, the headlight beams suddenly *bent* to the right side of the road. He saw a luminous, 25-foot-tall, cone-shaped UFO in a plowed paddock (on or near the ground). The bottom was brilliant white; the rest shone "all the colors of the spectrum." It rose soundlessly and shot away at very high speed. A three-foot-wide concave depression was found at the site. It was two to five inches deep. (Coincidentally, only two days later, a car driven by young Gary Taylor, of Carnegie, swerved off the same road at the same place for no apparent reason. It struck a tree, killing Taylor).[37]

This effect has been observed elsewhere. John Keel has this to say about it in *Disneyland of the Gods:*

> There is now strong evidence that some UFOs are surrounded by a force field which exerts a strong influence on the space-time coordinates of our reality. It is not a gravitational pull in the accepted sense of the term, yet it possesses some of the characteristics of gravity. The headlights of a car in England were diverted by such a space-time warp.[38]

One year to the day after Mr. Sullivan's unnerving sighting, Justice of the Peace John H. Demler was driving near Jones–town, Pennsylvania. At 7:45 P.M., his car's engine and lights failed. He saw a UFO 33 feet in diameter hovering low over the car, making a noise like an electric motor and producing sparks. Demler noticed an odor like "sulphur and camphorated oil." The UFO flew away, at which time the car rocked and was pulled. Twelve hours later, Demler suffered peeling skin and perspiration.[39]

A teenaged driver named Edward Bruns was the victim of a similar but more dramatic meeting with the unknown on December 20, 1965. He was driving a pickup truck to his farm a few miles from Herman, Minnesota. At 11:45 P.M., he came upon a bright, lighted UFO hovering six feet above the road and covering its entire surface. His truck's engine and lights failed. The UFO began an ascent. He could see inside and described it as red with something that looked like a man moving around inside it. Sparks shot from its underside. As the UFO rose, the truck *rose with it.* The truck ended up in a ditch on the south side of the road pointed north (instead of on the road, pointed west). Bruns'

36. Flammonde, *op. cit.,* p. 290.
37. Lorenzen, *Startling Evidence,* p. 268.
38. Keel, *Disneyland,* pp. 96-97.
39. From NICAP, May 1967, as reported in Vallée, *Magonia,* pp. 342-343.

father and a reporter from the Herman *Review* were unable to find tire marks leading to where the truck rested in the ditch.[40]

The word of a 15-year-old driver whose vehicle had left the road late at night might be ignored but for the fact that other such cases have been reported. One startling incident was witnessed by Adolfo Paolino Pisani on the Andean highway between La Victoria and El Vigia, Venezuela, in January of 1961. Pisani had pulled to the side of the road to let a truck pass, when a brilliant disc that looked like polished blue steel streaked down out of the sky "at incredible speed," coming extremely close to the truck's hood. It turned upward and left—still traveling at very high speed—until it had disappeared. When the UFO rose above the truck, *"the vehicle also rose a few feet in the air and overturned in the direction of the object."* The truck landed on its top.[41]

People and cars aren't the only things that have been bowled over or lifted—apparently accidentally—when they somehow become ensnared in the fields surrounding UFOs. There is at least one reported instance of a horse being affected! It happened on October 16, 1954, during the intense wave of close encounters in France. Guy Puyfourcat was leading a mare by the bridle at Cier-de-Riviere. A small gray UFO rose from the side of the road and flew over the mare, which *rose ten feet* into the air (Puyfourcat had to let go of the bridle) and then fell back to earth as the UFO flew away at a high speed. The animal was paralyzed and terrified by its experience.[42]

On more than one occasion during the same wave, ufonauts must have misjudged just exactly where the perimeter of their crafts' fields were—that is unless they intended to drag a load of dirt along with them as they flew off.

The first case occurred at Poncey-sur-l'Ignon at 8:00 on the evening of October 4, 1954. Yvette Fourneret saw an orange, luminous, elongated UFO nine feet in diameter hovering over the mayor's yard as if about to land. It was only 60 feet away. Frightened, she rushed her young son to the house of a neighbor. Two other neighbors investigated, and although the UFO had already gone, they found a very strange physical trace in the form of a hole 4 1/2 feet long and 20 to 27 inches wide. The dirt had been displaced as if sucked up by a powerful vacuum. Large clods were scattered for 12 feet all around the hole, and some hung from the inside edges. Roots and worms protruded from the edges of the hole unscathed, and the hole was wider halfway down than it was at the surface. There was no evidence whatever that tools had been used to make the excavation. In the center was a plant with a long root which was still attached to the bottom but stripped of all earth, and with all rootlets undamaged. Francois Bouiller then arrived, exclaiming that he had observed a fuselage-shaped, luminous UFO that seemed to turn green the faster it went. Police and military investiga-

40. Steiger, *Flying Saucers Are Hostile*, pp. 43-44.
41. Lorenzen, *Startling Evidence*, pp. 185-186.
42. Vallée, *Magonia*, p. 231.

tors spent days examining the area and interviewing the village's 140 residents and were forced to accept the account.[43]

An even larger crater was found by Italian peasants who watched a UFO landing and takeoff at Po di Gnocca, Italy, in afternoon daylight just eleven days later. The circular, silent craft floated, landed, sat on the ground for a few moments then ascended vertically. Where it had sat, dirt was sucked out of a hole 20 feet in diameter and scattered around its edges in the same manner as the Poncey hole. Nearby trees were "carbonized." Military authorities investigated right away.[44]

At this juncture it may be important to note an observation made by UFO investigator and author Ray Stanford as he considered why the famous Socorro, New Mexico, UFO (seen by police officer Lonnie Zamora in 1964) appeared to use two distinct modes of propulsion:

> *Within twenty feet or so above the ground, reaction propulsion might have been preferred because of a danger in using the silent (field type?) propulsion. Depending on the type of field involved, certain objects on the ground might have been pulled up in response to the field, perhaps to strike the craft and damage it.*[45]

Wilson Lutosa found that water is also affected. On April 15, 1958, Lutosa and many others watched a UFO near Paripueira, Brazil. It was 40 feet thick, shaped like a lens with portholes. It gave off a red glow and a "whirring" noise. As it hovered 50 feet above the ocean more than 130 feet away, the water underneath it seemed to be disturbed, as if attracted toward it. The craft ascended and descended for over an hour.[46]

Twelve boaters on Switzerland's Leman Lake caught sight of a saucer in broad daylight on August 16 of that same year. It had a windowed "cabin" and a spinning rim, and was about 33 feet in diameter. Without making a sound, it came close to the water, creating "a noticeable current." It made "several leaps in mid-air," then left at extreme speed.[47]

And it seems that ufonauts are able to use their fields as nets to "collect" people the way we collect butterflies. There have been many instances in which they have picked up cars or seized airplanes. John Jenssen may have been the victim of a temporary kidnapping of this sort while flying at 6,000 feet on July 23, 1947. Jenssen, the editor of an American aviation journal, noticed a bright light above his plane, then the plane's engine sputtered and quit! The air speed indicator read zero...but instead of nosing down toward the ground as would be expected, the plane remained in its normal flying attitude—with its nose to the horizon. Jenssen experienced a prickling feeling and felt as if he were being watched, then saw two disc-shaped UFOs above him. The closer one looked metallic. It had a "flanged and projecting rim"

43. Michel, *Straight Line Mystery*, pp. 132-136.
44. *Ibid.*, pp. 180-181.
45. Ray Stanford, *Socorro 'Saucer' in a Pentagon Pantry* (Austin, Texas: Blueapple Books, 1976), p. 76.
46. From *SBEDV Bulletin*, as reported in Vallée, *Magonia*, p. 271.
47. Vallée, *Magonia*, p. 272.

and portholes like those of a ship. Jenssen felt an urge to turn his magneto on, and control was returned to him.[48]

John Jenssen was lucky. He landed safely and was able to tell of his harrowing adventure. Others have not been so fortunate. Rivalino Mafra da Silva, for instance, faded away into nothingness right before his sons' eyes! On August 19, 1962, a neighbor, Antonio Rocha, saw two spheres flying over da Silva's house. Da Silva and his three young sons were unable to sleep on the night of the 20th because of voice-like noises and "shadowy figures" gliding through the house. The next morning, one of the sons, Raimundo, left the house and was immediately confronted by two humming, flickering spheres that hovered six feet off the ground. Each of them had, attached to it, something that looked like a tail and something that looked like an antenna. One of the objects was black, the other black and white. Raimundo called to his father, who seemed mesmerized and warned his sons to stay back, then walked toward the UFOs. When he was within seven feet, the objects came together, raising dust and foul-smelling yellow smoke which enveloped da Silva. When the smoke dissipated, da Silva and the spheres were gone. Authorities mounted an extensive investigation, but were unable to solve the mystery.[49]

Viewed one at a time, these anecdotes seem to be nothing more than interesting bits of nonsense. But there are hundreds of them, and the more such anecdotes are considered *en masse*, the clearer the picture becomes.

UFOs are able to carry around with them a protective envelope—like a tiny alternative universe—within the influence of which events normally thought to be impossible happen as a matter of course. Although invisible itself, this region can be detected indirectly by observation of the effects it exerts on matter and energy. Its sphere of influence can apparently reach from a few feet to a mile or more beyond the craft. Its influence can be either minimal or profound and, as is the case with a gravitational or magnetic field, seems to become progressively greater as one moves closer to its source. It is "a region of space characterized by a physical property"—in other words, a field.[50]

In an attempt to explain how UFOs move so quickly, turn at right angles, disappear, etc., we postulated that they might be surrounded by fields that warp space-time. Although the evidence is far from conclusive that these fields exist, it grows more compelling as we consider each account. Could the same time-warping fields cause the bizarre gravitational, electrical, magnetic and temporal anomalies reported by so many who encounter UFOs at close range? Did Nélson Leite lose all sense of time and discover to his surprise that he was no longer walking toward the UFO in Brazil because he had been "frozen" in time? Did

48. Harold T. Wilkins, *Flying Saucers on the Attack* (New York: Citadel Press, 1954; rpt. New York: Ace Books, Inc., 1967), pp. 70-71.
49. Lorenzen, *Startling Evidence*, pp. 213-215.
50. *American Heritage Dictionary*, Second College Edition (Boston: Houghton Mifflin Company, 1982).

John Jenssen's air-speed indicator read zero because he was frozen in time? When Rivalino da Silva disappeared, did he move into another time frame? Is he alive and well and living a hundred years in the future, a real-life Buck Rogers? Is this what happens to some of the thousands of people who disappear every year without a trace? Are they providing sperm and ova in laboratories in another era? Are they on "field trips" against their wills?

11

...contactees have reported that the beings are frequently interested in how time is measured here. There are numerous instances in UFOlogy of time being speeded up, slowed, or distorted. These aberrations in time may be a clue to the origin of the ufonauts.
—Warren Smith[1]

What Time Is It?

One July evening in 1957, a prominent Brazilian lawyer named João de Freitas Guimares had a jarring experience while walking on a Bela Island beach alone. He saw a UFO come up out of the ocean and approach him. Two men with long, blond hair and tight, green coveralls invited him aboard without speaking. He spoke to them in French, English, Italian, and Portuguese, but they did not respond. He climbed a ladder and was taken for a ride for an estimated 40 minutes, during which time his watch stopped. He felt cold in his genitals. The men showed him a star chart, apparently tried to convey that they would return to see him again, and took him back to his beach.[2]

The stopping of wrist watches has long been a trademark of UFOs. You may remember that Barney Hill's watch stopped and so did Betty's. Clocks are also affected. Ted Phillips, an investigator with the Center for UFO Studies (CUFOS) who has specialized in gathering physical evidence, investigated a case in a small Tennessee town in which a UFO flew over the home of a man who collected antique clocks, and every clock in his collection, electric or otherwise, stopped.[3]

Other mechanical equipment is apparently affected as well. According to a message from the American Embassy in Kuwait City to the U.S. State Department, automatic oil pumping equipment (which is designed to shut itself off when a damage condition occurs and can only be restarted manually) shut off and restarted by itself when a UFO passed over and then left the area in the northern oil fields of Kuwait.

1. Smith, *op. cit.,* p. 11.
2. Keel, *Trojan Horse,* pp. 202-203.
3. Stringfield, *Situation Red* (Doubleday), p. 197.

The incident took place on November 9, 1978.[4] The only logical answer to this mystery seems to be that the pumps did not actually shut off, but were running in slow motion during the time the UFO was present, so that it appeared that they were shut off.

If watch, clock and pump stoppages might be explainable in terms of electromagnetic effects (although most antique clocks are made of brass, which is nonmagnetic), other bizarre happenings are not. Mário Restier's incredible adventure is one example.

At 5:00 in the afternoon on December 4, 1949, Mário was returning to his home in Barra Mansa, Rio de Janeiro, Brazil, from Volta Redonda, when a disc 50 feet in diameter landed 30 to 50 feet from the highway. A voice spoke to him in Portuguese, and two people 5' 5" tall who wore "Roman" skirts and helmets invited him to take a ride. He was placed in a liquid bath to nullify the force of acceleration (the same claim has been made by Betty Andreasson and others) and was apparently flown to "another planet," where tall, hairless people lived in domed cities with elevated roadways.

After a few hours, he grew homesick and was returned in the same type of vehicle, again in a liquid bath. Although only three days had passed for him, it was now April 14, 1950—*four months later*. Restier felt compelled to study physics. He had another subsequent encounter in September of 1956. He believed he could build a spacecraft engine, and that he had permission from the entities to do so.[5]

Now if Restier were the only one who reported such an unbelievable "telescoping" of time, his testimony might be rejected. Or we might conclude that he had been placed in "suspended animation" for four months. But his claims are not unique.

On April 25, 1977, an astonishing thing happened in the northern tip of Chile, near Putre, in the Arica region. Cpl. Armando Valdés, leader of a border patrol of the Rancagua Regiment, Huamachuco Brigade of the Chilean Army (based at Arica) and his men watched one of two big, violet, glowing objects moving silently at a low altitude behind a low stone wall. Valdés had just recently shaved. At 4:15 A.M. (Valdés looked at his watch), he stepped over the wall and approached the UFO, challenging it. As Humberto Rojas, Iván Robles, Germán Riquelmo, Raúl Salinas, Pedro Rosales, Juan Reyes and Julio Rato looked on, Valdés suddenly disappeared as if by magic! Fifteen minutes later, he reappeared among them just as abruptly. He was dazed, mumbling something about someone returning soon. Neither he nor his men could explain where he had been or how he had returned, but he now had a five-day growth of beard, and his calendar watch, which had stopped, showed the date April 30![6] The governor of Arica Province, Col. Oscar Figueroa, immediately told the press nothing could be published about the case without his approval and confiscated infor-

---

4. Message 290606Z, Jan. 1979, from the American Embassy in Kuwait City to the U.S. State Department, as quoted in Fawcett, *op. cit.*, p.90.
5. Richard W. Heiden, "A 1949 Brazilian Contactee—Part 1," *Flying Saucer Review*, 27, No. 5 (1982), pp. 28-iii.

mation about it. A spokesman for the Chilean Ministry of Defense said the affair was undergoing an intensive investigation.[7, 8]

An even more bizarre case has been reported by Mr. Zhang Ke-Tao (Chinese UFO Research Society, Peking branch). In 1975, on a fall evening, two Chinese People's Liberation Army soldiers saw a huge, saucer-shaped UFO circling above them and giving off orange light beams. One ran to camp; the second stayed to observe. The second man could not be found until several hours later. When he was found, his memory was gone, his watch had stopped, and his hair, eyebrows and beard had *grown very long*. His weapons and watch were slightly magnetized.[9]

There are other instances of mysterious aging effects caused by UFOs. One occurred on January 8, 1981. On that day, an elderly man named Renato Nicolai watched as a six- foot-by-eight-foot, gray, saucer-shaped UFO crashed on his land in Trans-en-Provence, France, and then took off again. Groupe d'Étude des Phénomènes Aérospatiaux Non-Identifiés (GEPAN) investigators found two concentric circles on the ground. They took samples of the vegetation, which were analyzed at the Institut National de la Recherche Agronomique by plant traumatologist Michael Bounias. Bounias found that the leaves had aged in an unexpected way (and also lost a third of their chlorophyll). The effect could not be duplicated in the laboratory. Jean-Jacques Velasco, who headed GEPAN, suggested that the plants resembled those whose seeds had been bombarded by gamma rays—but the samples were not radioactive.[10, 11]

Something strange happened to Nicolai's plants. And to the Chinese and Chilean soldiers. And to Mário Restier. Were they caught in time warps? Do time warps exist? John Keel makes this observation in *Disneyland of the Gods*:

> ...*motorists have...traveled great distances in impossibly short periods of time. In a number of well-documented instances, airplanes have also passed through one of these inexplicable time warps. Such distortions of space can only be accounted for by some direct, mysterious warping of our physical reality.... Space itself can be folded somehow so that the immediate reality of a plane or car...and the seemingly fixed distance between points A and B are altered. Ma-*

6. Publishers Note: It is interesting to note that several witnesses reported seeing a clean-shaven Eduard Meier leave for a contact and return 24 hours later with a five-day growth of beard. Meier then slept for 24 hours. His time travels are referred to in Gary Kinder, *Light Years: An Investigation Into the Extraterrestrial Experiences of Eduard Meier* (New York: The Atlantic Monthly Press, 1987). Further information can be found in W.C. Stevens, ed. *Message From the Pleiades: The Contact Notes of Eduard Billy Meier, Vols. 1 and 2* (Tucson, Arizona: UFO Photo Archives, 1989 and 1990).
7. Gordon Creighton, "The Arica Encounter: Chilean Soldier's 'Trip Into the Fourth Dimension'?" *Flying Saucer Review*, 23, No. 5, pp. 8-9.
8. Fowler, *Watchers*, p. 210.
9. Paul Dong, *Fiedie Bai Wen Bai Da* (Hong Kong: Deli Shuju, 1983), as quoted in "Extracts from Paul Dong's *Fiedie Bai Wen Bai Da* (Questions and Answers on UFOs)," trans. Gordon Creighton, *Flying Saucer Review*, 29, No. 6 (1984), p. 17.
10. Jerome Clark, "Unsolved Mysteries: From France to New York, the Five Thorniest Sightings of the Eighties," *Omni*, Dec. 1990, p. 100.

chines and people caught in these space warps also experience a compression of time. [12]

A contractor from Boyup Brook, Australia, must have been caught in a time warp at 9:35 on the night of October 30, 1967. He was driving near Boyup Brook on the Kojonup-Mayanup Road when his engine and headlights failed. His car stopped, but he felt no deceleration. He looked up through a two-foot-wide beam that seemed to be aimed at him. He saw a pulsating, oval UFO surrounded by a blue glow. It appeared to be 30 feet in diameter. He watched for several minutes, then the UFO moved away, and *the witness suddenly found himself traveling along at 60 to 65 m.p.h.* (as he had been before the sighting), his engine and headlights functioning normally. [13]

During a wave of sightings in New Mexico, a motorist had trouble with a device that indirectly measures time—his speedometer. Trent Lindsey, his wife and his son Byron were driving on highway 54 on the morning of November 7, 1957, when the speedometer on their car began changing wildly between 60 and 100 m.p.h. They then saw a bright object like polished metal with sharply defined edges and no visible exhaust or propellers flying to the southwest. When it was gone, the speedometer once again worked normally. Lindsey never had speedometer trouble before the incident, nor has he since. [14]

Alan Cave's 1981 experience was even more perplexing. One morning in October, Cave, a salesman from Taunton, Somerset, England, who still says he doesn't believe in flying saucers, was on his way from Bath to Stroud. He knew his watch and digital pen were set to the right time; he had just checked them before he left. Precisely as he drove under an odd orange something that looked a bit like a cloud in the sky above the road, an announcer on his car's radio read the 11 A.M. news headlines. He checked his watch again. It said it was 8:00, not 11:00. Confused, he looked at his pen. It said 9:00. Then he watched his speedometer turn *backwards* 300 miles! The British Flying Saucer Research Bureau investigated several reports of UFO activity in the area. [15]

At 8:35 on the night of March 30, 1966, a woman and her four children saw a red-orange, oval UFO while driving near Lexisburg, Indiana. As it approached the car, they heard a pulsating sound that seemed to come from the car radio. This seemed to increase in frequency as the UFO came nearer (as if time were being compressed in proportion to their distance from it). The object followed the car for eight miles, then turned blue-white and accelerated out of sight. [16]

Charles Gilpin and his wife and two children encountered a time anomaly in rural Kentucky near Gravel Switch a few minutes before midnight on July 18, 1976. They saw a silent, disc-shaped UFO 75 feet

11. Vallée, *Confrontations*, p. 106.
12. Keel, *Disneyland*, pp. 96-97.
13. Keyhoe, *op. cit.*, p. 35-36.
14. Lorenzen, *Startling Evidence*, pp. 99-100.
15. Blundell, pp. 32-33.
16. From Air Technical Intelligence Center files, as reported in Vallée, *Magonia*, p. 325.

in diameter approach and fly along about 30 feet above their pickup truck. Gilpin felt he no longer had control of the steering wheel, and the speedometer indicated 85 m.p.h., although *scenery seemed to be passing at only about 15 m.p.h.* When they came to a lighted farmhouse, Mrs. Gilpin and the children ran to it, but Gilpin was then paralyzed and could not. The UFO flew away, and the Gilpins continued their journey home. En route they saw 18 other people watching the UFO.[17]

An even more incredible case was reported from Africa. At 2:15 one June morning in 1974, a South African couple drove south from Umvuma, Rhodesia, to Fort Victoria. They noticed they were paced by a bright, revolving light. Their headlights faded, and some external force took control of the car; accelerator, brakes and steering did not affect its progress. Temperature in the car fell about 30 degrees. When they neared Fort Victoria, the light sped away, and the car once again responded.

Soon after they resumed their trip south, two lights appeared and paced them, and they once again lost control. This time engine and road noise ceased, and they appeared to be traveling 100 m.p.h. (when their car was only capable of about 75 m.p.h.) on a straight road through swamps (although, in actuality, the road is winding and through arid land).

Under the hypnosis of Paul Obertick, M.D., of Durban, Natal, Peter recalled contact with beings and details of a craft, which he said was 80 or 90 feet wide. When the UFOs left, they seemed to vanish instantly. Also under hypnosis, Peter stated: "They can travel on time. Speed of light is too slow to cover billions of miles in seconds. If they want to go from point A to point B, they have to go back in time. They are time travelers, not space travelers."[18]

Percipients of UFO close encounters often talk about "slow motion." At 7:00 P.M. on November 16, 1973, two boys playing in a Lemon Grove, California, vacant lot came upon a gray, domed UFO about 20 feet in diameter hovering 18 inches off the ground. One of them rapped on it with a flashlight, producing a metallic sound. The dome lit red and illuminated the area, a row of green lights began blinking around the rim, and the UFO lifted to about three feet off the ground and started rotating and making a whooshing noise. The boys fled, feeling "chills, tingly and weak." They felt as though they were going to faint and seemed to be "running in slow motion." The UFO flew away southwestward and disappeared into the clouds. Traces were found at the landing site, including square depressions in the hard ground that seemed to have been made by a very heavy object. Five neighbors experienced television interference at the time on three different channels.[19]

At 5:15 on January 23, 1976, Shelley McLenaghan, 17, saw a house-sized, red-and-green lighted object with a flat top, sloping sides

17. Stringfield, *Situation Red* (Doubleday), pp. 211-212.
18. Bill Faill, "UFO Car-napping in Rhodesia," *Fate*, Jan. 1977, pp. 34-42.
19. Stringfield, *Situation Red* (Doubleday), pp. 116-118.

and tripod legs. She experienced vibrating teeth, an odd taste in her mouth and pressure on her head and shoulders. When she ran away, her limbs moved in slow motion, and when she screamed, she was unable to hear anything. The next day she suffered from a purple rash on the upper fourth of her body and aching joints. Some of her fillings came out and the rest deteriorated. The incident took place near Bolton, in the northern part of England.[20]

Just a few months before that, on a fall day in 1975, Monty Skelton was hunting quail with another man about 18 miles north of Joplin, Missouri. Skelton (who is the founder of Intercontinental Association Research Enterprises in Kansas City) noticed that their bird dog seemed to be moving in slow motion. He looked up and saw a metallic-looking, oval-shaped UFO 70 to 80 feet in diameter. It looked like it was preparing to land. Skelton noticed a complete absence of ambient sounds. The UFO then took off at incredible speed. A rural newspaper carrier reported that he had seen UFOs on numerous occasions during the 1970s while delivering newspapers after 11:00 P.M. in an area just a few miles from where Skelton had been hunting. He also reported the weird lack of bird and bug sounds when one of the UFOs was near. He said that although UFOs occasionally appeared to have landed, they usually flew slowly in a grid pattern, as if they were searching for something.[21]

An even more intriguing slow-motion UFO close encounter was reported that same autumn in the small, remote, northern California community of Happy Camp. On October 25, two electricians, Steve Harris and Stan Gayer, watching from Shivar Saddle, near Happy Camp, saw a red, glowing, oscillating UFO. Later they saw a similar object resting on the side of Cade Mountain.

On October 27, they went back to the spot where the landed object had been. They heard a noise that sounded somewhat like a siren and saw two silver, luminous eyes in the undergrowth. They shone a spotlight toward the eyes (it was dark out), but something prevented the light from it from illuminating anything, even the vegetation.

They drove back into Happy Camp, then returned to the site with 62-year-old Helen White (who brought a camera) and a 17-year-old student. When they arrived, Harris fired rifle shots into the bushes. Two figures with headgear similar to welders' helmets emerged and moved toward the witnesses, stopping 50 feet away. Helen White was unable to snap a photograph. The witnesses experienced oppressively hot, heavy, choking air. They fled down the mountain. A glowing, red object followed them.

On November 2, Helen, Stan, Steve and two other people drove back to Cade Mountain to investigate once again. On a dirt road in a canyon at the foot of the mountain, they encountered a heavy fog. From that point on, their recollection of events is incomplete. They later re-

20. From the *Australasian Post*, 30 Jul. 1987, as recounted in Vallée, *Confrontations*, p. 122.
21. *The Mike Murphy Show*, KCMO Radio, Kansas City, Missouri, 12 Jan. 1989.

membered seeing boulders fall to the ground around their truck from
the surrounding cliffs and seeing a hovering UFO. A being told Steve
he wouldn't need his gun. Helen remembered warning a man in a long
coat about the falling rocks. He responded that he would be in no danger.

Helen was then abducted. She rose into the UFO in a beam of light
(this is a commonly-reported occurrence in abduction cases). The ufonauts granted her permission to take a memento for proof of her experience, then later reneged (the same thing happened to Betty Hill and
others). This angered her, and she complained bitterly. She later told
Jacques Vallée that while the abduction was transpiring, everything
happened "in slow motion," and that she was perplexed by the fact that
the UFO was considerably larger inside than outside. Happy Camp
played host to numerous other strange phenomena in the late 1970s,
including UFOs pursued by jets, poltergeist activity and a huge tree
that was inexplicably snapped in half and tossed across a road.[22]

Coincidentally, the most famous UFO encounter involving slow
motion happened exactly one year to the day before the Happy Camp
affair and also involved an unidentified craft that appeared to be much
larger inside than it looked outside. It involved a Rawlins, Wyoming,
man named Carl Higdon. On the afternoon of October 25, 1974, Higdon shot at an elk in the Medicine Bow National Forest south of Rawlins. The bullet left the gun barrel silently and in slow motion and fell
to the ground about 50 feet away. He could hear nothing and experienced a tingling sensation in his spine. He then saw a 6-foot, 180-
pound humanoid that had no chin, eyebrows, lips, or ears.

The being asked him if he was hungry, then waved a pointed object
toward Higdon's hand. A packet of pills floated over to him. The being
told him to take one of the pills, saying it would last him four days. Higdon did so—as if he had no control over his actions. Behind the being,
Higdon could see a shining, featureless, box-shaped object. The being
asked him if he would like to come with him, and he suddenly found
himself strapped to a chair in what was apparently a craft with transparent walls. At one point, another being suddenly appeared beside
him.

He was taken to a "planet" that the beings said was "163,000 *light
miles*" away (instead of light years). Higdon concluded that time passed
differently for the humanoids. Also taken were the five elk at which he
had been shooting. The elk had been paralyzed and were in another
compartment behind a transparent wall. Higdon was bothered by brilliant, colored lights and was told he would be returned to Earth.

He then found himself wandering a dirt road in confusion. He located his truck and radioed for help. His truck was eventually towed
out of a ravine, where it had been stuck axle-deep. It seemed impossible to his rescuers that he could have driven his pickup (not four-wheel
drive) to the spot. Higdon was delirious and was admitted at Carbon

22. Vallée, *Confrontations*, pp. 164-169.

County Memorial Hospital. He was released on the 26th, but had to stay home for three weeks to recover mentally and physically.

The *Rawlins Daily Times* reported the incident. Dr. R. Leo Sprinkle (associate professor at the University of Wyoming) hypnotized Higdon, learning the following further details: The being was named "Ausso One." The beings hunted and fished on Earth for food and breeding stock. Higdon's truck was instantly "teleported" five miles to the sinkhole where the searchers found it.

Higdon kept the bullet he had fired when his bizarre adventure began. Ballistics experts could not explain how it had been "turned inside out." Higdon felt he might have been returned to Earth as soon as he arrived because the entities had discovered during an examination that he had had a vasectomy. The search party that found Higdon saw the forest become illuminated inexplicably and saw "an eerie light" in a nearby grove.

While on the "other planet," Higdon saw normal humans in normal dress. Ausso would have preferred to keep Higdon's rifle (because it was "primitive"), but this was not allowed.[23]

Like Helen White, Higdon was very puzzled by the fact that when he saw the UFO from the outside, it looked quite small, yet when he found himself (apparently) inside it, it seemed quite large—large enough, in fact, to accommodate several elk that appeared to have been captured and placed in a state of suspended animation.

Other percipients have been similarly perplexed by what seem to them impossible spatial relationships. The Heraldsburg, California, incident is a good example. At 8:30 P.M. on August 30, 1977, a Mrs. Cray, her son Bob (19), daughter Cathy (18), son Jeff and daughter Josette saw a lighted, 50-foot object very close to their car as Bob drove them home from a football game. They said time seemed to be passing very slowly, as if they were in a dream, running in slow motion. They were also confused about the direction and distance of the object. They questioned how it could be moving north, as it seemed to them to be doing, because it was following them and they were going south. And they could not grasp why it seemed they could touch the UFO, which was 10 to 20 feet away from them, or why the nearby house they were trying to reach seemed so far away. In all, there were nine witnesses to the Heraldsburg event. Some of them suffered nausea, vomiting, headaches and trouble sleeping and eating normally.[24]

A man who claims to have photographed a captured UFO and the autopsy of its dead occupants for the Air Force told UFO investigator John Lear of a disorienting spatial paradox. "Mike" said that the object, located in a secret underground installation two hours' drive from Norton Air Force Base in California, was only about 30 feet wide on the outside, but was too large to throw a football across on the inside.[25]

23. Smith, *op. cit.*, pp. 6-17.
24. Vallée, *Confrontations*, pp. 71-78.
25. Leonard Stringfield, "UFO Crash Retrievals: Is the Cover-Up Lifting?" in Good, *The UFO Report*, pp. 191-192.

The experiences of these witnesses and others imply that the fields surrounding UFOs can warp space as well as time. Perhaps this should not surprise us as much as it does, since physicists tell us that space and time are inextricably interlocked, and in fact may simply be two different abstract ways of describing what is more accurately labeled "space-time." Dr. Vallée has this to say about the curious paradoxes reported by witnesses:

> If there are more than four dimensions, as many theoretical physicists now suspect, it may be interesting to speculate: a hypercraft capable of topological inversion into our space-time continuum could indeed be larger on the inside than on the outside.[26]

A few witnesses have reported time *delays*. At 1:00 in the morning on December 30, 1980, a Bentwaters AFB security policeman rushed to Rendlesham Forest, an area of woods in the English countryside a few miles from Bentwaters, to staff a trailer-mounted light for illuminating large areas. Before leaving the base, he saw animals running out of the nearby woods. His jeep followed others in a convoy into the Forest. Their orders were to leave their weapons behind.

In a clearing around which men and cameras were assembled, he saw a transparent, disc-shaped UFO about 50 feet in diameter filled with a "bright, pulsating, yellow mist" and hovering a foot above the ground. A red light sped toward the disc, hovered above it for a minute, then disintegrated, whereupon the disc was replaced by a bright, white, domed disc with an intricate surface and two short, wing-like protuberances.

He and others walked around the object. They noticed that their own shadows (which were cast upon the UFO by the gas-powered lights they had brought) were bent up at the head and *took another step after they themselves had stopped, as if delayed*. They tested this effect several times, then the security policeman lost consciousness. He awoke in bed the next morning, fully clothed and with mud on his pants. He was warned to forget—not discuss—the incident.[27]

Time. Somehow it is simply not as it should be in the vicinity of UFOs. As Charles Bowen points out in *The Humanoids*, ufonauts are apparently able to enter and leave their vehicles instantaneously.[28] Cars quit and then start of their own accord, people become paralyzed or age years in hours, bullets fly in slow motion, clocks and speedometers don't work properly—even shadows misbehave.

The occupants of UFOs habitually refer to time. They frequently ask witnesses questions like "What time are we in?" or "What is your time cycle?"[29] The ufonauts tell the witnesses that they (the witnesses) are "caught in time." They also say they (the ufonauts) must leave because they haven't much time, but they promise to "return in time." And they often do. The same witnesses see UFOs—and even the same

26. Vallée, *Confrontations*, p. 169.
27. Fawcett, *op. cit.*, pp. 215-216.
28. Charles Bowen, "Few and Far Between," in Bowen, ed., *The Humanoids*, pp. 23-36.
29. Keel, *Trojan Horse*, p. 184.

individual occupants—time and time again, sometimes throughout their lives, as if the ufonauts are keeping track of them.

Occasionally a witness will encounter a UFO at the same spot in which he had an earlier encounter at the same time of day. This was the case with the rural newspaper carrier, who drove exactly the same lonely route through the sleeping countryside night after night at the same late hour—which happens to be when most UFO activity occurs. He noted that the craft seemed to float slowly over the fields in a grid pattern, as if they were searching for something. Could it be that ufonauts use a time-travel capability to jump ahead a day, a month, a year to survey the progress of earthly events? Could they be observing mental and/or physical changes in individual human beings? Could the BB-like implants in abductees' brains and bodies be homing devices to facilitate these efforts?

At 9:15 P.M. on Wednesday, July 25, 1972, Mrs. Maurine Puddy was driving near Dromana, Victoria, Australia, on the Mooraduc road, when she saw a blue light above and behind her car. She stopped, got out and saw an intensely glowing, blue, saucer-shaped UFO about 100 feet in diameter hovering at double the height of a telegraph pole over the road and producing a humming sound. She drove away in fright, and the UFO followed her for about eight miles. She reported the incident to the police.

Twenty days later, she was driving at about the same place at about the same time of day when her car was surrounded by blue light. She tried to speed up, but the engine failed and the car steered itself to the side of the road and stopped. She could see part of the rim of a glowing, hovering UFO above the car. A voice in her mind told her "All your tests will be negative...Tell media, do not panic, we mean no harm...You now have control." Mrs. Puddy, who had felt as if she were "in a vacuum," now felt released from the vacuum, and the "car engine started up."[30]

At 8:40 P.M. on January 7, 1974, a Belgian man was driving toward Warneton, Belgium, when his car's engine misfired and failed and its headlights and cassette player quit. He saw an orange-white UFO shaped like a World War I British soldier's helmet resting on three legs 492 feet away. Like so many others, it was about 25 or 30 feet wide and 8 or 10 feet high. Two helmeted "occupants" approached to within 13 feet of the witness' car. One wore a segmented suit like the "Michelin Man," and the other had a square helmet and "Sam Browne" belt. Both had arms reaching to below their knees and gray, pear-shaped faces. The witness felt a "shock" at the back of his head and heard a modulated sound. The entities then returned to the UFO with synchronous movements. It took off at an angle after hovering for a few seconds. During the encounter, the UFO changed color from orange-white, to blue, to red, to "electric blue."

30. Judith M. Magee, "UFO Over the Mooraduc Road," *Flying Saucer Review*, 18, No. 6 (Nov.-Dec. 1972), pp. 3-5.

On June 6, the witness encountered a similar phenomenon at the same spot at the same time of day. On that occasion, the entities vanished instantaneously—as if by magic.[31]

Another 1974 case of multiple encounters came from Horcajo, Spain. While driving his truck on Wednesday night, March 20, Maximiliano Iglesias Sanchez encountered a light 2,000 feet ahead on the highway. It was so brilliant that he could not continue. Finally it dimmed and he drove on, only to have his truck's engine and lights fail.

About 600 feet ahead, he saw a glowing UFO 30 to 36 feet in diameter resting on a tripod with round pads. It appeared to be metallic. Another similar UFO was in the air nearby. He then saw two six-foot humanoids in brilliant coveralls. They entered the UFO. Producing a humming noise, it rose to hover beside its counterpart. Sanchez could then start his engine and drove on. He paused to watch a bit, then drove home.

The following night, at about 11:15 P.M., Sanchez was again driving his truck along the same road at the same place and experienced a nearly identical encounter. This time his truck backfired when the engine and lights failed (again about 2,000 feet from the landed UFO), and there were two other similar craft to the right of the road. Four humanoids began walking in Sanchez' direction, and he fled on foot. The beings gave chase, but Sanchez eluded them by hiding in a ditch. He later returned to his truck, and as before, the landed UFO ascended, and he was able to start his truck and drive away. So great was his curiosity, though, that he parked about 600 feet further on and returned on foot to watch the humanoids piercing the ground with "T"-shaped and horseshoe-shaped tools. Traces were found at the landing site.[32]

The UFO literature is replete with "coincidences" of dates and times of sightings. For instance, a UFO caused a power failure at Salta, Argentina, on July 22, 1958.[33] On January 22, 1959—six months to the day after the first outage—electrical power in Salta again failed as a round, luminous UFO flew over the city.[34] But that did not end the coincidence. Exactly five months later, on June 22, yet another power failure occurred in Salta as a luminous sphere passed overhead. The outage blacked out the entire city for several minutes, then power returned.[35]

The Bentwaters/Rendlesham Forest case mentioned earlier (in which a witness reported that shadows continued on another step after people stopped walking) apparently involved two similar incidents in the same place 48 hours apart. A letter from Lt. Col. Charles Halt, Deputy Base Commander at the time, states that the first encounter took

31. J. M. Bigorne, et al., "The Robots at Warneton," *Lumières dans la Nuit*, No. 139 (France), Nov. 1974, trans. Gordon Creighton, *Flying Saucer Review*, 20, No. 5 (March 1975), pp. 6-9.
32. Brad Steiger, *Alien Meetings* (New York: Ace Books, 1978), pp. 158-164.
33. Edwards, *Serious Business*, p. 144.
34. Keyhoe, *op. cit.*, p. 207.
35. Lorenzen, *Startling Evidence*, p. 178.

place at 3:00 A.M. on December 27, 1980, and the second occurred sometime during the night of December 29-30.[36]

And, as Dr. Vallée astutely points out, what is most extraordinary about this case is that *military authorities knew in advance when and where the UFO would appear*. Forty personnel were assembled around a forest clearing in the dark before the UFO was sighted. They were not allowed to take weapons. They trained portable lighting units, movie cameras, video cameras, and still cameras on nothing but the ground fog that England is famous for. And wondered why. And waited. The fog was illuminated, but nothing was happening. Then (according to U.S. Air Force Security Guard Larry Warren) someone called out, "Here it comes!"

A red glow raced out of the north and stopped abruptly to hover 20 feet above the illuminated fog. It appeared to explode *in slow motion* and without a sound, scattering what looked like shards of light. When the "explosion" was over, Warren saw a solid arrowhead-shaped UFO—with a red light on top and several blue lights underneath—where the red glow had been. Then "Base Commander Col. Gordon Williams arrived on the scene and approached three life forms that had spilled out of a glowing light to the right." Warren says Williams actually communicated with the beings.[37]

Because the exact time and location of the Bentwaters event were known in advance, Dr. Vallée suggests that the military may have staged the entire event to test soldiers' reactions to an unidentified flying object.[38] This theory does not answer the question of how such an incredible "magic trick" could have been accomplished. Nor does it explain why the staging was not candid or why so much film of the object was taken (film that would later have to be confiscated and which would pose unnecessary security risks).

Could the date, time and place have been known not because present-day military authorities planned the event, but because someone from the future provided information? Was the 1980 U.S. Air Force working in cooperation with its 2080 counterpart and found it necessary or advisable to record a specific future event (after having been provided the precise date, time and coordinates at which that event was to occur)? Did officers tell airmen to leave their weapons behind to avoid an interplanetary incident—or to prevent them from shooting at future members of their own service?

Statistical analyses of the times and dates (and places) of large numbers of sightings have uncovered some very revealing facts.

To begin with, it is well known that UFO sightings occur in "waves" or "flaps." During a period of several weeks or months, no sightings at all will be reported. For the next few days a report or two will surface.

---

36. Fawcett, *op cit.*, pp. 214-219.
37. Jacques Vallée, *Revelations: Alien Contact and Human Deception* (New York: Ballantine Books, 1991), pp. 153-160. See also Jenny Randles, Dot Street, and Brenda Butler, *Sky Crash* (London: Neville Spearman, 1984).
38. *Ibid.*, pp. 159-160.

Then for a period of a few days, hundreds of sightings may occur. Just as investigators arrive, the sightings taper off again to a level of a very few each day. Finally, there are no sightings for another long period. The next group of reports will come from another part of the country, or a country halfway around the world. The wave phenomenon is well documented.[39] The Air Force's contention that it results from hysteria is unfounded, since witnesses usually report their sightings before reading or hearing of other sightings.

For a few years, waves coincided roughly with the closest approaches of Mars to Earth, and some researchers thought they had an explanation. But with time that relationship evaporated, as did the idea that UFOs were from a star system "x" light years from Earth and therefore appeared every "2x" years. It seems that no one can predict when a wave might occur. Could it be that waves of sightings correspond to searches made by ufonauts? Could they happen when people from our future see a need to travel back in time to their past (which is our present) to look for something they know should be there?

A tremendously disproportionate number of UFO sightings happen at night, when the fewest people are outside to see them. Graphs of the distribution of times show a huge spike around 10:00 P.M. and a lesser spike around 3:00 A.M. These data are also well established.[40, 41] Because there are so few people awake at 3:00 A.M., and yet a significant percentage of sightings occur then, researchers have concluded that:

(a) Most of the activity actually occurs around 3:00 A.M. rather than 10:00 P.M., and

(b) The times are chosen purposely for reasons of concealment.

There are other empirical data to support the concealment theory; statistics also indicate that the density of sightings is inversely proportional to the population density.[42] Indeed, most sightings occur in very brief spans of time on dark, lonely, country roads in very sparsely populated areas late at night. As Coral Lorenzen wrote, "The surreptitiousness of the UFO entities in the past years indicates an unwillingness for contact with humans."[43]

Visitors from other planets might have compelling reasons (other than the altruistic "policy of noninterference" that some devotees suggest) for staying hidden. They would surely discover almost immediately just from monitoring our television broadcasts that we humans are an untrustworthy, aggressive, warlike lot armed with horrendously devastating weapons. Our proclivity toward fighting would doubtless horrify the members of any peaceful civilization. Those who hadn't thought to watch TV or directly observe any of the murder, treachery

39. David M. Jacobs, "waves, UFO," in Story, *Encyclopedia*, pp. 389-390.
40. Hendry, *op. cit.*, p. 249.
41. Hynek and Vallée, *The Edge of Reality*, p. 20.
42. Hendry, *op. cit.*, p. 260.
43. Lorenzen, "UFO Occupants in United States Reports," in Bowen, ed., *The Humanoids*, p. 174.

and countless wars that have raged on this planet since man first arose would doubtless blunder into our bullets and missiles before having even a chance to contact us. We have shot both such weapons at UFOs on several occasions. Aliens may also wish minimal contact to protect both us and them from biological contamination, to protect our society from the economic and religious chaos that has been predicted if open contact should be announced, and/or for other reasons we cannot begin to imagine.

Visitors from our own future might also have a host of good reasons for clandestine operations. We might expect to find them sneaking around kidnapping, threatening and brainwashing unsuspecting individuals and performing other loathsome, spy-novel deeds—to insure that the future turns out the way they want it to. The list of possible missions, from historical research, to escape from the law, to the elimination of rivals, is endless. They might have an urgent need to visit any day in the earth's history, and they certainly would not want to be caught in the past, especially if their missions were unauthorized.

Several established statistics are puzzling when viewed in terms of "conventional" space travel, yet logical when viewed in terms of time travel. For instance, a significantly higher percentage of sightings occur in July than in any other month.[44] More sightings take place on the 24th of the month than on any other day. And incredibly, more UFOs are seen on Wednesdays than on any other day of the week.

"The Wednesday phenomenon," as John Keel calls it, seems preposterous. But it is well established. About 20% of the hundreds of reports Keel collected from 1966 described UFO encounters that happened on Wednesdays. This is far more than the 14% of the week that Wednesday occupies and therefore far above statistical probability, particularly since a great many more people are out and about late on Friday and Saturday nights and during the day on Saturdays and Sundays. Keel found the same curious condition when he examined data from the waves of 1967 and 1973. Dr. David Saunders (of the University of Colorado) ran a computer analysis of thousands of sighting reports and obtained similar results. And since then, other researchers have independently demonstrated the Wednesday pattern and confirmed that considerably fewer sightings occur on Saturdays and Sundays.[45, 46]

It seems ludicrous that a being from another planet on a trip spanning trillions of miles would be more likely to arrive on Earth on a Wednesday than any other day. On the other hand, a time traveler from our own future might have a very simple reason for doing so.

You may have noticed that when you unplug some digital electric clocks, they lose their memories. No matter what time you plug them back in, they will read "01:00." One o'clock is their "default value." Many gadgets have default values. Computers are a good example. If

44. Hendry, *op. cit.*, p. 253.
45. Keel, *Mothman Prophesies*, pp. 132-133.
46. Keel, *Trojan Horse*, pp. 19-20.

you don't give your word processor specific instructions not to justify the right margin of your page, it will automatically justify it. If you tell it not to, turn it off, then turn it back on, it will again have defaulted to the justify mode. Egg timers, volt meters and stop watches reset themselves to "0" if you leave them alone. Some pocket calculators turn themselves off and clear their memories if left unused for a few minutes. And American cars are designed to return to a straight-ahead path if you release their steering wheels while driving. These are all examples of default values.

If there really is such a thing as a time machine in our future, it would have to have controls. The "pilot" would have to have some way to designate the exact year, month, day, hour, minute and second he wanted to visit. But what if the day wasn't important, or even the month? What if he simply wanted to shoot for a particular year? He would switch on the time machine and the controls would automatically default to their default values. He would then punch in the year he wished to visit, leaving the month, day, hour and second controls alone. If the default values were "July," "day 24," "Wednesday" and "03:00," then he would emerge in whatever past year he had selected on Wednesday, July 24th at 3 o'clock in the morning (unless of course July 24th did not fall on a Wednesday that year, in which case the defaults would surely change automatically).

It seems obvious that 03:00 would be a good default value to choose if one were attempting to escape detection and/or abduct people, because most of the population is deeply asleep at that time. By the same token, Wednesday might be a good choice for a default value because the middle of the work week is when the fewest people are outside (and perhaps looking up). Most of the population ordinarily works indoors Monday through Friday and concentrates outdoor activity around Saturdays and Sundays. More holidays and vacation days are taken on Mondays and Fridays (and to a lesser extent Tuesdays and Thursdays) to extend weekends. Consequently, more people are likely to be outdoors (and perhaps looking up) on those days, while Wednesday is the least likely day for the bulk of the population to be outdoors.

The month of July might also be chosen as a default value for reasons of concealment. In the northern hemisphere, where most of the world's population resides, it corresponds to midsummer, when the peak growth of vegetation, heat shimmers, and moisture and dust that cause atmospheric haze combine to provide considerably more natural cover for a craft operating near the ground than does any other time of the year.

Why the 24th day of the month might be selected as a default value is not clear, but the fact that more sightings occur on that day would seem to point more toward Earth-based activity than toward visits from other planets, since the statistical probability of calendars developed by entities from alien worlds being identical to ours is near zero.

Yet another statistical pattern—also noted by Keel—is that UFOs are seen year after year in certain relatively small areas Keel calls "windows," and that their flights appear to coincide with state bound-aries.[47] He writes:

> If the UFOs are actually machines of some sort, their pilots seem to be familiar not only with our calendar but also with the political boundaries of our states. They not only concentrate their activities on Wednesday nights, they also carefully explore our states methodically from border to border.
>
> Does this sound like the work of Martians or extraterrestrial strangers? Or does it sound like the work of someone who is using our maps and our calendars...?[48]

Again we see that established data does not mesh well with the popular theory that UFOs are interplanetary spacecraft piloted by aliens from distant planets who travel trillions of miles to survey our planet and study us. While there may be some unknown reason why such intrepid astronauts might choose to make "planetfall" in the same places year after year, it is absurd to suppose they would have any interest in artificial boundaries of individual states. However, we can easily imagine why time travelers from our own future might observe or be constrained by state boundaries. And they might very well appear in the same "window" areas time after time if those areas correspond to the location of their home bases in the future. Time travelers from other planets may find it useful to frequent certain places as well, perhaps because they have charted them and therefore can calculate where in space they will be at any given moment, perhaps because they harbor special conditions that allow passage through time or facilitate ingress into or egress from our time frame.

47. *Ibid.*, p. 157.
48. *Ibid.*, pp. 20-21.

12

We believe that these objects have appeared before human beings in a guise or a frame of reference appropriate to the period, or one that might be expected in the near future (relative to that period).
—*Charles Bowen*[1]

Warnings, Rescues, and Anachronisms

On the 24th day of the month of April, 1959, Helio Aguiar took three photographs of a silver, domed disc as it maneuvered slowly in the sky near Piatã, Brazil. It had windows and markings like symbols. Aguiar felt as if he were being compelled to write something down and lost consciousness. He awoke to find a message in his own handwriting warning to stop atomic testing and saying the "balance of the universe is threatened." The note also declared, "We shall remain vigilant and ready to intervene."[2]

The Aguiar case smacks of the hypnosis techniques used by the CIA or the KGB in spy novels. He wakes up to find the message in his own handwriting and remembers having felt compelled to write, but very little else. Like hundreds of other abductees, he may have been given that distinctly human instruction—a posthypnotic suggestion not to remember certain things.

The content of the message is not uncommon. Juan Carlos Peccinetti and José Fernando Villegas were treated to a similar warning at 3:42 on the morning of September 1, 1968. While they were driving through Mendoza, Argentina, their car's engine and headlights failed and the car stopped. Peccinetti's watch stopped. The two men felt paralyzed. They saw an oval UFO 13 feet wide hovering 4 feet over a vacant lot. It shone a searchlight beam at the ground.

Five hairless, five-foot-tall humanoids with very large heads and coveralls stood nearby. Three of these floated across the ditch and approached the car. The witnesses heard a voice that told them not to be

---

1. Charles Bowen, "More Beliefs," *Flying Saucer Review*, 20, No. 6 (Apr. 1975), p. 2.
2. Keel, *Trojan Horse*, pp. 198-199.

afraid, that mathematics was the universal language, etc. At the same time, another entity was drawing pictures all over the car with a device like a portable welder. A circular, TV-like screen appeared beside the UFO. It showed pictures: "...a waterfall in lush country...a mushroom shaped cloud...the waterfall scene again, but no water." The humanoids then pricked a finger of each witness' left hand and ascended to the UFO along a light beam. The UFO then ascended with an "explosive effect" and a "vast radiance" and flew away.[3]

A Runcorn, Cheshire, England, resident was given a similar message at 2:15 on the morning of September 7, 1957. A luminous UFO changed color from blue, to white, to blue, to red and landed very close to James Cook. A voice invited him to come aboard by jumping (rather than stepping) onto the ladder, because of the danger of electrical shock. Another UFO containing 20 people considerably taller than Cook landed nearby. Cook was taken for a ride in space and told to warn Earth's people that they would "upset the balance if they persist in using force instead of harmony." When Cook complained that no one would listen to him, one of the men said with irritation (a distinctly human quality) that they wouldn't listen to anyone else either. They told Cook that they were from a planet in another solar system, but that their craft could only be used near the earth and did not work in space.[4]

UFO occupants have been issuing warnings to us for decades. According to John Keel:

> For the past twenty years the ufonauts have been repeating two phrases over and over again to the flying saucer contactees (who now number in the many thousands). "We are One," is one of their favorite declarations. "You are endangering the balance of the universe," is their warning. They are apoplectic over our atomic experiments....[5]

If the ufonauts who issue these warnings are from some distant planet, the message—that we are going to "upset the balance of the universe"—doesn't seem to make much sense. The atomic explosions we have triggered here are the merest trifle when compared to those constantly taking place in even a small star, and there are countless trillions of stars. Why should it concern them for a warlike race on an insignificant planet to blow itself to bits?

If, however, they share this planet with us—and their own admission that they have craft that are only used here seems to support that hypothesis—they would likely be terrified by our idiotic proclivity toward war and our stockpiles of enough weapons to destroy all life on this planet forever.

3. From *Los Principios* (Córdoba, Argentina), 2 Sept. 1968, from *La Crónica* (Buenos Aires), 9 Sept. 1968, from *Gente Y la Actualidad* (Buenos Aires), 5 Sept. 1968, and from *Ya* (Madrid), 3 Sept. 1968, as reported in Charles Bowen, "One Day in Mendoza," *Flying Saucer Review*, 14, No. 6 (1968); rpt. in Bowen, ed. *Encounter Cases from Flying Saucer Review*, pp. 131-138.
4. Keel, *Trojan Horse*, pp. 199-200.
5. Keel, *Disneyland*, pp. 121-122.

Does the oft-repeated declaration made by ufonauts that "We are One" mean that we and they are the same? Are they human? Do they have a vested interest in us? Is this why they have gone out of their way to rescue people on several occasions?

A British rail worker appears to have been "rescued" early on the evening of February 12, 1979. He was walking home from Headingly, Leeds, England, along the tracks when he saw a UFO in the form of a green light above him. When he had to dodge to another track to avoid being run over by the Harrogate-to-Leeds train, the UFO swooped low, somehow levitated him six feet into the air, then set him down further along the track. He turned around "and saw an oval with a misty vapour moving away." Interestingly, he had already stepped to safety.[6]

Had the witness not been staring at the UFO to begin with, he probably would have given the train a much wider berth. Did the craft's occupants think they were about to inadvertently cause the death of the witness, and then act quickly to assure that such a tragedy would not happen? The fact that the witness was already safe makes their action seem rather like that of a mother hen overly concerned for one of her brood. Had they been watching the Englishman with the express purpose of keeping him out of trouble? Was it their job to be a sort of "guardian angel" to him? Is he important to them in some way? Will his son or daughter or grandchild make some important discovery at some future date?

An early-morning incident that happened in British Columbia, Canada, in 1977 may bear some relation to the Leeds case. At 4:10 on January 5, Kirk Alore was driving between Prince George and Vanderhoof when he noticed a red light flying above an oncoming car. He then saw it was an oblong object with stubby, rounded, triangular wings, a red-lit dome and a counter-rotating circular appendage. It was 120 feet wide and 200 feet long. It shot toward him, causing him to swerve into another car's lane at 70 m.p.h.! The last thing he remembered was that his motor quit and he heard static on his radio instead of the station he had been listening to.

Both drivers lost consciousness. But 15 minutes later, they revived. The cars were stopped two feet apart, but there were no skid marks. Alore was in the passenger seat of his car, feeling as if he had been examined, and the other man was standing outside his car.[7]

As in the Leeds case, had the UFO not been present, the witnesses would probably not have been in danger. Alore would not have swerved into the path of the oncoming car. Once he had, both he and the other driver faced almost certain death, which the UFO apparently prevented. The 15-minute interval and the fact that Alore awoke feeling as if he had been examined imply that there was a subsequent abduction, and the fact that he has since seen UFOs on more than one occasion might mean that he is being watched.

6. Randles, *Conspiracy*, p. 105.
7. W. K. Allan, "The Fort St. James Sightings," *Flying Saucer Review*, 24, No. 3 (1978), pp. 8-11.

One of the most dramatic "saucer rescue" stories is the Coyne helicopter case. At 11:02 P.M. on October 18, 1973, Capt. Lawrence J. Coyne (commander), First Lt. Arrigo Jezzi (pilot), Sgt. John Healy (flight medic) and Sgt. Robert Yanacsek (Crew Chief) were flying a U.S. Army Reserve helicopter over the Mansfield, Ohio, area. Yanacsek saw a steady, red light approaching on a collision course. Coyne took the controls, started a 500-feet-per-minute dive and contacted Mansfield Tower. Radio contact failed, both UHF and VHF. The men could feel the deceleration from the dive.

The light still approached from the east and grew brighter. Coyne changed the rate of descent to 2,000 feet per minute. Just before colliding with the helicopter, the UFO stopped in midair and hovered above and in front of it. The helicopter's altitude had dwindled to 1,700 feet.

At this point, the UFO had an apparent length almost equal to the width of the windshield. It was gray, domed, cigar-shaped and appeared to be metallic. Something resembling windows were barely discernible on the dome. In addition to the red light in front, a white light shone from the rear and a cone of green light from the bottom. The green light then illuminated the helicopter's cockpit. After ten seconds, the UFO flew away, executing a 45-degree turn and disappearing in the distance over Lake Erie. The men felt a "bump" as it left.

At that point, the helicopter's magnetic compass was rotating at four RPM, the altimeter indicated 3,500 feet, and the helicopter was in a 1,000 foot-per-minute climb, even though the collective was in the down position as far as it would go. An altitude of 3,800 feet was reached before control was reestablished. Even though they had reversed from a steep dive toward a crash into the city of Mansfield, to an impossibly steep climb (gaining 1,800 feet in ten seconds), the men did not feel any of the tremendous G-force that should have accompanied their movement, and Captain Coyne was only faintly aware of a climb in progress.

Columbus researchers William Jones and Warren Nicholson located five people who independently reported having witnessed the encounter from the ground. The FAA later indicated that the Cleveland Hopkins airport radar room had contact with the helicopter and the UFO.[8, 9]

It appears that all three of these rescues were effected by enclosing the "rescuees" in a field and then manipulating the field. The British Rail worker and Captain Coyne's helicopter were lifted to safety inside some sphere of influence where gravity could not reach, just as cars, pickup trucks, loads of dirt and even horses have been lifted in other close encounters. The momentum of Kirk Alore's car and the other driver's car, which were hurtling toward one another at a relative speed of over 70 miles an hour, was reduced to nothing in the space of a few

8. Jennie Zeidman, "Coyne (Mansfield, Ohio) helicopter incident," in Story, *Encyclopedia*, pp. 93-95.
9. Stringfield, *Situation Red* (Doubleday), p. 189.

feet, just as Carl Higdon's bullet was slowed from its muzzle velocity of hundreds of miles per hour to nothing in the space of 50 feet, and just as cars, planes, rocks, and people have been stopped in other cases.

In all three cases, time itself seems to have been different than it normally is. The helicopter changed its attitude abruptly from plunging downward at 2,000 feet per minute to climbing upwards at 10,800 feet per minute (in other words a change of more than 6 normal Earth gravities) in 10 seconds. Imagine stepping into the elevator on the ground floor of a 22-story building and arriving at the penthouse a second later; you can readily see the crew would have noticed the change in attitude. But Coyne felt no more pull of gravity than he would have had the change been stretched over a much longer span of time. The G-force was so slight that the crew was not even aware of it. The speed of the climb after the UFO disappeared demonstrates that time had gone awry; at that moment, the helicopter was in a 1,000 foot-per-minute climb. Only seconds before, it had been in a 10,800 foot-per-minute climb. At that point, the crew's bodies should have been pulled upward against their seat belts with a force of five Earth gravities, but they felt nothing other than a "bump." We must conclude that *the helicopter did not actually climb 1,800 feet in 10 seconds—it only appeared to do so.*

The Coyne case is reminiscent of the John Jenssen case (see Chapter 10). Jenssen's plane remained in a level attitude, even though his airspeed indicator read zero. This condition persisted for several seconds, perhaps even several minutes, which would ordinarily be impossible. But if Jenssen and his plane had been included in a field within the influence of which the length of a second had been lengthened or shortened a dozen or a hundred times, it might suddenly become possible.

Kirk Alore had been driving down the highway at about 70 m.p.h. when the UFO caused him to swerve into the path of the oncoming car. We don't know how fast the other car was traveling, but we might guess the combined speed of the two cars was in excess of 100 miles an hour. When Alore swerved, the two cars were very close to one another. Both cars stopped without leaving skid marks on the pavement. Again, what actually happened seems impossible, until one considers that time may have been dilated in the vicinity of the UFO. If the length of an hour is varied by a factor of 10 or 20 or 100, then 100 m.p.h. may not be a high speed at all.

In all three cases, the rescues seem to be deliberate attempts to keep the presence of the UFOs from causing accidents that would not have occurred had the UFOs not been present in the first place. In the Leeds case especially, it looks as if an intelligence in control of the UFO went to some effort to assure that the rail worker was out of danger. The question is, would aliens from distant planets have a motive for rescuing a single member of a race of billions? What would they care if two more cars ran together on a highway? It happens thousands of times each year all over the world.

On the other hand, UFO pilots from our own future might have powerful motives for maintaining the status quo of their past. Imagine visiting the past and inadvertently causing the death of your spouse's grandfather before he had sired any children. When you went back home, you might not have a spouse! Possibly the witnesses are to be involved in some important future discovery or battle. A legitimate time-machine operator might suffer severe penalties from his superiors for accidentally bringing about the death or injury of such a person, just as a policeman who shoots an unarmed citizen might be penalized. And an illegitimate operator certainly would not wish to draw attention to himself and give away his hiding place in time by committing such a *faux pas.*

There are also cases in which witnesses have been "rescued" in other ways. Several have reported that they were given some sort of prophylaxes by UFO entities. Usually they are placed under a strong light and then told that a particular malady has been cured.

Another argument for the case that some UFOs may be from our own future is the fact that physical evidence left behind after encounters is often very mundane. A good example is the strange case of Oscar Heriberto Iriart. At midday on July 2, 1968, Oscar was horseback riding on his father's farm near Sierra Chica, Buenos Aires, Argentina. He saw two ordinary men of ordinary size but with short, white hair, red clothes and deep-set, unblinking eyes. They gestured for him to approach. When he did, he noticed he could see the grass through their semi-transparent legs. They told him they would at some time take him to see the world and handed him an ordinary envelope, instructing him to dip it into a puddle. When he did so, he found the envelope and his hands to be dry and saw this misspelled Spanish message written on the envelope in a preschooler's hand: "You are going to know the world. F. Saucer."

The men lifted the top of an elliptical UFO that rested on three legs in a nearby drainage ditch. They entered it and closed it behind them. The UFO then immediately shot straight up with flashing light and with such great speed that it dwindled to a speck in the distance almost instantaneously. Iriart felt as though he had been asleep and found his horse and dog paralyzed. They were not able to move for several minutes afterward. Precise depressions were found at the site. Several others saw a UFO at the site late that night.[10]

The misspellings and childish writing skills evident in the Iriart case are interesting. Computers are already making pen and paper obsolete. Dictation machines that convert speech directly into typescript are already in use. Software packages that correct spelling errors are everywhere. Handwriting and spelling skills might be museum curiosities to future humans, just as the knowledge of how to use a slide rule

---

10. From *La Razón*, 4 Jul. 1968, as reported in Gordon Creighton, "A South American 'Wave,'" *Flying Saucer Review*, 14, No. 5; rpt. in Bowen, ed., *Encounter Cases from Flying Saucer Review*. pp. 50-53.

has begun to disappear since the introduction of pocket calculators 20 years ago.

Iriart's experience is not unique. Ufonauts have given other witnesses notes. Sometimes they are written in strange codes. The Air Force gives them to cryptographers, who easily decipher them as trite messages written in coded English on ordinary paper. Officials therefore conclude that they are hoaxes perpetrated by the witnesses. But are they?

Messages are not the only bits of hard evidence that have been disregarded because they are not exotic enough. On several occasions, fragments of metal left behind by UFOs have been recovered. If witnesses manage to hold on to them long enough to have them analyzed, they are rarely found to be "alien" material with magical properties. Usually they are composed of ordinary metals like aluminum. Officials usually conclude they are fragments of ordinary metal that have nothing to do with alien spaceships.[11] UFO investigators breathlessly read the analysis reports, hoping to spot unusual characteristics like Major Marcel found at Roswell, then disgustedly toss them into their files with other such reports. They may never consider that if the fragments came from a few years in our own future they probably should not be the least bit exotic—just as paper and messages from a few years in our future probably wouldn't be exotic.

Perhaps the most famous examples of this pattern are the metal fragments recovered after a disc-shaped UFO exploded over a beach at Ubatuba, São Paulo, Brazil, in 1957. When they were subjected to very detailed scientific analyses, it was found that they were nothing more than pure magnesium with a slightly greater-than-normal density. "Big deal!" the skeptics sneered. (A few years later, though, another of the samples was found to contain an unexpected amount of strontium, which is normally not present in magnesium. Then in 1969, it was found that the fragments had been manufactured using directional crystallization, a strengthening process that had not yet been invented at the time the fragments were recovered.)[12]

Another Brazilian incident involving metal happened in Campinas three years before the Ubatuba affair. On December 14, 1954, many spectators watched a disc wobble and lose altitude. Two other discs followed it down until it stabilized about 300 feet above the ground. It squirted out a stream of hot, silvery liquid, some of which was recovered. According to researcher Kenneth Behrendt, a Brazilian government laboratory analyzed it and found it to be tin, with other metals present. According to journalist Frank Edwards, Dr. Risvaldo Maffei, a

---

11. Publisher's Note: Although when scientists analyzed metal samples obtained by Eduard Meier, the "metal specimen's general characteristics seemed to indicate a non-electrolytic, cold fusion synthesis process not generally known to earth technology." See Brit Elders, et al. *UFO...Contact From The Pleiades.*, Volume I (Munds Park, Arizona: Genesis III Publishing, 1980), p. 58.
12. Walter W. Walker, "Ubatuba (Brazil) magnesium," in Story, *Encyclopedia*, pp. 374-375.

private chemist, did another analysis and found the metal to be 90% tin.[13]

The Campinas incident is very reminiscent of the famous Maury Island affair (see Chapter 14). The Maury Island metal was said to have been identified as ordinary slag (although no analysis seems to have been done).

Swedish industrialist Gosta Carlsson came upon a domed, disc-shaped UFO that had landed outside Angleholm, Sweden, in May of 1946. He saw a "guard" in white coveralls, and then seven men and four women with black boots, gloves, belts and transparent helmets. They all had brown skin, and the women's hair was "ashen-colored." Some of them were apparently repairing a window. Carlsson heard one of the women laugh when she tossed an object away. The UFO was bathed in a purple light from a device reminiscent of a lamp shade above it. When it flew away, it ascended to 2,000 feet while producing a whine, then wobbled, changed from red to purple and flew away at "tremendous speed." Carlsson picked up the discarded object, which proved to be partly silicon, and, like most junk left behind by ufonauts, nothing out of the ordinary.[14]

UFOs leave behind oil, too. There are many instances on record of a purplish, oily substance resembling automatic transmission fluid being discovered at UFO landing sites. Investigators usually conclude that it is automatic transmission fluid—and disregard the entire encounter, considering it to be a hoax.

Spaceships from distant planets probably don't use automatic transmission fluid, but time machines from a few years in our future just might. In hundreds of cases, witnesses have reported that part of a UFO—usually the rim—was spinning. Kirk Alore, for instance, described a spinning component as a part of the UFO that caused him to swerve into the other car's path. It is conceivable that some sort of mechanical apparatus that needs oil is involved. The most common explanation for the spinning mechanism is that it may provide a gyroscopic stabilizing action. The transmission fluid calls to mind Frank Scully's claim that a crashed flying saucer was recovered, measured and dismantled. The measurements implied that the craft had been built using feet and inches, and a circular gear was found around the rim, which meshed with a gear on the "cabin."

If investigators were surprised to find transmission fluid, they must have been astonished at the analysis report returned from HEW's Food and Drug Laboratory on the "cookies" a 60-year-old chicken farmer named Joe Simonton had received from some ufonauts. It was broad daylight on April 18, 1961, when a sound like tires on a wet street prompted Joe to step outside his Eagle River, Wisconsin home. Hovering just slightly above his yard was a 30-foot saucer with a mirrored surface. A door opened, and Joe saw instrument panels and

13. Vallée, *Confrontations*, p. 49.
14. Jerome Clark and Loren Coleman, *The Unidentified* (New York: Warner Paperback Library-Warner Communications Company, 1975), pp. 28-30.

three swarthy men about five feet tall wearing turtlenecks and knit helmets. They handed him a shiny jug, which he filled with water. When he did so, he noticed they were cooking on a grill. Joe gestured at the food to show interest and was handed three perforated cookies. The ufonauts closed the door, and the UFO ascended 20 feet and shot away southward, bending trees in the process.

Trusting fellow that he was, Joe ate one of the things. He said it "tasted like cardboard," which was not surprising in light of the Air Force's findings. Air Force personnel sent one to be analyzed, and it was found to be an ordinary buckwheat pancake. They declared that it was from Earth.[15] Joe should have added some butter and blueberry syrup!

Simonton's pancake probably was of earthly origin. Aliens from a distant planet probably would not make pancakes with soybean hulls and wheat bran and buckwheat hulls any more than they would look like us or speak our languages or breathe our air or walk normally in our gravity. They would probably eat something completely alien to us, if they ate at all. And if we ate it, it might sicken or kill us. Visitors from the future, on the other hand, might very well choose such culinary fare. Buckwheats are one of the most nutritious foods known. The Food and Drug Laboratory analysis showed the pancake to be a complete dietary staple. It even contained dietary fiber. And, since Joe said the one he ate had little taste and the analysis report made no mention of salt, we can guess the pancakes must even have been low in sodium. We have grown more and more nutrition-conscious in the last few years. Why shouldn't we expect time travelers from our future to eat foods as nutritious as those our own astronauts eat?

Just as we might expect objects left behind by alien space travelers to be exotic and advanced, we might expect artifacts known to be millions of years old to be primitive. But that is not always the case. Miners and excavators have time and again stumbled onto anachronisms—artifacts not adequately explained by present-day archaeological theories.

Quarriers working near the River Tweed (Rutherford, Scotland) in 1844 discovered a length of gold thread in rock eight feet below ground.[16] Of course the rock was millions of years old. So who made the thread? Who dropped it millions of years ago, before the rock was formed?[17]

The following year, a nail was found in a block of rock from Kin

15. From Air Technical Intelligence Center files, as reported in Vallée, *Magonia*, pp. 23-25, 281.
16. From the *London Times*, 22 Jun. 1844, as reported in Carroll C. Calkins, ed., *Mysteries of the Unexplained* (Pleasantville, New York: The Reader's Digest Association, Inc., 1982), p. 47.
17. Publisher's Note: Other researchers suggest that extraterrestrial involvement with our planet extends into our past by perhaps millions of years. See, for example, Richard C. Hoagland, *The Monuments of Mars: A City on the Edge of Forever* (Berkeley, California: North Atlantic Books, 1987) and Zecharia Sitchin, *The 12th Planet* (New York: Avon Books, 1978).

goodie, another quarry located in the north part of England.[18] In 1851, at least two important anachronisms surfaced. A Springfield, Massachusetts resident, Mr. Hiram de Witt, dropped a million-year-old formation of auriferous quartz, which broke open, revealing a cut iron nail. And a bell-shaped metal object that looks like a chalice or candleholder and is inlaid with silver in intricate floral patterns was found 14 feet down inside of solid rock at Dorchester, Massachusetts, when workmen blasted.[19, 20]

In 1891, a Mrs. Culp, of Morrisonville, Illinois, broke open a lump of coal that was millions of years old. Inside was an intricately-worked chain of gold. Another intriguing object was found inside a piece of coal that came from Salzburg, Austria. It is a cube of steel that has obviously been machined. Its top and bottom are formed into convex domes, and a precise groove circles it. Nobody knows what it is, but it should not have been inside a lump of coal.[21, 22, 23]

In 1927, Albert E. Knapp found the fossilized imprint of a leather shoe, complete with hand stitching with fine thread, in the Triassic limestone of Fisher Canyon, Pershing County, Nevada. Mr. Knapp's find is mysterious, because while men only began walking the earth less than a million years ago, Triassic limestone is between 180 million and 225 million years old.[24]

In June of 1968, amateur fossil collector William J. Meister discovered, inside yet another rock, what seems to be the fossilized imprint of a sandaled foot. The rock came from the Antelope Spring area west of Delta, Utah. The step had apparently crushed a living trilobite, which should not be possible, since trilobites became extinct 280 million years ago. On July 20 of the following month, Dr. Clifford Burdick found a fossilized child's footprint in the same area, and in August, Mr. Dean Bitter of Salt Lake City said he discovered two more of the fossilized sandal prints.[25]

One of the most fascinating of all anachronisms is what has become known as the "Piri Reis map." In 1513, a Turkish admiral named Piri Reis made a chart of the world. One of his sources of information was a map that Christopher Columbus had used on his famous American voyage in 1492. What Reis did not know, and what was only discovered centuries later, was the fact that the map he copied was strangely distorted because of the curvature of the earth. In fact, tests performed by the U.S. Navy Hydrographic Office and retired sea captain A. H. Mallery showed that Columbus' map was incredibly accu-

---

18. Charles Fort, *The Complete Books of Charles Fort* (New York: Dover Publications, Inc., 1974), p. 133.
19. From the *London Times*, 24 Dec. 1851, as reported in Calkins, p. 46.
20. From *Scientific American*, Vol. 7 (5 Jun. 1852), p. 298, as reported in Calkins, p. 46.
21. The Morrisonville, Illinois, *Times*, 11 Jun. 1891, as reported in Calkins, p. 46.
22. Otto O. Binder, *Flying Saucers Are Watching Us* (New York: Belmont Books-Belmont Productions, Inc., 1968), pp. 88-89.
23. Jessup, *op. cit.*, pp. 87-92.
24. Brad Steiger, *Mysteries of Time and Space* (Englewood Cliffs, New Jersey: Prentice-Hall, Inc., 1974), p. 18.
25. From *Bible-Science Newsletter*, Aug.-Sept. 1969 and *Creation Research Society Quarterly*, Dec. 1968, as reported in Calkins, pp. 37-38.

rate. It included minute detail of the Antarctic coastline as it had existed thousands of years ago—a fact that was only substantiated by subsequent seismic mapping of the actual coastline under the ice cap that now covers that continent. It has now been determined that the map could only have been made via photography of the Atlantic Ocean from a vantage point in orbit far above the earth at a time before the Antarctic ice cap formed—which was thousands of years ago.[26]

The list of these anachronisms is long and perplexing. They may be of extraordinary importance, but most of them lie gathering dust in the basements of museums around the world, along with outdated displays and broken chairs. They don't fit the accepted paradigms of history and prehistory, so they are ignored in the hope they will go away.

Are they clues that a civilization very much like ours thrived on the earth millions of years ago? "No," archaeologists, anthropologists and evolutionists agree. They are certain that man did not develop enough to produce a civilization until a few thousand years ago, and no other creature capable of making nails and chalices ever evolved on Earth. Could they have been dropped by ancient alien astronauts who visited the earth millions of years before man evolved? Perhaps, but why would such spacefarers have been carrying around ordinary terrestrial iron nails?

Could it be that the fossilized foot marks were left by time travelers who never thought they wouldn't be brushed away by the very next tide? Were chalices, chains, nails and threads lost by time travelers who once explored (and who are perhaps exploring as you read this) both our present and our remote past? Were they cast away carelessly, like Gosta Carlsson's silicon rod? Could these anachronisms be a cosmic version of the trail of gum wrappers and Polaroid film sheaths thoughtlessly dropped by the awed visitors who tramp our national parks today? Will future humans still not have learned to refrain from littering, even when they are away from "home?"

UFO lore is filled with anachronisms like the use of laparoscopic procedures (sometimes called "belly-button surgery"), "stun guns" and lasers years before they were invented. The craft themselves are anachronisms. For example, in the late 19th century, there were innumerable witnesses to UFOs in the form of giant, dirigible-like "airships" that toured the United States and other countries with great facility years before such contraptions were invented. Some witnesses even met and talked to the crews, who they sometimes described as human beings (some noted they looked Asian or foreign). They made flights in a fraction of the time that was possible for the technology of the time or even years later. The story of the airships is well documented and appears in dozens of books.[27, 28]

During World War II, pilots and air crews on both sides wondered how the now-famous "foo fighters" out-flew their best planes. Then the

26. Keyhoe, *op. cit.*, pp. 231-232, 236.
27. Loren E. Gross, "airship wave of 1896," in Story, *Encyclopedia*, pp. 8-10.
28. Lucius Farish, "airship wave of 1897," in Story, *Encyclopedia*, pp. 10-11.

green "ghost rockets" appeared over Scandinavia in 1946 and traveled faster than anything that man had invented—yet.[29, 30] Then people started seeing unmarked helicopters and airplanes. On the surface they looked like ordinary aircraft that had been painted black, but they did things aircraft of the day were not advanced enough to do. They flew in blizzards without navigation lights, and in mountainous areas no pilot would dare approach. Some had brilliant light streaming from *inside* their cockpits—light so bright it would have blinded a pilot. Others had odd configurations—eight engines, for instance (which no plane had at the time)—or flew equally well whether their propellers were turning or not.[31] When supersonic flight began, UFOs were there, and they were faster. The faster our planes became, the faster the UFOs became. And they remain just a step ahead, just a bit more advanced, than aircraft of every era in which they appear—like anachronisms. According to Dr. Vallée:

> *...UFOs seem to represent an alien force that anticipates our own scientific development by decades, mocking our efforts to identify its nature and its long-term intentions. Understandably, the military establishment does not feel comfortable with the disclosure of our weakness any more than the scientific establishment feels inclined to confessing its ignorance.*[32]

It has often been speculated that ufonauts might purposely appear in vehicles somewhat more advanced than ours to stimulate our own development of such machines. The idea is that if we know something can be done, we will successfully accomplish it, whereas otherwise we might not even try. But why would aliens want to speed the entry into space of a warlike species (us) that daily demonstrates bents toward violence and treachery? And if they did want to, why not simply land at Cape Canaveral or some other space center and hand over their technology?

If some UFOs are from the future, however, their pilots may have good reason to use vehicles that are almost, but not quite, appropriate to the era they are visiting. By doing so, they can perform their missions without getting shot down and captured, while we pass off sightings as misperceptions of our own developmental aircraft or guess their craft might be some secret weapon of another government. Thus, they accomplish their objectives and at the same time avoid encouraging us to develop time-travel capabilities of our own before we are supposed to (which would no doubt pose serious problems for them).

So we might ask ourselves: If we were to discover how to generate a field that warps time, would we do so? Would we use it to visit the past? If we did, what sort of vehicle would we choose to make our visits? Would we prefer a craft that could avoid being destroyed or captured? And how would we behave? Littering is practically a way of life

29. Ronald Story, "foo fighters," in Story, *Encyclopedia*, pp. 135-136.
30. Loren E. Gross, "ghost rockets of 1946," in Story, *Encyclopedia*, pp. 147-149.
31. Keel, *Trojan Horse*, pp. 122-143.
32. Vallée, *Confrontations*, p. 230.

for a lot of folks in the present; would some of us litter in the past? If we knew nuclear and toxic pollution was going to ruin the earth and the people in the past didn't know, would we try to warn them? And if our mistakes put someone in mortal danger, would we stand idly by (or hover idly by) and let him die? Or would we rescue him?

13

*...UFOs, if they are spacecraft en-gaged in a general survey of our planet, must have landed here no fewer than **three million times** in two decades....*

This number is totally absurd. Using a single probe the size of a beer keg in orbit a thousand miles above the earth, human technology as it exists today would be able to capture in a few weeks most of the important facts about the planet's geography, weather, vegetation and culture....

*The theory of random visitation does **not** explain it. Either the UFOs select their witnesses for psychological or sociological reasons, or they are something entirely different from space vehicles.*

—Jacques Vallée[1]

"Impossible" Variety

With trembling hands, a 21st-century inventor tries his experiment again. He notes meter readings, records numbers and watches his apparatus fade into nothingness. Breathlessly, he performs measurements where the object had been. There has been no mistake. The apparatus is not invisible; it is gone! His mind whirls as he paces his basement laboratory. What should he do? Who should he tell?

A loud noise from behind startles him. He peers through the maze of wires and gadgets to the far side of the room and draws a quick breath; there, lying broken on the floor, is his apparatus! It must have materialized in the air and fallen!

But his shock is not over yet. As he squats to examine the device, he notices that its clock is still working...but it's five minutes slow. For the first time, the real significance of his experiment dawns on him. The rotating fields he has discovered don't just make things disappear; they send them into the future!

In a few weeks, he has perfected a working model of a device that can travel through time—into both the future and the past. He takes into his confidence a patent attorney, who doesn't believe his wild claims, but who is nevertheless happy to take his money.

A few days after his patent application is filed, government agents burst into his makeshift laboratory, pack his equipment and notes into plastic bags, then load everything into a truck. He is given a terse explanation—he must cooperate because national security is at stake.

He is blindfolded and taken to a secret underground installation hours away. He is offered full use of a completely equipped laboratory for life plus a huge amount of tax-exempt money—if he agrees to teach

---

1. Vallée, *Dimensions*, p. 258.

government scientists how to build time machines. It is insinuated that his cooperation can be arranged against his will, if necessary—and without the bonus.

He is told his invention will be used for historical research and space exploration. This makes him feel better about the situation, so he agrees to cooperate. But after he teaches others how to build the devices, he is disgusted to learn that time machines will also be mass-produced for military use.

Then foreign agents capture a time machine in the field. Another is stolen by political extremists. Soon there is a black market. Criminals use them to avoid the law by escaping into the past. Hostile governments use them to abduct politicians and nuclear devices. Terrorists use them to bring terrifying weapons back from the future. Some gutsy opportunists kidnap children from the past to sell to barren couples for adoption. Others collect huge fees to take clients back past the ice ages to hunt mammoths and dinosaurs.

In desperation, governments hastily cooperate to form an international, interdimensional police force to prevent unauthorized use of time machines. But their job is next to impossible, since their quarry can be anywhere on—or off—the earth during any time period.

Meanwhile, the same invention makes space travel easy. Astronauts discover that other intelligent beings use the same method. They eventually contact other races. Some of them are at war with others. Some have studied the earth throughout its history. Their aid is enlisted in the policing effort.

Governments in the past manage to shoot down and capture a time machine. Some of those who learn of the secret are taken bodily into the future to prevent them from leaking it. Others are kept quiet with threats. Still others are quieted permanently....

For 45 years, people have been saying it is very improbable that UFOs are extraterrestrial spacecraft. Many of those making such statements have not been ordinary lay persons but people like Dr. Carl Sagan, whose opinions have carried much weight because they are highly qualified to give them.

The velocity-of-light "speed limit," declared by Henri Poincaré and later "proven" by Albert Einstein, forms the foundation of most arguments against extraterrestrial visitation. It works something like this:

According to theory, as an object having mass is accelerated, its mass increases and its length shortens in the direction of travel. At the slow speeds of our current spacecraft, the amount of increase and foreshortening is negligible. But mathematics indicate that if an object were to approach the velocity of light (about 186,000 miles per second), its mass would become enormous (as its time dilates). Theoretically, just before light speed could be achieved, the object's mass would reach infinity (so that an infinite amount of energy would be required to accelerate it any faster) and it would become infinitely foreshortened. Thus, the velocity of light, "c," becomes, for all practical purposes, a speed limit for any physical object.

Based on observations made possible by space probes, astronomers believe no intelligent life exists anywhere in our own solar system except on Earth. They also believe they have established that although there are countless trillions of stars in the known universe, only about 1,000 stars lie within 55 light years of the earth (which is about as far as they can imagine anyone traveling in a lifetime). And only about 46 of those stars are likely to have spawned planets capable of producing life. Even if some such planets do exist, it is considered statistically improbable that life would have formed on more than a handful of them. It is even less likely that such life might include one or more intelligent species. And the probability that even one such intelligent species might have already developed a technology capable of interstellar flight approaches zero.

Consequently, when astronomers are confronted with the enormous number of UFO sightings that are reported (and the even greater number of those that are not), when they consider that rarely is one UFO described to be exactly like any other, when they look at the wide variety of occupants witnesses swear they have seen, they cannot believe UFOs are extraterrestrial spacecraft. Because to do so, they must accept that thousands of alien beings representing dozens of different species have, since recorded history began, traveled for dozens, perhaps thousands of years in thousands of different types of vehicles just to come to Earth and collect rocks, sticks, hair samples and bits of fingernails, and to perform bizarre experiments involving the human reproductive system.

Because they believe no spacecraft could ever exceed, or even approach, the speed of light, many astronomers consider contact with extraterrestrials a one-in-a-million chance. Many of them believe that if it ever happens, it will be in the form of radio signals transmitted decades ago or centuries ago by an alien race and picked up by gigantic radio telescopes on Earth. The chances of ever making any sense of such signals are considered slim, and even if we can decipher their meaning, both the human race and the alien race may be long dead before our answer reaches the alien planet. Therefore, the thousands of reports of actual contact are either completely disregarded or are believed to be hoaxes, hallucinations, misperceptions of normal phenomena or manifestations of some local phenomenon other than extraterrestrial visitation.

But if time travel in the manner we have postulated is possible, these arguments may have no validity whatsoever, because the speed of light would no longer be a limit. Instead of making journeys lasting dozens or hundreds or even thousands of years, aliens using time machines may be able to traverse the gulfs of interstellar space in minutes or hours. Instead of being a destination that can be reached from only a handful of other stars via a lifetime of travel, the earth may be a good place for an afternoon outing—for intelligent races from thousands of different solar systems.

And time travel also opens up another possibility that could explain the tremendous diversity of vehicles that appear to be visiting us. Because if time travel is indeed possible, human beings are bound to eventually discover how to use it themselves or buy the technology from alien visitors who use it. Once that happens, we could expect to be visited by innumerable time machines from our own future.

Let's suppose for a moment that the time machine is indeed invented on Earth in the 21st century, and that a few years later, several manufacturers are making them. Assuming there were 100 different models of time machines (there are hundreds of different models of automobiles) that changed somewhat each year, and this condition persisted for, say 100 years, then there might be 10,000 different *models* of time machines, any one of which could be visiting any place on Earth right now or on any other day in our history. If there were 100 of each model produced (automobiles are produced now by the tens of thousands), there might be 1,000,000 time machines involved from Earth alone.

If out of the billions of other planets that probably exist in the universe there are just 99 other planets on which intelligent creatures have similarly developed time machines, then there might be 100,000,000 different time machines involved. Since many of the builders would be alien species to each other and to us, designs would differ greatly. And just as there are hundreds of different ways you can order a new Chevrolet, different time machines of the same model may look different.

Since there might be an infinite number of different purposes for using time machines, one might imagine that there would be some specialization. Most of our space probes and satellites, for instance, are unique in appearance because each has a different, highly specialized purpose. Perhaps, then, a better analogy might include not only automobiles, but also different makes and models of trucks, trains, boats, submarines, airplanes, helicopters and spacecraft.

An electronics instructor named W. E. (Eddie) Laxson encountered what may have been one of the first human-made time machines at 5:05 on the morning of March 23, 1966 near Temple, Oklahoma. Laxson was driving on Highway 70 near the Oklahoma/Texas state line. He stopped and got out to inspect a landed, silver UFO with clear identification markings—either "TL-41" or "TL 4768." Although he was familiar with military aircraft, he couldn't identify it. It was comparable in size to a C-124 Globemaster (but had no wings or engines) and rested on legs and pads in the road. On top was a transparent bubble canopy similar to that of a B-26, and each end of the craft had a bright light.

A "plain old G.I. mechanic" or "crew chief" dressed in "G.I. fatigues" was using a flashlight to inspect something on the bottom of the craft. He wore something similar to a baseball cap. Laxson was sure he would recognize the man, were he to see him again. He turned to get his camera, but the G.I. ascended a ladder, and the UFO made a noise like a "high-speed drill" and flew away vertically. A truck driver named Anderson was also a witness to the incident.[2, 3]

Was the Temple UFO an American military craft from our near future? Did the "T" in its I.D. number stand for time?

Another witness saw a UFO that could have been from a future United Nations military unit. Haskell Raper, Jr. was driving near Provencal, Louisiana, at 11:00 one rainy November night in 1957. An oval, army-green UFO 16 feet long bearing the letters "UN" and some numbers shone a light beam on his car. The car slowed to a stop by itself 16 feet away. The car became very hot, and Raper fled as it caught fire. The UFO ascended with a noise like a diesel engine. Raper ran to Provencal to report the encounter. His car was completely destroyed.[4]

Another saucer camouflaged olive-drab was seen in the summer of 1952 near Garden City, Texas, by Mrs. Flora Rogers. It was shaped like two turtle shells about 10 feet by 15 feet and had three paddle-like protuberances and a flaming spout that resembled a tail-pipe. It flew, with a wobbling motion, to within 20 feet of her. She stopped her car and leaned out the window to watch it for a few minutes. It suddenly flew away at tremendous speed, "almost too fast for the eye to see," and was beyond her sight in seconds.[5]

Probably the earliest sighting of an olive-drab UFO was made in late April or early May of 1928 by Floyd Dillon, who was then a young man 17 years old. Dillon was driving a Model T Ford along a dirt country lane 10 miles west of Yakima, Washington, at 4:00 in the afternoon when he encountered the object. It was hexagonal, with a dome on top and a smooth, rounded underside. It was about 22 feet wide, 7 feet from top to bottom and appeared to be metallic, with rivets at each edge and a metallic frame around a two-foot-by-three-foot window. When he looked through the window, Dillon saw the upper third of a man, who looked to him like an Italian. He wore a dark blue uniform, and his hair was parted in the middle. The UFO made no sound and swung as it flew slowly over the landscape. Its occupant looked toward the Ford. Then the craft rotated on its axis, passed over the road and flew away "at a terrific speed."[6]

Despite cases that point to military involvement, the idea that present-day U.S. military units have been testing secret aircraft seems improbable (especially in 1928). If they did have aircraft capable of such radical flight, they probably would have kept them under wraps, as they did the stealth bomber. They would not have tested them over populated areas, especially not in the daytime. Nor would they have risked losing them over practically every other country in the world.

2. Lorenzen, "UFO Occupants in United States Reports," in Bowen, ed.,*The Humanoids*, pp. 175-176.
3. From Air Technical Intelligence Center files, as reported in Vallée, *Magonia*, pp. 148, 324.
4. From Ray Palmer, ed., *Flying Saucers* (Amherst, Wisconsin), Oct. 1958, as reported in Vallée, *Magonia*, p. 261.
5. Barker, *op. cit.*, pp. 63-66.
6. Vallée, *Confrontations*, pp. 147-149.

And why would they have continued to request billions of taxpayers' dollars on just such projects as the stealth bomber if they already had something superior to them? Once the technology used by UFOs is learned, all other forms of weapons delivery—and for that matter, all other types of transportation—will instantly become obsolete.

If, on the other hand, UFOs are something that will be invented at some time in our near future, you can bet your bottom dollar our army will do everything in its power to get its hands on some of them. It would even be completely consistent with present policy if they were to attempt to monopolize the use of them. And all manner of future military and paramilitary operations—from intelligence-gathering sorties, to policing of escaped criminals, to combat—may require that they occasionally expose themselves to public view.

The "plain old G.I." Eddie Laxson saw is not unique. Hundreds of witnesses have reported seeing human UFO occupants.

During the same month as Haskell Raper's encounter in Louisiana, a Bakersfield, California, grain buyer named Reinhold Schmidt related meeting ordinary people aboard a UFO. Schmidt was driving near Kearney, Nebraska, on the afternoon of November 5, 1957, when his engine failed. He saw a four-legged, silver, blimp-shaped UFO 30 feet wide, 100 feet long and 14 feet tall landed about 60 feet away. He approached it, and two "middle-aged men" wearing ordinary clothes took him aboard after checking him for weapons. Inside, he saw two middle-aged women—also dressed in ordinary clothes. Schmidt said they were working on wiring; they told him they would have to stay there for a while. They said to "tell the people they were doing no harm" and inferred that Schmidt would soon understand who they were. They asked Schmidt to leave, and the UFO ascended vertically without a sound. He subsequently was able to start his car and drove to Sheriff Dave Drage's office to report his experience.[7]

The pilots and crews of UFOs must have a good reason for assuring witnesses that they will at some point in the future understand who they are—because they do so frequently. Those who appear entirely human, like the ones Reinhold Schmidt met, are especially prone to such statements. Could their reason be that they know time travel will soon be discovered? And that once we are aware that people can speed up or slow down time, we will deduce their origin? Is that why some of them look so human? Do they seem to have such an abiding interest in us because we are their ancestors?

At 6:30 on the evening of March 18, 1950, at Lago Argentino, Southern Argentina, a rancher named Wilfredo Arévalo saw two disc-shaped UFOs. One landed and emitted a green-blue gas and an odor like "burning benzine." It looked to be made of aluminum and had a flat rim, which revolved. The witness could see "four tall, well-shaped men" with pallid faces and transparent suits working inside it. They saw him and shone a bright light on him. The UFO became illuminated with a

---

7. Lorenzen, *Occupants*, p. 123.

blue light, the vapor increased, and the landed UFO ascended on red and green flames, producing a humming sound. It and the second UFO, which had been hovering above it, flew away toward Chile, leaving blue trails behind them. Burnt grass was found at the site the next day.[8]

Like many, many other witnesses, Arevalo did not describe the ufonauts as "creatures," as one might expect the denizens of distant worlds would be viewed, but as men. Except for the pallor of their faces, they apparently looked normal.

Joseph Matiszewski heard a noise like a whistle at Sonderberg, Denmark, at noon on June 19, 1951, and watched as a UFO settled to earth. When he approached to within 164 feet, he discovered he was paralyzed, as were nearby cows and birds. Four "handsome," brown-complected men dressed in shiny black suits and "translucent helmets" came out of the UFO. Matiszewski also saw other men inside the object and on its deck who appeared to be making repairs. In addition, he saw eight other objects, which "emerged from the craft and hovered above it."[9]

A pair of "fair-complexioned men" got out of a small craft that landed near a miner named Rafael Aguirre Donoso, who was in his car near Arica, Chile, on June 15, 1964. Speaking partly in English and partly in Spanish, they asked for water. Donoso complied, and they returned to the UFO, which "rose rapidly and vanished."[10]

A retired prison officer named E. A. Bryant was walking through a scenic part of the English countryside (Scoriton Down, South Devon, Dartmoor) when he encountered a large UFO that "appeared 'out of thin air',," executed a pendulum motion, then hovered three feet above the ground 120 feet ahead of him. A door opened and three human-shaped beings wearing garments akin to diving suits emerged, beckoned to him, then removed their "headgear." Two were blond and blue-eyed with high foreheads; the third had dark hair and eyes and normal features but was smaller. Bryant estimated his age at 15 years. He spoke to Bryant in English, saying they were from Venus and promising to return in a month. Interestingly, comments made by the young ufonaut seemed to have some enigmatic connection to George Adamski (the famous, controversial contactee, who had died the previous day), and Capt. Thomas Mantell (the American military pilot, whose plane had crashed while pursuing a UFO in 1948). Metal fragments were found at the site. The incident occurred at 5:30 P.M. on April 24,

8. From *La Razón* (Buenos Aires) 13 Apr. 1950, and from Cristian Vogt, *El Misterio de los Platos Voladores* (Buenos Aires: Editorial La Mandrágora, 1956), p. 75, as reported in Gordon Creighton, "The Humanoids in Latin America," in Bowen, ed.,*The Humanoids*, pp. 89-90.
9. From *UFO Nachrichten*, May 1959, as reported in Vallée, *Magonia*, p. 196.
10. From *La Razón*, 21 Jun. 1964, and from *Flying Saucer Review*, March/April 1965, as reported in Creighton, "The Humanoids in Latin America," in Bowen, ed.,*The Humanoids*, p. 108.

1965.[11]

Winsted, Minnesota, was the scene of a landing on January 25, 1967. One resident related that at 4:30 that morning, the engine of his pickup truck stalled, then he saw a brightly-lit UFO 80 feet in diameter settle to the road on a tripod landing gear. A man dressed in blue coveralls and a fishbowl-like helmet descended in an elevator and appeared to inspect something before leaving.[12]

Travis Walton described similarly attired people. Walton's incredible story, which began at dusk on November 5, 1975, is one of the most extensively investigated and documented UFO stories in history. Walton and six fellow workers were driving on a remote forest trail near Turkey Springs, Arizona, after a day's work thinning the Apache-Sitgreaves National Forest in the Mogollon Rim area, south of Heber. They saw, hovering 15 feet over a clearing, a luminous, gold, disc-shaped UFO that appeared to be constructed of panels. Walton approached it while the others watched. He was struck, thrown into the air and knocked unconscious by a blue-green light beam. The other witnesses fled in panic as fast as Mike Rogers could drive on the rough trail, then returned when they saw lights fly away from the area. Both Walton and the UFO had disappeared. They drove to Heber and reported the incident to Deputy Ellison, who noted that they were too excited and upset to be perpetrating a hoax.

For the next several days, a thorough search of the area was made by sheriff's deputies, volunteers and helicopters, but no sign of Walton was found, even though numerous deer hunters were in the area. On November 10, at about 11:30 P.M., Walton found himself on a road near Heber. He called for help from a pay telephone, and relatives came to his aid.

He was weak, disoriented, suffering from hunger and extreme thirst, and several pounds lighter, and had a five-day growth of beard. He gradually remembered having awakened in a white, hospital-like room and seeing three identical, five-foot-tall humanoids with "round, domed heads, large eyes, and tiny noses, mouths and ears." They had no fingernails and were wearing tan-orange coveralls. Walton threatened them and they fled. He followed a curved corridor to a round room, where he could see stars through the ceiling. He then moved a lever, which made the stars' positions change.

Then an ordinary-looking man about six feet tall with brown hair and eyes, normal teeth and a normal haircut entered the room. Like the Winsted ufonauts, he was wearing a blue coverall and a transparent helmet. He escorted Walton down a ramp and into a hangar-like place where Walton saw that they had just exited a UFO identical to the one he and the others had seen in the forest. There were also other

11. From an address of the British UFO Research Association by N. Oliver and Miss E. Buckle, 26 Feb. 1966, and from the Plymouth, Devon, England Independent, 8 Aug. 1965, as reported in Charles Bowen, "Few and Far Between," in Bowen, ed., The Humanoids, pp. 20-21.
12. From Air Technical Intelligence Center files, as reported in Vallée, Magonia, p. 339.

metallic-looking objects he took to be craft. He was taken to a room oc-cupied by two men and a woman (also dressed in blue coveralls, but without helmets) who strongly resembled the first man. He was asked to get on a table, and something like an oxygen mask was placed over his face. He lost consciousness and did not remember anything else until five days later.[13]

The Walton case rocked the world, not just because it received widespread publicity, but because six separate witnesses passed poly-graph examinations, and because Walton's testimony placed ordinary humans and "aliens" together in the same craft. But a study of other cases shows this is actually not uncommon.

One example is the Bodega Bay, California, incident of November 26, 1972. Under hypnotic regression, Judy Kendall remembered that she and her sisters Danon and Becky were abducted from their car somewhere near the Cash Creek bridge. Three distinct types of entities were seen—one entirely human, the others hairless and milky-skinned. The witness was apparently given a posthypnotic suggestion not to remember.[14]

In another case, a mother and at least three of her seven children were apparently abducted while sleeping in their home in Utah, "float-ed" aboard a UFO, examined and returned. Details of the encounter were not recalled until two of the abductees, Pat Roach and her daugh-ter, Betty, were hypnotically regressed by Dr. James Harder. Pat then recalled that several short humanoids with claw-like hands and one normal, bald man with horn-rimmed glasses and a fringe of gray hair unclothed her, examined her, pushed a needle into her abdomen and somehow extracted her thoughts against her will.

During one hypnotic session, Pat volunteered—and repeated twice—that her abductors somehow "limited time" in a way we do not. Another daughter, Dottie, remembered the chilling detail that she had seen several people standing in line to enter the UFO, including two neighbor children she recognized. The abduction took place about mid-night on October 16, 1973.[15, 16]

Horn-rimmed glasses?! Do aliens wear horn-rimmed glasses? Do they look like ordinary men, fringe of gray hair and all? Probably not. The ufonauts who look exactly like ordinary human beings probably are ordinary human beings.

But why would ordinary human beings appear aboard alien flying saucers populated by short, hairless, large-headed beings, as reported by Travis Walton and others? Why would a normal man be working with similar humanoids to perform what must have been a laparoscop-ic procedure on Pat Roach? Are these people kidnap victims? Are they "subjected to some kind of diabolic alien mind control and forced to tor-

13. Lorenzen, *Abducted!*, pp. 80-113.
14. From B. Ann Slate, "The Story of the Kendall Abduction," *UFO Report*, Dec. 1979, pp. 55-62, as reported in Hopkins, *Missing Time*, pp. 73-75.
15. Lorenzen, *Abducted!*, pp. 9-24.
16. Randle, *The UFO Casebook*, pp. 145, 206.

ture unsuspecting women to amuse some warped alien villain," as a science-fiction cartoon might suggest? Is that what is behind the pattern of abduction that appears to have been going on for at least several generations?

Perhaps. Almost anything is possible. But it sounds ludicrous, doesn't it? It just doesn't make any sense.

But maybe we're making assumptions we shouldn't be making. Maybe the "aliens" are not alien at all. Maybe they are simply advanced forms of human beings.

Biologists have developed various models to study our evolution. Many of them predict that man will eventually evolve—in response to pollution, increasing technology, etc.—into a being that looks very much like the "dwarf aliens" reported by Betty Hill, Travis Walton and hundreds of others. Several UFO investigators have made this connection. According to Aimé Michel:

> ...these small humanoids, as I say, usually fit in with the idea of an interpolation, in the future, of the past evolution of mankind...as though a biological and genetic technique had 'done a job' on human nature...'stepping up the performance' in those features peculiar to it (which are linked to the use of the brain), and artificially accelerating the natural rate of evolution of mankind.[17]

Charles Berlitz and William Moore put it this way:

> If the validity of the various descriptive reports is debatable, one must still admit that the features of head enlargement, hairlessness, muscle deterioration, elongation of arms, loss of height, etc., might be said to be a perceptive guess of how **we** will look in the far future, the point from which the "aliens" may conceivably have come.[18]

If humans begin colonizing space soon, as futurists predict we will, those who are born and raised in environments having little or no gravity may exhibit an abnormal appearance even without natural or artificial selection. It is a well-established fact that extended periods of weightlessness cause our bodies to atrophy. As Brenda Forman puts it:

> The absence of gravity does very nasty things to the human body. After even a few days, astronauts lose bone calcium, cardiovascular conditioning, and electrolytes.[19]

The atrophy of bones and muscles occurs because they are not constantly working against one another in dynamic tension. Astronauts who have stayed in space for months have had to perform regular rigorous exercises to lessen this effect, and they have still had a difficult readjustment period after returning to Earth. Humans who live in weightless environments outside the earth's gravitational field for generations (possibly to escape pollution, wars, biological contamination, overpopulation, cataclysm or perhaps even the aging process) will probably look quite alien to us, since they would have had no fa-

17. Aimé Michel, "The Problem of Non-Contact," in Bowen, *The Humanoids*, pp. 249-256.
18. Berlitz, *op. cit.*, p. 102.
19. Brenda Forman, "Voyage to a Far Planet," *Omni*, Jul. 1990, p. 84.

cility for (and no reason for) what we consider normal body development since birth. They may very well resemble mature babies. Yet they will still be identical to us genetically—in other words, they will be able to interbreed with us.

And the ufonauts might have good reasons for interbreeding with us and performing genetic "experiments," according to some experts. Richard Neal, a medical doctor specializing in obstetrics and gynecology at Beach Medical Center in Lawndale, California, thinks they may be attempting to create new genotypes by isolating mutant genes and using selective breeding over generations.[20] This is an intriguing concept in light of the time-travel hypothesis, because such an undertaking would be very difficult if researchers had to wait for generations to see results, but it would be quite easy if they were able to leap forward to the next pregnancy or the next generation in a matter of minutes or hours.

Michael D. Swords, Ph.D., Professor of Natural Science at Western Michigan University, proposed a slightly different scenario in 1985. In an article titled, "Ufonauts: Homo sapiens of the Future?" Dr. Swords suggested UFO occupants may be our descendants—improved by genetic engineering methods that will be developed in the future—who are coming back in time to repair their gene pool, which may be damaged by changes in the environment.[21]

In *The Watchers*, Raymond Fowler speculates that extraterrestrial beings may have come to Earth since man's beginnings and may have produced both us and the humanoids.[22]

Betty Andreasson says she was told by these "Watchers" that they are doing genetic manipulation because they know that the human race will become sterile in the future.[23]

Fowler's investigation into testimony from Betty and others indicates that some of the humanoids look like human fetuses because they *are*. They are apparently extracted from their human mothers long before term, prevented from breathing air, and placed in some type of apparatus we can surmise must be an artificial womb. This meshes well with data gathered by Budd Hopkins and others.

If Dr. Neal's guess that new genotypic individuals are the object of these bizarre acts (which several researchers now contend involve thousands of individuals) is correct, then we can begin to deduce a small measure of rhyme and reason from the frightening—and heretofore incomprehensible—pattern of abduction.

Dr. Swords points out that Caesarean sections are becoming more common as prenatal care and proper nutrition cause fetuses to develop larger craniums (despite the fact that human beings have not had time to evolve a larger pelvic size to accommodate the passage of larger

20. Fowler, *Watchers*, p. 238.
21. Michael D. Swords, "Ufonauts: Homo sapiens of the Future?" *MUFON UFO Journal*, Feb. 1985, pp. 8-10.
22. Fowler, *Watchers*, p. 224.
23. *Ibid.*, pp. 340-341.

heads through the birth canal). At the same time, a great deal of evidence exists to support the theory that human births may be triggered when the fetuses' brains have grown to the point that they begin to asphyxiate because the mother cannot supply enough oxygen to them.[24]

Swords and Fowler speculate that if this is indeed the case, the human brain (and head) might develop further if fetuses were removed before this stage of development was reached, and allowed to develop outside the mother's womb in an artificial, womb-like environment that supplied all the oxygen they needed. Thus, the ufonauts may be forcing the development of superintelligent human beings long before our natural evolution has had a chance to produce a pelvic size and womb-oxygen capacity capable of mothering such a development.[25] (In fact, we may have arrested our own natural evolution in this direction indefinitely. Survival of the fittest is no longer in full effect for the human species. Due to our social values, we are keeping weaker individuals alive and enabling them to reproduce through intense, even heroic medical efforts. And at the same time, women with extremely wide pelvises may actually have *less* chance of procreating instead of a *better* chance because cultural concepts of what characteristics a man should desire in a mate have made them less attractive to men in many parts of the world, and the stereotype of "slim is beautiful" has become self-perpetuating.)

There may be more arcane reasons for allowing fetuses to grow outside the womb. Survival may be one reason. Some experts believe that differences between the nervous systems of men and women start in the womb, when an estrogen, or so-called "female hormone," DES (diethylstilbestrol), bathes the fetus and "masculinizes" it, causing differences in brain anatomy, which, in turn, may alter not only sex and sexual behavior, but also mental attitudes and even "memory, cognition, perception, imagination, and control of bodily movement."[26, 27] Since psychological studies suggest it is male aggressiveness that is at the root of war (which at any moment could cause the destruction of all life on Earth), the human species may be able to survive in the future only if that male aggressiveness is removed from the species. Removing fetuses from the womb before masculinization occurs might be an effective way to do that. Of course the method would presuppose asexual procreation via cloning or some other artificial means—or through the use of sexual surrogate parents. Could Betty Andreasson have been such a surrogate?

Communication may be another reason. Removing a fetus prior to the hormonal changes mentioned above (or prior to other factors we are completely unaware of), or allowing the brain to develop further in the mother's body, might remove barriers to mental communication. Tests

24. Swords, *op. cit.*, p. 10.
25. Fowler, *Watchers*, pp. 223-224.
26. Kathryn Phillips, "Why Can't a Man be More Like a Woman...and Vice Versa," *Omni*, Oct. 1990, pp. 44, 48.
27. Douglas Stein, "Interview Roger Gorski," *Omni*, Oct. 1990, p. 72.

have shown that some human beings are capable, albeit sporadically and incompletely, of nonverbal communication with others (telepathy) over great distances. If this ability could be fostered, refined and mastered by the majority of the population, everyone might be able to communicate with almost everyone else with almost perfect understanding, regardless of nationality, religion or race. Enormous social problems resulting from misunderstanding and prejudices—problems that now cause terrible strife and may some day threaten the very existence of civilization—might evaporate. And spiritual and technological advancements might blossom beyond imagination.

Investigations done by Fowler, Hopkins and others indicate it is the diminutive, large-headed humanoids (often called "grays" because of their pallid skin tone) that are most often reported to be involved in breeding experimentation. And time after time, people who have been abducted by these humanoids report that they communicate via telepathy.

Whatever reasons ufonauts have for their "experiments," the fact that they perform them may not be as "inhuman" and "monstrous" as it looks at first glance.

For centuries, man has been biologically and/or mechanically altering living things—including human beings—to serve specific purposes. Most of our major food animals and plants, most of our pets and many of our flowers and trees have been "domesticated" through selective breeding and/or hybridization. We prune fruit trees, flowering plants, horses' manes and dogs' tails and ears, often just to make them more appealing to our eyes. We have castrated men to create eunuchs who could be trusted to guard harems. We have circumcised women to prevent them from enjoying sex "so they would become better mothers and wives." We routinely circumcise men for religious reasons or to make their lives more comfortable. We pierce our ears and noses (sometimes grotesquely), tattoo our skins, paint our faces, tan our bodies, shave our hair, distend our lips and breasts. We regularly alter the workings of our minds and bodies with diets, drugs, and surgeries, even changing our sex. We replace our organs with organs cut from live humans, dead humans, animals and hunks of metal and plastic. We terminate pregnancies if they are not convenient. Most of us would pay *anything* to substantially lengthen our lives. Many have already paid to have their bodies or heads frozen for the day when they can be brought back to life. It is perfectly logical to conclude that once methods become available whereby human beings can be "improved" (made more intelligent, less animalistic, long-lived) human beings will use them. In fact, it would be almost impossible not to draw such a conclusion.

Using gene splicing, DNA replication, cloning and in vitro fertilization, scientists can now practically create new forms of life to meet specific requirements. Already they have produced bacteria that can digest crude oil and toxic wastes and attack other specific bacteria. And some geneticists contend only a few years and a few legal and moral barriers separate us from the proliferation of "artificial species."

If our past is any indication of our future, the "invincible soldier" and the "perfect servant" will no doubt be priorities. We will also likely create organisms capable of surviving in hostile environments, such as alien planets. There has already been much discussion among NASA scientists and science-fiction writers about "terraforming" other planets by introducing organisms capable of metabolizing their crusts and atmospheres and excreting air and water. There has been much speculation among biologists, ufologists and scholars studying ancient history that the legendary "missing link" between early man and the apes may never be found because we ourselves are an engineered species an order of magnitude more human than our immediate ancestor. And many ancient myths and religious writings contain material that would seem to support such a hypothesis.

The hypothesis that at least some of the dwarf-like "aliens" are really human would help explain several characteristics of UFO phenomena that have posed thorny problems to proponents of the extraterrestrial hypothesis. One such characteristic is the way the "aliens" act. As Peter Gersten, a criminal defense attorney in New York, has pointed out, the things that happen during UFO abductions seem more consistent with what people do to other people than with what we might expect aliens to do to people. One researcher believes that the BB-like "monitoring devices," the patterns of electroshock, drug experimentation, hypnosis and posthypnotic suggestions that become "screen memories" are so similar to the methods used by our own CIA that abductions might be clandestine terrestrial operations similar to the "mind control" experimentation that we now know was carried out in the 1960s.[28]

Another argument for their humanness is that their equipment seems to be designed specifically for humans. As Fowler correctly notes, their abilities to easily paralyze our bodies without injuring them and to precipitate "out-of-body experiences" with small gadgets on their belts reflects an understanding of the human nervous system and the human mind that is superior to our own.[29] Their demonstrated ability to insert probes into several areas of abductees' brains, again without causing serious injury, adds weight to this idea, as does the fact that other hardware, such as the seat used to transport Betty Andreasson, was apparently designed to fit humans perfectly.[30]

Of course, not all ufonauts need be humans or near-humans for the time-travel hypothesis to be accepted, particularly since the ability to manipulate time will probably make space travel over vast distances possible. And not all ufonauts are. Almost everything, from ten-foot-tall green monsters with red-glowing eyes, to disembodied brains, to beer-can-shaped creatures with pencil-like appendages, has been observed.

Many UFO occupants have been described as robots. They probably are. Once figments of science-fiction writers' imaginations, robots

28. Patrick Huyghe, "UFO Update," *Omni*, Jul. 1990, p. 73.
29. Fowler, *Watchers*, pp. 72, 183.
30. *Ibid.*, p. 118.

have become a reality. Hundreds of different types are in use all over the world. Many are designed to perform tasks that humans wish to avoid, such as disposing of bombs, photographing radioactive areas, welding car bodies—and exploring other planets.

We will certainly have robots in the future, and some may be so sophisticated as to be indistinguishable from living beings (already much effort has gone into the development of robots that look, act and think like human beings). They will no doubt be used for dangerous missions (like exploring other planets and perhaps other eras). And there is no reason to suppose that the residents of other planets will not build robots of their own for similar missions.

If we use the time-travel hypothesis as a guide, we can explain the vast number and variety of craft that witnesses have reported, and that have caused mainstream science to disbelieve that UFOs could possibly be spacecraft. We can also explain the variations in occupant types. Because the hypothesis is based on fields, and because fields usually take on some variation of a spheroid shape, we should expect the variations of craft to be approximately round in at least one dimension, which is almost invariably the case. Because visitors from our own future could be expected to have numerous reasons to travel back to their past (our present), we should expect a great many UFO occupants to be human or near-human, which is exactly what the data indicate. And because aliens who can breathe our air and who resemble us would probably be much more interested in us than those who have little or nothing in common with us (for reasons of trade and exchange as well as for the sake of curiosity), we should expect a fair proportion of our nonhuman visitors to be humanoids—which appears to be the case.

14

If they use slang, they might come up with archaic terms like "twenty-three Ski-doo" or "hubba hubba."
—John Keel[1]

Men in Black

Between 1:00 and 4:00 one morning some years ago (the exact year has not been established), a West Virginia man named Jennings Frederick was awakened by a flash of red light. He saw an apple-sized canister bouncing around the floor. He was grabbed, felt a needle prick, then saw three men in black turtleneck sweaters, dark slacks and ski masks. They said the dogs had been darted and the people in the house gassed. One of the intruders asked another about Frederick and was told that he was about to lose consciousness and that he might later experience a sore arm from the injection. Both men spoke in common American idiom. Frederick remembers something being pulled over his face and being asked questions about UFOs. What did he think they were? What time was it? *What did he think of the future?* Then he did lose consciousness. No one else in the family remembered anything about the incident the following day.

Years earlier, Frederick's mother had seen a creature, tethered to a UFO, gathering samples of dirt and grass near the house. Frederick was a UFO "buff," perhaps because of an earlier encounter with a strange creature as a school boy, so he investigated the site. He found tracks that looked like something made by animal claws. In them were strands of hair. He sent samples of the hair and plaster casts of the tracks to the Air Force, which "explained" that his mother had seen a weather balloon! They never returned the casts or hair. Later, Frederick joined the Air Force. It was after his discharge that the abduction occurred.[2]

---

1. Keel, *Mothman Prophesies*, p. 173.
2. From *Gray Barker's Newsletter*, Mar. 1976, as reported in Steiger, *Alien Meetings*, pp. 58-60.

The Frederick encounter sounds suspiciously like a covert operation by the CIA or some other supersecret government agency. The methods and manner of speech were very human and very present-day. But why would the perpetrators ask their victim what time it was? This is the same question UFO occupants so often ask their abduction victims. Why would they ask him what he thought of the future? Was it important to them that he think what he was supposed to think? Was there a connection between the package of clues he sent to the Air Force and his abduction? Is there a connection between the hypodermic-brandishing cat burglars in the hill country and the grim humanoids who use their flying saucers to stall cars on lonely back roads, who poke and prod the bodies and minds of social workers and forestry workers and lawyers? Is the government cover-up more than a cover-up? Is it part of an alliance?

Methinks something was rotten in the state of West Virginia.

Something was definitely rotten in the state of Washington on June 21, 1947, just three days before Kenneth Arnold's famous Cascade Mountains sighting catapulted us into the "age of flying saucers." At about midday on that date, salvager Harold Dahl, his teenaged son and two crewmen on Dahl's boat observed six silvery-golden, doughnut-shaped objects over Maury Island. Dahl estimated they were 100 feet in diameter and hovering 2,000 feet above Puget Sound. Each had regularly spaced "portholes" around its perimeter, a dark, round "observation window" on its underside and a center "hole" one quarter its diameter. None had visible projections. Five of the objects seemed to be aiding the sixth, center one, which descended as if damaged and hovered 600 feet overhead. One of the other UFOs attached itself to it for several minutes, whereupon it spewed out a shower of aluminum-foil-like flakes, followed by an estimated *20 tons* of hot, heavy, slag-like material, some of which injured Dahl's son's arm, killed his dog and damaged the boat they were on.

The following day, an unfamiliar man in a black suit appeared at Dahl's door and described the entire event as if he had been there. He warned Dahl that he had seen things he shouldn't have, and that he and his family would be in danger if he told anyone. Two Air Force officers who investigated Dahl's claims were later killed when the Air Force plane carrying them and a large amount of the recovered slag-like material exploded and crashed under mysterious circumstances. Sabotage was suspected.[3]

The Maury Island encounter was later branded a hoax. But why should we believe it was? It was never proven so, and as we know, debunkers employed by the government have a habit of calling close encounters hoaxes even if they're not.

If it was a hoax, it is similar to many other UFO reports that have surfaced in later years. The visitor who knows more about a sighting than he could possibly know is a familiar theme to UFO researchers.

---

3. Flammonde, *op. cit.*, pp. 144-147, 166-183.

Julio Ladaleto was visited after he saw a UFO at Cojutepeque, San Salvador, El Salvador. At 11:35 P.M. on November 23, 1958, Ladaleto's car struck a can rolling in the road. He stopped, then saw a landed UFO 40 feet in diameter 115 feet away. It looked like a lamp shade resting on three half-spheres and had a transparent sphere on top that gave off a pulsating blue light. He then saw a bald, eight-foot-tall being wearing luminous boots and blue coveralls. He photographed it as it crossed the road to inspect the UFO. After ten minutes the UFO flew away with sparks, smoke and a "whining" noise.

The very next day "strange 'newsmen'" who seemed to know all the details of Ladaleto's encounter contacted him before he had had a chance to reveal anything about it to anyone.[4] If Ladaleto's visitors were newsmen—or even intelligence agents—how could they have known the details of the sighting? The witness hadn't told anyone—*yet*.

Angleton, Texas, Deputy Robert Goode stepped into the same "Twilight Zone" seven years later. At 11:00 P.M. on September 3, 1965, the same day as the New Hampshire encounter that inspired John Fuller's book, *Incident at Exeter*, Goode and Chief Deputy B. E. McCoy were driving between West Columbia and Damon when they saw a brilliant, purple glow. They turned their patrol car to watch. The UFO approached from five to seven miles in three or four seconds (which computes to 4,500 to 8,400 m.p.h.) and hovered silently 150 feet away at an altitude of 100 feet. It was gray, cigar-shaped, about 200 feet long with a rectangular, pulsating purple light as bright as a "welder's light" on one end, a hump in the middle and a smaller, dimmer, blue light on the other end. The light lit the pasture, the highway and the patrol car (inside and out).

Goode felt heat and panicked. He drove away at 110 m.p.h., while McCoy watched the UFO return to its original position at astonishing speed—as if it were a ball attached to a rubber band. The purple light brightened to tremendous brilliance as the UFO suddenly shot upward and disappeared. An infected pet alligator bite on Goode's hand that had been swollen and painful immediately before the incident was inexplicably nearly healed after having been exposed to heat from the UFO.

Later, two men came to the sheriff's office to warn Goode to keep quiet and to cooperate with any "occupants" he might meet in the future. They described the UFO in detail *before* he could tell them what it had looked like. They were never identified.[5, 6]

At 7:00 P.M. on November 2 the following year, two men saw a dark cylinder descend to interstate 77 in front of their car near Parkersburg, West Virginia. A grinning man in a dark coat emerged. Keeping his hands under his armpits, he asked them who they were, where they came from, where they were going, and what time it was. Even though

4. From *Settimana Incom*, 16 Sept. 1962, as reported in Vallée, *Magonia*, p. 273.
5. Keel, *Trojan Horse*, pp. 253-254.
6. Lorenzen, *The Whole Story*, pp. 248-251.

the sighting had not been publicized, they were later warned by an unknown "scientist" to forget the whole thing.

An appliance salesman named Woodrow Derenberger had an almost identical experience in about the same place. He described the
cylinder as charcoal gray, and shaped somewhat like a kerosene lamp
chimney. The occupant, "Indrid Cold," did not speak; Derenberger
sensed the words. Cold told Derenberger to report the sighting to the
authorities; he would come forth and confirm it. Cold and/or the object
were witnessed independently by Mrs. Frank Huggins and her two children and others.

Derenberger suffered threatening phone calls and other harassment, particularly from foreign-looking men who told him to forget all
about his experiences. Instead, he claimed continued mental contacts
and subsequent visits to Cold's planet, "Lanulos." In December, 1966,
he underwent electroencephalogram testing at St. Joseph's Hospital in
Parkersburg. He was pronounced normal. Derenberger considered the
ufonauts "time travelers," because trips he supposedly took with them
seemed to take days, but when he returned, he found that only hours
had passed. Indrid Cold referred to himself as a "searcher."[7]

At the same time on the same day, across the Ohio River in Gallipolis, Ohio, a professional woman was leaving work when she saw a
camera-like flash and was paralyzed while she watched a cylinder land
20 feet away. Two dark-complected men with angular features who
wore coveralls emerged to quiz her in "singsongy, high-pitched" voices.
They asked where she was from, what she did for a living, and "What
is your time?" (They asked this two or three times.) She later saw the
same two walking down the main street of Gallipolis in normal clothes.
She was plagued by further sightings, telephone problems, poltergeist-
type activity and even cattle mutilations on her farm.[8]

Ohio was to host more of the uninvited visitors. At 11:30 on the
night of July 13, 1967, Robert Richardson and Jerry Quay were driving
between Maumee and Whitehouse at about 40 m.p.h. when they
rounded a bend and saw a brilliant blue-white light blocking the road.
Richardson was unable to stop, and the car struck something. Both
men closed their eyes during the collision; when they opened them, the
object had disappeared. They reported the incident to police and highway patrolmen at the Maumee police station. They later found a lump
of metal at the site.

On the 16th, at 11:00 at night, two young men came to Richardson's home and questioned him about the incident. They didn't identify
themselves, but Richardson noticed they were driving a black 1953 Ca-
dillac with license 8577-D. Toledo police later found that number had
not yet been issued.

A week later, two foreign-looking, dark-complected men in black
suits came to Richardson's home and tried to make him think he had

7. Keel, *Mothman Prophesies*, pp. 55-236.
8. *Ibid.*, pp. 126-129.

not had the collision on the 13th. They made vague threats against his wife if he did not give them the lump of metal.[9]

The threats are not unique to the United States. Carlos Antonio de los Santos Montiel encountered them in Mexico. While in flight to Mexico City, Carlos' light plane started to shake. He saw three dark gray discs—one just beyond each wing tip and one coming straight toward him. He tried to lower his landing gear to touch the oncoming object, but the gear did not respond. The UFO scraped the underside of the plane's fuselage. For a time before he finally landed, he was unable to get the plane's controls to respond. Emilio Estanol, an air-traffic controller, told reporters that the UFOs had made a 270-degree turn at 518 m.p.h. in an arc of only three miles, whereas a plane would usually require eight to ten miles for such a maneuver.

While the witness drove to a TV interview, two brand-new-appearing, black Galaxie limousines forced his car over, and four tall, broadshouldered men (who never blinked) with black suits and very white skin threatened him and his family if he didn't keep silent about his experience. One of the same odd strangers threatened him again when he attempted to meet with Dr. Hynek (the UFO investigator) at Hynek's hotel.[10]

At 9:30 on the night of October 2, 1981, a student named Grant Breiland spotted a UFO through the view finder of his camera at Victoria, Vancouver Island, British Columbia, Canada. It was a bright, starlike object that appeared to be an inverted, domed disc. It was surrounded by four white lights attached to it by multiple light beams, and a diamond-shaped red light moved around its surface. When he asked on CB radio whether anyone on a nearby mountain could see the object, another young man replied affirmatively.

Three days later, Grant was approached by two very odd men dressed in strange, near-black clothing (including their shirts, which were fastened tightly at the neck, although no buttons were visible). They had no fingernails, deep suntans, lips the same color as the rest of their skin, rectangular ear lobes, no eyebrows and perfect, regular teeth. They spoke to Breiland in monotones without moving their mouths, asking his name, where he lived and what his number was. When he refused to answer, they walked stiffly (without bending their knees) into the rain and across a muddy field (where they left no footprints) and seemed to vanish. During the encounter (which took place in the vestibule of a busy K-Mart store near Breiland's house), he observed that all activity seemed to have inexplicably ceased.

Grant apparently suffered a time loss. That night he dreamed that the strangers had abducted him, taken him to a circular room and told him to forget his experience. The next day, he discovered an odd, inexplicable welt on his leg. He later received crank phone calls.

9. Lorenzen, *UFOs Over the Americas*, pp. 41-43.
10. Jerome Clark, "Carlos de Los Santos and the Men in Black," *Flying Saucer Review*, 24, No. 4 (1979), pp. 8-9.

A few hours earlier, the other witness had received a similarly pointless visit by two weird men (dressed identically to Breiland's visitors, also without fingernails but with extremely pale skin) at the gas station where he worked. They asked for "petrol" (not "gas"), grossly overpaid for it and then brought it back unused. No car was ever seen. Dr. P. M. H. Edwards, who investigated the affair and wrote an article for *Flying Saucer Review,* also received crank calls.[11]

Scores of witnesses of close encounters have complained of harassment by men who are usually dressed entirely in black, but occasionally don uniforms. The "Men in Black," as they have come to be called, or "MIBs," are often reported to ride around in big black cars, usually older model cars in "mint" condition (sometimes the cars even smell new). Often the windows are tinted black, and the license numbers, like those on secret-government-agency cars, are always unissued.

MIBs often show up at a witness' door the day after his sighting, before he has had a chance to mention it to anyone. Sometimes they appear to have trouble breathing and/or speaking, and occasionally ask for a glass of water to take a pill. On occasion, witnesses notice that they are wearing very thick soles on their shoes, as if they feared electrical shock, or as if they had club feet. Often witnesses notice other oddities about their clothes and/or mannerisms. They are likely to dress in a style that has been obsolete for years and use ridiculously outmoded expressions. Sometimes they walk about in frigid weather without any type of coat. Occasionally they seem to be baffled by common things. For instance, one was given a bowl of gelatin dessert and tried to drink it.[12]

These eerie characters usually know about and want any physical evidence the witness has, such as photographs, pieces of metal, etc. They usually warn the witness not to tell a soul about his encounter, sometimes making threats against him or his family (these threats are usually empty, but there is some evidence that they are occasionally carried out). They try to convince the witness that he hasn't seen anything. Before they leave, they frequently ask for an insignificant object, such as a ball-point pen, and seem elated if they are allowed to take it with them or manage to steal it.

It is impossible to tell where the government conspiracy to deny the existence of UFOs and to keep information about them secret ends and similar action by the ufonauts themselves begins. Even the Air Force is not sure. On March 1, 1967, Gen. Hewitt T. Wheless issued an official memorandum to a dozen Air Force departments, stating:

> *...persons claiming to represent the Air Force or other Defense establishments have contacted citizens who have sighted unidentified flying objects. In one reported case an individual in civilian clothes, who represented himself as a member of NORAD, demanded and re-*

---

11. Dr. P. M. H. Edwards, "M. I. B. Activity Reported from Victoria, B.C.," *Flying Saucer Review,* 27, No. 4, pp. 7-12.
12. Keel, *Mothman Prophesies,* p. 27.

*ceived photos belonging to a private citizen. In another, a person in an
Air Force uniform approached local police and other citizens who had
sighted a UFO, assembled them in a school room and told them that
they did not see what they thought they saw and that they should not
talk to anyone about the sighting....*[13]

Author Brad Steiger has this to say about MIBs in *Alien Meetings*:

*Those who have taken photographs of UFOs have been called on
by rather unusual individuals who confiscated the pictures and the
negatives—often by claiming government affiliation....*

*After a percipient has experienced a confrontation with the
MIB...telephones ring at all hours with threatening or nonsensical mechanical voices. Television and radio programs are interrupted by
alien signals. Network video and audio are blotted out, to be replaced
by images of robed, sometimes cowled, figures, who instruct the saucer sighters to cooperate and to keep all UFO information confidential.
In exchange...the mysterious entities promise the percipients key roles
in marvelous projects which will benefit all mankind.*[14]

Warren Smith writes the following in *UFO Trek*:

*Witnesses will almost invariably receive a call from a man selling
books, encyclopedias, pots and pans....They seldom talk about their
product and never close a deal. But they enjoy talking about UFOs.
They go over what the witness saw in great detail....If the witness
might have something physical from a UFO landing site, the salesman
gets even more interested. A few hours, no more than a day, after the
salesman leaves, the witness receives a visit from two or more men.
The newcomers display various credentials, some show cards as
members of Air Force Intelligence, NASA, or other agencies. The witness ends up giving his artifacts to what he presumes are government
investigators.*[15]

The MIBs seem to be as interested in UFO investigators as they are
in witnesses if it suits their purpose. After having obtained a piece of
metal from a farmer who said he had found it on the ground under
where a UFO had hovered, Warren Smith suffered break-ins and
searches of his hotel room, interference with his telephone messages
and with hotel records, and a visit by two men who made veiled threats
against his wife, children and publisher. After thus forcing Smith to
hand over his artifact, the men left in a car. Smith later determined the
license number had never been issued.[16]

John Stuart was cofounder of Flying Saucer Investigators, of
Hamilton, New Zealand. Sometime in 1952, about 30 minutes before
midnight, he received a telephone call from a mechanical voice that
claimed to be from another planet. The voice warned him to stop interfering in matters that did not concern him. Stuart and his partner,
Doreen Wilkinson, were plagued with paranormal phenomena and
threats until they discontinued their research. The final decision to

13. Memo from USAF Assistant Vice Chief of Staff Lt. Gen. Hewitt T. Wheless to ADC,
    AFCS, AFLC, AFSC, ATC, AU, HQCOMD USAF, CAC, MAC, SAC, TAC, and
    USAFSS, 1 March 1967; rpt. in Fawcett, *Clear Intent*, Appendix A, fig. 3.
14. Steiger, *Alien Meetings*, pp. 112-113.
15. Smith, *op. cit.*, p. 213.
16. *Ibid.*, pp. 210-219.

quit was made when a man visited Stuart, told him something that badly frightened him and took Stuart's prized proof—a piece of metal that had fallen from a UFO—away with him. This occurred in February of 1955.[17]

In April 1952, Albert Bender, a Bridgeport, Connecticut, resident, founded the International Flying Saucer Bureau. He was working on the first issue of that organization's publication, *Space Review*, when, beginning with a crank telephone call on July 30, 1952, he found himself besieged by unimaginably bizarre manifestations.

Strange, shadowy figures with glowing eyes and dark complexions and dressed entirely in black would appear in a dark theater or street. They finally began appearing in Bender's home. Each time this happened, he would experience swollen, painful sinuses, dizziness, nausea, headaches, etc. Each time, he detected a sulfurous odor and found his radio inexplicably turned on and tuned to a vacant channel.

Eventually, three of these MIBs materialized in his home—*Star Trek* fashion—and gave him a coin-sized, Saturn-shaped disc of metal. They explained that it would act as a transmitter in conjunction with his radio. Following their instructions to use the disc, Bender was transported instantly into an unknown place, which he took to be a flying saucer. There he was told by "alien" beings that their race had been visiting Earth for years to gather a particular chemical from the oceans. It was explained that while they were here they assumed human form, and that many of them had infiltrated the Pentagon and other sensitive places for intelligence purposes.

Bender was not to tell the aliens' secret. He was shown pictures of their planet and of terrestrial stockpiles of atomic weapons. He was warned that if Earth people learned what they were doing and tried to interfere, they had the capability of detonating all of the stockpiles simultaneously. Bender lost consciousness and awoke in his room.

On August 1, 1953, with the help of the MIBs, he was transported to a huge Antarctic ice cave. He was shown flying saucers, enormous, cigar-shaped craft and the process by which the aliens recovered the chemical from sea water. He saw aliens in their natural form, which he described as outlandishly horrible. A nine-foot-tall humanoid with silver hair, referred to as the "exalted one," answered Bender's questions about cosmology, religion, cancer cures, etc. He was again warned not to discuss anything he had seen and was returned to his room.

On one of his visits to the alien realm, Bender was stripped of his clothing, washed with a chemical and irradiated with a purple light. He was told this was a preventative for serious disease. He was also warned that his actions could now be minutely observed (perhaps he was fitted with an implanted transmitter). It seems he was to be under constant surveillance until the beings' Earth visit was finished, at which time he would be able to tell all to anyone he chose.

17. Barker, pp. 159-184.

Frightened of the nuclear threat, Bender declined to tell anyone the details of his ordeal until years later, when he published the story. Meanwhile, working on the assumption that since he already knew all the answers there was no reason to continue investigating the UFO enigma, he discontinued all such efforts. The International Flying Saucer Bureau dissolved.[18]

Aware that Bender was responding to some sort of pressure but unaware of the circumstances, many ufologists drew the conclusion that government agencies were responsible. For some years afterward, many regarded subsequent MIB actions to be the work of clandestine agencies like the supersecret National Security Agency (this was of course long before Lt. Col. Oliver North and the Iran-Contra hearings made the NSA a household word).

Albert Bender may have come too close to the real answer to the UFO riddle. The subsequent nightmarish chain of events just described may have been staged (or perhaps planted in his brain while he was in a highly suggestible state) to keep him from uncovering the truth. Although his terrifying abductions may have been real enough, the sea-water story seems preposterous—as if it were a cover story that totally ignores the thousands of close encounters on land. The real answer may be what Bender was pursuing when his weird ordeal began.

Bender's experiences cause one to wonder if he might not have been drugged, brainwashed or hypnotized and left with implanted memories. Investigators have uncovered other evidence that would seem to result from just such a scenario. John Keel, for instance, taped interviews with UFO witnesses on Long Island, New York. When he returned a year or two later, the people had no idea who he was, had no memory of their UFO experiences, and were genuinely shocked when Keel told them about their UFO connections.[19]

Whether due to posthypnotic suggestion or some later action, the New Yorkers in question appear to have been brainwashed. Perhaps if witnesses do not heed the warnings of the MIBs, arrangements are made to erase their memories?

I have had similar experiences myself. I once spent more than an hour discussing UFOs with a friend in the presence of three other people. She was keenly interested in my plan to write this book because a close relative of hers had had a close encounter. She volunteered a detailed account of it and told me she intended to ask her relative for more details. The next time I saw her, I casually asked if she had yet spoken to the woman who had had the encounter. She had no idea what I was talking about, even after I explained it to her at great length. She didn't remember a word of our previous conversation, or about any relative of hers ever seeing a UFO. She was not a close friend, but she was quite normal, a calm, open, friendly person. I had never known her to lie about anything else, and if she was lying about this, she had be-

18. Bender, *op. cit.*
19. McWane, *op. cit.*, pp. 28-29.

come an excellent actress without my knowledge. Her astonishment plainly showed on her face, and she clearly thought I was joking when I told her about our earlier conversation about her relative's encounter. But the others who had been present did remember the conversation.

There is some evidence that methods even more stringent than those used on Bender or Smith have been employed to silence investigators. Mrs. Jennifer Stevens of Schenectady, New York, was an active UFO researcher in 1968. She suffered a wide range of crank calls and phone problems the telephone company could not explain on her unlisted phone. Her husband, Peter, sketched an odd man who approached him to issue a cryptic warning about looking for UFOs. Peter gave a copy of his sketch to Keel. Later the Stevens' house was burglarized and ransacked. Nothing but the sketch was missing. Keel showed his copy to MIB witnesses, who usually responded that the sketch resembled the MIB they had seen enough to have been his brother. Two months after the warning, Mr. Stevens died very suddenly. Mrs. Stevens, convinced that Peter's death had been somehow related to UFOs, abandoned UFO research.[20]

Several UFO investigators have, over the years, died under somewhat unusual circumstances. For instance, both Morris K. Jessup and Dr. James E. MacDonald were the apparent victims of suicides. Recently, D. Scott Rogo was stabbed to death in his own home by an unknown assailant. Although there is no evidence to support their allegations, some UFO buffs believe these and other investigators, among them commentator Frank Edwards, who died some years ago, may have been "silenced" by MIBs.

Considered singly, each of the MIB stories sounds like nonsense; considered *en masse*, they paint a chilling picture of surveillance, kidnapping, death threats, burglary, brainwashing and murder. MIBs' methods often smack of the involvement of agencies like the CIA and the KGB. We now know, for example, that unsuspecting citizens were covertly used as guinea pigs to find out the effects of LSD and radiation on humans (just as we now know that radiation was routinely and intentionally released from the Hanford nuclear facility and the effects on citizens secretly monitored, a fact that the government covered up for 40 years). The MIBs' black cars with tinted windows and phony license numbers are straight out of the spy manuals.

But MIBs have been seen driving their black cars to and from landed UFOs, and have even been observed entering and leaving the craft.

According to R. Perry Collins, seven members of a family saw a flying saucer land in a field in central Long Island, New York, on a June afternoon in 1967. As they watched, a car left the road and drove across the field to the saucer. When it arrived, a door opened in the saucer. Two men emerged. They got into the sedan, which returned to the road and departed. The saucer ascended and grew smaller with distance until it could no longer be seen.

20. Keel, *Mothman Prophesies*, pp. 74-76.

A grocer and two policemen watched a dark UFO lower two cylinders to the ground as it hovered less than 50 feet over a field near Miami, Florida. The cylinders split and dissolved completely, revealing a large car and several men in business suits carrying briefcases. The UFO flew away. The men entered the sedan, which drove across the field to a road and left. The policemen refused to follow and implied that they intended to forget the entire incident.

Sometimes ordinary people are seen rendezvousing with UFOs. A high school science teacher watched a faintly luminous disc land in a Connecticut drive-in theater at 10:00 one night in August of 1983. It rose again almost at once, then the witness noticed a normal-looking man and woman in their mid-twenties walking away from the landing site. They walked out of the theater, entered a Volvo that was parked across the street and drove away. Two other people saw the UFO circling prior to the landing.[21]

Some MIBs may indeed be present-day operatives employed by government agencies like the CIA. We have already established that several intelligence agencies know more than they're telling about UFOs and that they have gone to great lengths to cover up the entire subject. Several Americans claim to have knowledge of a treaty between aliens and the U.S. government that gives the aliens rights to abduct and study certain people and mutilate cattle, provided the situation is kept secret, and provided the U.S. benefits by receiving advanced technology. Except for the curious tendency of people who make such claims to disappear, no convincing evidence has surfaced to establish the treaty rumor. But if these claims are even partially true, we can logically deduce that some U.S. intelligence agency is involved. Its operatives are no doubt kept informed of who has seen what where and when, and so would know which people to threaten.

Some intelligence agency would also almost certainly be similarly involved if the ufonauts are from our own future—particularly if they are from a future U.S. government.

Other MIBs are definitely something more exotic than CIA agents. Brad Steiger describes them as:

> ...short men, probably five foot six or less, with dark complexions and somewhat Oriental features...eyes that were noticeably slanted, but slanted in a way somehow different from...Orientals...pointed or peculiarly misshapen ears....MIB have difficulty in speaking properly because of short-windedness.[22]

John Keel also noticed this strange respiratory affliction:

> They seem to be gasping for air when they speak, as if they were suffering from asthma.
>
> This labored breathing is a common factor in many contact cases and in many Men in Black episodes as well.[23]

21. R. Perry Collins, "Playing the 'Reality' Game," *UFO Universe*, Jan. 1990, pp. 16-17.
22. Steiger, *Alien Meetings*, pp. 112-113.
23. Keel, *Disneyland*, p. 151.

So some MIBs look like ufonauts, they sound like ufonauts; they must be ufonauts—without their UFOs. Present-day CIA agents wouldn't have trouble breathing (but aliens or people from far in the future might very well be adapted to breathing a different type of atmosphere). They would know better than to try to drink Jell-O, and they would never ever draw attention to themselves by driving outdated cars or wearing odd clothes.

MIBs probably don't want to stand out either, but they often do. To once again quote Keel:

> They often arrived in old model cars which were as shiny and well kept as brand-new vehicles. Sometimes...wearing clothes that were out of fashion or...would not come into fashion until years later. Those who posed as military officers obviously had no knowledge of military procedure or basic military jargon. If they had occasion to pull out a wallet or notebook, it would be brand-new....like the fairies of old, they often collected souvenirs from the witnesses...delightedly walking away with an old magazine, pen, or other small expendable object.[24]

How can one possibly make sense of the seemingly nonsensical aspects of the MIBs' behavior? Imagine if you will that the scenario outlined in Chapter 13 is at least partially correct. That is, at some point in our future, someone will discover a way to slow the passage of time in a finite space, so that, in effect, he can arrange to have time "catch up" with him. As with every other discovery man makes, individuals who are greedy or stupid or desperate will eventually abuse the discovery, and that abuse will increase until society will have no alternative but to establish an interdimensional police force to preserve the integrity of history.

In recent years, crime in the United States has grown to such proportion that police forces are overwhelmed. Thousands of cases go unsolved each year. Imagine the enormity of the task that would face you as an undercover agent of an interdimensional police force in the future. The strategies, tactics and technology used by future criminals will be more complicated and more deadly than those used today. And hunting criminals down may be thousands of times more difficult. They might be able to escape not only to other locations on Earth, but also to thousands of other years in the past and future and to thousands of other planets during any one of those years. Finding them may be a million times as formidable a task as finding a needle in a haystack, especially if they disguise themselves as "natives" of the particular time zone to which they escape.

We have already established that time is not the flowing river we envision it to be. There may be no cause and effect, no linear progression from past, to present, to future in the real universe as there is in the model of the universe that exists in our minds.[25] Instead, the past, present and future may all be present simultaneously, so that what time really represents is an infinite number of coexistent parallel uni-

---

24. Keel, *Mothman Prophecies*, p. 28.

verses. Or time may be something we are unable to even imagine because of the dimensional limitations of thought.

At any rate, finding a person who has escaped into the past may not be a simple matter of moving forward along an accelerated version of your own "time line" to see if you found him. And both you and the refugee you are pursuing may run the risk of triggering any number of different types of paradoxes, the consequences of which would be unimaginably complex and extremely dangerous. There may be mechanisms, for instance, by which you could make some blunder that would erase your own existence and all memory of it. A typical example of such a paradox would be to go back into time before you yourself were conceived and prevent your own parents from ever meeting one another. This sounds ludicrous to us because our minds are in the habit of thinking of time as a linear progression, but since time is not linear, it may be entirely possible. In fact it may be happening constantly and we have no way of knowing about it.

The undercover agent in an interdimensional police force would face tremendous logistical problems. Anyone who has ever been involved in theater will recognize the staggering scope of trying to match wardrobe, props, vernacular, accents, mode of transportation, etc. for any place on Earth for any period throughout all of history at a moment's notice—perhaps for a force of thousands of agents! An incredibly extensive—and expensive—amount of research and props would be required. The only viable method of proceeding would be to make rough matches—within a decade or two—and learn a few basic phrases in each language or rely on computers capable of understanding thousands of languages.

Anyone who has ever worked for any government will be able to appreciate the profound effect budget restraints would have on such an operation. In many cases, the right costume or car simply would not be available, and you would simply have to make do with what you had—even if it was 20 years out of date. You would have to rely heavily on stealth, surprise, propaganda, hypnosis, drugs, disinformation, threats, etc. to maintain any semblance of your cover.

You would also undoubtedly have to employ a "mop-up" crew to follow you to erase any trails of telltale clues you may have been unable to avoid leaving scattered throughout time. Otherwise, you would constantly run the risk of having someone in the past deduce how time travel works, build a time machine and begin time travel prematurely—which could cause still more catastrophic paradoxes. The mop-ups' job would be as difficult as your own, as they would have to relieve witnesses of any physical evidence such as photographs or artifacts, then try to either erase their memories or scare them into keeping their

25. Publishers Note: In precognitive remote perception, "substantive information about geographical targets inaccessible by any known sensory channel has been acquired by remote percipients, with a degree of fidelity that appears to be statistically insensitive to the intervening space or time." See Robert G. Jahn and Brenda J. Dunne, *Margins of Reality: The Role of Consciousness in the Physical World* (San Diego: Harcourt Brace Javanovich, Publishers, 1987).

mouths shut, then disseminate false stories to discredit them and assure that serious investigations failed—and all with the same wardrobe
and prop limitations of the agents. The antique cars are logical, since
they could be used throughout a span of 20 years or more. Advanced
cars used even a year or two in the past, on the other hand, would be
obvious anachronisms.

Piled atop all this complication would be the even more mind-bog-
gling fact that time machines, by their very nature, will make interstellar travel possible, which means that criminals may escape to other
worlds and alien criminals may escape to Earth. Men, robots, androids, engineered species and alien beings from any one of countless
alien worlds and future Earth colonies may be visiting Earth's history
for an infinite number of reasons, and, of course, their respective interdimensional police forces would be obliged to follow. When one considers this, the apparent connections between UFOs and fairies,
leprechauns, bigfoots, "mothmen," mystery panthers and so forth
(which several UFO investigators have insisted exist) suddenly fall into
perspective. The reason these phantoms have been reported throughout history to make brief appearances but authorities have never been
able to capture them may be because they are only "passing through"
on a journey through time.

The description of dusky MIBs with Asian features is interesting.
Much of the earth's population is already centered in China and India,
and the proportion is growing constantly. Allowing for the ever-increas-
ing efficiency of transportation and communication, especially through
the use of computerized universal language translators (which we may
now be only a few years away from developing), a trend toward the mix-
ing of the various nations into a more homogeneous form seems inevi-
table. Our children are already fast becoming citizens of the world—
instead of nationalists or racists—because of the way satellite TV has
shrunk the world. War is fast becoming impractical because we now
have weapons that can destroy us all; eventually man will realize nobody can win. The necessity of world trade to support a burgeoning
population is already on the verge of forcing us to use universal cur-
rency in the form of computer credits that are instantly transferable via
satellite, and is tearing down isolationist barriers. Both communist
and capitalist nations are learning that they must cooperate if they and
our increasingly polluted planet are to survive. Barriers to free association—language differences, trade restraints, bigotry, etc.—will inevitably fall as man becomes more educated and more sophisticated. And
the development of telepathy would doubtless intensify that trend.

A more homogeneous race is sure to follow. We can only speculate
what the future human will look like, but dominant genes like dark
hair and dark eyes will surely survive, and the sheer numbers of Asian
peoples may insure that their stature and features will become the
norm.

MIBs' apparent breathing difficulties may, as I said, result from
being accustomed to breathing a different atmosphere. If they are from

Earth's not-too-distant future, they are probably adapted to breathing more polluted air, and because of our deforestation they are almost certainly used to more carbon dioxide than we are. Chances are good that they would tend to hyperventilate here. They could probably learn to control their breathing so they could operate in our cleaner air, or they could take pills to make the transition easier. (MIBs have asked witnesses for water to take pills that appeared to allow them to breathe more comfortably.) If they are from the remote future, they may be used to pristine air (assuming they have solved air-pollution problems or constructed their habitats so as to keep them out). If they are from some other world, they may breathe something else entirely.

The fact that the MIBs sometimes seem overjoyed by the prospect of getting to keep a common, highly portable, seemingly insignificant object poses a fascinating question: Could the ball-point pens be trophies—antique mementos to add to a collection of similar objects MIBs display in glass cases in their dens? Will they reminisce about them with their buddies over a glass of brandy and a cigar far in the future, just as many American servicemen discuss Japanese daggers they picked up during World War II?

A member of an interdimensional police force probably would not want to take anything of significance for such a collection. By doing so, he might inadvertently change the course of history. But the chances that an object as insignificant as a pencil or magazine would have an important effect on future events would be infinitesimal—well within the range for an agent to gamble on removing them for a prized collection. The practice might be just the ticket for making an unconscionably stressful job tolerable.

Apparently, MIBs usually succeed in depriving witnesses of their evidence. If a witness doesn't buy the line that the Air Force needs his pictures as a matter of national security, threats usually scare him into releasing them. If not, the photos usually disappear mysteriously within a few days. One day the witness goes to find them and they aren't there. He begins to doubt his own sanity, wondering if he ever saw anything at all. The visit by the MIBs seems so ridiculous to him that it only serves to strengthen his doubts. He usually decides not to tell anyone. Even if he does tell, nobody will believe him without the evidence. They will certainly doubt that the evidence disappeared of its own accord.

The method of acquisition should be fairly simple for someone capable of time travel. A personal time-warping field would probably be most convenient. The MIB could simply materialize inside the witness' house while the witness was away or asleep, take the photograph or fragment of metal, and dematerialize. If for some reason that method was impractical, a simple cat burglary should suffice. Imagine how easy such an operation would be for a present-day James Bond were he to travel a hundred years into the past with all his modern burglar-tool gadgets.

Considering the extent of the investigation undertaken by the Air
Force and the subsequent sudden, drastic changes of policy and obvious cover-up, it seems likely that somebody in the government found
the answer to the UFO/MIB mystery years ago, perhaps at the time of
the Roswell crash. It is not unreasonable to suppose that answer was
given in exchange for present governments' complete cooperation with
governments of the future in an attempt to control unauthorized time
travel and keep the secret of time travel under wraps until the date
when it is supposed to be introduced.

If this is indeed the case, present-day operatives would be working
covertly to support the investigations and actions of the future government. Their primary tasks would probably be to monitor all forms of
communication (which is exactly what the National Security Agency is
responsible for) in order to spot unauthorized time travelers, to debunk
sighting reports (which the Air Force and CIA have obviously been doing successfully for decades) in order to protect the secret until it is
time for it to be released, to quiet witnesses and to recover physical evidence. They would be working in tandem with operatives from the future (MIBs) and would only be used on a compartmentalized, need-to-
know basis when the MIBs were unable to handle the situation on their
own. The need for secrecy would be so great that they may be required
to submit to hypnosis or some mechanical type of therapy after their
tasks are completed, in order to erase even their own memory of the
mission.

It would seem that once our government officials were aware of
what was happening, they would have no choice but to cooperate. Not
only would the superior technology of visitors from the future or from
other planets give them the upper hand in any contest of wills, but also
cooperation with them would be in our best interests. The fact that
they exist at all is of paramount importance—it means we have a future. In this crazy world where young men and women on both sides of
the earth sit anxiously in silos deep underground, poised over buttons
that could end all life here, that fact alone outweighs all other consid-
erations. Surely no sane person would choose to jeopardize that delicate balance, even if a few of his countrymen must die from time to time
to protect it. And once any rational person learns that a time traveler
has the power to arrange for his entire existence to be canceled, he is
very likely to do everything in his power to keep that from happening—
which of course would mean cooperating, joining the conspiracy.

Without cooperation, history itself could easily become a disorder-
ly free-for-all, subject to the whims and mistakes of anyone who controls a time machine. A single security leak could have catastrophic
results. A single careless or unscrupulous individual could upset the
earth's entire history by tampering with the past purposely or accidentally. Imagine, for instance, what kind of a world we would live in now
if Adolph Hitler had been given nerve gas or atomic bombs.

There are other reasons for a cover-up—the economic and political
ramifications of the time machine itself. Once time machines become

available, all other forms of transportation and many forms of communication may instantly become obsolete. Why would anyone spend hours traveling via car or plane or train when he could use a time machine and arrive immediately? Why write letters to relatives in other states; why not visit them in person? The world's automotive, air, rail, trucking, shipping, telephone and postal industries could collapse virtually overnight. Economic chaos would result, including a global stock-market crash. Fortunes would be lost, millions would starve, seats of government would shift.

And just one time machine, if used properly, could easily allow a terrorist to hold the entire planet up for ransom. It would make stealing atomic weapons as easy as driving to the beach. The owner of the first time machine may decide to rule the world.

If some MIBs are indeed agents from the future trying to cover up the true nature of the UFO phenomenon, our tendency to believe in the romantic notion that all UFOs are spacecraft from distant planets that traveled here through space instead of through a space-time warp may be one of their most powerful tools. As long as we believe that, we are likely to continue scanning the far reaches of the universe for signals from those distant planets and building bigger and better rockets to penetrate space the hard way, thus leaving them free to go about their business unhindered. There is a great deal of evidence to support the idea that ufonauts have fostered the idea to throw us off the scent. To quote Jenny Randles:

> ...the visitors themselves might wish to create the false impression that they were from space. That could explain why they play games and act out roles based on our current science-fiction concepts. In this way the truth is not perceived by us, but if that truth is suspected by authorities, then it offers an even bigger incentive to cover-up.[26]

UFO occupants have been lying to us for centuries. They tell us it won't hurt when they stick needles into our abdomens—but it does. They tell us they will return on a certain day at a certain place. We gather our families and friends and TV cameras and wait dutifully at the appointed time on some lonely mountain top; they never show up. They tell us very soon they will land openly and reveal everything, but they have been saying that for decades at least. Meanwhile they sneak around in sparsely-populated areas in the middle of the night, abduct us and tell us they are from a city on Mars. But of course we have sent probes to Mars, and we know perfectly well there are no cities there. Next they assure us they are from the forests of the moon (but of course we know there are no forests there), or the galaxy of Ganymede (Ganymede is the fourth moon of Jupiter, not a galaxy). They tell us their names, and we later find out the names mean something like "visitor" or "searcher" in some obscure or ancient Earth language. They invite housewives and sign painters (instead of spacecraft designers or nuclear engineers) aboard their "spaceships," and show them their

---

26. Randles, *Conspiracy*, pp. 131-132.

"star drive engines," which usually turn out to be some nonsensical ball of glass or coil of wire. They convince these simple, honest people to join the lecture circuit so they can further confuse the rest of the population by repeating tired utopian ideas and ridiculous stories of beautiful, naked space maidens from nonexistent planets they themselves have visited.

Paranormal event investigator and author D. Scott Rogo thought ufonauts may have some way of extracting the thoughts of people they have taken captive, finding out what their beliefs are or what the current myths consist of, and then telling or showing them what they want or expect to hear or see.[27]

Several abductees, among them author Whitley Strieber, have suggested that the ufonauts may have been wearing costumes—masks or suits.[28, 29, 30] This is consistent with numerous descriptions of smooth gray skin, sometimes with a suggestion of a seam in the middle of the head, or a corrugated surface like the "Michelin Man," no fingernails, huge, shiny, black, opaque eyes like sunglasses (which could be lenses in a helmetlike head covering), and so forth. Some abductees say their captors told them the suits were prophylactic—to avoid spreading unfamiliar (and therefore potentially dangerous) germs back and forth.[31] That may be, but they may also be stage costumes designed to perpetuate the idea that they are from other planets. All sorts of other theatrical props and performances have been reported that would make no sense at all unless the purpose was deception—like the airplanes with eight engines that fly along silently while their propellers do not turn, and perhaps even the car/saucer rendezvous.

The ufonauts supplement the illusion by subjecting their victims to a form of mind control. Witnesses commonly describe being struck by a "light beam," or say a device which shocked them into paralysis was placed against their necks. Then they report telepathic communications with the ufonauts and rides in flying saucers to other planets.

Witnesses are convinced they are conversing with aliens. In reality, some are probably being drugged or hypnotized so screen memories can be planted in their minds by a "virtual reality" apparatus similar to a sophisticated video game, or so they can be taken to the future Earth and told it is "the planet Lanulos."

Curiously, "alien" planets are usually populated by people who look and talk just like humans, though the civilizations *are usually more advanced than ours.* It is important to note that the most outlandishly non-human-appearing examples of both ufonauts and MIBs are often described as robot-like. They move stiffly, speak in monotones without moving their mouths, have glowing eyes, etc. Many of the "aliens" witnesses have confronted may not be alien at all, but animat-

27. D. Scott Rogo, ed., *UFO Abductions: True Cases of Alien Kidnappings* (New York: Signet-New American Library, Inc., 1980), p. 109.
28. Strieber, *op. cit.,* pp. 67, 80.
29. Hopkins, *Intruders,* p. 137.
30. Edith Fiore, *Encounters* (New York: Doubleday, 1989), p. 312.
31. *Ibid.,* pp. 300-301.

ed mannequins in stage makeup. Similar "monsters" have been made for motion pictures. Walking, talking, gesturing copies of presidents and celebrities that are so lifelike as to be almost indistinguishable from the real thing can be seen now at amusement parks.

It is perfectly reasonable that we ourselves will eventually unravel the scientific principles that will allow us to communicate telepathically, either through mental training or through the use of some yet-to-be-invented gadget. Parapsychologists have been studying extrasensory perception (ESP) for years and have already made some progress. Some day they may understand the wordless communication that exists between mother and child in times of extreme danger. The conclusion that because ufonauts speak to us telepathically they must be aliens is unfounded. A truly alien race will probably find the way our minds work a complete mystery and vice versa. The idea that aliens will learn all about us and use the knowledge to invade us is probably nothing but science fiction. But it is quite possible that the tiny, BB-like implants that ufonauts have placed in abductees' brains may be futuristic receivers that facilitate telepathic communication with ufonauts fitted with transmitters or devices to stimulate areas of the brain that are the seats of telepathic ability.

It is only a matter of time before we develop beam weapons that can stun and paralyze. Prototypes have already been built. And stun guns—cattle prod affairs that paralyze a victim at a touch—are already in widespread use. We know that epileptic seizures can be triggered by strobe lights, and that flickering lights in sync with the normal brainwave patterns of humans can cause trance states and hallucinations. Neurosurgeons learned how to stimulate certain areas of the brain long ago, and in a few years we will doubtless be able to create whole experiences. Perhaps we will be able to direct television signals directly into the brain to simulate real experience.

The implants may also receive signals from distant transmitters that cause abductees to become paralyzed or to think they are having physical experiences when in reality they are in dreamy trance states. Hypnotists can make subjects experience vivid experiences simply by suggesting them. For example, subjects under hypnosis have actually formed blisters when told that a pencil placed against their skin was a lighted match. Certain drugs can create a similarly suggestible state. The so-called "truth serums" like sodium pentothal are good examples, but there are others that are more effective, and intelligence agencies around the world have been working overtime for decades to perfect them.

A similar state of mind can doubtless be induced by the right electrical stimulation in the right place. A subject so entranced can probably be made to believe *anything*. Perhaps this is why psychic manifestations like shadowy ghosts and objects which move by themselves and ringing telephones that are not plugged in are reported by abductees after their experiences. Of course it is also possible that the psychic centers of their brains have been stimulated into actually, physically producing these manifestations.

The methods of some MIBs are no more alien than those of some ufonauts. They too are sometimes just a bit more advanced than the methods of our own present-day secret agents—which is what we should expect if they are from our future. Whether a particular MIB is a present-day agent, a member of a mop-up crew from a time machine, a psychic manifestation or an induced hallucination, the result of his visit is the same—it confuses and scares us. By confiscating physical evidence, threatening family members, convincing a witness he did not see what he thought he saw, or appealing to his sense of patriotism, the MIB effectively stops the flow of information about UFOs. His theatrical performances, like the performances of the pilots of UFOs, are just ridiculous enough to ensure that a witness who describes them will not be believed.

Then our government discredits the witness publicly by issuing a cover story most people want to believe, and the job is neatly completed. We have once again been prevented from discovering the answer to the UFO mystery. We are left with the vague idea that UFOs probably don't exist, but if they do, they must be spaceships piloted by beings from distant galaxies who have spent centuries traveling through space to come here and study us or save us from ourselves. *That is what we are supposed to believe.*

Meanwhile, the ufonauts continue their clandestine surgeries and impregnations and "fetus-nappings" unhindered. The Men in Black stroll our shopping malls unnoticed. If we are to believe the claims of Albert Bender and other contactees, some even work at the Pentagon!

Contemporary supersecret organizations like the CIA and the NSA employ thousands and spend billions to spy. Undercover agents ("spooks") sneak all over this planet, using electronic surveillance, deception, disinformation, threats, brain–washing, drugs, hypnosis—all the same methods that ufonauts and MIBs employ. Their techniques and technology are so sophisticated that they would seem supernatural if they were to use them on people 100 years in the past.

Similar, but even more sophisticated teams will undoubtedly be operating in the future. They will go anywhere covert missions like intelligence gathering are needed—which is everywhere. When humans learn to travel into the past, they will follow. From time to time they will be called upon to perform burglaries, kidnappings, even assassinations. They will do so without question because they are protecting national security. They may even be protecting world security. Their gadgets will be so advanced that they will probably never get caught, but if they do, the diplomatic status their secret agreements with governments in the past will give them will allow them to go free while a cover story is circulated. The public won't hear anything about them except secondhand anecdotes.

As I was readying this book for publication, I heard a new rumor from an informant. It seems President Kennedy was supposedly assassinated by a government agency because he believed the American public had a right to know the real truth about UFOs, and he was determined to tell us, but let word of his plans slip before he had a chance to.

The Kennedy rumor is probably absolute rubbish. Most such rumors are. But it is just *barely* possible that there is a grain of truth in it. Several authors contend they have incontrovertible evidence that the *Warren Commission Report* was a whitewash. The photographic evidence clearly shows that the President was shot from in front, not from behind as the official story goes. And would the First Lady have tried to climb out the back of the car if the shots were coming from the rear? Suspects that should have been apprehended were ignored, and Lee Harvey Oswald, who could not possibly have done what he was accused of doing, became the scapegoat. And fishy things went on with other presidents and UFOs. Congressman Gerald Ford tried hard to get investigations of UFOs, but President Gerald Ford's lips were sealed. Governor Carter vowed to release UFO information once he was elected president, but President Carter simply made a halfhearted request that NASA look into the subject. NASA turned him down. Then there is the MJ-12 document that purports to be a supersecret briefing for a newly-elected President Eisenhower about a supersecret UFO project set up under President Truman.

So was the Kennedy assassination an MIB operation as my informant implied? I doubt it. As I said, it's probably rubbish. But it does serve as an excellent example of how a time traveler could change history dramatically with a ten-second effort.

Think about it the next time you're in an elevator, or on the street, or at a cocktail party, and you overhear a stranger say, "I wasn't born yesterday, you know."

If you're like me, you might catch yourself unconsciously wondering...was he born tomorrow?

15

The visitors could be...from this dimension in space but not in time. Some form of time travel may not be impossible...We cannot assume that time travel is out of the question.

—Whitley Strieber[1]

The Hypothesis

The background has been laid. A working hypothesis can now be proposed:

We do not understand the true nature of the universe as well as we think we do. Time is elastic, nonlinear and inconstant. Our ideas of time are illusions caused by (or confused by) the convoluted pattern of motions that our earth, our solar system and our galaxy follow. Time, like space, is not a thing, but an abstract concept used to describe certain aspects of space-time. It is possible to warp space-time, thus to, in a manner of speaking, "step outside the universe," and then return to it at other coordinates.

An analogy would be moving a pencil point from one end of a sheet of paper to the other by folding the paper instead of by drawing a line along its entire length. Understanding of the laws that govern this process makes possible the development of technology capable of a form of spatial transference equivalent to faster-than-light space travel. It also makes possible a number of paradoxes that could not occur if time were linear and fixed. At present, we are incapable of understanding the mechanics of this reality because our minds are trained to function in only four dimensions; however, we are able to grasp the concept subconsciously, because the subconscious mind is not restricted by linear thinking.

UFOs are not manifestations of a single phenomenon, but of a complex tapestry of many different phenomena. After the hoaxes, hallucinations and misperceptions of natural objects and occurrences have been removed, many of the remaining reports of unidentified flying objects describe real objects that are as tangible as automobiles.

---

1. Strieber, *op. cit.,* pp. 223-224.

Many of these UFOs are not spaceships in the common sense of that word, but vehicles designed to travel through time in the manner described above. Many of them are not from other planets, but from a future Earth.

These time machines are peopled by a complex mixture of human beings, evolved forms of human beings, genetically engineered life forms, androids, robots and/or alien life forms. These occupants make use of advanced technology based on principles that will be discovered at some point in our near future to produce fields around their craft that warp space-time. By manipulating those fields, they are able to traverse what we think of as space and time almost at will.

UFOs appear to us to be capable of impossible speeds and flight characteristics because they are moving through time at different rates and in different directions than we are. The fields are able to vary their space-time coordinates to match ours. The effect of the time-warping fields on light and other forms of electromagnetic radiation can make the UFOs seem to appear, disappear and change color and shape, and emit enormous quantities of electromagnetic radiation of all frequencies. The fields can stop automobiles, electricity and mechanical devices, and can paralyze people and animals and affect human perception.

UFO occupants visit all areas of the earth throughout its history for reasons ranging from scientific research to law enforcement. Their visits have inspired various myths throughout our history.

Some ufonauts observe our political boundaries and calendars and use our languages because they are from our own future. They do not want us to know this or to know the extent of their presence among us, so they discharge their missions in secrecy whenever possible. When their security is compromised, they send agents to cover up any evidence they have left behind.

Our government and the governments of other countries know who and what ufonauts are because they have recovered and studied crashed UFOs. They cooperate with them in keeping their identity and purpose secret because government officials deem cooperation to be in our best interests.

Some ufonauts are very frightened of our use of atomic energy and other things dangerous to the environment because they are from a future Earth, and, due to the nonlinear nature of time and the consequent possibility of paradoxes, can be directly affected by events in their past (which is our present).

Some ufonauts are engaged in an ongoing program of human husbandry designed to "improve" the human species to promote its survival in the future. They regularly and systematically abduct generations of human beings at various times throughout their lives to facilitate this program. They implant transmitters in their victims to monitor their conditions and movements in the same way we install portable transmitters on endangered animals. They have an intimate knowledge of the human organism, and of our future. They use surgical procedures, "mind-control" techniques, and terrorism and propaganda methods similar to, but more advanced than, ours.

Several different methods, including the following, can be employed to test this hypothesis:

(1) Equipment capable of detecting temporal anomalies can be designed and used. This needn't be horrendously complicated or expensive; we possess technology capable of producing large numbers of extremely accurate clocks, placing them at points all over the world, and linking them by computer. Such a system might show the path of a UFO surrounded by a strong time distortion as clearly as our radar systems track orbiting spacecraft. Results could then be compared with visual data and anecdotal data. The extremities of the jet airplanes the world's air forces use to pursue UFOs could be fitted with similar timepieces, and their times compared after close pursuits of UFOs.

(2) UFO investigators could redirect their inquiries with the time-travel and the implanted-transmitter ideas in mind. They could coordinate their efforts so the data they gathered might be less anecdotal and thus more useful for statistical analyses.

(3) Research projects designed to discover the true nature of time could be funded. They might begin with the clues already afforded us: relativistic theory, tachyons, black holes, quasars, the Doppler effect, etc. They should assume that time is variable, nonlinear, and inconstant as a starting point.

(4) Statistical analyses of the direction of travel of UFOs could be undertaken using computer databases compiled from reports where exact date, time of day and direction are known. The objective of this study would be to discover if there is indeed a correlation between the movements of the UFOs and the complicated mixture of loops and spins the earth follows as it makes its way through space. Studies could also be done to determine if these same movements actually influence our perception of the universe—specifically if they affect what we think of as the flow of time.

(5) Computer models that speculate on the direction human evolution might take could be compared to beings described by people who have been taken captive.

(6) Abductees who are experiencing frequent abductions could be monitored to alert others when such abductions are taking place, and can be given accurate clocks to place at different parts of their homes to record any temporal anomalies.

(7) Campaigns could be mounted to locate, remove and study those tiny implants lodged in the bodies and brains of hun-

dreds or thousands of abductees—before UFO occupants
are able to retrieve them.

Although I arrived at this hypothesis independently by studying
UFO encounters (many of which I summarized in these pages) over a
period of more than 20 years, I want to make it clear that I do not claim
to be the originator of—or even a pioneer in—the time-travel idea. It has
been used by science-fiction writers since H.G. Wells penned *The Time
Machine: An Invention* in 1895.

Throughout this text, I have mentioned authors who referred to
time travel in one way or another. In addition, it was studied and written about by Wilbert Smith, A.G. Cadman, Adrian R. Cox and Hernani
Ebecken de Arujo.[2, 3, 4, 5] René Fouéré speculated in 1966 that UFO
occupants might be time travelers from the future.[6] Ronald Story's *Encyclopedia of UFOs* lists time travel as one of eight explanations for
UFO phenomena, mentioning both the "policy of noninterference" and
the similarity of ufonauts to human fetuses as support for it.[7]

UFO investigator and author William Hamilton writes:

> It is generally agreed that alien vehicles are surrounded by and
> embedded in a field: electric, magnetic, and gravitational; and by the
> manipulation of this field an [sic] propel at great velocities or hover in
> place or do sharp-angled vector changes. By means of field control,
> they can disappear or change shape or change density so as to merge
> two independent structures into one. It is also possible to imagine that
> these vehicles can travel in a mode that warps space-time and permits
> them to span enormous distances separated by light-years.[8]

In *Healing Shattered Reality: Understanding Contactee Trauma*, Alice Bryant and Linda Seebach write:

> It is possible that the UFO phenomenon, as it has been experi-
> enced in the past 40 years, is a tantalizing glimpse of the break-
> through into heretofore unbelievable dimensions that are outside the
> time and space boundaries. If that is true, then the keys are already
> at hand in the new quantum physics.[9]

> It is highly possible that all of the universe(s) simultaneously oc-
> cupy the same nonlinear time and space. When it can be accepted that
> the universe functions like a hologram, that reality itself is the life force
> acting on the energy particles, then the next step is space and time
> travel, which, it appears, UFOs have already accomplished.[10]

2. "Another Speech by Wilbert B. Smith," *Flying Saucer Review*, 9, No. 6 (Nov.-Dec.
   1963), pp. 11-14.
3. A. G. Cadman, "A Layman's Time and Space," *Sphere*, 13 Jun. 1964; rpt. *Flying Saucer
   Review*, 10, No. 6. (Nov.-Dec. 1964), pp. 19-21.
4. Adrian R. Cox, "A Question of Time," *Flying Saucer Review*, 10, No. 4 (Jul.-Aug. 1964),
   pp. 7-9.
5. Hernani Ebecken De Arujo, *Einstein, espaço-tempo*, (Rio de Janeiro: the author, 1965).
6. René Fouéré, "Seraient-ils des revenants du futur?" *Phénomènes spatiaux*, Jun. 1966,
   pp. 11-14.
7. J. Richard Greenwell, "theories, UFO," in Story, *Encyclopedia*, p. 363.
8. William Hamilton, "Could this Be Magic?" *UFO Universe*, 2, No. 1 (Spring 1992), p. 23.
9. Alice Bryant and Linda Seebach, *Healing Shattered Reality: Understanding Contactee
   Trauma* (Tigard, Oregon: Wild Flower Press, 1991), pp. 176-177.
10. *Ibid.*, p. 177.

> *The current construct of time and the lack of understanding of vi-*
> *brations may be preventing the true breakthrough, if, in the other di-*
> *mensions, time is nonlinear and simultaneous, i.e. the eternal now.*
> *This may already be being demonstrated in instances of accelerated*
> *time. While not as common as missing time, accelerated time is still*
> *part of the UFO phenomenon.[11]*

Raymond Fowler hints that ufonauts are time travelers throughout *The Watchers*. He remarks:

> *...somehow they are able to know the future! Needless to say,*
> *this not only provokes some pretty hefty philosophical questions but it*
> *also raises equally mind-straining questions about the nature of* **time**
> *itself.[12]*

> *...the aliens told Betty about* **time***. They insisted that our concept*
> *of time was* **localized** *and that time as we understood it did not really*
> *exist. The human concept of time was illusory. All is* **Now***. Until recent-*
> *ly such statements would have been scoffed at by scientists. But the*
> *New Physics seems to be hinting at this very concept.[13]*

> *...Betty Andreasson was told some very incredible things about*
> *the aliens and their relation to time....In essence, the aliens informed*
> *Betty that they had the capability to freely move through time and*
> *space. The past, present, and the future are the same to them.* **Time,**
> *as we know it, does not exist for them![14]*

Dr. Vallée states in *Confrontations*:

> *I do not believe any more that UFOs are simply the spacecraft of*
> *some race of extraterrestrial visitors. This notion is too simplistic to ex-*
> *plain their appearance, the frequency of their manifestations through-*
> *out recorded history, and the structure of the information exchange*
> *with them during contact. Instead, I have argued that an understand-*
> *ing of the UFO phenomenon would come only when we expanded our*
> *view of the physical universe beyond the classic four-dimensional*
> *model of space-time. Like other paranormal phenomena, UFOs seem*
> *to be able to operate outside of known space-time constraints.[15]*

In *Revelations: Alien Contact and Human Deception,* he adds:

> *The genuine UFO phenomenon, as I have shown in* **Confronta-**
> **tions,** *is associated with a form of nonhuman consciousness that ma-*
> *nipulates space and time in ways we do not understand.[16]*

> *It is curious to observe that even scientifically trained researchers*
> *who accept the idea of multiple universes, or the few ufologists who*
> *understand the idea that space-time could be folded to allow almost*
> *instantaneous travel from one point of our universe to another, still*
> *cling emotionally to the notion that any nonhuman form of conscious-*
> *ness is necessarily from outer space.[17]*

> *...we could hypothesize extraterrestrial travelers using radical*
> *methods of space-time manipulation, notably the use of four-dimen-*

---

11. *Ibid.*, p. 178.
12. Fowler, *Watchers*, p. 125.
13. *Ibid.*, p. 185.
14. *Ibid.*, p. 209.
15. Vallée, *Confrontations*, pp. 99-100.
16. Vallée, *Revelations*, p. 236.
17. *Ibid.*, p. 237.

*sional wormholes for space and possibly even time travel....Such trav-
elers could perform many of the physical feats ascribed to ufonauts,
and they could also manifest simultaneously throughout what appears to us as different periods in our history. This hypothesis represents an updating of the ETH where the "Extraterrestrials" can be from
anywhere and any time, and could even originate from our own
Earth.*[18]

In *Communion*, Whitley Strieber writes:

> *...they might have really, physically arrived sometime in the fu-
ture, and then spread out across the whole of our history, in effect going back into time to study us. This might mean that they could be here
only a short time—say a few weeks or months—but are carrying out a
study that would seem to us from our position in sequential time to
have extended over our entire recorded history....If time travel can exist and is involved, God only knows what the travelers would look like
to us as they reached back from the future.*[19]

Jenny Randles sums the situation up splendidly in *The UFO Conspiracy: The First Forty Years*:

> *...UFOs might be 'timeships,' not 'spaceships'. They are flown by
intelligent beings far past our level of technological development and
they **are** extremely interested in us at this critical time in the planet's
history. However, they are human. Humans from our far future.... For
UFOs **not** to be 'timeships' we will virtually have to rule out any prospect of time travel **ever** becoming possible. For if it does—even thousands of years from now—surely the era when we entered space and
built our first weapons capable of destroying the planet would have
sufficient interest to attract visitors.*[20]

Finally, there are those who claim to have actually worked on and
used time machines built by human beings here on Earth.

Contactee Fred Bell, for instance, claims entities from other solar
systems taught him how to build a working time machine that he could
actually use to transport things.[21] I have not seen Bell's machine in operation, so I cannot vouch for him, but I can say that he is not alone in
his assertions. In fact, people have now come forward to publicly pro-
claim that humans began traveling through time as early as 1943!

According to several witnesses, including Alfred Bielek, Preston B.
Nichols and Carl Allen (who often referred to himself as Carlos Miguel
Allende), a group of scientists working for the United States Navy made
a ship disappear from a Philadelphia dock in 1943. This event, which
has popularly become known as "the Philadelphia Experiment," was
apparently one of a long series of experiments sponsored by the Navy
in an attempt to achieve invisibility, which would give U.S. ships a powerful edge over Axis submarines during World War II.

18. *Ibid.*, p. 255.
19. Strieber, *op. cit.*, p. 225.
20. Randles, *Conspiracy*, p. 131.
21. For information on Fred Bell, see *International UFO Library Magazine*, Vol. 2 (1991),
    p. 28.

According to these witnesses, the project was called Project Rainbow. Nicola Tesla, the brilliant inventor responsible for alternating current, and Dr. John von Neumann, the brilliant mathematician, were the primary designers of special high-voltage equipment installed on the U.S.S. *Eldridge*. At 9:00 on July 22, 1943, the equipment was turned on. The ship became invisible, both optically and to radar. When it was turned off, some of the crewmen were found with parts of their bodies intermingled with the steel of the ship's bulkheads and decks, others were burning, invisible, floating in the air or unable to move. Most were hysterical with fear.

The equipment was changed to achieve only radar invisibility, not optical invisibility, and a new crew was assembled. On the morning of August 12, the switches were pulled again. For a minute or more, the *Eldridge* was invisible to radar. Then there was a flash and it disappeared. It was not invisible, it was gone completely. There was not even a line in the water where it had been.

Once again, the crew "went crazy." Fearing the worst, Alfred Bielek (known at that time as Edward Cameron) and his half-brother, Duncan Cameron, both physicists in charge of starting and stopping the experiment, jumped overboard. They did not land in Philadelphia Harbor, but on the grass at New York's Montauk Army Base on Long Island! And though it had been morning, it was now night!

Their adventure was soon to become even more shocking. They were expected at Montauk. Military Policemen were waiting for them. They ushered them into an underground complex, where they were greeted by Dr. von Neumann—the same man whose presence they had left moments before—who was now *forty years older*. Von Neumann told the stunned scientists they had been sucked into hyperspace and into the year 1983 through the interaction of time-warping fields created by the equipment aboard the *Eldridge* and time-warping fields generated by an experimental time machine being tested at the Montauk site.

I asked Bielek if there was any possible way von Neumann could have been disguised with makeup to fake being forty years older for some unknown reason.

"Absolutely not," he said.

"How can you be certain?" I asked.

"Because we saw modern computers, computer graphic displays, color TV, etc. and watched the content of TV for several hours."

The elderly scientist then told them they would have to return to the *Eldridge* to turn off the equipment—by destroying it if necessary—because a serious rift in time had resulted from the incident. It had to be closed or it could have disastrous effects.

"How will we get back there?" they asked.

"Don't worry, we'll get you back there," von Neumann told them. "With this station we have complete control over space and time, and we can send you anywhere in space or time."

Von Neumann did send them back, they did destroy the equipment, and the Navy declared the Project Rainbow impractical and abandoned it. Then, many years later, Bielek and Duncan both worked on Project Phoenix at Montauk with Dr. von Neumann—the same project that had transported them through time back in 1943.[22]

Bielek details his story about Project Rainbow in *The Philadelphia Experiment and Other UFO Conspiracies*, which he coauthored with Brad Steiger and Sherry Hanson Steiger.[23]

In *The Montauk Project: Experiments in Time*, Preston Nichols describes in great detail how he, Bielek, von Neumann and others explored thousands of years into the earth's past and future using the Phoenix Project time machine.[24] This took place between 1979 and 1983, when the project was abandoned. It included the transport of the *Eldridge* from 1943.

The stories that Allen, Bielek, Nichols and others tell are extremely difficult to believe, even for researchers who have spent years delving into the bizarre details of the UFO mystery. In addition to time travel, they involve mind control, psychic projections, age regression, transfer of souls from one body to another, trips inside pyramids on Mars and financing of secret projects with billions of dollars' worth of stolen gold. Nichols says the time machine he worked with may have been based on an alien design; Tesla claimed frequent communication with aliens; and Bielek told me he personally saw and worked with several different groups of aliens, including the now-famous, diminutive "grays," which he said were "all over the place" in the underground facility at Montauk. He said aliens "provided the technical expertise to make the project possible."

The stories are even harder to document. The government officially denies that any of the experiments ever took place. The underground portion of the former Montauk Army Base has been sealed with concrete plugs. Each witness says that he and his peers were brainwashed and given new identities, and only remembered their involvement much later, when a movie about the Philadelphia Experiment, a visit to the Montauk site, etc. triggered his buried memories. (It is rumored that intelligence agents routinely submit—voluntarily—to drug therapy and hypnosis to remove memories dangerous to national security and replace them with harmless screen memories. A similar process may be the cause of some of the more bizarre aspects of Bielek's and Nichols' stories.)

Nevertheless, others who claim to have been involved in Project Rainbow and/or Project Phoenix continue to surface. Stories of the Philadelphia Experiment stubbornly refuse to die. This might simply be

---

22. Telephone interview with Alfred Bielek, 7 Aug. 1992.
23. Brad Steiger, Alfred Bielek and Sherry Hanson Steiger, *The Philadelphia Experiment and Other UFO Conspiracies* (New Brunswick, New Jersey: Inner Light Publications, 1990).
24. Preston B. Nichols and Peter Moon, *The Montauk Project: Experiments in Time* (New York: Sky Books 1992).

because so many people love a mystery. Then again, maybe it is because the stories are at least partially true.

When I submitted the original manuscript for this book, I was aware of the Philadelphia Experiment in invisibility, and had even read claims that the ship had been somehow transported instantly from one harbor to another, but I had never heard of Fred Bell, Alfred Bielek, Preston Nichols, Project Phoenix or any other alleged time-travel experiments. These things were only brought to my attention during final preparations for printing *Visitors From Time*. Had I not done the research that led to the writing of this book, I am certain I would have considered these tales the most outrageous fiction. But, although I am cautiously skeptical, I cannot dismiss them out of hand. I believe I have shown that it is likely UFO occupants are able to manipulate space-time. Why should it not be equally likely that a group of brilliant scientists, backed by huge sums of money and possessed of supercomputers and other space-age technology, might have learned to do so too? Why couldn't they have accomplished a crude form of time travel as early as 1979—whether they had alien help or not? And why couldn't they have continued to use time travel, and to refine the process to the point where they themselves are now zipping around throughout space and time, perhaps even abducting unsuspecting people on dark, lonely highways?

I have no doubt that skeptics and debunkers will attempt to discredit this book, as they have tried to discredit others, by proclaiming that a detail is in error here and a witness is unreliable there. They will subsequently demand that the entire book and all its premises, including the time-travel hypothesis, be ignored because they can find inconsistencies.

Let me save them some effort by admitting in advance that it is quite possible some, perhaps many, of the accounts in these pages are spurious or at least partially incorrect. At the same time, I would suggest that these people will be entirely missing the point. Because with these accounts, as with all bodies of anecdotal data, it is not the veracity of individual details or witnesses that determine value, but rather the collective weight of the whole volume of data. To treat empirical data skeptically is wise, particularly if peer review and refereeing finds inconsistencies in those data. But to ignore unmistakable patterns in preliminary anecdotal data because this detail or that is suspect is to champion ignorance merely for the sake of argument. Such an attitude demonstrates an inelegant obtuseness akin to that of a man who starves to death in a supermarket because he suspects a few of the foods it contains are not nutritious.

Clearly the question of whether UFOs exist was answered long ago. Clearly they are real. Clearly they cause temporal and spatial anomalies. And clearly their occupants have been kidnapping us, performing unauthorized surgeries on us and lying to us about the whole project.

It is true that the UFO enigma that has defied solution for nearly half a century may never be resolved. Indeed, we may be incapable of recognizing or understanding its solution even if we find it. But if we apply the scientific method to our search for answers—if we use existing data to formulate working hypotheses, then design repeatable experiments to test those hypotheses, building on what we learn until we can construct theories and finally arrive at facts—we may have a chance to someday say with certainty, "These are the answers."

If, on the other hand, we fail to test hypotheses because we have decided beforehand that they are impossible, we can only delay the completion of the puzzle. We will have fallen into the same trap that ensnared astronomers a hundred years ago—the men who refused to believe meteors existed, declaring that stones could not fall from the sky because, as everyone knew, there were no stones *in* the sky. And if, instead of proposing hypotheses that can be tested experimentally, we simply continue to gather more and more anecdotal data to pile atop the mountain we have already collected, all the while hoping the perfect encounter case with the ultimate, definitive answer will someday magically appear, then we will probably still be hoping after another half a century.

I cannot establish scientific fact because I am a writer, not a scientist. But I believe the chronicles in the pages of this book make the time-travel hypothesis I have outlined a valid working platform for scientific research. And I believe the methods I have suggested warrant consideration. I challenge those who *are* scientists to test the hypothesis, and I challenge those who underwrite scientific research to make funds available for such tests.

Doing so will not be an easy task. For decades, government officials in key positions have gone to great lengths to ensure that certain information about the UFO mystery remains hidden. And they have done a competent job. Even now the mere mention of UFOs is likely to elicit jeers and snickers from almost any group. And I'm sure that even after reading this entire book, some people will insist on asking me, "Do you believe in UFOs?"

Nevertheless, the "dark ages" of ufology may be behind us now, at least in the U.S. Polls show a majority of Americans admit UFOs exist. Millions admit sightings and thousands claim abductions. Many of those who scoff at UFOs in public privately confess personal encounters. As a rule, witnesses are less fearful of ridicule and retribution than they were a few years ago, and many are now allowing their real names to be used. Distinct patterns concerning abductions are being documented, and psychologists are taking them seriously.[25]

After scandals like My Lai, Chappaquiddick, Watergate, Iran-Contra, the savings & loan debacle and "Read my lips," people have learned not to blindly trust the words of government officials. A lot of them are angry about the Air Force's obviously false "explanations" claiming UFOs are weather balloons and swamp gas. Some have vowed to force

25. See David M. Jacobs, *Secret Life: Firsthand Accounts of UFO Abductions* (New York: Simon & Schuster, 1992).

the CIA and NSA to honor Freedom of Information requests for UFO information whether they want to or not. Others have already unraveled the Roswell cover-up beyond anyone's ability to keep a lid on it and are disclosing more facts all the time.[26]

The ufonauts have been telling us for decades that we would soon understand who they are and where they are from. Maybe this is the time. Maybe the "New World Order" former president Bush talked about will involve more than the fall of Communism. Maybe we will find out who has been kidnapping us and why.

Maybe someone from our future has made a decision to allow this book to be published because the proper time to announce the discovery of the time-warping field is just around the corner.

---

26. See Stanton T. Friedman and Don Berliner, *Crash at Corona* (New York: Paragon House, 1992).

16

I don't know what the "aliens" are. They could be a product of government or military mind control. We must keep our minds open to all possible explanations until we are certain of the truth.

—Leah A. Haley

Beyond Time

This book was never intended as an argument that *all* UFOs are from our own future. It does attempt to establish that many (perhaps not all) UFOs appear to be surrounded by, and encased in, fields capable of warping space-time in a way that is somewhat similar to the way a black hole warps space-time. This process could make space travel and even interdimensional travel very easy. This could mean that UFOs might be coming here from literally millions of *different* places, including other planets, other star systems, other galaxies, parallel universes that we have not yet discovered *and* the past and future of each of these places. For all we know, these fields might even enable our visitors to travel here physically from the dimensions we ourselves go to "astrally" when we dream or when we die.

So the time-travel hypothesis does not necessarily *conflict* with the ET hypothesis, it is just more complete. As I pointed out earlier, the ET hypothesis does not fit the data for some cases. But that certainly does not mean that it is wrong for all cases. Some ufonauts may be time travelers, others may be space travelers, and still others may be both—or neither. Some may also be angels, demons, atmospheric animals, etc. Because our minds want to be linear, because we have been taught since we were children to file facts away in neat little pigeon holes, we tend to assume unknown phenomena must fall into one category or another, rather than considering that they may represent many different categories.

Before we can truly solve this mystery, we may have to learn to think differently. As researcher Stanton Friedman tells us, breakthroughs often come when people learn to think about things in a different way. Unfortunately, in the UFO community, as in any other arena, people often resist change of any kind. We often become so enamored with certain opinions and pet theories that we begin to treat them as facts, and then hang on to those "facts" long after they have been proven to be in error.

Some people who experience contact with the occupants of UFOs refer to themselves as "abductees." They describe how they are the unwilling victims of small beings from Zeta Reticuli or some other star system who kidnap them from their beds, callously perform business-like examinations, inseminate them, rob them of their fetuses and unfairly block their memories of the entire process. Many abductees suffer trauma similar to posttraumatic stress disorder and believe that "all aliens are evil, or at least uncaring." Some become angry when others talk about "benevolent ETs" and refuse to read books about the "space brothers."

Others call themselves "contactees," "selectees" or "experiencers." They tell me about taking wonderful rides on fabulous alien ships piloted by gentle, loving people from Saturn, Andromeda, Arcturus and other places. Some report that they have happily sired or given birth to numerous half-human/half-alien children, and a few even say they are married to aliens as well as to their human spouses. They often believe the "space brothers" are here to help deliver us from ourselves, and say they are given messages like "stop using nuclear power and stop polluting the planet," and "learn to love one another unconditionally." Many of these people feel outrage, sorrow or hurt when they hear the stories of the abductees, and contend that all extraterrestrials (they dislike the term "aliens") are good.

Another large group of experiencers prefer the name "channelers." These people recount how they receive telepathic messages by mentally "tuning in" to thought waves generated by intelligent beings who live in space, on other planets, or in other "higher planes of vibration" that are sometimes referred to as other dimensions or other universes that co-exist with ours. Channelers often talk about consciousness expansion; upcoming Earth changes; the transformation of humans into more spiritual, more intelligent, more powerful and purer beings. Many of them consider themselves citizens of the universe who are only temporarily living on Earth. Some say their souls chose to be born here to fulfill a particular purpose, and will return to the "higher planes" after death (and perhaps be born again in a different body on Earth, on a different planet, or in a different universe). Many believe the abductees are misguided.

Still another group interprets all contact with other intelligences in terms of Christian religious beliefs. What is an abduction by unfeeling aliens to one abductee might be one of Satan's tests to another. A contactee-like experience might be a communication with Mother Mary, a guardian angel, or Jesus Christ. And channeling might be talking to God, speaking in tongues, or manifesting a demonic possession. Many of these people take a dim view of the whole idea of advanced extraterrestrial life because they have been taught that the human being is the apple of God's eye.

And, of course, there are the ufologists, who are trying to accumulate enough physical evidence to prove, once and for all, that ufonauts are either ET astronauts from another planet, ultraterrestrial beings from another dimension, "Deros" and "Teros" from the center of the earth, or something else entirely. Each ufologist seems to have a pet theory. Some of them are skeptical about the possibility that ETs could be visiting us in the great numbers that have been reported, because they believe that Einstein's theory of relativity proves the speed of light cannot be exceeded, and therefore the ETs could not live long enough to visit here.

It seems to me that members of all of these groups (and others) share a few similar ideas. For instance, most of the people in each group believe "non-human intelligences" exist. Most of them seem to be excited and a little anxious about something momentous and imminent, and many believe they are being somehow groomed or trained to play a special role in this event. But the similarity that I have found most striking is that each group seems to be completely faithful to its own chosen interpretation as the one and only possible explanation for all visitations and is unwilling to even consider that other explanations might have validity. In other words, they are not open to the idea of thinking differently.

But if the hypothesis presented in this book is correct, each of these groups might have the right answer—to *part* of the mystery. Not all "non-human intelligences" need necessarily be from one particular place. Some could be from Zeta Reticuli, some from Andromeda, some from Earth, some from a dimension where psychic energy reigns and so on, *ad infinitum.* Nor do all of them need necessarily come from the year 1994. Some might be from 2999, some from 2000 B.C., and so on. And, of course, each might have a different motivation and a different agenda than any other.

So perhaps we students of ufology are not as open-minded as we thought. Yes, we're all light years ahead of the official positions of the *New York Times* and the U.S. Air Force. But perhaps we should all try to pry our minds open just a little further. Perhaps the opinions of abductees, contactees, channelers, Christians, ufologists and a great many other groups are *all* valid. Perhaps we should all learn to be tolerant enough to at least listen to others' ideas.

It was with this idea of tolerance for different viewpoints in mind that Wild Flower Press and I began publishing a newsletter, titled *CONTACT FORUM (The Round Table of Universal Communication),* which promotes open discussion of encounters, findings and opinions among experiencers of all types, researchers and therapists. (Another major reason for the newsletter is to help experiencers cope with their encounters.) The response to our first few issues has been very gratifying. We have received scores of articles.

Time travel and the warping of space-time are not obscure New Age concepts. They are staples of the state-of-the-art quantum physics that is taught in our most prestigious universities. Some of our most respected physicists have said for years that time travel is theoretically possible.

In his marvelous book, *Parallel Universes*, physicist Fred Alan Wolf deftly illustrates—in terms lay persons can understand—that quantum physics not only predicts that time travel *can* happen, it shows us that it *must be happening.*[1] He also describes how Frank J. Tipler, a professor of physics and mathematics at Tulane University, has deduced exactly how backward-through-time travel might be accomplished by passing very close to a series of rotating neutron stars.[2]

Michael Talbot goes a step further. In his extremely important book, *The Holographic Universe*, Talbot shows us that the very nature of reality is not at all what we think it is. Rather, he says, it appears that there is a vast quantity of evidence to indicate that our universe is structured somewhat like a hologram.[3] Talbot's ideas are shared by a growing number of scientists. It may be the difference between our commonly-held beliefs and actual reality that has kept the existence of time travel and space-time warps obscured from us in the past. Perhaps we have not understood our surroundings because thinking about things in a different way is a prerequisite to such understanding.

Several abductees have told me that they have received telepathic instructions about the nature of the universe and the nature of time. These "lessons" usually contain simple analogies.

Michelle LaVigne, whose encounter memories are mostly conscious, says she was told to think of the different dimensions of time as if she were walking through a peanut butter and jelly sandwich. She was to imagine that she could only walk sluggishly through the peanut butter, but if she jumped up into the jelly, she could walk much faster, then return to the peanut butter at a place further along than she would have been had she stayed in the peanut butter. She was told this type of dimension hopping could be accomplished in different directions as well—i.e., one could travel backward in time. She explains that people can be abducted on a Monday, kept until Friday, and then returned an hour after they were taken, then abducted again on Tuesday, so that they actually exist in two different locations (parallel universes?) at the same time.

Leah Haley, an abductee whose fascinating story is unique because she appears to have been aboard a flying saucer when it was shot down by our Air Force, says a telepathic "silent voice" told her: "Time is no more linear than the earth is flat. Time is like a Slinky [the springlike child's toy]. It can be bent, stretched, contracted and overlapped. Because of this, choices we make today can affect not only our future but whether or not certain aspects of our past ever occurred. Actually, time as we know it is nonexistent; it's space that's important."

---

1. Fred Alan Wolf, *Parallel Universes* (n.p.: Youniverse Seminars, 1988; rpt. New York: Touchstone/Simon & Schuster, 1990).
2. *Ibid.*, pp. 234-238.
3. Michael Talbot, *The Holographic Universe* (New York, HarperCollins, 1991).

Another experiencer whose name I am not at liberty to mention says, "They not only can travel backward and forward through time, they also have a machine that can see through time...time unfolds like a flower; it's fantastic!"

Before it can be considered complete, any hypothesis that attempts to explain the UFO enigma satisfactorily must offer some reason for "the government cover-up." It must address the frequently asked question: "Why won't the U.S. Air Force tell the public what is really going on; what do 'they' know that is so terrible that they won't tell us?"

To begin with, it appears that UFOs and contact with other intelligences may not really fall under the jurisdiction of the U.S. Air Force at all. For twenty years, Air Force officers "investigated" UFO sighting reports. But it now appears that all three of their investigation projects—Sign, Grudge and Bluebook—were in actuality nothing more than public-relation ploys designed to mollify citizens who became interested in the subject. These three projects dealt mostly with reports of UFOs that could be explained as known objects, that could not be substantiated, that were not particularly dramatic, etc. Meanwhile, the spectacular multiple-witness reports with no earthly explanation were covertly sent to a top-secret group within Naval Intelligence or some other branch.

So, although Freedom of Information Act requests and other evidence prove that some Air Force personnel know a whole lot more than they are telling, clearly nobody in the Air Force knows everything about what is going on, and the same may be the case with many other government/military groups as well. Many groups appear to be covering up what they do know, while at the same time trying to find out more.

Here is just one example. In *Lost Was the Key*, an intriguing account of her personal encounters, Leah Haley relates how an unknown group of uniformed men (she calls them "OMAGS," for "obnoxious military and government scoundrels") abducted her on several occasions.[4] They drugged her and questioned her using torturous methods in an apparent attempt to discover what she had learned during previous abductions by aliens. Obviously, if they knew the answers to their questions, they would not be going to such extreme lengths to ask them; yet, at the same time, they have covered up their involvement and even their existence.

Since then, other men with military/government connections have interrogated Leah and/or questioned others about her. As is the case with other abductees—and with others who have simply reported seeing UFOs—men from one agency or branch ask questions about another agency or branch. Or they issue warnings to be careful of other "OMAGS."

---

4. Leah A. Haley, *Lost Was the Key* (Greenleaf Publications; P.O. Box 70563; Tuscaloosa, Alabama 35407-0563, 1993).

This type of activity is common not only in this arena, but in others as well. It is not rare for the FBI to accidentally arrest an undercover policeman, an agent of the Bureau of Alcohol, Tobacco and Firearms, etc. Nor is it uncommon for one branch to feud with another over jurisdiction. One answer is that anywhere governments are involved, the right hand may not know what the left hand is doing.

That leaves us with those who *do* know all the answers. Why aren't *they* telling us (if they exist)? That question may have many different answers. I suggested earlier that some of the UFO occupants may be from our own future. They may even be government agents or military personnel from our own future. If so, the very fact that they exist may mean that we *have* a future—that we will not blow each other up or pollute our environment to the point where we will no longer be able to survive as a species. And it would be logical for agents of our present-day government to cooperate with them in keeping the very existence of "time machines" secret. Because as soon as we know that time machines can be built, some of us will figure out how to build them. And then we will begin to use them. And then we will begin to cause all sorts of the paradoxes discussed in earlier chapters—like the theoretical son who goes back into time and prevents his parents from ever meeting one another.

But there may be many other very valid reasons for a widespread, systematic cover-up of contact with alien intelligences.

One involves the destruction of our civilization. Since the Roswell crash, studies have been done to determine what happens when a technologically advanced civilization comes into contact with one that is less advanced. Historically, the less advanced structure has ceased to exist, either through outright conquest or because it was literally absorbed into the more advanced one. (The fate of Native Americans after coming into contact with European settlers is a good example.)

Imagine what would happen if a flying saucer landed on the White House lawn—in full view of all the TV networks' cameras—and alien beings emerged. Imagine how we would react if the President of the United States (or perhaps the Secretary General of the United Nations) announced publicly that alien beings had been abducting millions of people at will for decades. The next day, half the American population might sit at home and watch for news of the aliens on TV instead of going to work. As a result of that one detail, the U.S. stock market could crash overnight and other markets all over the world could follow. And that would only be the very tip of an enormous iceberg of calamity that could topple religions, unseat governments, foment panic and rioting in the streets...and eventually result in the end of our civilization as we know it.

If MJ-12 or something very much like it really was launched because of the Roswell crash in 1947, one of its first priorities might have been to develop a plan to prevent just this sort of catastrophe. That plan might very well have included an immediate and total cover-up, followed by a comprehensive metered release of information designed to systematically educate the public a little bit at a time.

The idea that there is a government education program has been championed by Donald Ware and others in the field for some time now. It appears that certain television programs, for instance, are used to subtly expose the public to images, concepts and information that they would otherwise have avoided or missed. So are advertisements, motion pictures, magazine articles and perhaps a host of other media. At the same time, a few UFO investigators are actually given classified information—a bit at a time—to disseminate to the ufological community.

The officials who covered up the Roswell/Corona crash had to decide whether to make news of the crash public right away, make it public later, or try to keep it secret forever. If they knew about the history of the conflict between advanced and less-advanced technological societies, that knowledge may have influenced their decision. The decision may also have been influenced by postwar jitters, a security-conscious military mindset, intelligence manuals stating that secrets cannot be kept forever, even instructions handed down from ufonauts. At any rate, they appear to have discarded the first and last avenues, which left them with the problem of how to best manage an eventual disclosure.

That problem appears to have been solved by adopting a policy of denial, ridicule and disinformation, while at the same time slowly educating the public through the metered release of information. In this way, those of us who were ready to receive knowledge without panicking had plenty of access to it through popular literature, UFO conferences, etc. Meanwhile, those whose fear would have caused unmanageable problems were insulated from the knowledge until they had seen enough ET-adorned T-shirts and heard enough subtle references that they were able to assimilate the concept of contact.

Like any large undertaking, the cover-up/education program appears to be plagued by money problems, policy disagreements, political infighting, unmanageable growth and a host of other obstacles. Both experiencers and investigators have told me that they have seen evidence of power struggles between two groups of intelligence agents—one that is pushing for full public disclosure and another that insists on less disclosure. And some even tell of in-between groups that disagree with both of the other two groups.

Michael Lindemann and others have suggested that the enormous impact that knowledge of contact would have on our civilization could be used as a lever to influence public opinion. In order to secure huge quantities of money and political power for themselves, those who know the most about contact (and about future Earth technology and/or alien technology) might be working very hard to keep certain facts from the public. And they might be releasing facts, disinformation and/or outright fabrications at specific times in prearranged ways in order to have the maximum effect.

History is full of accounts of people giving up their civil rights because their leaders convinced them they must do so in exchange for protection from enemies of one kind or another. We may be seeing this happen right now in the United States as more and more stringent laws are passed in the name of "stamping out drugs." We, the citizens, are now subject to several kinds of searches and seizures that were illegal just a few years ago, and we are on the verge of being disarmed by gun legislation. The fact that the so-called "war on drugs" cannot be won as long as key people within the U.S. government continue to promote the spread of drugs rather than oppose it does not ameliorate the deterioration of our rights because it is continually covered up. Our attention is constantly directed away from the fact that our governments are gobbling up more and more of our money and personal power. It is focused instead on the medical tragedies, crime and gang violence that are byproducts of the drug trade.

This is all possible because a few government officials have convinced us that we as individuals are powerless to combat a relatively understandable "enemy"—drugs. Imagine how much sway they could have over us if they were to convince us that we were being invaded by sinister, bloodthirsty creatures beyond any understanding, and that, as individuals, we were helpless victims.

History is also littered with cases of technological breakthroughs being used as levers to acquire massive fortunes and enormous political power. Alfred Nobel's invention of dynamite, for instance, earned him a fortune that is still burgeoning today, years after his death. And we have all read how the births and deaths of nations and the entire course of history were determined by the development of the axe, the bow, gunpowder, the machine gun, the airplane, the atomic bomb and so on. Imagine how much money and power could be amassed by the first person who managed to duplicate the types of technology discussed in this book. He (or she) would be able to use materialization/dematerialization and incredible speed and maneuverability to steal nuclear weapons and deliver them anywhere, undetected. He would be able to offer for sale a craft many times more efficient than any previous one—a craft capable of traveling to other stars and perhaps into the past or future. His inventions would render all other forms of communication, transportation, weaponry, anesthesia, surgery, surveillance, and so on pathetically obsolete.

The stakes in this game might be even higher. Many abductees and contactees say they have been told by the ufonauts that some sort of struggle is being waged between "good" forces and "evil" forces, and that the fate of "Earthlings" may hang in the balance. Some speak of satanic and angelic influences. Some imply that ETs that are visiting the earth now were involved in the genesis of human beings. Others say the human body was designed to be a container for souls, that it has been redesigned several times in the past, and that the hybridization of humans with the gray "Zeta Reticulan" aliens is a joint project to develop a better container for our souls. Still others believe our visitors are here to harvest our souls for their own purposes.

There does seem to be a very deep spiritual component to the whole subject. Perhaps the evangelists who have interpreted biblical prophesies to mean that we are living in the "end times" are correct. Maybe UFOs are the "signs in the heavens" that they tell us will be the harbingers of a one-world government, an antichrist, Armageddon, etc. If so, and if some of our government officials found out about it, would they tell us? Or would they be afraid to talk about it? Or would they try to use their knowledge for their own gain?

Similarly, would government officials tell us if they knew that our species was in danger of being exterminated? When contactee Alex Collier addressed the International UFO Congress and EBE Awards in Las Vegas in December of 1993, he broke a chilling story. He claimed that, for many years, he had been in contact with entities from Andromeda who sat on a "Galactic Council." Part of this council's business, he said, is to determine the fate of Earth and its inhabitants. And they are evenly divided as to what that fate should be. Half of them contend that we human beings are of questionable value because we do not respect ourselves, each other or our environment. Of course, Collier's claims, like those of Alfred Bielek, Robert Lazar and others in the field, are very controversial, and no one can prove their validity. But, by the same token, nobody can prove they are false.

Collier also mentioned a subject that has been widely predicted by other contactees, and by abductees, channelers and a few geologists— a "pole shift." Many other experiencers have told me that ETs have shown them graphic pictures of a future mass evacuation of millions of humans aboard extraterrestrial "mother ships." Some of them firmly believe that the purpose of the evacuation will be to save us from an impending slippage of the earth's crust that will be so sudden and so severe that it could not fail to wipe out our entire civilization, kill billions of people and hurl the survivors back into the Stone Age.

Scientific evidence to support their apocalyptic vision does exist. Some geologists believe that studies of iron-bearing lava deposits on either side of the Mid-Atlantic Ridge indicate that the earth's magnetic poles have shifted scores of times in the last few million years. So far, no accurate method of predicting when the next such shift will occur or how long it will take has been established, because we are not sure what triggers these shifts. But someone in our government may know. Someone may have determined that pole shifts are triggered by comet impacts, planetary alignments, the build-up of polar ice or something we have not yet even imagined. If so, would they tell us and then sit back and watch—and perhaps fall victim to—the panic and chaos that would be sure to follow when we realized our civilization was doomed? Or would they keep the knowledge to themselves and try to use it for their own personal gain, perhaps use it to plan a Noah-style escape for themselves and a select few cronies?

These possibilities of why the truth about UFOs and abductions is being covered up are just a sampling of the speculations that pervade ufology. I put more stock in some possibilities than in others, but, like many of my colleagues, I feel I can neither subscribe to nor condemn any of these ideas "for the record" because I simply do not have enough information. I can only present them as possibilities that should be considered seriously.

Regardless of which hypothesis each of us leans toward, regardless of which one finally proves correct regarding the UFO enigma, each of us involved in ufology occasionally has an obligation to set aside academic musings and nut-and-bolt investigation in order to help address the urgent and growing human need engendered by contact with other intelligences.

After almost every speech I make, people say to me, "I think I am an abductee, but I'm not sure and I'm thinking about being hypnotized. What should I do?" Like many of my colleagues, I am very concerned about these people, but, since I have no formal training in psychotherapy, I do not feel qualified to offer counseling. The best I can do is to first ask, "Are you a danger to yourself or others and/or having trouble sleeping, eating, working, forming and maintaining relationships, etc.?" If they answer, "No, I am just curious," I recommend that they not seek therapy (if it ain't broke, don't fix it). This is because I know of others who have unwittingly opened a Pandora's box this way, and were later sorry they had done so. If they answer, "Yes, this thing is interfering with my life," or "I am so obsessed with knowing what happened to me that night that I can't think of anything else," I recommend a therapist.

At this writing, there is an acute shortage of qualified therapists who are knowledgeable about contact phenomena. If I send subjects to a therapist who doesn't believe the contact is real, he (or she) can do them more harm than good. But if I send *every* one to the few therapists who understand that these experiences are real, they will not have enough time to counsel them all. So, even though I am not qualified to counsel people, I have found it necessary to devise an informal screening questionnaire to determine which people I should encourage to see the "pro-alien" therapists and which I should advise to seek regular therapists of their choice. This has taken the form of the list of 21 questions shown below. Some of these questions come from the Roper surveys commissioned by Budd Hopkins and David Jacobs and sponsored by The Bigelow Holding Corporation.

1. Have you seen a UFO (an alien)? On how many occasions?

2. Do you have a deep, abiding interest in UFOs and/or aliens?

3. Do you have recurring dreams about UFOs or ETs?

4. Have you awakened and felt paralyzed (unable to move, scream, open your eyes, etc.) and felt that there was a presence in your room?

5. Have you seen anomalous lights floating around in your bedroom (or elsewhere)?

6. Have you had a sensation that you were flying or levitating, or dreamed that you were flying?

7. Have you had periods of missing time?

8. Have you felt a compulsion to go to a specific place, usually a remote location or a place like Sedona, Arizona, and don't know why?

9. Have you awakened to find inexplicable scars (usually already healed or nearly healed), bruises, triangular rashes, etc., on your body and neither you nor your family members can remember where they came from?

10. Have you awakened with unusual body sensations?

11. Have you experienced miraculous healing?

12. Do you feel homesick even when you are at home or feel like you are different from other people—that you don't belong, don't fit in?

13. Do you have miraculous abilities (for instance, can you repair the electronics in a TV set even though you have no training in electronics)?

14. When people say how bad ETs are, do you feel like defending them? Do you sometimes identify more with them than with humans—perhaps even feel love for them?

15. Do you consider yourself an environmentalist? (That is, do you feel angry or sad when you see how we are polluting, cutting down the trees, etc.?)

16. Do you consider yourself a human-rights advocate? (That is, do you feel angry or sad when you see how minorities are treated, etc.?)

17. Do you consider yourself an anti-nuclear advocate? (That is, do you think we should get rid of all nuclear weapons?)

18. Are your parents and/or children experiencers?

19. Do you feel anxiety or fear about UFOs or ETs?

20. Do you feel as if you are being monitored, watched or telepathically communicated with?

21. Have you experienced a disappearing pregnancy?

If the subjects answer yes to more than a few of these questions, I usually recommend a therapist who I know understands that contact is real. If not, I recommend that they choose a therapist on their own. (Readers should keep in mind that these questions do not necessarily indicate a subject is an abductee. You may answer yes to many of these questions and still have nothing to do with the abduction phenomenon.)

ADDITIONAL READING

Thousands of books and articles about UFOs and abductions are available. Recommending reading is always difficult because important works will always by left out, either because the author has not yet read them or because space simply does not allow for all of them. Below is a brief list of well-known works that should acquaint readers with a variety of viewpoints. Further references may be found in the bibliography.

AUTHOR	BOOK(S)
Bowen, Charles, ed.	*The Humanoids* *Encounter Cases From* *Flying Saucer Review*
Boylan, Richard	*Close Extraterrestrial Encounters:* *Positive Experiences with* *Mysterious Visitors*
Bryant, Alice and Linda Seebach	*Healing Shattered Reality*
Cooper, William	*Behold A Pale Horse*
Fowler, Raymond	*The Andreasson Affair* *The Andreasson Affair, Phase II* *The Watchers* *The Allagash Abductions*
Good, Timothy	*Above Top Secret* *Alien Liaison*
Haley, Leah A.	*Lost Was the Key*
Hopkins, Budd	*Missing Time* *Intruders*

Keel, John A.	*The Mothman Prophesies* *UFOs: Operation Trojan Horse*
Marciniak, Barbara	*Bringers of the Dawn*
Strieber, Whitley	*Communion*
Talbot, Michael	*The Holographic Universe*
Turner, Karla	*Into the Fringe* *Taken*
Vallée, Jacques	*Passport to Magonia* *Dimensions* *Confrontations* *Revelations*
Wolf, Fred Alan	*Parallel Universes*

PERIODICALS

Bulletin of Anomalous Experience
2 St. Clair Ave. West, Suite 607
Toronto, ON M4V 1L5
Canada
(416)963-8700

Contact Forum
P.O. Box 726
Newberg, OR 97132
U.S.A.
(800)366-0264

Flying Saucer Review
FSR Publications Ltd
P.O. Box 162 High Wycombe
Bucks HP13 5DZ
England

MUFON UFO Journal
103 Oldtowne Rd.
Seguin, TX 78155-4099
U.S.A.
(210)379-9216

Bibliography

Books

American Heritage Dictionary, Second College Edition. Boston: Houghton Mifflin Company, 1982.

Barker, Gray. *They Knew Too Much About Flying Saucers.* New York: University Books, Inc., 1956 (paperback).

Bender, Albert K. *Flying Saucers and the Three Men.* New York: Paperback Library, Inc., 1968 (paperback).

Berlitz, Charles, and William L. Moore. *The Roswell Incident.* New York: Grosset & Dunlap, 1980.

Binder, Otto O. *Flying Saucers Are Watching Us.* New York: Belmont Books-Belmont Productions, Inc., 1968 (paperback).

————. *What We Really Know About Flying Saucers.* Greenwich, Connecticut: Fawcett Gold Medal-Fawcett Publications, Inc., 1967 (paperback).

Blum, Howard. *Out There.* New York: Simon & Schuster, 1990.

Blum, Ralph, and Judy Blum. *Beyond Earth: Man's Contact With UFOs.* New York: Bantam Books, Inc., 1974 (paperback).

Blundell, Nigel, and Roger Boar. *The World's Greatest UFO Mysteries.* London: Octopus Books Limited, 1983. Rpt. New York: Berkley Books, 1990 (paperback).

Bowen, Charles, ed. *The Humanoids.* Chicago: Henry Regnery Company, 1969.

——, ed. *Encounter Cases from Flying Saucer Review.* New York: Signet-New American Library, Inc., 1977 (paperback).

Boylan, Richard J. *Close Extraterrestrial Encounters: Positive Experiences with Mysterious Visitors.* Newberg, Oregon: Wild Flower Press, 1994.

Bryant, Alice, and Linda Seebach. *Healing Shattered Reality: Understanding Contactee Trauma.* Newberg, Oregon: Wild Flower Press, 1991 (paperback).

Calkins, Carroll C., ed. *Mysteries of the Unexplained.* Pleasantville, New York: The Reader's Digest Association, Inc., 1982.

Clark, Jerome, and Loren Coleman. *The Unidentified.* New York: Warner Books, Inc., 1975 (paperback).

Cooper, William. *Behold A Pale Horse.* Sedona, Arizona: Light Technology Publishing, 1991.

Davies, Paul. *Other Worlds.* New York: Simon & Schuster, 1980.

De Arujo, Hernani Ebecken. *Einstein, espaço-tempo.* Rio de Janeiro: the author, 1965.

Deardorff, James. *Celestial Teachings: The Emergence of the True Testament of Jmmanuel (Jesus).* Newberg, Oregon: Wild Flower Press, 1991.

Edwards, Frank. *Flying Saucers—Here and Now.* New York: Lyle Stuart, 1967.

——. *Flying Saucers: Serious Business.* New York: Lyle Stuart, Inc., 1966. Rpt. New York: Bantam Books, Inc.-Grosset & Dunlap, Inc., 1966 (paperback).

Elders, Brit, et al. *UFO...Contact From The Pleiades, Volume I.* Munds Park, Arizona: Genesis III Publishing, 1980.

Emenegger, Robert. *UFO's Past, Present and Future.* New York: Ballantine Books-Random House, Inc., 1974 (paperback).

Fawcett, Lawrence, and Barry J. Greenwood. *Clear Intent.* Englewood Cliffs, New Jersey: Prentice-Hall, Inc., 1984 (paperback).

Fiore, Edith. *Encounters.* New York: Doubleday, 1989.

Flammonde, Paris. *UFO Exist!* New York: G. P. Putnam's Sons, 1976.

Fort, Charles. *The Complete Works of Charles Fort.* New York: Dover Publications, Inc., 1974.

Fowler, Raymond E. *The Andreasson Affair.* Newberg, Oregon: Wild Flower Press, 1994 Reprint.

———. *The Andreasson Affair, Phase Two*. Newberg, Oregon: Wild Flower Press, 1994 Reprint.

———. *Casebook of a UFO Investigator*. Englewood Cliffs, New Jersey: Prentice-Hall, Inc., 1981. Will be reprinted 1995, Wild Flower Press.

———. *UFOs: Interplanetary Visitors*. Jericho, New York: Exposition Press, 1974. Will be reprinted 1995, Wild Flower Press.

———. *The Allagash Abductions*. Newberg, Oregon: Wild Flower Press, 1993.

———, and Betty Ann Luca. *The Watchers*. New York: Bantam Books, 1990.

Friedman, Stanton, and Don Berliner. *Crash at Corona*. New York: Paragon House, 1992.

Fuller, John G. *Incident at Exeter*. New York: G. P. Putnam's Sons, 1966. Rpt. New York: Berkley Medallion-Berkley Publishing Corporation, 1967 (paperback).

———. *The Interrupted Journey*. New York: Dial Press, 1966.

———, ed. *Aliens in the Skies* (Testimony by six leading scientists before the House Committee on Science and Astronautics, July 29, 1968). New York: G. P. Putnam's Sons, 1969.

Gaddis, Vincent H. *Mysterious Fires and Lights*. New York: David McKay Company, Inc., 1967.

Good, Timothy. *Above Top Secret*. London: Sidgwick and Jackson Limited, 1987. Rpt. New York: William Morrow and Company, Inc., 1988.

———. *Alien Liaison*. London: Century, 1991. Rpt. London: Arrow Books Limited, 1992 (paperback).

———, ed. *The UFO Report*. London: Sidgwick and Jackson, 1989. Rpt. New York: Avon Books, 1991 (paperback).

Haley, Leah A. *Lost Was the Key*. P. O. Box 70563, Tuscaloosa, Alabama: Greenleaf Publications, 1993.

Hendry, Allan. *The UFO Handbook*. Garden City, New York: Doubleday & Company, Inc., 1979 (paperback).

Hoagland, Richard C. *The Monuments of Mars: A City on the Edge of Forever*. Berkeley, California: North Atlantic Books, 1987.

Hobana, Ion, and Julien Weverbergh. *UFO's from Behind the Iron Curtain*. Trans. A. D. Hills. London: Souvenir Press Ltd., 1974. Rpt. New York: Bantam Books, Inc., 1975 (paperback).

Holzer, Hans. *The Ufonauts: New Facts on Extraterrestrial Landings*. Greenwich, Connecticut: Fawcett Gold Medal-Fawcett Publications, Inc., 1976 (paperback).

Hopkins, Budd. *Intruders: The Incredible Visitations at Copley Woods*. New York: Random House, Inc., 1987.

———. *Missing Time*. New York: Richard Marek Publishers, Inc., 1981.

Hoyle, Fred. *Frontiers of Astronomy*. New York: Harper & Row, Publishers, 1955.

Hynek, J. Allen. *The UFO Experience*. Chicago: Henry Regnery Co., 1972.

———, and Jacques Vallée. *The Edge of Reality*. Chicago: Henry Regnery Co., 1975 (paperback).

Jacobs, David M. *Secret Life: Firsthand Accounts of UFO Abductions*. New York: Simon & Schuster, 1992.

Jahn, Robert G. and Brenda J. Dunne. *Margins of Reality: The Role of Consciousness in the Physical World*. San Diego: Harcourt Brace Javanovich, Publishers, 1987.

Jessup, M. K. *The Case For the UFO*. New York: The Citadel Press, 1955.

Kannenberg, Ida. *The Alien Book of Truth*. Newberg, Oregon: Wild Flower Press, 1993.

———. *UFOs and the Psychic Factor: How To Understand Encounters With UFOs and ETs*. Newberg, Oregon: Wild Flower Press, 1992.

Keel, John A. *Disneyland of the Gods*. New York: Amok Press, 1988 (paperback).

———. *The Mothman Prophesies*. New York: The Saturday Review Press/E. P. Dutton & Co., Inc., 1975.

———. *Our Haunted Planet*. Greenwich, Connecticut: Fawcett Publications, Inc. 1971 (paperback).

———. *UFOs: Operation Trojan Horse*. New York: G. P. Putnam's Sons, 1970.

Keyhoe, Donald E. *Aliens From Space*. Garden City, New York: Doubleday & Company, Inc., 1973.

Kinder, Gary. *Light Years: An Investigation Into the Extraterrestrial Experiences of Eduard Meier*. New York: The Atlantic Monthly Press, 1987.

Lorenzen, Coral E. *The Great Flying Saucer Hoax: The UFO Facts and Their Interpretation*. New York: William-Frederick Press, 1962. Rpt. *Flying Saucers: The Startling Evidence of the Invasion from Outer Space*. New York: Signet-New American Library, Inc., 1966 (paperback).

————, and Jim Lorenzen. *Abducted!*. New York: Berkley Medallion Books-Berkley Publishing Corporation, 1977 (paperback).

————, and Jim Lorenzen. *Flying Saucer Occupants.* New York: Signet-New American Library, Inc., 1967 (paperback).

————, and Jim Lorenzen. *UFOs Over the Americas.* New York: Signet-New American Library, Inc., 1968 (paperback).

————, and Jim Lorenzen. *UFOs: The Whole Story.* New York: Signet-New American Library, Inc., 1969 (paperback).

Marciniak, Barbara. *Bringers of the Dawn.* Sante Fe, New Mexico: Bear & Co., 1992 (paperback).

McWane, Glenn, and David Graham. *The New UFO Sightings.* New York: Warner Paperback Library-Warner Books, Inc., 1974 (paperback).

Michel, Aimé. *Lueurs sur les Soucoupes Volantes.* Paris: Mame, 1954. Rpt. *The Truth About Flying Saucers.* New York: Criterion Books, 1956. Trans. Paul Selver. Rpt. New York: Pyramid Books-Pyramid Communications, Inc., 1974 (paperback).

————. *Mysterieux Objets celestes.* Paris: Arthaud, 1958. Rpt. *Flying Saucers and the Straight Line Mystery.* New York: Criterion Books, 1958. Trans. Civilian Saucer Intelligence of New York.

Meier, Eduard. *Unpublished Contact Notes.* F.I.G.U. Semjase-Silver-Star-Center, CH-8495 Hinterschmidrüti, Switzerland.

Nichols, Preston B. and Peter Moon. *The Montauk Project: Experiments in Time.* Westbury, New York: Sky books, 1992 (paperback).

Randle, Kevin D. *The UFO Casebook.* New York: Warner Books, Inc., 1989 (paperback).

————, and Donald R. Schmitt. *UFO Crash at Roswell.* New York: Avon Books, 1991 (paperback).

Randles, Jenny. *The UFO Conspiracy: The First Forty Years.* Poole, England: Blandford Press, 1987.

————, Dot Street and Brenda Butler. *Sky Crash.* London: Neville Spearman, 1994.

Rashid, Isa, Eduard Meier, J.H. Ziegler and B.L. Greene. *The Talmud of Jmmanuel: The Clear Translation in English and German.* Tigard, Oregon: Wild Flower Press, 1992 (paperback).

Rogo, D. Scott, ed. *UFO Abductions: True Cases of Alien Kidnappings.* New York: Signet-New American Library, Inc., 1980 (paperback).

Ruppelt, Edward J. *The Report On Unidentified Flying Objects*. Garden City, New York: Doubleday and Company, Inc., 1956. Rpt. New York: Ace Books, Inc., n.d. (paperback).

Saunders, David R., and Roger R. Harkins. *UFOs? Yes! Where the Condon Committee Went Wrong*. New York: World Publishing Company, 1968. Rpt. New York: Signet-New American Library, Inc., 1968 (paperback).

Scully, Frank. *Behind The Flying Saucers*. New York: Henry Holt and Company, 1950.

Sitchin, Zecharia. *The 12th Planet*. Briarcliff Manor, New York: Stein and Day, 1976. Rpt. New York: Avon Books, 1978.

Smith, Warren. *UFO Trek*. New York: Zebra Books-Kensington Publishing Corp., 1976 (paperback).

Stanford, Ray. *Socorro 'Saucer' in a Pentagon Pantry*. Austin, Texas: Blueapple Books, 1976.

Steiger, Brad. *Alien Meetings*. New York: Ace Books-Charter Communications, Inc.-Grosset & Dunlap Company, 1978 (paperback).

———. *Mysteries of Time and Space*. Englewood Cliffs, New Jersey: Prentice-Hall, Inc., 1974.

———. *Strangers from the Skies*. London: Universal-Tandem Publishing Co. Ltd, 1966. Rpt. London: Tandem Publishing Ltd, 1975 (paperback).

———, and Joan Whritenour. *Flying Saucers Are Hostile*. New York: Universal Publishing and Distributing Corporation, 1967. (paperback).

———, Alfred Bielek, and Sherry Hanson Steiger. *The Philadelphia Experiment and Other UFO Conspiracies*. New Brunswick, New Jersey: Inner Light Publications, 1990 (copyright Timewalker Productions) (paperback).

Stevens, W.C., ed. *Message From the Pleiades: The Contact Notes of Eduard Billy Meier, Vols. 1 and 2*. Tucson, Arizona: UFO Photo Archives, 1989 and 1990.

Story, Ronald D., ed. *The Encyclopedia of UFOs*. Garden City, New York: Dolphin Books-Doubleday & Company, Inc., 1980 (paperback).

Stranges, Frank E. *Flying Saucerama*. New York: Vantage Press, Inc., 1959.

Strieber, Whitley. *Communion: A True Story*. New York: Beech Tree Books-William Morrow and Company, Inc., 1987.

Stringfield, Leonard H. *Inside Saucer Post ...3-0 Blue*. Cincinnati, Ohio: Civilian Research, Interplanetary Flying Objects, 1957.

———. *Situation Red, The UFO Siege.* Garden City, New York: Doubleday & Company, Inc., 1977.

———. *Situation Red, The UFO Siege.* Rpt. New York: Fawcett Crest Books, 1977 (paperback revised edition with additions).

Talbot, Michael. *The Holographic Universe.* New York: Harper-Collins, 1991.

Turner, Karla. *Into the Fringe: A True Story of Alien Abduction.* New York: Berkley Books, 1992 (paperback).

———. *Taken: Inside the Alien-Human Abduction Agenda.* Roland, Arkansas: Kelt Works, 1994.

Vallée, Jacques. *Anatomy of a Phenomenon: Unidentified Objects in Space—a Scientific Appraisal.* Chicago: Henry Regnery Co., 1965. Rpt. *UFOs in Space: Anatomy of a Phenomenon.* New York: Ballantine Books-Random House, Inc., 1974 (paperback).

———. *Confrontations: A Scientist's Search for Alien Contact.* New York: Ballantine Books, 1990.

———. *Dimensions: A Casebook of Alien Contact.* New York: Contemporary Books, 1988.

———. *Messengers of Deception.* New York: Bantam Books, Inc., 1980.

———. *Passport to Magonia.* Chicago: Henry Regnery Co., 1969 (paperback).

———. *Revelations: Alien Contact and Human Deception.* New York: Ballantine Books, 1991.

———, and Janine Vallée. *Challenge to Science.* Chicago: Henry Regnery Co., 1966.

———, in collaboration with Martine Castello. *UFO Chronicles of the Soviet Union: A Cosmic Samizdat.* New York: Ballantine Books, 1992.

Vesco, Renato. *Intercettateli senza sparare.* Milan, Italy: U. Mursia & C., 1968. Rpt. *Intercept—But Don't Shoot.* New York: Grove Press, Inc. 1971. Trans. Grove Press, Inc.

Wells, H. G. *The Time Machine: An Invention.* Holt, 1895.

White, Dale. *Is Something Up There?* New York: Doubleday and Company, Inc., 1968. Rpt. New York: Scholastic Book Services-Scholastic Magazines, Inc., 1969 (paperback).

Wilkins, Harold T. *Flying Saucers on the Attack.* New York: Citadel Press, 1954. Rpt. New York: Ace Star-Ace Books, Inc., n.d. (paperback).

Wolf, Fred Alan. *Parallel Universes: The Search for Other Worlds.* n.p.: Youniverse Seminars, 1988. Rpt. New York: Touchstone-Simon and Schuster, 1990 (paperback).

Articles and Other Sources

"Abandoned Jet Kills 3 in Car, 1 in House." *New York Times*, Late City Ed., 3 July 1954, Sec. A, pp. 1, 6.

Air Force Regulation 200-2. Aug. 1953.

Allan, W. K. "The Fort St. James Sightings." *Flying Saucer Review*, 24, No. 3 (1978), pp. 8-11.

Anderson, Tim. "Smokey and the UFO." *UFO Report*, Sept. 1979, pp. 14-17.

"Another Speech by Wilbert Smith." *Flying Saucer Review*, Vol. 9 (Nov.-Dec. 1963), pp. 11-14.

Apps, David. "Fighter Pilot's Sighting Over Egypt." *Flying Saucer Review*, 26, No. 1 (1980), pp. 32, iii.

Azhazha, Vladimir Grigorievich. "Life in the Cosmos." Lecture. Trans. Gordon Creighton. *Flying Saucer Review*, 25, No. 1 (1979), pp. 25-29.

Benitez, Juan José. "Jetliner 'Intercepted' by UFO Near Valencia." *Flying Saucer Review*, 25, No. 5 (1980), pp. 13-15. Trans. Gordon Creighton.

Berry, Kevin R. "The Kaikoura Controversy." *Flying Saucer Review*, 26, No. 2 (1980), pp. 13-15.

Bielek, Alfred. Telephone interview, 7 Aug. 1992.

Bigelow Holding Corporation. *Unusual Personal Experiences: An Analysis of Three Major Surveys Conducted by the Roper Organization*. Las Vegas, Nevada: Bigelow Holding Corporation, 1992 (pamphlet).

Bigorne, J.M., et al. "The Robots at Warneton." *Lumières dans la Nuit*, No. 139 (France, Nov. 1974). Trans. Gordon Creighton, *Flying Saucer Review*, 20, No. 5 (March 1975), pp. 6-9.

Binder, Otto O. "10,000,000 UFO Witnesses Can't Be Wrong!" *Mechanix Illustrated*, June, 1967, pp. 61-63, 144-145.

Bowen, Charles. "A South American Trio." *Flying Saucer Review*, 11, No. 1 (Jan.-Feb. 1965), pp. 19-21.

———. "More Beliefs." *Flying Saucer Review*, 20, No. 6 (Apr. 1975), pp. 1-2.

Buehring, J. M. "Invisible Barriers." *Flying Saucer Review*, 29, No. 5 (1984), pp. 19-22.

Buhler, Walter. "Brazilian Cases in 1968 and 1969—4." *Flying Saucer Review Case Histories*, Supplement 5 (June 1971), pp. 9-10, 13. Trans. Gordon Creighton.

———. "Brazilian Cases in 1968 and 1969—Pt. 6." *Flying Saucer Review Case Histories,* Supplement 7 (Oct. 1971), pp. 15-16. Trans Gordon Creighton.

———. "Extraterrestrial Dwarves Attack Farm Worker." *SBEDV Bulletin* No. 136/145 (Sept. 1981-Apr. 1982) Brazil. Rpt. *Flying Saucer Review,* 28, No. 1 (1982), pp. 5-8. Trans. Gordon Creighton.

Bulletin of Anomalous Experiences. Toronto, Ontario.

Cadman, A. G. "A Layman's Time and Space." *Flying Saucer Review,* 10, No. 6 (Nov.-Dec. 1964), pp. 19-21.

"CE II in Iowa." *International UFO Reporter,* 2, No. 12 (Dec. 1977), pp. 4, 8.

Clark, Jerome. "Carlos De Los Santos and the Men in Black." *Flying Saucer Review,* 24, No. 4 (Jan. 1979), pp. 8-9.

———. "Unsolved Mysteries: From France to New York, the Five Thorniest Sightings of the Eighties." *Omni,* Dec. 1990, p. 100.

"Cloud Hides UFO." *The A.P.R.O. Bulletin,* 22, No. 3 (Nov.-Dec. 1973), pp. 1, 4.

Collins, R. Perry. "Playing the 'Reality' Game." *UFO Universe,* Jan. 1990, pp. 16-17.

Contact Forum. Newberg, Oregon: Wild Flower Press.

Cox, Adrian R. "A Question of Time." *Flying Saucer Review,* 10, No. 4 (Jul.-Aug. 1964), pp. 7-9.

Creighton, Gordon. "Amazing News from Russia." *Flying Saucer Review,* 8, No. 6 (Nov.-Dec. 1962), pp. 27-28.

———. "The Arica Encounter: Chilean Soldier's 'Trip Into the Fourth Dimension'?" *Flying Saucer Review,* 23, No. 5., pp. 8-9.

———. "Dr. Zigel and the Development of Ufology in Russia: Part II." *Flying Saucer Review,* 27, No. 4 (1982), pp. 13-19.

———. "Itaperuna Again." *Flying Saucer Review,* 18, No. 2 (Mar.-Apr. 1972), pp. 13-15.

Dong, Paul. *Feidie Bai Wen Bai Da.* Hong Kong: Deli Shuju, 1983, as quoted in "Extracts from Paul Dong's Feidie Bai Wen Bai Da (Questions and Answers on UFOs)." *Flying Saucer Review,* 29, No. 6 (1984), pp. 14-20. Trans. Gordon Creighton.

Druffel, Ann. "California Report: The Mystery Helicopters." *Skylook,* Feb. 1976, pp. 8-9.

Edwards, P. M. H. "M.I.B. Activity Reported from Victoria B.C." *Flying Saucer Review,* 27, No. 4 (1982), pp. 7-12.

Evans, Alex. "Close Encounters in Argentina." *UFO Report,* Sept. 1979, pp. 18-20, 58-60.

Faill, Bill. "UFO Car-napping in Rhodesia." *Fate*, Vol. 30, No. 1, Issue No. 322 (Jan. 1977), pp. 34-42.

Farrow, Richard. "Landing on Winkleigh Airfield." (Readers' Reports) *Flying Saucer Review Case Histories*, Supplement 8 (Dec. 1971), p. 16.

Flying Saucer Review. Bucks, England: FSR Public Ltd.

"Follow Up." *The A.P.R.O. Bulletin*, 22, No. 1 (Jul.-Aug. 1973), pp. 6-7.

Forman, Brenda. "Voyage to a Far Planet." *Omni*, Jul. 1990, pp. 34-36, 38, 80, 83-86.

Fouéré, René. "Seraient-ils des revenants du futur?" *Phénomènes spatiaux*, Jun. 1966, pp. 11-14.

Fowler, Omar. "UFO Seen from 'Trident' near Lisbon." *Flying Saucer Review*, 22, No. 4 (Nov. 1976), pp. 2-4, 19.

Gouiran, Charles, et al. "Report on a Landing at Uzès." *Flying Saucer Review*, 24, No. 4 (1979), pp. 3-7. Trans. Gordon Creighton.

Graber, Gary. "Two Occupants in Craft." *Skylook*, Feb. 1976, pp. 3-4.

Haines, Richard F. "Commercial Jet Crew Sights Unidentified Object—Part 1." *Flying Saucer Review*, 27, No. 4 (1982), pp. 3-6.

———. "Commercial Jet Crew Sights Unidentified Object—Part 2." *Flying Saucer Review*, 27, No. 5 (1982), pp. 2-8.

Hall, Richard. "Woman Says UFO Restarted Her Auto." *Skylook*, Feb. 1976, pp. 10-11.

Hamilton, William. "Could This Be Magic?" *UFO Universe*, 2, No. 1 (Spring 1992), p. 23.

Harris, Leslie. "UFO & Silver-Suited Entity Seen Near Winchester." *Flying Saucer Review*, 22, No. 5 (Feb. 1977), pp. 3-6.

Heiden, Richard W. "A 1949 Brazilian Contactee—Part 1." *Flying Saucer Review*, 27, No. 5 (1982), pp. 28-iii.

Hopkins, Budd. Telephone interview. 1 June 1992.

Huyghe, Patrick. "UFO Update." *Omni*, Jul. 1990, p. 73.

———. "What the Government Isn't Saying About UFO's." *Omni*, Dec. 1990, pp. 93-94.

Keatman, Martin. "The Llanerchymedd UFO." *Flying Saucer Review*, 25, No. 5 (1980), pp. 16-23.

———, and Andrew Collins. "Physical Assault by Unidentified Objects at Livingston—Part 1." *Flying Saucer Review*, 25, No. 6 (1980), pp. 2-7.

Kenney, Dave. "1952 Catalina Sighting." *The A.P.R.O. Bulletin*, 27, No. 10 (Apr. 1979), pp. 4-5.

Korcsmaros, Geza, Jr. "Radar—Clue to UFO Propulsion?" *Fate*, Aug. 1957, pp. 64-69.

Liss, Jeffery. "UFO's that Look Like Tops." *Fate*, Nov. 1964, pp. 66-72.

Louange, F., and J. L. Casero. "Unusual Encounter in Jaraba, Spain." *Flying Saucer Review*, 26, No. 2 (1980), pp. 4-5.

Maccabee, Bruce. "UFOs—Still Unexplained, Part II." *Fate*, Mar. 1984, pp. 68-75.

Magee, Judith M. "UFO Over the Mooraduc Road." *Flying Saucer Review*, 18, No. 6 (Nov.-Dec. 1972), pp. 3-5.

McDonald, James E. "UFO Encounter I." *Astronautics and Aeronautics*, Vol. 9, July 1971, pp. 66-70.

Mebane, Alexander D. "The 1957 Saucer Wave in the United States." Appendix in Michel, Aimé. *Flying Saucers and the Straight Line Mystery*. New York: Criterion Books, 1958.

Mendenhall, Jonathan. "Hastings UFO: 'Moonlight' Says Observatory." *The News*, 8 Oct. 1981 (Hastings, East Sussex, England), as quoted in "World Round-up." *Flying Saucer Review*, 27, No. 4 (1982), pp. 25-26.

Michel, Aimé. "Flying Saucers in Europe: The Crisis of Autumn in 1954." *Fate*, Aug. 1957, pp. 28-35.

The Mike Murphy Show. Prod. Chris Stoner. KCMO Radio, Kansas City, Missouri. 12 Jan. 1989.

———. 6 Feb. 1989.

———. 14 May 1992.

Mufon UFO Journal. Seguin, Texas: Mutual UFO Network.

Oechsler, Bob. "Investigation: The Gulf Breeze Sightings." *International UFO Library Magazine*, 1, No. 3 (1992), pp. 6-9, 50.

Osborn, Richard D. "UFO Over Toledo." *Fate*, Nov. 1964, pp. 31-37.

Peters, Ted. "Warm Light Stops Everything!" *MUFON UFO Journal*, Feb. 1977, pp. 3-6.

Phillips, Kathryn. "Why Can't a Man Be More Like a Woman...and Vice Versa." *Omni*, Oct. 1990, pp. 44, 48.

Phillips, Ken. "Bedfordshire Cross-country Chase." *Flying Saucer Review*, 25, No. 3 (1979), pp. 28-31.

Phillips, Ted. "UFO Events in Missouri, 1857-1971." *Flying Saucer Review Case Histories*, Supplement 13 (Feb. 1973), pp. 9-11.

Pinotti, Roberto. "Landing, E. M. Effects and Entities at Torrita di Siena." *Flying Saucer Review*, 25, No. 4 (1979), pp. 3-6. Trans. Maurizio Verga.

Rutkowski, Chris. "The Falcon Lake Incident—Part 1." *Flying Saucer Review*, 27, No. 1 (1981), pp. 14-16.

Stacy, Dennis. "Close Encounter with Dr. J. Allen Hynek." *MU-FON UFO Journal*, Feb. 1985, pp. 3-6.

Stein, Douglas. "Interview Roger Gorski." *Omni*, 13, No. 1 (Oct. 1990), pp. 70-72, 74, 76, 78, 134, 138, 140.

Swords, Michael D. "Ufonauts: Homo sapiens of the Future?" *MUFON UFO Journal*, Feb. 1985, pp. 8-10.

Thayer, G. D. "UFO Encounter II." *Astronautics and Aeronautics*, Vol. 9, September 1971, pp. 60-64.

Toft, Ron. "The Alleged Landing at Winkleigh." (Readers' Reports) *Flying Saucer Review Case Histories*, Supplement 13 (Feb. 1973), p. 16.

UFO Cover-up...Live. Narr. Mike Farrell. Prod. LBS Communications and Michael Seligman. 14 Oct. 1988.

"UFO Update: Turn off the Lights." *UFO Report Annual*, 10, No. 1 (1981), pp. 6-10.

Vertongen, Jean Luc. "The Vilvorde Humanoid." *Inforespace*, No. 18 (1974). Rpt. *Flying Saucer Review*, 20, No. 6 (Apr. 1975), pp. 13-17, 22. Trans. Gordon Creighton.

Webb, Bob. "Amoeba-like UFO Over Oxfordshire." *Flying Saucer Review*, 24, No. 4 (1979), pp. 26-27.

Weintraub, Pamela. "Secret Sharers." *Omni*, Vol. 10, No. 3, (Dec. 1987), pp. 53-58, 136-145.

Index

The Book Shopper®
A Division of Greenleaf Publications

So busy that you cherish every second of leisure time?
Want someone else to take care of unpleasant tasks for you?
Loathe traffic, crowds, and waiting in line?
Lack transportation?
Stumped every time you must buy a gift for someone?

Never fear! **The Book Shopper®** *is here!*

We established our company with your needs in mind. You can now buy books by simply dialing our toll-free number. We'll ship right to your home or work place! *We'll even gift wrap or ship to a third party at no extra charge if you like!*

📖 Novels 　📖 Cookbooks 　📖 Romances 　📖 Westerns

📖 Children's books 📖 Sports Books 📖 Any kind of book!*

1-800-905-8367

(615-896-1549 outside the U.S.)

*applies only to books currently in print and carried by major U.S. distributors. It does not include out-of-print titles.

Alienated
A Quest to Understand Contact

Jeanne Marie Robinson

The long-awaited true account of alien abductions & information about our future from Missouri abductee Jeanne Marie Robinson.

Available August, 1997

Quality paperback
6" x 9"
200 pages
Photo section

To order, fill out the information below and mail, along with $18.95 + $4.00 S&H or credit-card information to:

Greenleaf Publications
P.O. Box 8152
Murfreesboro, TN 37133
U.S.A.

or call
800-905-8367
with MC, Visa, or American Express card

Name _____Address_____
City _____State _____Zipcode _____Country_____
Credit-card # (if using card) _____Exp. Date _____Phone #_____

Leah Haley's Latest!

ORDER

YOURS

TODAY

new IN HEAVEN

A delightfully humorous look at life that lets each of us escape from the massive weight of our everyday concerns and daydream about a more utopian existence. Written in a format reminiscent of the enormously popular *Life's Little Instruction Book, In Heaven* lists just one attribute of the author's idea of heaven on each page. Page one: " In heaven I can walk anywhere I want and never step on gum." A perfect stocking stuffer.

THE AUTHOR is a CPA and former English instructor with masters degrees in education and business administration. An internationally known lecturer, she is the founder and owner of Greenleaf Publications. Her last book, *Ceto's New Friends,* has delighted children throughout the English-speaking world.

Publication Date: January 1997
$8.95 • ISBN 1-883729-04-1
Quality Paperback, 4 x 6, 104 pp

GREENLEAF PUBLICATIONS
P.O. Box 8152
Murfreesboro, TN 37133
U.S.A.
Fax: (615) 896-1356

Shipping and Handling:

In U.S.A....$4 first item
$1 each additional item

Outside U.S.A....$5 first item
$1.50 each additional item
PLUS: $3 each item if
shipped by air.

Toll-Free Order Line:
1-800-905-8367